G

15 -

Kirtland Cutter

Architect in the Land of Promise

KIRTLAND CUTTER

Architect in the Land of Promise

Henry Matthews

For Bob and Marsha

Henry Matthews

February 24 1999

A McLellan Book

University of Washington Press   *Seattle and London*
in association with Eastern Washington State Historical Society, *Spokane*

This book is published with the assistance of a grant from the
McLellan Endowed Series Fund, established through the generosity
of Martha McCleary McLellan and Mary McLellan Williams

Copyright © 1998 by the University of Washington Press
Printed in the United States of America

Library of Congress Cataloging-in-Publication Data
Matthews, Henry.
    Kirtland Cutter : architect in the land of promise / Henry Matthews.
        p.   cm.
    "A McLellan book."
    Includes bibliographical references and index.
    ISBN 0-295-97609-8 (alk. paper)
    1. Cutter, Kirtland Kelsey, 1860-1939—Critcism and interpretation.
    2. Eclecticism in architecture—United States.   I. Cutter, Kirtland Kelsey,
    1860-1939. II. Title.
    NA737.C89M38   1998
    720'.92—dc21   98-14470
                                                                                      CIP

The paper used in this publication meets the minimum requirements of
American National Standard for Information Sciences—Permanence of Paper
for Printed Library Materials, ANSI Z39.48–1984.

Contents

Preface

UNTIL RECENTLY THE LACK OF DOCUMENTARY EVIDENCE
limited opportunities for research on Kirtland Cutter's life and work.
Then in 1984, after years of searching, Larry Schoonover of the Eastern Washington State Historical Society (EWSHS) discovered a
cache of 290 sets of drawings as well as office accounts, letters, and
books. It is the acquisition and cataloguing of this material by the
Society that made my study possible. In 1985, Schoonover contacted
the architect Richard Poper, Cutter's successor in Long Beach, California. Although the firm had not retained the working drawings
and office records from Cutter's time, they had kept a collection of
preliminary drawings, many of them colored pencil sketches. Mrs.
Phyllis Poper, who developed a strong interest in Cutter's work, had
already located some of his buildings from the drawings.

My own interest in Cutter dates back to the late 1960s, when the
talented and thoughtful Spokane architect Kenneth W. Brooks introduced me to his work. I wish that I had begun my investigation then,
when so many people who knew or worked for Cutter were still alive.
In 1985, I was precipitated into the research leading to this book by
the television producer Ivan Munk, who was looking for an architectural historian to help with a documentary on Cutter for KHQ
TV of Spokane. I agreed to help and found myself almost immediately on location with his camera crew in Spokane, on the Washington coast, and in California. At that stage, I think I learned more
from Ivan than he ever did from me. His 1986 documentary, *Vision
of an Era: Kirtland Kelsey Cutter,* attests to his knowledge and under-

standing, and I have been indebted to him on many occasions since then. Larry Schoonover also joined us in California, where we had the pleasure of working with Phyllis Poper, who had made important contacts for us with the owners of Cutter houses as well as arranging interviews with two of his former assistants and some clients who provided valuable insights. Without the generous assistance of Phyllis and Richard Poper, my study of Cutter's California work would have been very difficult. They also supplied many photographs and drawings.

I am grateful to the Eastern Washington State Historical Society for their support over the past ten years. Time and wisdom were generously contributed by Glenn Mason, the director; Larry Schoonover, the curator for history; Edward Nolan, the archivist; his successor, Laura Arksey; and Marsha Rooney, curator of the Campbell house. I am indebted to them for providing many of the illustrations in this book. The cataloguing of the drawings, by Dennis Andersen and Nancy Compau, made my work easier. Both of them continued to provide me with information and advice. My many hours in the archives were rewarding, but there were major problems to be faced. Very few of the drawings were dated; no financial accounts were available for the years before 1910; and correspondence was limited to a few commissions. Furthermore, Cutter, a prolific builder, appears to have put little in writing about his views on architecture. No documents from either of Cutter's partners, John C. Poetz and Karl Gunnar Malmgren, have come to light; existing records do not explain the degree of their responsibility for specific jobs; and correspondence and accounts give only limited information about their activities. Malmgren's daughter, Frances M. Hannaford, supplied some useful information to Dr. Robert Maudlin of Spokane, and he has passed it on to me.

Although Spokane's folklore is rich in anecdotes about Kirtland Cutter, little documentation of his personal life has been found, and no private correspondence. His only known surviving relative, his great-niece Peggy Hoyt Bayless, has a collection of family papers, mainly concerned with earlier generations in Connecticut and Ohio. She has generously donated material relating to Kirtland Cutter, including many photographs, to the EWSHS Archives.

I am indebted to the National Endowment for the Humanities for a grant that helped with my travel costs, and to Washington State University for awarding me professional leave to initiate research for this book.

In the course of writing the book I have received generous help and valuable advice from many architectural historians and scholars in other fields. I am grateful to all of them. My wife, the art historian Susan Platt, has given me support, encouragement, and insightful criticism. I particularly want to thank the late David Gebhard, who did much to reassure me of the value of this project. He painstakingly read preliminary drafts as well as the revised version, and provided constructive criticism. Dennis Andersen, Malin Dollanger, John Fahey, Leonard Garfield, Grant Hildebrand, Donald Meinig, Marsha Rooney, and Larry Schoonover also read the manuscript and gave useful information and advice. Nancy Compau, Sarah Bradford Landau, Leonard Eaton, Mark Alan Hewitt, Jeffrey Karl Ochsner, and Gavin Townsend helped me by reading and commenting on specific chapters. Catherine Bicknell, Arthur Hart, Lawrence Kreisman, and Jean Oton have also given me valuable assistance.

I also want to thank the editors of several journals and books who graciously published my articles on Cutter: David Nicandri, editor of *Columbia;* Jeffrey Karl Ochsner, one of the editors of *Arcade* and editor of *Shaping Seattle Architecture;* David Stratton, who was responsible for the book *Spokane and the Inland Empire;* and Nicola Gordon Bowe, who assembled and edited *The Search for Vernacular Expression in Turn-of-the-Century Design.* Their insights, editorial advice, and encouragement proved invaluable.

Those who helped me at museums and archives are too numerous to mention, but I feel particularly indebted to Leonore Blume of the Palos Verdes Public Library, Karen Clements of the Long Beach Heritage Coalition, Nancy Compau of the Spokane Public Library, Lawrence Dodd of the Whitman College Archives, and Richard Engeman of the Special Collections and Preservation Division, University of Washington Libraries.

Others who helped me obtain pictures were Richard Cardwell, Glen Cloninger, Arthur Hart, Lawrence Kreisman, Mary Randlett, and my son Zachary Matthews.

I want to thank the owners and residents of many of Cutter's buildings who welcomed me into their private spaces and gave me useful information. Indeed it is to them that this book is dedicated. May they long enjoy and respectfully maintain Cutter's legacy.

For the sake of simplicity, I have only occasionally used the full name of the firm—Cutter and Poetz or Cutter and Malmgren. I have generally used Cutter's name alone. This is not intended to

imply that all credit for the buildings discussed should go to
Cutter; the reader should constantly be aware that he could not
have achieved what he did without the help of others.

Henry Matthews
1998

Kirtland Cutter

Architect in the Land of Promise

Introduction

IN THE 1890S A DUTCH BANKER WHO WAS MAKING
investments in the Northwest visited Spokane, Washington, and
was amazed by the ambitious architecture he saw there. He wrote:
"I have never seen a small town which offers such an overwhelming
impression of monumental buildings."[1] The people who rapidly
rebuilt this northwestern outpost after the catastrophic fire of 1889
had gone far beyond necessity to erect grand structures of brick and
granite. In an age when citizens nationwide competed with each
other to proclaim their achievements through the medium of architecture, Spokane outreached many long-established cities in both
scale of building concepts and quality of execution. The most celebrated of the architects responsible for these impressive new buildings was Kirtland Kelsey Cutter, who began practicing architecture
in Spokane in 1888.

In 1905 the well-known polemicist Elbert Hubbard, founder of
the Roycrofters' Arts and Crafts workshops and a self-styled successor to William Morris, declared Spokane "the most beautiful city
ever created within so short a time in the history of the whole
world." Comparing Spokane to ancient Athens, which he said took
ten years longer to reach its pinnacle, he credited its citizens with
"the Spirit of the hive."[2] The following March, in his journal *The
Philistine,* he confirmed his judgment by describing Spokane as "the
model city of America," surpassing all others "in its attention to the
excellent and fit in architecture."[3] Hubbard did not usually hand
out such accolades; indeed in his copious writings he tended to crit-

icize the cities he visited. It is clear that he had discovered architecture in Spokane that rose above prevailing standards. Furthermore, he was not likely to be impressed by mere ostentation and grandeur, or lavish such praise on buildings that did not respect Arts and Crafts ideals.

In 1921 the California journal *Architect and Engineer* also singled out the architecture of Spokane for praise. Devoting the June issue to the city, the editors compared its architecture favorably with that of Los Angeles and Portland, Oregon. They spoke of the city's distinctive character and high proportion of excellent design.[4] Both Hubbard and the professional jury who reported their findings to *Architect and Engineer* named Kirtland Cutter as the individual responsible for the outstanding urban environment of Spokane. Hubbard described him as "a designer and architect who has keyed Spokane in an artistic way"; the jury wrote of his "rare architectural force and genius for design."[5] One of the jurors was Charles Cheney, an architect and city planner who worked tirelessly to raise aesthetic standards in American design.

Such recognition from contemporary critics reinforces the acclaim that Cutter still commands in Spokane, where he is celebrated as the leading turn-of-the-century architect and in some quarters has attained the status of folk hero. But Cutter's true significance is based on a half century of work executed throughout the West and even further afield. One major aim of this monograph is to establish him as a western architect whose contribution should not be overlooked by those studying American architecture as a whole. Even in his early days, his sphere of influence stretched far beyond Spokane. His career provides a fascinating study of the frontier architect who through fortuitous economic circumstances had the opportunity to bring civilization to a remote region, and subsequently to a much broader field. He began to practice in 1888, only a few years after the railroad linked Spokane with the great cities of the East. His reputation soon brought him commissions on the coast of Washington, and in Oregon, Idaho, and Montana; and it was not long before he had erected buildings in the East and even one in England. After an illustrious career in the Northwest that ended in financial ruin, he made a new beginning in southern California, where he spent the last sixteen years of his life. During that fruitful period he designed a series of award-winning houses in an emerging regional manner. He continued to work until 1939, when he died at the age of seventy-nine.

Like many of his American contemporaries in that era of ambition and enterprise, Cutter exploited an astonishing range of styles and types, drawn from diverse sources and freely adapted to meet new expectations and changing patterns of life. Moralizing modernist critics of a generation ago, intent on establishing the primacy of the International Style, despised the eclectic architecture of Cutter's era. Arguing that the twentieth century should have an architectural aesthetic based on advanced technology and new spatial concepts, they gave their support to a series of building designs and critical statements that appeared to culminate in an ideal modernist vision. Such critics would have characterized Cutter's experiments with such a profusion of past styles as shameless promiscuity, seeing his architecture as failing to respond to the imperatives of the modern world. Today historians and critics are taking a broader, more inclusive view of history and giving serious consideration to many talented architects who were sidelined in the search for a mythic holy grail of progress. Furthermore, postmodern architects are again studying historic precedent, and quoting liberally from traditional vocabularies in order to invoke time-honored designs and valued principles. Today we can easily admit that no single, unified style could express the values, aspirations, and desires of a dynamic and multifaceted society. The historicism in Cutter's architecture was an inevitable response to the life of his era.

The product of a career that stretched from the Gilded Age to the Great Depression, Cutter's architecture provides a record and interpretation of society at two major turning points in American history. His surviving buildings in the Northwest are emblems for the opening up of a territory rich in water power, lumber, silver, gold, and other natural resources. They mark the transition from frontier settlement to modern city. We can see Cutter as a mediator between his clients, many of whom were embroiled in the ruthless pursuit of wealth, and the wild landscape they had appropriated. We can witness his attempts to bring civilization to this rugged country by invoking the architectural diversity he had experienced in Europe. The styles he had studied as a young man, traveling in England, France, Germany, Switzerland, and Italy, the books he collected, and the new designs published in American journals provided him with a richly expressive architectural language capable of infinite permutations. It was, moreover, a flexible language that could evolve to meet new needs and respond to fresh opportunities. Underlying the styles that Cutter exploited were principles, many of them rooted in the Arts and Crafts movement, to which he constantly returned. His work in California, initiated almost four decades later, represents an alternative vision, distinct from the creative eclecticism of his early years; it sought a unified expression of regional identity, a common preoccupation of many architects at that time.

When Cutter arrived in the Northwest in 1886, he found the prominent citizens of Spokane building in pretentious late Victorian styles. Vertically clustered houses in the French Second Empire and Queen Anne styles stood aloof from the land in formal gardens. Like his more progressive contemporaries in the East, he disdained this type of architecture and looked for guidance in the principles of the Arts and Crafts movement. H. H. Richardson and the creators of the Shingle Style also helped show him the way to a more vigorous and natural architecture. Making his own interpretation of their concepts, and drawing inspiration from vernacular traditions, he began in 1889 to build houses that were closely associated with the rugged terrain of the South Hill of Spokane. Here he exploited rough native basalt to anchor rambling, many-gabled houses to rocky hillsides. Fifty years later, when he was designing houses of Hispanic inspiration at Palos Verdes near Los Angeles, he was true to the same principles. He integrated these houses subtly into their settings in a way that respected the character of each site on the steep peninsula jutting out into the Pacific. Cutter also carried his love of nature sometimes to an extreme by designing rustic buildings using natural materials in their raw state. In such structures as the Idaho Building at the World's Columbian Exposition of 1893 and Lake-McDonald Lodge, built in Glacier National Park in 1913, he contributed significantly to a unique American type that celebrates the grandeur of wilderness.

While he believed in the Arts and Crafts ethic of simplicity and fitness to purpose, he was also excited by exotic and extravagant architecture. Thus he indulged in experiments drawing inspiration from Islamic and oriental sources. His 1897 residence for the mining magnate Patrick Clark in Browne's Addition, Spokane, is the quintessential millionaire's mansion, expressing not only the wealth and status of its owner but also the architect's fantasy on the potential of wealth. This house still presents a unique synthesis of romantic ideas and practical considerations. The two extremes of the rustic picturesque and exotic extravagance, both of which fascinated Cutter, represent polarized directions.

It was Cutter's good fortune to be presented with a clean slate on which to work: a fledgling city waiting for his imagination to bring it to life, and sites still in their natural state that could inspire an architectural response. When he opened his office there were few qualified architects in Spokane to show up his inexperience, but skilled craftsmen were available to realize his designs. His patrons, the enterprising men and women who helped create the wealth and culture of the region, offered him extraordinary freedom and at the same time placed demands on him that stretched his talents and expertise. Cutter did not merely fulfill his clients' requirements; he influenced their desires, gently persuading them to temper pragmatism with romantic inclinations. Although his buildings functioned as efficient settings for complex and often formal social rituals, he considered how to make them comfortable as well as impressive. They were rarely without playful touches.

The role of Kirtland Cutter's partners and draftsmen in the practice is not entirely clear. He was in partnership with John C. Poetz from 1889 to 1894 and with Karl Gunnar Malmgren from 1894 to 1917. It appears, however, that Cutter was always the dominant partner and that he initiated the major designs. He needed the help of experienced colleagues to deal with the large volume of work that passed through the office. Indeed they brought technical skills he did not have, but there can be no doubt that he set the artistic direction of the firm and personally attracted the majority of the commissions.

Although it might have been easier for me and for the general reader if I had simply selected a few of Cutter's best works and analyzed his career based on the high points, I think that to understand an architect we need to look at the entire body of work. In each of his types of architecture, certain examples stand out which seem most fully to realize his intentions. But others, exploring variations on the same themes, help to explain his approach to the concepts he followed and demonstrate the range of his creativity. I also believe that there is a need for a comprehensive guide to help those interested in the architecture of his period identify particular buildings and place a broad range of examples in their historical context. This book both selects highlights and demonstrates the breadth of his accomplishment.

Since a monograph this detailed on an architect who practiced for fifty years and was responsible for hundreds of buildings could read like a catalogue of projects, I have attempted to group them in a way that allows for continuity in the discussion. Although I have in general taken a chronological approach, much of the book is organized thematically, with chapters on particular topics that help to interpret his work. The themes relate to aspects of the architect's practice, specific building types, architectural styles, and facets of Cutter's life. Some chapters focus on relatively short time spans; others deal with buildings that reveal a single design concept over a longer period. The chapter discussing the first boom in Cutter's practice immediately after the Spokane fire of 1889 covers his work during two busy years, while the one on summer camps in the wilderness traces through two decades a particular architectural type to which Cutter made a significant contribution.

Cutter left little in the way of theoretical writings. Like many of his contemporaries, he was much more interested in practice than in theory.[6] We find evidence of his interests by examining the books he possessed and the few statements he made in letters and newspaper interviews. As far as is known, he published only one article—a short piece on domestic architecture that appeared in 1909. His own architecture must therefore speak for him. Many of Cutter's works stand today and enrich their surroundings. The majority of these are still in their original use as residences, hotels, clubs, or commercial premises, but others have been successfully adapted to new purposes and therefore preserved. Few have suffered seriously from inappropriate alterations; and with the help of owners who respect them, some have recently been restored. Most notable of these is the Davenport Hotel in Spokane, a symbol of the city's success. After years of mistreatment and even the threat of demolition, it is in the process of restoration. Kirtland Cutter's imagination and design skills are still a delight to those who occupy his buildings, as indeed they are to those who pass by.

CHAPTER ONE

Whippoorwill Farm

KIRTLAND KELSEY CUTTER WAS BORN AUGUST 20, 1860, in the village of East Rockport, near Cleveland, Ohio. He spent his first seventeen years at the home of his mother's grandfather, Jared Kirtland, a distinguished physician and naturalist. His father, William Lemen Cutter, a prosperous bank official, and his mother, Caroline Atwater Pease, both came from pioneer Ohio families. His parents must have felt a deep involvement with the thriving city of Cleveland, for so many of their ancestors had played important roles in its founding and development. Their marriage linked families active in business on William's side and distinguished in the learned professions on Caroline's. They brought into the world a child so well provided with enterprising and successful relatives and ancestors that he had no reason to doubt his own worth or question his ability to achieve his ambitions. Joined by his sisters Laura in 1862 and Caroline (known as Caddie) in 1866, he benefited from the company of four generations of his family.

His mother's forebears on both sides had been among the first explorers, settlers, and public officials of the Western Reserve. Her great-uncle Seth Pease accompanied General Moses Cleveland on his first expedition in 1796, as a surveyor and astronomer. The next year he laid out the plan of Cleveland with a grid of wide streets and a public square.[1] Seth's brother Calvin, her grandfather, helped to establish law in the new territory. He began his career from a log cabin, and as a circuit judge rode over rugged terrain between distant townships. Family legend claims that to carry out his duties he

1.1 William Lemen Cutter, Kirtland's father. Photo by J. F. Ryder. Eastern Washington State Historical Society, L94–60.2.

1.2 Caroline Pease Cutter, Kirtland's mother. Photo by Green of Schwerdt, Cleveland. Eastern Washington State Historical Society, Peggy Bayless Collection, L94–60.3.

made a point of choosing horses that could swim well. At the peak of his professional life he became chief justice of the Ohio supreme court.[2]

In 1798, Caroline's great-grandfather on her mother's side, Turhand Kirtland, had also led a survey party to the new territory. Born in Wallingford, Connecticut, where his family had farmed since arriving from England in 1633, Turhand became one of the founders of the Connecticut Land Company, which purchased title to the Western Reserve. He made the arduous boat journey west several times with parties of emigrants via the Niagara River, hauling boats around the falls and reaching the future state of Ohio by Lake Erie. Settling permanently in Poland, Ohio, in 1803, Turhand worked as an agent of the company, selling tracts of land, promoting settlements, and "introducing schools and various improvements." He gained respect among the settlers, who elected him a judge and then a state senator.[3] The house he built for himself in Poland still stands, a witness to the simple elegance and good proportions of the Federal Period.

When Turhand left New England, his young son Jared Potter Kirtland (1793–1877) stayed behind in Connecticut to be educated by his grandfather, Dr. Jared Potter, a pioneering physician who kept a medical school. Potter became his mentor and taught him to question common beliefs. Under his tutelage Jared became an acute observer of nature, and even as a young man carried out original research in botany and entomology.

At the age of seventeen, summoned west because of his father's ill health, Jared rode to Ohio with two companions. Excited by the unfamiliar flora and fauna he found along the way, he took notes, even stopping at the lakes to dissect fish specimens that were new to science. By the time he finally arrived in Poland, Jared found that his father had recovered from his illness. He spent the next year there teaching school and recording scientific information about his new surroundings.

When his grandfather, Dr. Potter, died leaving him his medical library and enough money to attend medical school, Jared enrolled at Yale University and followed in his benefactor's footsteps, practicing medicine in Wallingford and studying the natural world. He was described as "a veritable human worm, boring his way to knowledge by a precocious system of analysis and investigation applied to everything he touched and saw." On the death of his wife and one of his daughters in 1823, he returned to Ohio to join his father and soon became one of the leading medical men and scientists in the West, passing on his knowledge to many doctors, farmers, and naturalists. He possessed an irresistible personal magnetism that inspired others: "The man who came to him with a stolid contempt for book-learning and with no sense of the beautiful as distinct from the profitable left him with higher views and nobler impulses. With an art beyond all art, because it was nature, the clod, the miser, were lured out of themselves and brought to see the world through the eyes of a magician."[4]

This was the man who helped guide young Kirtland Cutter through his formative years, who taught him observation, analysis, and the appreciation of natural beauty. By the time the two were together at East Rockport, Jared had risen to a position of eminence with many achievements to his name. He served three terms in the Ohio State Legislature, and assisted in the geological survey of Ohio. He became professor of theory and practice of medicine at the University of Cincinnati and later at Cleveland Medical College, which he helped to found. He was also a founder of the Cleveland Academy of Sciences and the author of a catalogue of the mammals, birds, reptiles, fishes, and mollusks of the state, complete with his own drawings. As an expert taxidermist he prepared specimens for his own vast collection as well as for other institutions, including the British Museum. Although an active member of many national learned societies, he was always ready to give time to private pupils and to his great-grandson. His advanced age was apparently no impediment.[5]

Jared Kirtland's greatest pleasure was in his model farm at East Rockport. In 1840, tired of living in the city, cut off from the natural phenomena he loved to observe, he had purchased eighty-three acres on the shore of Lake Erie. Here he built Whippoorwill Farm, a modest house of stone dredged from the bed of the Rocky River two miles to the north.[6] He surrounded it with a large, private arboretum stocked with many species of trees, including magnolias of spectacular size. Over many years, he carried out experiments in the cultivation of fruit trees and developed new varieties best adapted to the climate.[7]

Young Kirtland Cutter spent happy hours on the farm, in the orchards, and in the arboretum on the edge of the lake. He could also explore the private museum where Jared kept his outstanding natural history collection. In a letter, his great-grandfather described him at the age of ten "as being of bronze molasses color with his frame rapidly developing in height, breadth and grace into the model of Abram Lincoln. His time is mostly spent out of doors on the farm, and the hens, turkies, rats and mice all are embraced in his charge and jurisdiction, snakes and fishes included."[8]

Years later, Kirtland Cutter admitted that when he was young he had wanted to be a naturalist himself, and acknowledged his debt to his great-grandfather.[9] No doubt the old man loved to explain for him the mysteries of nature, and it may have been under his tutelage that the boy did his first drawings. With scholars coming from distant places to visit the "sage of Rockport" and so many phenomena to awaken a sense of wonder, Whippoorwill Farm must have seemed a very important place in a rich and intriguing world.

It was also a place where moral values and humanitarian concerns could be absorbed. Jared Kirtland was not a religious man; he had acquired a skepticism from his mentor, Dr. Potter. However, he was a man of strong moral convictions who believed in the fundamental rights of the individual. He spoke out vehemently against the execution of John Brown, volunteered at the age of sixty-nine to

1.3 Kirtland Cutter
as a child. Eastern
Washington State
Historical Society,
L85–174.2.

assist as a doctor in the Civil War, and pioneered legislation in penitentiary reform.[10]

His obituary in the *Cleveland Herald* portrays him as a veritable Saint Francis of the Middle West: "He was a diligent student of nature, and nature repaid him in a charming way. The birds, the bees, the insects, the trees he planted, tended, and engrafted with his own hands, the flowers, and the grasses under his feet, all seemed to know and love him. . . . Amidst swarms of bees he went unharmed and the very birds around his dwelling scarce moved at his approach."[11]

1.4 Dr. Jared Potter Kirtland, Kirtland Cutter's great-grandfather. Painting by Allen Smith. Cleveland Museum of Art, Neg. 1397.

Jared Kirtland's daughter Mary Elizabeth married Charles Pease, the son of Judge Calvin Pease. Charles did not follow family tradition by studying for a learned or scientific profession, but entered the world of business and became involved in property and railroad development. His success enabled the family to live in comfort and prosperity. In 1836 the couple moved from the Pease home at Warren, Ohio, to Cleveland, and in 1850 they joined Jared Kirtland at Whippoorwill Farm, which they helped to rebuild.

Mary Elizabeth gave birth to four children, two of whom survived childhood: Charles and Caroline, Kirtland Cutter's mother. Uncle Charles, who also lived at Whippoorwill Farm, carried on the family tradition as a naturalist and explorer. In 1862 he joined a party of young naturalists from the Smithsonian Institution to explore the Yukon River in Alaska. After the members of the expedition had endured "all manner of hardship and privation," the leader died and it fell to Charles to bring his body back, over eight hundred miles "by the water of the great lonely river." He "earned the proud title of being the first American, if not the first white man, who had ever passed down the great flood of the Yukon to the sea."[12]

While the Pease and Kirtland families gained their prominence through achievements in law, science, and the exploitation of land, the Cutters were involved in trade and commerce. But they too had played a part in the opening of the Western Reserve, and like the Peases and Kirtlands they belonged to old American families whose ancestors had come from England in the early seventeenth century. Orlando Cutter, Kirtland Cutter's paternal grandfather, certainly had tales to tell about his life and adventures as a pioneer, but he could also offer the young boy words of wisdom about hard work and honesty.

Orlando was born in New Hampshire, but moved to Boston where he worked for "a large jobbing house." He must have made an exceptionally good impression on his employers, for when he was only twenty-one they "offered him credit for dry goods to the amount of ten thousand dollars, with which to go West to seek his fortune." Orlando decided to make a preliminary trip to select a suitable place to open a business. He borrowed four hundred dollars and set off on horseback in the spring of 1818: "He started with a pair of well-filled saddle bags as an outfit, and in due time arrived in Cleveland. He reached this city by water on the 30th of June 1818, having spent nine dismal days on the schooner Ben Franklin, en route from Black Rock. . . . Cleveland then contained but two hundred inhabitants and four stores. Water Street was the only thoroughfare to the lake that was cleared sufficiently for travel. . . . Twenty or thirty teams driven by Germans from Pennsylvania . . . were encamped in Superior Street on the night of Mr. Cutter's arrival and they gave the town such a business-like appearance that he became quite enchanted with it."[13]

Orlando judged well in his choice of site, but made an unfortunate choice of partners. The business started well, but his partners absconded, leaving him alone to face a debt of thirty thousand dollars. Rather than shirk his responsibilities, he spent "ten years of hard labor working to pay off his indebtedness to the company which had put their trust in him." Orlando was joined by his brother

Abilene, who worked for him as a clerk before setting up on his own as a dry goods merchant in Cleveland. Orlando himself branched out into auctioneering and for many years ran a successful auction house, handling everything from furs and stuffed birds to the materials from demolished buildings.[14]

Grandfather Orlando Cutter married twice and fathered twelve children, eight of whom survived and were living in Cleveland during Cutter's childhood. Only the eldest, Edwin, went into the family business. William Lemen, Kirtland's father, started work at the age of sixteen as messenger boy for the Merchant's National Bank. Within eight years he had "worked his way up step by step to the cashiership, learning thoroughly the entire routine of the banking business."[15] He held this responsible position, equivalent to bank vice president today, until his death. William's brothers John and Horace also entered banking; and Norman, the youngest son, was a bookkeeper for a Cleveland iron works.

Kirtland's father remains a somewhat shadowy figure. While the Cleveland newspapers abound with references to members of the Cutter clan, the only notices referring to him are concerned with his role at the bank. They suggest that he was an efficient and respected banker.[16] Living at East Rockport with his parents-in-law, Charles and Mary Elizabeth Pease, and Jared Kirtland, it is reasonable to assume that William Cutter was absorbed in his work and family.

Whether young Kirtland spent much time with his grandfather Cutter is unknown. Orlando was a patriarchal figure, possibly rather dour and frightening to a little boy. The sermon preached by the Reverend H. C. Hayden in the Presbyterian Church at the time of his death, in 1875, paints a vivid picture of him as "a man of the old time . . . of unimpeachable integrity" but with "almost excessive devotion to worldly affairs." While to a stranger he may have seemed "brusque and cold" the minister credited him with a "pleasant vein of humor, and . . . a warm, tender heart."[17]

The old auctioneer may well have doted on his little grandson, the only male child of his own hard-working son William Lemen. Perhaps young Kirtland was welcomed into the auction rooms by a genial grandfather and proudly shown the paintings, fine furniture, and bric-a-brac. Or this may have seemed to him a spooky place presided over by a gruff old man who would not let him touch the objects on view. In any case, Cutter's auction rooms presented a constantly changing world of mystery and wonder that might fuel the imagination of a sensitive child.

At Whippoorwill Farm, Kirtland lived in an extended family. Four generations shared the house and estate, including Uncle Charles the explorer and his children.[18] It was a place of large family gatherings with countless visitors and lively conversation. There was probably much talk of the early family members who had played such a significant part in creating the state of Ohio.

2.1 Brooks School, Cleveland, built in 1875. Described in the Cleveland press both as English and as Swiss in style. From Rose, *Cleveland: The Making of a City* (Cleveland, 1950).

CHAPTER TWO

The Education of an Artist

IN THE FALL OF 1874, WHEN KIRTLAND WAS FOURTEEN
years old, he was enrolled along with the sons of many prominent
citizens in the newly opened Brooks School. The first headmaster,
a Harvard man, organized a curriculum including Greek, Latin,
French, German, geology, and botany. The school had a variety of
music classes, but apparently did not offer drawing or painting.
Because "increased patriotism and preparedness" were considered
"essential to national security," military training was required. Indeed
the school, sometimes described as Brooks Military Academy, was
known for its well-drilled school battalion, which appeared in
parades "dressed in handsome new uniforms." Capacity crowds
attended "complimentary drills" at which the boys entertained
spectators with "bayonet practice executed with perfect timing"
and "candle snuffing at 10 feet with only a cap on the gun." The
drills were often combined with the recitation of stirring poetry
such as "The Captive Knight" and "How Horatio Kept the Bridge."[1]

Nothing in Kirtland's later life suggests that the discipline of military training would have appealed to him. Reports of prizes for
scholastic and athletic achievements do not include his name. But
in one respect the school may have influenced him significantly. In
1875, Brooks School moved from temporary classrooms in a commercial block into a new, specially designed building near Sibley
and Hayward Streets (fig. 2.1). The half-timbered schoolhouse, with
prominent diagonal cross braces, was unlike anything Cleveland
had seen before. Critics described it variously as English or Swiss,

2.2 Michigan State Building, Centennial Exposition, Philadelphia, 1876, by Julian Hess. Architectural character is created by forceful expression of the framing. *McCabe Illustrated History of the Centennial Exhibition* (Philadelphia: Jones Bros. and Co., 1876).

2.3 George Kirtland house, Poland, Ohio, ca. 1830. Displays the classical formality of the Greek Revival Style. Ohio Historical Society.

but in fact it belonged to a uniquely American type, based only remotely on the vernacular traditions of Europe. The bold expression of the framing and the huge brackets of the corner towers were characteristic of the Stick Style, which developed on the East Coast in the 1860s and 1870s. American architecture in the eighteenth and early nineteenth centuries, attempting to reproduce in wood the surface effect of brick or stone, had denied the existence of a building's wooden frame.[2] In contrast, the Stick Style accentuated the inner structure.

In the mid-1870s an elaborate version of the Stick Style emerged with a new infusion of Swiss influence in the form of broad, overhanging eaves supported on dominant brackets. This phenomenen reached its peak in the Michigan Building at the Philadelphia Centennial Exposition of 1876, which offered fantastic variations on a Swiss theme (fig. 2.2). The slightly earlier Brooks School was by no means as elaborate, but appears to belong to the same type. While English half-timbered houses tended to have blackened beams and the mountain chalets of Switzerland were generally built with a natural wood finish, the framed houses of southern Germany and the lower regions of Switzerland were often painted a reddish brown. Brooks School followed this palette, with beams colored chocolate and vermilion.[3] The excitement of moving into the new building may have initiated Kirtland's lifelong fascination with half-timbered buildings.

Meanwhile, American architecture was in a state of flux. Jared Kirtland's generation had built their houses in the classical tradition which had prevailed since about 1700. His brother George erected an elegant house in Poland Ohio, in 1830 in the Federal Style (fig. 2.3). Close by in the same town his other brother Billius built one in the more up to date Greek Revival Style.[4] Whippoorwill Farm was comparatively simple when first built (fig. 2.4), for Jared wanted to create a pleasant retreat from the city with little outward show. But later, when Charles Pease and his family came to live there with his father, the house was rebuilt in the rambling asymmetrical manner of the Gothic Revival (fig. 2.5). Its irregular roofline and informal porches show the architectural influence of Andrew Jackson Downing, who had advocated less formal design to fit the landscape and the lives of the inhabitants.

The Greek and Gothic revivals had flourished side by side until the Civil War. Then, with hostilities over and reconstruction under way, public tastes changed. An explosion of business activity inspired

2.4 Whippoorwill Farm, home of Jared Kirtland, as originally constructed. Historical Division, Cleveland Health Sciences Library.

2.5 Whippoorwill Farm, rebuilt in a rambling, picturesque style, ca. 1870. Historical Division, Cleveland Health Sciences Library.

2.6 R. K. Winslow house, Euclid Avenue, Cleveland, 1878, design by Levi Schofield. A combination of French Second Empire and Gothic Revival. Western Reserve Historical Society.

ambitious building projects. Huge fortunes were made and the newly rich took pleasure in displaying their wealth. Kirtland would have witnessed the transformation of the center of Cleveland from an old town of small-scale buildings to a city where new, larger, highly ornamented structures were going up everywhere. Out on Euclid Avenue, near the Brooks School sports fields, impressive mansions were rising in the High Victorian Styles. Based on grandiose Italian villas or the florid palaces of Second Empire France, they were often eclectic in detail. The house built in 1878 to a design by Levi Schofield for Jared Kirtland's friend Rufus K. Winslow (fig. 2.6) combined the steep mansard roof and central tower of the French Second Empire Baroque with Gothic windows and dormers.[5] It alludes to the French chateau of the fifteenth century but belongs without doubt to the American Age of Enterprise. Whether Kirtland took much notice of such architectural evolutions can only be speculated, but we do know that soon after he left Brooks School he had made up his mind to study art.

Kirtland's introduction to drawing was probably through scientific illustration at the home of his great-grandfather. In a relatively tasteless age, there was perhaps more to be learned from a naturalist's drawings of plants or birds than from the pictures on the walls of most middle-class living rooms. While this was an era of significant experimentation, popular artists of the seventies and eighties showed strong sentimental tendencies. American historical works, and biblical and genre scenes, often stressed morality or invoked sickly pathos. Such subjects as The Wayward Son and The Wise and Foolish Virgins took their place on parlor walls beside wood nymphs in sylvan landscapes. Engravings of Renaissance masters and plaster casts of Greek and Roman art were displayed in many homes. Academic art prevailed, and innovation was generally regarded with suspicion.

Young Kirtland's imagination may have been stirred by scenes of the frontier that were available in engravings. Paintings such as Albert Bierstadt's *Among the Sierra Nevada Mountains, California* (1868) dramatized the opening of the West through sublime interpretations of the western landscape. Emanuel Leutze's *Westward the Course of Empire Takes Its Way* proclaimed the heroic nature of Manifest Destiny. Another source of visual education was to be found in weekly and monthly magazines, such as *Harper's* and *The Century Magazine.* These publications brought the work of major painters and sculptors into the living rooms of readers in cities where there were no art galleries. And they ran travel articles that projected visions of an exciting and romantic world beyond the shores of America, explored and recorded by intrepid artists and illustrators. Their engravings and line drawings, which conveyed vivid, romantic images of artistic cities and picturesque landscapes, could hardly have failed to stimulate a desire for travel in an impressionable young man.

Kirtland entered the field of art at a time when many American artists were turning to Europe for teaching and guidance; it was also a time of profound changes. The academies of Europe, which had maintained their power as arbiters of public taste for many years, were now assailed by young artists challenging the principles of classical art on which their authority was based. One major American artist who chose to work in Europe was James McNeill Whistler, who as early as the 1860s contradicted the traditional concepts of subject matter. He described his works as arrangements in light, form, and color and titled them "symphonies," "harmonies," or "nocturnes" in white, blue, silver, or black.

In the same decade, the French Impressionists used broken brush strokes to convey their observations of the fragmentation of form by light. Painting outdoors rather than in the studio, they interpreted contemporary life as they saw it. Some American artists, such as Mary Cassatt and Theodore Robinson, also played an active role in redefining the nature of landscape. William Merritt Chase, working under the influence of Impressionism in the 1880s, succeeded in gaining recognition among the American art establishment. By this time in Europe, Postimpressionists such as Gauguin and Van Gogh again altered the foundations of art by emphasizing emotion, conveyed with simplified color and line.

While New York and Philadelphia were the principal centers for artistic activity in America, Ohio was not a complete backwater. Though Cleveland lagged behind as it gradually became an industrial center, Cincinnati, known as the Paris of the West, was enjoying a cultural boom. Its Conservatory of Music, Art Academy, and University attested to its citizens' appreciation of the arts.[6] In the 1870s, Ohio produced a surprising number of important artists, including several associated with Impressionism. Frank Duveneck, born near Cincinnati in 1849, was an outstanding painter who succeeded in developing his own style, combining the bold brushwork of the modern painters with the "mellow tones of an old master." Although his parents were struggling immigrants, Duveneck studied at the Royal Academy in Munich, which rivaled the École des Beaux Arts in Paris as the leading school in Europe. After distinguishing himself at the academy, he went back to Cincinnati to teach at McMicken School of Art. But after a year he returned to Munich, where in 1878 he opened his own school. His American pupils there were soon known as "the Duveneck boys." The following year he moved with ten students to Florence, where they spent two winters. Passing the summers in Venice, the group met frequently with Whistler, who was working there at the time. One of Duveneck's pupils in Cincinnati, the Impressionist John Twachtman, went with him to Munich and in 1880 joined the staff of the school in Florence. The Impressionist painter Theodore Butler, who was almost the same age as Kirtland, studied at Marietta College in Ohio before going to New York.[7]

While such progressive tendencies were germinating in Ohio, Kirtland probably came in contact with the conservative, academic painter Kenyon Cox. Born in Warren, Ohio, where Cutter's grandfather Charles Pease lived, Cox was only four years older than Kirt-land. His father, General Jacob Cox, was both governor of Ohio and president of the University of Cincinnati, where Jared P. Kirtland had taught in the medical school. Since he was also a scientist, and microscopist, it is certain that he and Jared Kirtland were acquainted. Cox was determined from an early age to be an artist. When he was only thirteen, he studied under Duveneck in Cincinnati. In 1877, at the age of twenty-one, he went to study at the École des Beaux Arts in Paris under Gérôme, whom he greatly revered. He emerged from his European education as a rigidly classical painter.[8]

If Kirtland took art classes in Cleveland, he would probably have studied with Archibald Willard, who in 1876 founded the Cleveland Art Club, otherwise known as the Old Bohemians. Willard, whose fame rested on a highly patriotic painting exhibited in Philadelphia that year, *The Spirit of '76,* gave lessons in his studio on the top floor of City Hall. Among the young artists in his circle, while Kirtland was still in the city, were Max Bohm, who later studied in New York and Paris, and Otto Bacher, a talented illustrator who followed Duveneck to Munich, Florence, and Venice. Bacher befriended Whistler and is perhaps best known for a piece he wrote for *The Century Magazine:* "With Whistler in Venice."[9]

In the absence of detailed information on Kirtland's life in the early eighties, there is little choice but to accept a brief account based on an interview with him written almost forty years later: "Early in life Mr. Cutter wanted to be an illustrator—or at least so he thought at the time. After a course at the Art Students' League in New York under Beckwith and Kenyon Cox, it was his privilege to continue his studies in the old world atmosphere, particularly in Dresden and Florence."[10]

Unfortunately, the newspaper article presents us with a problem: Kenyon Cox did not join the faculty of the Art Students' League until 1885.[11] It is possible that Kirtland studied at the League under Beckwith in the early eighties and returned, after a period in Europe, to continue his education under Cox.[12] Or he may have visited Cox in Paris as a family friend and taken some lessons from him there.

The Art Students League offered a freedom found in few other art schools (fig. 2.7). It was formed in 1875 by the students them-selves, after the directors of the National Academy of Design, tired of rebellious pupils, announced that they would close their school. Refusing to be discouraged, a group of students persuaded Profes-sor Wilmarth, their favorite teacher, to run classes modeled on the

2.7 Carroll Beckwith's antique class at the Art Students League.
Harper's Magazine.

Parisian ateliers. Soon the Art Students' League was able to open
its doors to all who were prepared to work hard and pay the modest dues.[13] It offered students the chance to "get the strictest classical training" from masters of the academic camp or study under
more progressive artists. As an early graduate of the school
explained: "They made a school entirely independent, entirely
free—free of control, of advice, of obligation; the sort of school
they themselves wanted. They hired the teachers they thought well
of. It was a school made by students, supported by students and
managed by students."[14] It was a system that encouraged self-reliance
and independent thinking, in which the student had to provide his
own discipline.

Kirtland Cutter was fortunate to study under Carroll Beckwith,
a talented painter with a breadth of outlook derived from recent
European study. In Paris, Beckwith had studied classical techniques
of draftsmanship under Carolus-Duran, a pillar of the Beaux Arts
establishment, but he also came under the influence of the French
Impressionists and shared a studio with William Merritt Chase.
Beckwith is best known for his Impressionist style and for his
efforts to introduce Impressionism in America.[15]

Cutter would have received a more traditional type of teaching from Kenyon Cox, whose studies in Paris under Gérôme had been quickly rewarded with success. Having exhibited in the Paris Salon between 1879 and 1882, he returned to America and took a studio in New York. Soon he found that he could fulfill American dreams of a classical past through large-scale public commissions. Two decades later in *The Classic Point of View* he expressed his conservative views on art: "The Classic Spirit is the disinterested search for perfection; it is the love of clearness and reasonableness and self-control; it is above all, the love of permanence and of continuity. It asks of a work of art, not that it shall be novel or effective, but that it shall be fine and noble."[16]

Cox found the virtues he described in Puvis de Chavannes's great murals in the Paris Pantheon, but he sneered at Impressionism, recognizing in it only an interesting technique. He considered

2.8 Group photograph taken in Dresden in 1882. From left: Maurice Clark, Louise Corbin, Laura Cutter, Douglas Schneider, Mrs. Cutter, Caroline Cutter (Caddie), Miss Ruggles, Kirtland Cutter, Austin Corbin, future client and brother-in-law. Photo by M. Scherer and Engler, Dresden. Eastern Washington State Historical Society, L85–174.10.

the Postimpressionists utterly despicable, attempting "pure self-expression—to the exaltation of the great god Whim."[17]

How long Kirtland stayed at the Art Students League is uncertain; but it is clear that at some time in the early 1880s he decided to travel to Europe and continue his studies there. During this period it was widely accepted that serious students of art must go to European art schools. In 1879, the American artist Frank Millet wrote: "London and Paris are the centers of the world and the best artists will congregate there." For others, Munich was the Mecca. As the "Duveneck boys" moved from Munich to Florence and to Venice, these European cities were home to many American art students. One of their favorite gathering places, the Piazza San Marco in Venice, has been called the "living room of Europe" and "a popular center of international society."[18]

Cutter's travels were probably well financed, but many students lived bohemian, communal lives, crowded into cheap boarding houses and mingling with intellectual travelers in outdoor cafes.[19] Some studied in official academies or in the studios of painters who took pupils; others moved from place to place, absorbing new ideas and influences in a more casual way. Only a few scraps of evidence can be used to construct a picture of Kirtland's European study. Since we know he was in both Venice and Florence, it would be tempting to think that he was one of the "Duveneck boys." However, if he had studied under such a successful artist, he would certainly have claimed the association, as he did with Kenyon Cox. But he could easily have met some of Duveneck's protégées in Florence or Venice.

In April 1880, when Kirtland was only nineteen years old, his father died suddenly of heart disease,[20] leaving his wife a forty-two-year-old widow. In August of the same year, Caroline Cutter made a bold decision to travel in Europe with Kirtland's younger sisters, Laura and Caddie.[21] The itinerary included Switzerland, where Laura attended a young ladies' boarding school in a chateau.[22] It is not clear whether Kirtland traveled with them at that time, but the whole family was in Dresden two years later. They appear together in a group portrait by a Dresden photographer dated 1882 (fig. 2.8). Mrs. Cutter and her three children are shown with Austin Corbin, the son of an American railway magnate, his sister Louise, and three other Americans. The men are wearing outlandish headgear and six of the group are carrying shepherds' crooks. It is said that Kirtland Cutter met Austin Corbin at the Anglo-American Club in Paris

2.9 Kirtland Cutter, age twenty-two, showing signs of early baldness. Inscribed on back: "Very lovingly, Kirt, Lucerne, Suisse, 1 Aug 82." Eastern Washington State Historical Society. L85–174.3.

and that they went on a walking tour of Switzerland together.[23] Cutter later claimed to have studied the design of the Swiss chalet while traveling in the Alps.[24] He may have done so on this tour. Cutter's association with Austin Corbin in Europe is of interest because Austin and his family were to play an important role in Kirtland's future.[25] Another photograph (fig. 2.9), taken in Dresden in 1882, shows Kirtland as an earnest young man with prematurely thinning hair.

It seems clear that Kirtland spent some time studying in Dresden, a city that offered outstanding opportunities. It was regarded at that time as the Florence of Germany—one of the great art cities of Europe—with fine art galleries and a splendid architectural setting. Here Kirtland could see buildings from nine centuries intermingled, providing constant variety as well as historic continuity. In comparison, the American cities he had experienced were so new and quickly built. When Charles Dickens visited New York, he noted the gaudy colors of the signboards, the brilliant paint on the buildings, "and all so slight and insubstantial in appearance—that every thoroughfare in the city looked exactly like a scene in a pantomime."[26] Dresden, on the other hand, with its medieval and Baroque architecture forming a dramatic skyline, might have seemed more like a series of scenes from grand opera. Its Royal Palace—with lively Dutch gables—and its civic and religious build-

ings possessed a heroic quality. Playful Baroque and Rococo town-
houses lined the streets and even the seedier parts of town were
picturesque.

In the nineteenth century, important classical architecture,
including Gottfried Semper's opera house of 1871, was built there.
Under the influence of Semper, who held the post of professor of
architecture at the Dresden Academy, the city had developed a reputation as a progressive center for architectural education.[27] At the
time of Cutter's visit, the Judgendstil, Germany's equivalent of Art
Nouveau, was in vogue in the city. Several architectural firms were
doing avant-garde work in Dresden—work that appears to have
influenced some of Cutter's designs. His early architectural work
makes it clear that the classic solemnity of Dresden's public architecture appealed to him less than the picturesque qualities to be
found in the small towns and villages of Saxony. The irregular pattern of half-timbered walls and gables around marketplaces, and
the clusters of farm buildings in the countryside, appear to have
offered him more inspiration (fig. 2.10). Years later, he described
Nuremberg as possessing "what American cities lack most, namely
the quaint architectural unity and interesting skyline that gives that
city an indescribable charm."[28]

2.10 Title block of
*Alte Fachwerkbauten
der Provinz Sachsen*
(1903), a book in
Cutter's library on
traditional timber
framed buildings
in Saxony. Eastern
Washington State
Historical Society.
Rare Books.

Of all the cities in Italy, Florence was the best known to English-speaking art lovers. While Rome, shaped by emperors and popes, was unmatched for its grandeur, and waterborne Venice, poised between East and West, had a magic of its own, Florence was the place where the spirit of the early Renaissance was most accessible to the visitor. In Dresden the main art collections were displayed in museums and therefore divorced from their original contexts. But in Florence, in addition to seeing works of art in the Uffizi and Pitti Galleries, the visitor could enjoy paintings in the very places where the citizens of the thirteenth and fourteenth centuries first set eyes on them. In the church of Santa Croce, the student could imagine the amazement of those who first perceived the realism in Giotto's frescoes. Gazing at Masaccio's *Tribute Money* in the Brancacci Chapel, one could understand the momentous discovery of linear perspective. A student could enter the tiny cells at the convent of San Marco and see the frescoes of Fra Angelico, from the physical viewpoint of a quattrocento monk.

Like Dresden, Florence was a city of variety and contrast. Many of the streets were narrow, dominated by forbidding palazzi, whose rusticated walls once protected the fortunes of wealthy bankers and merchants. But within them one could catch glimpses into peaceful courtyards, enlivened with flowers. The city also offered spacious and welcoming public squares where pedestrians could linger in the shade. Under Brunelleschi's graceful arches in the Piazza Santissima Annunziata, the traveler could sense the democratic spirit and enlightened patronage that launched the Renaissance in architecture. Above Florence towered Brunelleschi's proud dome, Giotto's Campanile, and the brooding watchtower of the Signoria. From the eleventh-century church of San Miniato on the hill across the river Arno to the south, Kirtland may have looked out over the city and dreamed of his own artistic career.

If he stayed long in Florence, he may have made excursions into the hills of Tuscany and sketched the picturesque villages and farmhouses, standing as naturally in the landscape as outcroppings of rock. While the classicism of the High Renaissance does not appear to have been a major influence on him, the rustic structures in the Tuscan hills have qualities he was to emulate in many of his own designs.

There is much evidence in Kirtland Cutter's early work, indeed throughout his career, that the English Arts and Crafts movement was the source of his most important influence in architecture and

2.11 Kirtland Cutter as a young man, now wearing a luxuriant wig. Eastern Washington State Historical Society, L94–9.4.

design. Launched by William Morris and his mentor John Ruskin in the 1850s, this movement produced not so much a unified style as an ethic. Their followers valued craftsmanship and simplicity in design, seeking inspiration in cottage furniture and humble, vernacular buildings. They despised the pretentiousness of Victorian taste and greatly preferred the medieval era to the Renaissance. The aspiring architect could have absorbed the teachings of Ruskin and Morris in the United States, and seen the designs of architects working under their spell in journals; but his own earliest houses suggest a familiarity with the rural traditions of England that they admired most. On the other hand, he had clearly been seduced by the quest, in the Aesthetic movement, for beauty of a more sensual and exotic type.[29]

According to legends current in Spokane, Kirtland returned to America with suits tailored in Savile Row, leading to the conclusion that he also passed through London. Few other clues shed light on his travels; however, it is certain that he was back in the United States by 1886.[30] And by this time he had given up his ambition to be an artist. Early in life he wanted to be an illustrator, but from his own recollections thirty years later we know that he began to set his sights on a career in architecture instead. One factor was what he called a "little kink in his color discerning apparatus," an inability to see the

Break, break, break,
At the foot of thy crags, O Sea!
But the tender grace of a day
that is dead
Will never come back to me.

Break, break, break,

On thy cold gray
stones, O Sea!
And I would that my tongue
could utter
The thoughts that arise in me.

2.12 Pages from a book made and illustrated by Cutter in 1885 of Tennyson's poem, "Break, Break, Break." Eastern Washington State Historical Society. Rare Books.

color red at a distance. He was apparently not color blind, but his condition affected his ability as a colorist.

He may have harbored some doubts about his artistic talents, or he may simply have developed a stronger interest in architecture. Many years later he gave this explanation: "In my art work I always felt a certain lack of satisfaction which was rather indefinite to me at the time. Everything that I had been doing seemed to appeal to the eye and to the intellect rather than fitting in to the daily life of my fellow beings. I soon came to feel that it was entirely different with architecture." Cutter clearly did not consider architecture inferior to painting or sculpture, and he invoked the eminent critic Ruskin's authority to support his view: "It was Ruskin, I believe, who said that architecture is the finest of the useful arts and the most useful of the fine arts. . . . To me [architecture] is art incarnate. . . . And above all, in it are expressed every form of art with the ultimate end of not only pleasing the eye of a man and ministering to his esthetic nature, but contributing to his comfort and convenience as well."[31]

2.13 Venetian Scene. Oil painting by Kirtland Cutter, 1885. Collection of the Washington Trust Bank, Spokane.

Only three examples of his student work have survived. One is a little book, dated 1885, in which he drew illustrations to Alfred Tennyson's poem "Break, Break, Break" (fig. 2.12). Its handwritten pages, with vignettes from the poem, give no hint of study among avant-garde artists in Europe, but suggest a sympathy for the sentimental tastes of the time. Another example is an oil painting of a gondola on the Venetian lagoon with the city of Venice in the background. Since it is dated 1886, it could have been painted in Spokane from sketches done in Venice (fig. 2.13).[32] The composition is classical and traditional, with the gondola placed centrally in the foreground; and the quality of light on the water and of the distant buildings shimmering under the hazy sky suggest an accomplished artist. However, the conservative style of painting is more reminiscent of seascapes executed by Monet's teacher Boudin thirty years earlier. The glassy surface of the water is undisturbed by the aggressive brush strokes characteristic of the Impressionists. There is a hint of dark underpainting and precise, carefully modeled detail. This picture would indicate that Carroll Beckwith was not a major influence on Cutter. Indeed, its brushwork is similar to that of Kenyon Cox's landscapes of the early 1880s. The third example of

2.14 Charles Pease, Cutter's maternal grandfather. Portrait bust by Kirtland Cutter. Undated photograph, inscribed on the back in Cutter's handwriting: "Charles Pease by Kirtland Cutter." Eastern Washington State Historical Society, L94–609.

his work is a portrait bust of his grandfather Charles Pease, a competent work in the academic American tradition of portrait sculpture (fig. 2.14).

Returning to America with a desire "to devote all of my efforts to architecture,"[33] Cutter needed to find a place where he could pursue his chosen profession. He was perhaps reluctant to enter a long apprenticeship in an established practice or to start formal training. In any case, his uncle Horace appears to have provided the solution. Horace Cutter had followed his brother William Lemen into a banking career in Ohio, but falling ill he had moved to Colorado to recover his health. Later, when passing through San Francisco on the way to Japan, he was persuaded by an acquaintance to stay in California and join in a banking venture. In 1882, after ten years in California, he traveled to the Washington Territory, where he helped to found the First National Bank of Spokane Falls and became its cashier.[34] It seems likely that Horace Cutter lured his nephew westward with glowing tales of the rich prospects to be found in Spokane Falls. As Kirtland recounted many years later, he was gripped by the impelling "call of the West."[35] In making his decision, he was following in the footsteps of his forebears, the Cutters, the Kirtlands, and the Peases, who had set off for the Western Reserve with high hopes of bringing civilization to a wild and savage place. Having completed his education, he was now ready to make his mark in the world.

CHAPTER THREE

Spokane Falls:
Architecture on the Frontier
(1886–1889)

IN OCTOBER 1886, KIRTLAND CUTTER MADE THE LONG
train journey on the recently opened Northern Pacific Railroad to
Spokane Falls in Washington Territory.[1] As he approached his destination, he was in a sense reenacting his grandfather's experience on
his first visit to Cleveland sixty-eight years earlier. Orlando Cutter,
completing a far more rigorous journey on horseback, had been
sufficiently impressed by the "business like appearance of the city"
to settle there. Now, two generations later, it was Kirtland's turn to
stake out his future.

Only ten years before his arrival, Spokane Falls had been little
more than a cluster of shacks at a river crossing above a dramatic
cataract. James Glover, the "father of Spokane," had ridden to the
area in 1873, bought out two squatters, and obtained for himself
what he believed to be a perfect townsite. At first Glover had run a
sawmill and a trading post whose main customers were the Indians
who camped near the falls. Then, in 1876, he persuaded Frederick
Post to relocate his flour mill from Rathdrum to Spokane Falls by
offering him a valuable property by the falls. In 1881, the railroad
finally reached the town, but it was the discovery of gold in the
Coeur d'Alene mountains to the east that brought prosperity.
Spokane Falls became the principal source of supplies for the
mines, and by 1885, after the opening of Bunker Hill Mine, it
was already attracting many investors.[2]

When Cutter arrived there were only a few brick blocks, one
of which housed James Glover's bank,[3] but others were under con-

struction. The principal hotel was the California House, a three-story frame building surrounded by a shady porch. The rest of the town consisted mainly of hastily erected timber buildings. Cutter, who had recently come from Europe, described it as "new and architecturally savage."[4] Nevertheless, as his uncle took him around to meet the important people, the town may have seemed encouragingly businesslike. There was potential here for an aspiring architect.

Further exploration revealed the falls of the Spokane River. A little way downstream from the California House the broad river, after meandering across a plain, encountered rapids, divided itself around some small rocky islands, united again, and then plunged over a series of cataracts into the gorge below. Falling seventy feet in a short space, the surging waters produced a constant roar and sent up a cooling spray (fig. 3.1).

With the arrival of white settlers, the beauty of the scene had suffered the effects of exploitation. A rickety wooden bridge with its supports in the boiling water crossed the river just above the deepest plunge. Makeshift structures along the banks stood on stilts in the water. Sheds, machine houses, flumes, and platforms all added to the confusion. The C and C Flour Mill, standing on the largest island, was the most substantial structure.[5] But the water power had also attracted a far more progressive industry. The Electrical Illuminating Company's dynamo, installed in 1885 to supply electrical power for the streetlights of the town, was the first hydroelectric power plant west of the Mississippi.[6]

To the south of the town, half a mile from the river, the ground began to rise gently. Then, as the incline became steeper, the sparsely treed plain gave way to wooded slopes, crowned by cliffs. Strange, domelike outcroppings of volcanic rock protruded from the hillside, the remnants of an ancient lava flow.[7] In the hot summer weather, the north slope of this craggy hill seemed to have a climate of its own. It not only caught the breezes when the city streets were stifling; it also offered pleasant, shady places under the trees and cliffs. Rich vegetation grew in moist, cool hollows, while down below, where most of the people lived, the streets were brown and dusty.[8] Furthermore, the South Hill afforded splendid views over the city and to distant mountains beyond. It is not surprising that Cutter chose this as the ideal place to live.

Surveying the domestic buildings of the town, he would have found simple pioneer homesteads and a few log cabins, but also houses showing some architectural pretensions. The recently built

3.1 A detail from the Bird's Eye View of Spokane Falls, Washington Territory, 1884, engraving by Henry Wellge. Although the growing city, recorded here with remarkable accuracy, had expanded further by the time Kirtland Cutter arrived in 1886, the upper slopes of South Hill seen in the distance were still clear of houses. At this time Howard Street, running south from the mill on Havermale Island (lower left), was the principal commercial thoroughfare, but Riverside (the third street in from the river) was beginning to assert itself as a choice location for business. Within four years of his arrival, Cutter was to build two banks at the intersection of those streets and to situate his office in one of them. Eastern Washington State Historical Society.

homes of the wealthiest people were mostly in the Queen Anne Style, which had been popular for a few years. Among these, James Glover's house on Riverside was large but not extravagant looking.[9] The most ostentatious residence in Spokane Falls belonged to Anthony Cannon, who had arrived in 1878 and opened the first bank. Built in the French Second Empire Style and surrounded by formal gardens, it occupied an entire city block on the southwestern edge of town (fig. 3.2).[10] In composition it was much like the Win-

3.2 The Anthony Cannon house on the South Hill, Spokane, by architect Herman Preusse. It combines features of the Italianate style of the 1860s and the French Second Empire of the 1870s. Demolished. From *Spokane Falls Illustrated.*

slow house on Euclid Avenue in Cleveland, built in 1878 (fig. 2.6), but it was constructed of wood. The mansarded roofs and the slim tower emphasizing the center of a compact, symmetrical block were typical of the French style. However, the design was already old-fashioned when it was built.[11] The more progressive American architects had abandoned such vertically clustered compositions, typical of the late 1870s, and were often building in a less formal manner. Anthony Cannon's house represented the end of one era in the architecture of the city, and Kirtland Cutter was looking forward to opening a new one.

But launching a career as an architect was not easy without professional training or experience. Horace's partners, James Glover and F. Rockwood Moore, were both active in many business ventures, but they had already employed an established architect, Herman Preusse, in 1882 to design the First National Bank building. Preusse, whose stepfather was a successful architect in Germany, had studied for several years in Halle and Holzminden and gained experience in the family office before coming to the United States. He had practiced in California and Kansas before moving on to Spokane Falls and had a good practical knowledge of building in a frontier town. Preusse was busy with commercial blocks and houses, and in the year of Cutter's arrival he completed the first building for the Catholic Gonzaga College. By 1888 he was employing six assistants and was responsible for buildings worth half a million dollars.[12]

Compared with this diligent German who had already proved his ability, Kirtland Cutter was an unknown quantity. To the self-made

3.3 Kirtland Cutter, probably photographed soon after he arrived in Spokane. Cutter evidently liked the youthful quality of this portrait: he used it in a journal article twenty years later (*Pacific Builder and Engineer,* December 11, 1909). University of Washington Libraries, Special Collections Division, Neg. UW 4977.

men of Spokane Falls, his artistic ideas may have seemed out of place. Elegantly dressed and wearing a wig to conceal his premature baldness and to appear more masculine, he could even have been the subject of ridicule in this rough pioneer town. However, a photograph probably taken at about this time shows him with an eager and determined expression (fig. 3.3). At first, lacking architectural commissions, he had to fall back on working for his uncle as a teller in the bank.[13] Thirty years later, he gave his own explanation of his debut as a designer: "Some of my first house sketches came into the hands of practical builders who seemed pleased with their appearance and buildings were modelled after them. They were crude enough, but they gave me my introduction to my life work."[14]

Cutter is said to have worked for Preusse after serving for a time in the bank, but his first real contribution to the artistic life of the city may have been in the theater. In January 1887 he painted the scenery for an amateur production of Gilbert and Sullivan's *The Mikado* at Joy's Opera House. Among the cast were some of his future clients. They gave three performances to packed houses, followed by one in Coeur d'Alene.[15]

Regardless of Kirtland's promise as a scenery painter, Moore and Glover did not offer him a commission for the new First National Bank building constructed that year. Presumably the contract went

3.4 Horace Cutter house at the head of Stevens Street, Spokane, 1887. Demolished. From *Spokane Falls and Its Exposition* (1890). Eastern Washington State Historical Society.

to Preusse. But Horace did allow Kirtland the opportunity to design a house for him, and it seems likely that the architect influenced the choice of site. They selected a four-acre property on the South Hill at the head of Stevens Street, which offered a "sweeping view of the landscape [and] the snow-capped mountains, ninety miles to the north." With "great walls of basaltic rock and pine clad bluffs . . . in the rear," the terrain, enlivened with "basaltic rock piles in their naked condition," was far more dramatic than the residential areas established on the plain below.[16] Cutter's original plan, later scaled down, was for a fifteen-thousand-dollar mansion, but they built a stone stable block first as a temporary dwelling while construction was in progress. Horace, his wife Emily, and Kirtland were already living there by January 1887.[17] They built a scaled-down version of the house that summer, and Horace and Emily remained there for several years (fig. 3.4).

The aspiring architect's first known work demonstrated his break with the prevailing styles in Spokane and began to set a direction for his career. Although the Horace Cutter house was described in a guide to the city as a Queen Anne cottage, it was by no means a characteristic Queen Anne design; indeed, its chief virtue was its simplicity. The roof was almost oriental, having a low-pitched hipped form out of which rose a steeper gable roof. The horizontality of the lower roof related it to the ground, while the steeper upper roof responded to the hill above. The chimney and walls of local basalt anchored the house to the rock-strewn slope. But the unity of the design was somewhat compromised by a projecting wing on the north side which included a shady upper-story balcony and, surprisingly, a Gothic window below. The elaborately turned posts supporting the balcony and roof seem out of keeping with the heavy chimney, but the idea of creating a private outdoor room on the upper floor was an inspired one.[18]

In this design Cutter seems to have been exploring concepts which were to be more fully developed a decade later in the Prairie Houses of Frank Lloyd Wright. The oversailing, low-pitched roof symbolizing shelter, and the massive chimney of indigenous rock signifying both the warmth of the hearth and the connection to the ground, were clearly expressed. The house may have been an immature work, but the young architect was nevertheless cutting his teeth precociously.

No plan survives, but sketches and descriptions of the interior hint at a bohemian atmosphere. The house included a "Japanese room," and a Moorish arch separated the hall and dining room. In one room a large draped curtain and a guitar, leaning casually against a piano, give a theatrical appearance. Kirtland had probably encountered the vogue for chinoiserie and Japanese art in Europe; however, wealthy Americans in the late nineteenth century also indulged in the fashion of building exotic rooms.[19]

Having produced an unusual design for his uncle, Kirtland Cutter began work on his own house on a hillside site not far away. We do not know whether the funds were obtained from his family in Cleveland or he had earned or borrowed the money in Spokane, but in August 1887 he was able to purchase a lot on the south side of Seventh Avenue below Horace's property and a little to the west. By late November he had completed the construction of a small house on this site. He then bought three adjoining lots to the south and by August 1888 was in possession of two city blocks between Mill Street and Lincoln.[20] This property had plenty of trees and the ground fell away steeply, ensuring good views over the city. He may have bought the land partly as an investment, for within a few months he had sold some of the lots. But he chose for himself a site with a frontage of 106 feet on Seventh Avenue on the corner of Mill

3.5 Design for a Swiss cottage. From Andrew Jackson Downing,
The Architecture of Country Houses (New York, 1850).

Street. This property had the attraction of a picturesque basalt outcropping near the entry, which he exploited as a natural rock garden.

In the design of his own house, Cutter chose to emulate the Swiss
chalet, a type he had admired on his European travels. He must certainly have known Andrew Jackson Downing's popular and influential pattern book, *The Architecture of Country Houses;* first published
in 1850, it had the most profound effect on American taste in
domestic architecture and was issued in many editions.[21] Its essential message was that houses should be carefully related to their
sites. In his introduction, Downing defined The Beautiful and The
Picturesque. While The Beautiful is "the embodiment of unity, proportion and harmony," giving buildings the quality of repose, "The
Picturesque, is seen in ideas of beauty manifested with something
of rudeness, violence or difficulty. The effect of the whole is spirited
and pleasing, but parts are not balanced, proportions are not perfect, and details are rude. We feel at the first glance at a picturesque
object, the idea of power exerted, rather than the idea of beauty
which it involves." Downing discussed the virtues of many architec-

tural styles, particularly in their relationship to landscape. Indeed, he perceived landscape as a determinant of architectural form: "The scenery, amid which it is to stand, if it is of a strongly marked character, will often help to suggest or modify the character of the architecture. A building which would appear awkwardly and out of place on a smooth plain may be strikingly harmonious and picturesque in the midst of wild landscape."[22]

Downing pleaded for unpretentious building in simple, strong materials. He preferred the more picturesque and asymmetrical styles such as Tudor because of their natural fit with the landscape. In the section on designs for cottages, he presented a design for a Swiss cottage and discussed the merits of the type:

> The genuine Swiss Cottage may be considered the most picturesque of all dwellings built of wood. Bold and striking in outline, and especially in its widely projecting roof, which is peculiarly adapted to a snowy country, rude in construction, and rustic in quaint ornaments and details, it seems especially adapted to the wild and romantic scenery where it originated. . . . There is no need, however, in the copying a Swiss Chalet, that we could copy all its defects; we may retain much of the picturesqueness of the Swiss cottage without making its basement a stable for cows, or piling large stones on the roof.[23]

Cutter appears to have taken Downing's remarks about modifying the Swiss chalet for American use as a challenge. The South Hill in Spokane was picturesque enough to qualify as a suitable site. The rough outcroppings of basalt and the coniferous trees clinging to the slope provided a perfect setting for "the most picturesque of all dwellings built of wood." But Cutter had been in the Alps and seen real mountain architecture. To him, Downing's illustration of a Swiss cottage could have seemed weak and emasculated (fig. 3.5). Downing's example exerts little power and its details seem pretty and genteel rather than rude or inspiring. If Cutter was influenced by any model in a pattern book, it might have been one from P. F. Robinson's *Rural Architecture* (1823), which shows a highly sculptural chalet standing in a sublime Alpine landscape (fig. 3.6).[24] In any event, Cutter built his own chalet confidently, like a real Alpine house, of solid logs. Although he gladly eliminated the stable for cows, he was authentic in many details, including the use of rocks on the roof and sturdy consoles of projecting logs under the eaves (fig. 3.7).

3.6 Design for a Swiss cottage. From P. F. Robinson, *Rural Architecture* (London, 1823). "Bold and strong in outline."

3.7 Chalet Hohenstein, Cutter's own house, Seventh Avenue, Spokane. Undated drawing by K. K. Cutter. Eastern Washington State Historical Society, L.95–12.132.

Other American architects of the previous generation had built houses based on the chalet, and several popular pattern books included designs for them.[25] Most examples use elaborate fretwork ornamentation and tend toward fantasy, but some, like the design of the Michigan Building at the Philadelphia Centennial Exposition (fig. 2.2), display an astounding complexity of form. The most authentic looking American chalet was probably the one built for Mrs. Colford Jones at Newport, Rhode Island, in 1866 by Richard Morris Hunt.[26] However, Cutter's chalet appears more robust and sculptural than Hunt's. Having studied the construction of chalets in Switzerland,[27] Cutter may have been the first to spurn Downing's caution and reveal the rude and inspiring character of the Bernese Oberland.

When first constructed, Cutter's "Swiss Cottage" was quite small, built only for himself as a young bachelor (fig. 3.8). Next door was the modest home of four of Kirtland's unmarried friends, Lane

3.8 Cutter's "Swiss Cottage," the Chalet Hohenstein, as originally built in 1887. In front, from the left: Lane Gilliam, Mr. Flannagan, John B. Fiskin (electrical engineer), Kirtland Cutter (holding mandolin), Bertie Nichols, Henry M. Hoyt (attorney), Judge Kinnaird on "Monte," and Yick, the Chinese cook. Gilliam, Hoyt, Kinnaird, and Fiskin boarded in the house to the right. Eastern Washington State Historical Society, L87–362.

3.9 Chalet Hohenstein, south side, facing Seventh Avenue, after enlargement in 1906. To the left is one of the many basalt outcroppings that Cutter integrated with his houses. Demolished. Eastern Washington State Historical Society, L84–487.55.

Gilliam, Henry Hoyt, Judge Kinnaird, and John Fiskin.[28] With the assistance of Yick, Cutter's Chinese cook, the group of young men lived a carefree, communal life.

Sometime in 1887, Kirtland's domestic life changed. His widowed mother, Caroline, arrived from Cleveland with his two sisters, Laura and Caddie, to live with him in the chalet. Once again he was in a well-run family home with women in important roles. The new arrivals were probably there in December when the Bachelor's Ball was held at Concordia Hall. This entertainment was described as the society event of the season; Lane Gilliam helped organize it and Kirtland served on the refreshment committee.

The winter that followed was a hard one, with temperatures of thirty degrees below zero. For a short time Spokane was isolated from the outside world, and building came to a standstill for several weeks. The new year also brought personal tragedy to the Cutter family. On February 15, Caddie, who had never fully recovered from a long illness in Europe, died. She was finally laid to rest in Cleveland the following June.[29]

By 1889, Cutter had enlarged his chalet and a few years later expanded it still further (figs. 3.9, 3.10).[30] It soon became a gather-

3.10 Chalet Hohenstein, north side, showing the deep eaves on powerful brackets. Bayless collection.

3.11 The entry to the "Turkish Divan" in the Chalet Hohenstein shows Cutter's taste for the exotic. *Spokane Falls Illustrated.*

ing place for Spokane society that offered a change from the pretentious formality of Spokane's principal homes. The chalet had a strong Germanic flavor, suggesting that the architect retained an affinity for German culture. An undated perspective drawing shows the house with the title "Friederichsruhe" (fig. 3.7),[31] but as early as 1888 it was known as the Chalet Hohenstein. A German inscription in Gothic letters over the front door has been translated as: "Old Age Falls, Time Changes, and New Life Grows Out of the Ruins."

It is hard to establish what changes Cutter made as the house grew; the available photographs date from after the later remodeling. While from an exterior point of view the chalet was plausibly Swiss, the interior was full of surprises. Cutter was not, of course, a farmer from the Bernese Oberland, but a sophisticated much-traveled artist living in an eclectic age. Like most architects of his day he did not suppress his taste for the exotic in favor of architectural consistency. Emulating the designs of smoking rooms in fashionable houses of the time, he included a slender Moorish arch leading to the "Turkish Divan" (fig. 3.11).[32] A view from the hall into the den, framed by curios and oriental rugs hanging from the ceiling, also shows Cutter's unconventional approach. (fig. 3.12). The rough stone fireplace is an early example of the rustic character that he was often to achieve in the future. The living room, with built-in seats flanking a simple, tiled fireplace, epitomized the Arts and Crafts approach (fig. 3.13). Cutter gave the dining room a richer character, combining illumination through stained glass windows with elegantly designed woodwork (fig. 3.14).

While the "mansion" built for Horace Cutter was small, his partners, Moore and Glover, were ready by 1889 to begin the construction of grand residences. Both chose Kirtland Cutter as their architect. F. Rockwood Moore had come to Spokane in 1879 and opened a store. In 1882 he became the vice president of Glover's bank; he also speculated on property and other ventures in the expanding city. His most notable role was as the first president of the Washington Water Power Company.[33] Moore selected a building site under the rocky cliff immediately to the west of Horace's land. Glover built his house to the east, a little higher up the hill on Eighth Avenue. Both had commanding views over the town.

The homes Cutter offered his clients were very different from those of other successful capitalists and civic leaders. J. J. Browne, who was developing a new residential district on the bluff above the river gorge to the west of downtown, had followed the lead of

3.12 View from the hall into the den in the Chalet Hohenstein, Seventh Avenue, Spokane. Cutter acquired the Japanese suit of armor on a trip to Japan (date unknown). Photo by Bailey. Eastern Washington State Historical Society, L84–207.4.201.

3.13 Living room fireplace in the Chalet Hohenstein. The Arts and Crafts simplicity that Cutter chose for his own living room is in sharp contrast to the ostentatious interiors expected by many of his clients. Eastern Washington State Historical Society, Peggy Bayless Collection.

3.14 Dining room in the Chalet Hohenstein. *Western Architect,* September 1908. Eastern Washington State Historical Society, L84–487.62.

Anthony Cannon by building a house with tall mansard roofs.[34] Indeed, under Herman Preusse, the leading architect in Spokane Falls, the Second Empire Style still flourished in the city.[35] Gonzaga College, as well as several commercial buildings and schools, displayed towers with steep mansards. The more common Queen Anne houses, which Cutter despised, also showed a vertical emphasis. In contrast, Cutter's new designs were long and low. Rather than rearing up proudly, they seemed to grow naturally out of the landscape.[36]

Cutter's early work gives evidence of his sources and of the rapid formation of his ideas. He did not follow the classical principles that his teacher, Kenyon Cox, had so fervently espoused. He found inspiration in the irregular, picturesque dwellings of England and Germany. While in England he may have seen the work of Norman Shaw, who, in the spirit of Arts and Crafts, based much of his domestic architecture on rambling, vernacular types. Cutter could also have been aware of Shaw's influence on the work of East Coast architects. For example the Thomas Dunn house in Newport,

Rhode Island, by Charles Follen McKim (fig. 3.15), with its picturesque arrangement of dormers, gables, and tall chimneys, was illustrated in *American Architect* in 1877.[37] Cutter also seems to have been familiar with an indigenously American style that had emerged in the Northeast in the 1880s at the hands of McKim, Mead and White, as well as John Calvin Stevens and others, which has since been named the Shingle Style.[38] Drawing on the simple shingled dwellings of Colonial New England and on the English Queen Anne Revival, they produced houses devoid of applied ornament, with low-pitched roofs sweeping down over porches.

While Cutter's design philosophy appears to be rooted in the English Arts and Crafts movement, the architectural climate of the late eighties offered bewildering choices. He was clearly excited by the many possibilities and found it hard to limit the themes to be explored in any one building. It was as if the history of architecture offered an overflowing cornucopia from which the designer could freely select whatever enticed him. Cutter was experimenting with progressive ideas and developing principles on which he would base his approach to architecture for the next fifty years.

3.15 The Thomas Dunn house, Newport, Rhode Island, 1877, by McKim, Mead and White, appropriates the picturesque massing and vernacular sources of the English Queen Anne Revival. *American Architect and Building News,* July 18, 1877.

3.16 F. Rockwood Moore house, Seventh Avenue, Spokane, 1889–90. A rambling house, giving the appearance that it had been built gradually by several generations of owners. Demolished 1940. Undated pen and ink drawing by Cutter. Eastern Washington State Historical Society.

He built the lower walls of the Moore house (fig. 3.16) of the basalt that broke out in unruly heaps upon the site. He used the same material for the sturdy chimney that projected forward on the main front and rose to make its mark on the jagged skyline. The second-story wall was shingled, and above that a half-timbered gable bridged between an octagonal turret on the left and a bay window to the right. Beside the half-timbered turret, whose lower level served as a porch, a porte cochère sheltered residents and visitors as they alighted from their carriages. At the other end, a small lean-to was attached as if added later.

When this house was first built, the inhabitants of Spokane did not like it. One of their criticisms was that it looked old before it was even finished. That effect was exactly what Cutter was trying to achieve. In the countryside of England or France he must have seen many comfortable, livable houses whose diverse forms spoke of their long histories. Perhaps the walls of an old stone cottage provided

the foundations for a later house to which successive additions were
made before the comforts of the nineteenth century were introduced. Houses such as these were surely inhabited by families with
long pedigrees. They had their ancestors and their friendly ghosts.
Gertrude Jekyll, writing in England in 1901 about her own house
newly built by Sir Edwin Lutyens, may have perfectly expressed Cutter's aim: "From the way it is built it does not stare with newness; it
is not new in any way that is disquieting to the eye; it is neither raw
nor callow. On the contrary it gives the impression of a comfortable
maturity of something like a couple of hundred years."[39]

The interior of the Moore house offered a series of contrasts.
Entering through the porte cochère, one passed through the octagonal porch at the foot of the turret into an entrance hall exotic
enough to be a setting for the *Arabian Nights.* This tall space, lit by
a skylight, opened through tiers of Moorish arches to the upper
flights of the staircase and galleries leading to the bedrooms. The
carved and polished wood contrasted with the polychrome brickwork of the fireplace and arched doorways (fig. 3.17). At the foot
of the stair Cutter devised a richly upholstered built-in seat, and
elsewhere opulent hangings were draped over doorways leading

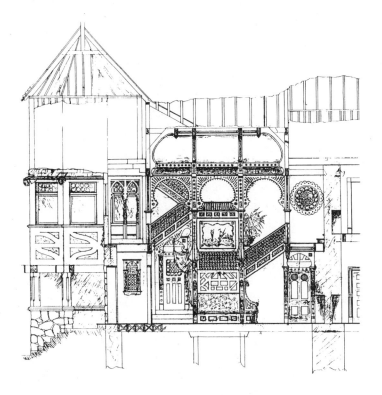

3.17 F. Rockwood
Moore house, sec-
tion. The grand
living hall is in the
Moorish style. East-
ern Washington State
Historical Society,
L84–207.138.

into formal reception rooms. The staircase, with a cherry wood balustrade of unusual design, led to the spacious gallery from which one could look down through Moorish arches to the hall below, or up at the elaborately coved ceiling around the skylight. Walking around this space one would reach a double arch, also of Islamic design, leading into a kind of loggia in the middle level of the turret. This octagonal room had a continuous built-in seat under the six windows, each of which looked out in a different direction. Less formal than the Louis XV reception room below, which Cutter designed in pea green and gold,[40] it was the perfect place for a conversation.

At the opposite end of the gallery another arch opened into the "promenade," a broad passage leading to a billiard room. This space, which looked south to the hillside through a continuous row of windows, must have been inspired by the long galleries of Elizabethan country houses in England. Intriguing and picturesque as the Moore house may have been, the design was clearly not the work of an experienced or well-trained architect. The grandiose character of the galleried hall is not matched by the planning of the rooms. The three bedrooms and single bathroom on the upper floor appear as mere appendages to the design of the hall. The house seems to have been conceived from the outside in, with the rooms as subdivisions of whatever space was left after the hall had taken its greedy share.

The Glover mansion (figs. 3.18, 3.20), built of local granite rather than basalt, has much in common with the Moore house. It is asymmetrical: its facade is divided by a monumental stone chimney; half-timbered gables rise above rough stone walls; and there is a sheltered outdoor room and a convenient porte cochère. But in this design Cutter demonstrated a firmer grasp of architectural principles and greater consistency in design. At the western end of the main front, a monumental stone arch clearly indicates the entrance. Above it the Tudoresque half-timbered gable of the main roof makes a huge triangle, echoed on the other side of the chimney by a smaller and lower gable. To the west the roof slope extends over the porte cochère. The low sweep of the roof, relating the house to the ground on which it stands, is somewhat reminiscent of Shingle Style designs, such as John Calvin Stevens's 1885 project for a "House by the Sea" (fig. 3.19).

The sheltered porch behind the large stone arch leads into an oak-paneled staircase hall in keeping with the Tudoresque exterior

3.18 Glover mansion, Eighth Avenue, Spokane, 1889–90. A Tudoresque house that shows some influence from the Shingle Style. Eastern Washington State Historical Society, L92–91.8

3.19 John Calvin Stevens's project for a "House by the Sea," 1885, Stevens and Cobb. The roof sweeping down over the spacious porch is typical of the Shingle Style. *Examples of American Domestic Architecture* (1889).

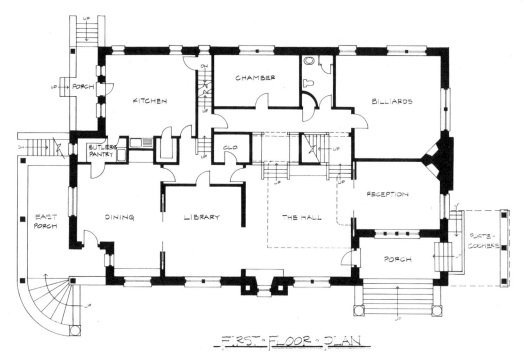

3.20 Glover mansion, first floor plan. Drawing by Terry Mourning.

(fig. 3.21). Cutter designed this impressive room, rising through two stories with galleries around on three sides, as a center for social occasions. The baronial fireplace offered the warmth of good hospitality; the grand staircase provided a setting for dramatic entries by superbly dressed ladies; the painted ceiling suggested that the owners were cultured patrons of the arts. Although the living hall may have conveyed the ambiance of the Tudor or Jacobean period, it was in fact characteristic of Shingle Style houses on the East Coast and the American Aesthetic movement. Over the doorway from the vestibule, a balcony, opening through glass doors off the billiard room, projects out over the hall. This balcony is like a spacious opera house box, a place where the master of the house and his chosen guests could participate in the events below or sit back in privacy almost unnoticed. In effect the entire hall, with its upper galleries, is like a theater for entertaining.[41]

The arch, following the theme of the entrance, is echoed on the opposite wall in a door leading to the bedrooms, and a third arch under the staircase encloses an intimate conversation space with built-in seats. Although this feature has no precedent in the halls of Tudor houses, it is similar to designs executed in Europe in the

3.21 The living hall of the Glover mansion, a space typical of Shingle Style houses. The balcony above the entry opened off the billiard room. The arch under the stair can be seen on the left. Photo by Bailey. Eastern Washington State Historical Society, L92–91.11.

3.22 Curiel and Moser, Villa Baumann, Baden, Switzerland. The arched aedicule under the stair is a more modern expression of the concept Cutter used in the Glover hall. From *Moderne Bauformen,* Cutter library. Eastern Washington State Historical Society.

3.23 The hall ceiling of the Glover mansion, executed by an unknown artist. Watercolor rendering, probably by Cutter. The recent restoration was based on this painting. Eastern Washington State Historical Society.

1880s. We know that Cutter was interested in such innovative work, because he owned several books illustrating the designs of avant-garde architects who designed simple built-in seating to avoid the clutter of ornate furniture so characteristic of the Victorian era. Cutter's library included books with illustrations of work by architects in Dresden who designed cozy recesses with seating for small groups. It is likely that he was aware of such designs while in Dresden.

One design, for the Villa Baumann in Baden, Switzerland, by Curiel and Moser of Karlsruhe (fig. 3.22), is more modern in its detail, but strikingly similar in concept to the arch under Glover's staircase.[42] This was illustrated in a book in Cutter's library that was published after the Glover house was finished. The two designs may have shared a common source.[43] Built-in seats were also hallmarks of the sumptuous interiors by McKim, Mead and White on the East Coast.

The painting on the hall ceiling (fig. 3.23) included heraldic shields and representations of the four muses on a background of vine leaves. Two peacocks that subtly dominate the design confirm the influence on Cutter of the Aesthetic movement. To the east of the hall, the space flowed into the oak-paneled library and the dining room beyond. The arch under the stairs led to the conservatory (now converted into rooms), which faced south toward the wooded hillside. From the shady porch outside the dining room one can walk out into the gardens and up the slope at the back, where it is almost level with the rooftops. From here the house looks more irregular and eccentric. While the front has a carefully composed balance, the back is a complex assembly of roofs, dormers, and chimneys.

With the Moore and Glover houses, Kirtland Cutter launched his career as architect to the leaders of Spokane Falls. By creating houses growing naturally out of the hillside, as if they had stood there for centuries, he sought to give his clients the legitimacy they desired. And the public, whose judgment had been so harsh, began to relent. Years later, Cutter told the story of the changing public reaction to the Moore house:

> In this structure we aimed to secure an old effect, using native basaltic rock for the walls and a tile roof. When it was completed, although Mr. Moore expressed satisfaction, the public was very plainly not pleased, and how they did pick that poor old thing to pieces.

But while the house showed no ill effects, these criticisms came pretty near to taking the foundations from under my aspirations. I was heart sick. It was my first big effort and it meant much to me to know that the thumbs of the populace were down. I was truly disconsolate. And then like a good prince in the story book, Dr. Seward Webb[44] came to visit our city, one of the early notables to honor us. While being escorted about the city to view its wonderful sights, the Moore place attracted his attention. In true fairybook style he insisted upon a close-up view of the house and his verdict in the case of alleged architectural crime was "not guilty." It is needless to say that this incident succeeded in loosening my spirits from the brambles of discouragement in which they had been so cruelly entangled.[45]

To Cutter's potential clients, it was probably Dr. Webb's exalted status as a railroad magnate and son-in-law of W. H. Vanderbilt that gave credibility to his critical judgment. But the accolade was indeed significant: Seward Webb was himself a notable patron of progressive architects. Furthermore, as a pioneer in the opening of the Adirondacks to wealthy summer visitors, he had played a role in the development of rustic architecture in America, a type that Cutter was to exploit. The young architect had indeed opened his career in a promising manner.

CHAPTER FOUR

Cutter and Poetz: Rebuilding Downtown Spokane (1889–1891)

IN THE SUMMER OF 1889, AS THE IMPOSING WALLS OF the Glover and Moore houses rose, Cutter faced the difficulties of practice on the frontier. Stone and timber could be obtained (the granite for the Glover house came from a quarry ten miles away) and good craftsmen were available for hire; but because of the isolation of Spokane Falls, many materials had to be ordered from faraway cities. For an architect with little experience, the business of specifying and ordering roof tiles, doors, windows, and high-quality interior finishings was taxing. Long before such products were required, detailed designs had to be sent out so that estimates could be received and orders placed.

Needing expertise in such tasks, Cutter recruited John C. Poetz, a young draftsman who had recently arrived from Los Angeles (fig. 4.1). Born in Minneapolis in 1859, Poetz was Cutter's opposite. He lacked his employer's privileged education, but he had spent seven years studying the "practical construction of buildings," first at a trade school, then under a civil engineer named Sackville Trehern. After gaining experience in Minneapolis, he moved to Los Angeles and, in about 1888, to Spokane.[1] John Poetz did not possess Cutter's imagination or knowledge of art; nor did he have the social graces and connections which had helped launch Cutter's career. But he could supply what the fledgling architect lacked: experience of the building process and its management. Furthermore, he knew suppliers of building materials in eastern cities such as Minneapolis who were directly linked to Spokane by rail.

Before the end of August 1889, Cutter and Poetz formed a partnership, and were busy on several commissions. Cutter remained the dominant partner, dealing with the clients on issues of design, while Poetz concerned himself mainly with practical matters of construction.[2] Their first joint projects included a business building for Theodore Cushing downtown and a house for Cyrus Burns on the South Hill.[3] These were stylistically different from Cutter's previous work. While the Glover and Moore houses seemed to grow naturally from the rocky slope of the hill, the Cyrus Burns house (fig. 4.2) stood out from its site. Composed somewhat like an elaborate Shingle Style house, it was ornamented with Moorish detail. A slim cylindrical tower surmounted by an onion dome dominated the north facade. Beside it, a covered balcony with six elaborately carved arches projected from the gable end. The lower walls of local granite were accented with arched openings of polychrome brick, whose red color was echoed in the Spanish roof tiles.[4]

The Cushing building (fig. 4.3), begun by Cutter and Poetz early in 1889, also displayed a flamboyant onion dome, in this case capping a turret corbeled out from the corner of the block. It is possible that Poetz was responsible for introducing this type of design, but it should be remembered that, before Poetz arrived, Cutter had given

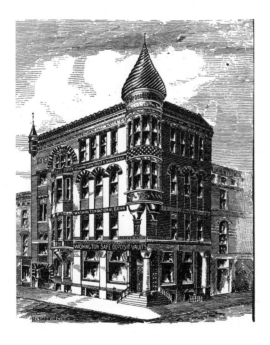

4.2 Cyrus Burns house, South Hill, Spokane, 1889–90. An early example of Cutter's fascination with the exotic. Demolished 1899. From *Spokane Falls and Its Exposition.*

4.3 Theodore Cushing Building, Spokane, 1889–90, northwest corner of Sprague and Howard Streets. Cutter's first commercial building, begun before the fire and continued afterward. Demolished. *Spokane Falls Illustrated.*

the Moore house an interior in the Moorish style, quite at variance
with its outer form. It seems equally likely that Poetz's presence gave
Cutter confidence to indulge his eclectic taste.

On August 4, 1889, a tragic event occurred that gave a dramatic
boost to Cutter's fortunes. A devastating fire, fanned by high winds,
destroyed thirty-two blocks in the heart of the city. Nothing remained of the former commercial center but smoldering heaps of
rubble. However, as in many towns that burned to the ground in
the late nineteenth century, the will to rebuild was strong. For those
who carried insurance, the prospects of reconstruction were good;
even on the first day after the fire, land began to change hands at
unprecedented prices. Three banks bought corner lots on Riverside
and Howard, and two of the commissions went to Cutter and
Poetz.[5] James Glover and Horace Cutter gave them the commission
for the new First National Bank; they also received contracts for the
Rookery, which housed the Spokane National Bank and a building
next door for Augustine, Bean and Hoyt, a prominent firm of attor-
neys.[6] Although the architects had lost their office, their equipment,
and their records, their future seemed assured in a city determined
to rebuild on a grander scale.

The Theodore Cushing block was already under construction on
the corner of Sprague and Howard and had reached second-floor
level when the catastrophe occurred.[7] The Cushing building shows
their inexperience, but the architects demonstrated considerable
progress in architectural quality as they moved on to the Rookery
and the First National Bank (figs. 4.4–4.6).[8] This evolution in the
course of a few months reflects the advance in the design of commercial buildings that took place in the mid-1880s in such cities as
Chicago and New York, under the influence of George Post and
H. H. Richardson.

On the five-story facades flanking the corner turret of the Cushing building, the architects combined the windows of the second
and third stories between tall brick piers under dominant granite
arches, almost in the manner pioneered by Richardson. However,
they did this without real conviction, allowing belt courses and brick
spandrels to break the upward thrust of the piers. Neither the wide
openings of the first floor nor the narrow windows of the top floor
were aligned with the pier and arch system of the middle levels. The
architects gave the longer wall facing Sprague Avenue such a variety
of architectural treatments that it seemed almost as if three separate
buildings had been erected under one cornice. The corner entry, hid-

4.4 The Rookery Building, Spokane, on the left; the Spokane National
Bank on the corner; Augustine, Bean and Hoyt on the right. Southeast
corner of Riverside and Howard, 1889–90. The three sections were built
together, but each had its own architectural identity. Although the structure was originally designed with five stories, a sixth was added at the
time of construction. Demolished. Eastern Washington State Historical
Society, L94–19.189.

ing behind a monstrous column, and the complicated support of the
turret, on bulging corbels, added to the confusion.

In the Spokane National Bank, the architects showed a far stronger
grasp of design principles. The ground-floor walls, faced in granite,
provided a strong base for the brick upper facade. An early drawing
(fig. 4.5) shows the composition of the longer elevation on Howard
Street as originally intended. It was organized around a dominant
central feature consisting of three tall, arched openings rising
through three stories. The lines of the supporting piers extended
upward to define three windows on the top floor and a pediment

4.5 The Spokane National Bank, Spokane, 1889–90. The original Howard Street elevation to which a sixth story was added. Demolished. This building occupied the corner of the Rookery Block. Eastern Washington State Historical Society, L84–207.185.

above. To either side, separate windows were aligned horizontally with the three central ones. Arches on the flanking windows on the third floor were echoed by a single arch in the pediment above the fifth floor. Thus the principal elements of the composition stepped up to the center. The shorter front on Riverside was only wide enough for a single arch uniting the three floors.

The bow windows at the corner were corbeled out above the second floor and rose through four stories to a little cupola breaking the roofline. They admitted extra light to the interior and emphasized the turning of the corner. Less dominant than the grotesque

4.6 First National Bank, Spokane, 1889–90 (later the Exchange National Bank). Demonstrates a greater sense of architectural unity than the two previous bank buildings. Demolished. Cutter and Poetz had their office on the sixth floor. Eastern Washington State Historical Society, L94–36.231.

turret of the Cushing block, this corner construction did not over-shadow the successful design elements described. The effect was somewhat weakened by the client's decision, after construction started, to add a sixth story. The architects did their best to revise the design appropriately, but the result was a compromise.[9]

In the First National Bank (fig. 4.6), Cutter achieved a more unified composition. He designed a compact block six stories high with two similar facades, each clearly divided into three bays. Above a ground floor of rusticated granite, a central arch rose up through three stories while the lower arches on either side covered only two.

The upward thrust of the center bay continued in a tall window, whose pointed gable broke through the cornice. On either side of it, chimneys were aligned vertically with the piers below. The pyramidal roof gave the building a sharp skyline.

The First National Bank was striking in its texture and color. The red Lake Superior sandstone for the rusticated base was cut, as the architect had specified, to appear bold and massive.[10] Even the lintels over the broad ground-floor windows had a jagged surface. The upper walls were of a deep red pressed brick shipped from Minneapolis; the smooth, precise finish contrasted with the roughness of the stone below.[11] The roof was of red Spanish tiles. The details of the building were crisply modeled. For example, window reveals were formed of molded brick.[12] At the entry, reached by a flight of ten steps, the huge sandstone arch sprang from a cluster of little colonnettes.

The greater integrity of the design may have been the result of a visit by Cutter to Chicago, where he could have seen recent work by Richardson, Burnham and Root, and Sullivan.[13] Another factor may have been the arrival in the office of a new assistant, Karl Gunnar Malmgren, a young Swedish architect who had been trained in his native land (fig. 4.7). Two years younger than Cutter, Malmgren was born in Örebro, near Stockholm. From the age of eight he had been sent away to school "in many parts of Europe," including a period of study in Berlin.[14] Back in Sweden, he had studied architecture and practical construction with an architect named P. L. Anderson, for whom he had also worked for seven years.[15] He traveled to the United States in 1888 and appears to have had an excellent command of the English language. The following April, "though his destination was Seattle . . . as it reminded him so much of the waters around Norway and Sweden," he met his future wife, Mary Arneson, in Spokane and decided to settle there.[16]

Malmgren was an excellent draftsman and brought a new professionalism to the office, which was much needed. Cutter could turn out beautiful watercolor or pen and wash perspectives, but his working drawings were poor. While technically proficient, Malmgren was also artistic. With his superior architectural education, interest in the decorative arts, and administrative skills, he could easily have challenged Poetz's position as Cutter's right-hand man.

The architects also benefited from the assistance of a good clerk of works (superintendent and inspector of construction) for the First National Bank. For that job Horace Cutter hired Frederick

4.7 Karl Gunnar Malmgren at about the time he joined Cutter and Poetz as a draftsman. Eastern Washington State Historical Society, L95–12.205.

Phair, who later became one of Spokane's leading contractors. The completion of this building was heralded by the *Spokane Review,* which reported that the bank had "as magnificent quarters as any bank on the Pacific Coast," and that "the interior fittings are pronounced to be unexcelled by any, even in New York City."[17]

Kirtland Cutter showed an enthusiasm for art glass. In his principal houses and business buildings, he took special care in ordering elaborate glass from Brown and Haywood of Minneapolis. He tended to divide the larger windows with mullions into three lights, the leaded upper panes of which were designed to soften the light and create subtle effects of color. He described the glass ordered for various projects as leaded, clear or muffled glass, leaded and copper ribbed, or crystalline; and he made much use of roundels, spun discs, and crown discs in various shades. For the First National Bank, he specified a large order of crystalline glass. The windows of the main banking hall were of plate glass with leaded transom lights above. One of Cutter's sketches shows a second-floor window with a border of spun discs in a light shade of green, and an inner border of the same discs in a lighter shade; the center was made up of two rows of clear roundels. To ensure accuracy, the oak window frames, made by another Minneapolis firm, were delivered to Brown and Hayward to be glazed directly.[18]

It was in the First National Bank that Cutter and Poetz decided to settle their office. After touting for business from a tent among the ruins of the fire and working in makeshift accommodations, perhaps studios in their own homes, they had the pleasure of designing the interior of their permanent headquarters on the fifth floor. Not only was everything thoroughly up to date, with an elevator and such details as mail chutes, but it was also finished with workmanship of high quality.[19]

A bird's-eye view of the city, published in the *Spokane Falls and Its Exposition,* showed "sixty acres of ruins . . . transformed by magic into a prosperous and handsome city within twelve months." The impressive rebuilding of Spokane after the fire put many of the owners of buildings deeply in debt. As historian John Fahey has noted: "They overbuilt in high-spending competition, ornate, fire-resistant structures of brick and granite." Dutch mortgage banker I. Jolles wrote a few years later: "Its people were too extravagant during [Spokane's] development and many overreached themselves to force its development."[20]

In the year after the fire, Cutter and Poetz also designed a building for John Sherwood, in whose Washington building Cutter had established his office just before the disaster struck.[21] They built it in the spring of 1890 on the same site, a block east of the First National Bank, "of heavy arched construction to avoid another similar calamity" (fig. 4.8).[22] The surprisingly plain facade was penetrated at the center by a large semicircular arch flanked by two lower arches. The deep reveals of these openings give the impression of walls at least two feet thick. The flat surface of this facade made a strong statement among its ostentatious neighbors on the street.[23]

They also built a brick building farther west on Riverside for the E. L. Powell Grocery Company, a three-story frame building for William Quirin, an investor from Boston, and some commercial properties for F. Lewis Clark.[24] They entered, but did not win, a competition for the administration building of Washington State College, which had been founded that year at Pullman. Their design was a curious combination of classical symmetry with picturesque massing and detail. The prize went to Herman Preusse, whose design was also resplendent with turrets, gables, and dormers. However, like Cutter's proposal, the winning design remained on paper. The

4.8 The Sherwood Building, 1890–91. The flat facade of heavy arched construction stands out among eclectic neighbors. At the extreme left is the First National Bank. Demolished. Eastern Washington State Historical Society, L86–399.2.

board of regents had commissioned a building for which there was little financial backing, and only a small structure was built at this time. Preusse and Zittel received further commissions at Washington State College, but Cutter never built there.[25]

Cutter showed his romanticism in a house design for the flamboyant Spokane capitalist, F. Lewis Clark (fig. 4.9). This unbuilt project, for which drawings have survived, illustrates Cutter's fascination with the eruptive geology of the hill and his creative approach to the site. Rather than flattening one of the mounds of basalt on the slope to make way for the house, he proposed to build the half-

4.9 F. Lewis Clark house, first design, ca. 1890. The house, bridging onto a natural outcropping of basalt, shows Cutter's desire to integrate house with landscape. From *Spokane Falls and Its Exposition.*

timbered upper story as a bridge spanning from the natural pillar of volcanic rock to the stone walls of the ground floor. The passage underneath it would conveniently provide a porte cochère at the front door.

In a mortuary chapel built at Fairmont Cemetery in Spokane in 1890, Cutter exploited local materials to good effect (fig. 4.10).[26] Its plan was the cruciform shape typical of Christian churches. Built of local wood and stone without any applied ornament, it expressed the belief, central to the Arts and Crafts movement, that there is inherent beauty in natural materials and simple construction. The walls of rough-hewn basalt with heavily buttressed corners proclaim the quality of the volcanic rock as it is found nearby on the cliff faces and outcroppings of the Spokane River canyon. The shingle roof shows the lightness of split cedar as well as its ability to curve to the shape of roof framing. Over the bold arch at the entry the

shingles on the gable end lift in a wave; the roof slope sweeps up to the bases of the lanterns, each capped with a pyramid. While the massive walls are earthbound, the roof is almost playful. The interior is plain, with plastered walls relieved only by four niches for flowers. The nave focuses on a rose window of art glass, executed in subtle colors.

The source for Cutter's design in rough stone was probably H. H. Richardson's Ames Gate Lodge (fig. 4.11) built at North Easton, Massachusetts, in 1880.[27] This structure, which Cutter could have seen illustrated after his return from Europe,[28] made a powerful statement about the nature of the materials of which it was constructed. While generations of architects and craftsmen had transformed building materials by smoothing them or applying artificial

4.10 Fairmont Cemetery Chapel, Spokane, 1890–91. Built of the rugged basalt found in outcroppings on the site, and cedar shingles, this chapel expresses a belief in the inherent beauty of natural materials and simple building methods. Photo by the author.

4.11 Ames Gate Lodge, North Easton, Massachusetts, 1880, by H. H. Richardson. *American Architect*, 1885.

4.12 F. Lewis Clark lodge gate, Seventh Avenue, Spokane, 1889. Built of rough-hewn basalt. The wall in the foreground divides the street into two levels. Photo by the author.

textures, Richardson allowed the great boulders of which the lodge walls are built to speak for themselves. And above these massive walls the red tile roof, curvaceous in form, almost floats like a canopy. Further, if Cutter had seen Richardson's Robert Treat Paine house at Waltham, Massachusetts (1883–86), he would have observed the combination of glacial boulders forming a great arch at the entry and a projecting apron of shingles undulating above it.[29] A similar arrangement of rough stone and shingles curving over an arch, almost in the manner of thatch, appears in Ernest Coxhead's diminutive Church of Saint John the Evangelist at Monterey, California, built the same year as Cutter's chapel. Both architects worked in the same idiom to convey a rustic simplicity.[30]

While the chapel was under construction, Cutter was at work on another building even closer in some respects to the Ames Gate Lodge. This was the gateway to an estate for F. Lewis Clark (fig. 4.12), opposite Cutter's chalet on Seventh Avenue.[31] The architect used rough basalt to build an imposing arch attached to a small lodge. It was in this cottage that F. Lewis Clark lived while awaiting completion of a mansion designed by Cutter a few years later. Since there was a sharp change of level between Clark's property on the uphill side of the street and the chalet below, Cutter took the unusual step of dividing the road and raising the upper half on a strong basalt retaining wall. Thus the lodge gate was easily entered from one level while Cutter's own driveway opened comfortably from the other.

Cutter's interest in the Shingle Style is confirmed in three perspectives of relatively simple houses covered entirely in shingles, except for lower walls of stone. One, a rendering labeled "As I Am" and "As I Might Be," shows a proposal to transform a Victorian cottage by the addition of a broad porch with basalt columns.[32] Another depicts a house with gambrel roofs in an ell shape, and a long porch in the angle between them (fig. 4.13). On one corner a vast stone chimney hints at an inglenook fireplace within. This was to be a spacious dwelling, unpretentious like a farmhouse, rooted to the ground on which it was built, yet light in structure. This design shows that Cutter could appreciate simplicity in building. However, two shingled houses actually constructed by him, in 1890 and 1891, belong to more elaborate Shingle Style types.

The first was built for James Wardner, a colorful character who made a fortune in the Idaho silver and lead mines and lived for a while in Spokane. In 1889 he decided to invest in the town of Fair-

4.13 Unidentified house in the Shingle Style. The gambrel roofs give it a simple, barnlike character. Eastern Washington State Historical Society.

haven on the coast north of Seattle.[33] While a boom lasted there, he profited from real estate dealings and banking. By the end of the year he had commissioned Cutter to design a house (fig. 4.14).[34] Facing south from a fine position overlooking the town and Puget Sound, the Wardner house was designed to benefit from the views. Balconies and covered porches run around it on two sides, and a corner turret with windows facing in five directions provides a more protected lookout.

It appears that the inspiration for this design came from Kragsyde, a large summer home at Manchester-by-the-Sea, Massachusetts, built by Peabody and Stearns in 1882–84 (fig. 4.15).[35] Towering above the sea on craggy rocks, this house was a complex assemblage of forms, responding both to the site and to the planning of the interior. The space within flowed from a large hall through the living rooms to covered piazzas, opening toward the views on three sides. On the exterior, porches, bay windows, and

4.14 James Wardner House, Fairhaven, Washington, 1889–90. Although in many respects this house is similar to Kragsyde (Fig 4.15), Cutter clearly preferred the broad, overhanging eaves, appropriate to the Northwest coastal climate. Photo by the Ellis Post Card Company, Arlington, Washington.

4.15 Kragsyde, Manchester by-the-Sea, Massachusetts, ca. 1882, by Peabody and Stearns. The shingles were stretched like a taut skin over the complex form of the house. *American Architect*, 1885.

dormers appeared where they were needed, not where a predetermined symmetry decreed. Two wings came together at an obtuse angle, their steep roofs of different heights intersecting boldly. The driveway passed under one wing through a great shingle-covered arch. Above this opening a covered piazza—an outdoor room protected with a roof—occupied the entire end of the house; next to it an octagonal turret with a bell-shaped roof stood out on the skyline, and from a gable end a broad bay window two stories high protruded from the wall.

Although the Wardner mansion was smaller, and lacked the spacious central hall, Cutter gave it a real openness to the outside and included many of the same exterior elements described at Kragsyde. Most obviously similar is the bold entry arch and above it a covered piazza the size of a large room. At the other end of the house a bell-shaped roof caps the turret, and in the center a cross gable projects out over a bay window. But whatever the similarities of the two houses, their expression is different. At Kragsyde the shingles were like a taut skin stretched over the house, smoothing the transition between the various forms. Since the eaves had little overhang, the surfaces of roof and walls were almost continuous. At Fairhaven, however, Cutter articulated each of the elements separately. The turret, the main hipped roof, the cross gable, and the canopy over the piazza all stand out clearly, and the broad eaves cast shadows. The two houses refer to their different roots: the asymmetrical gable at Kragsyde is not unlike the end wall of a New England Salt Box; the equivalent at Fairhaven is symmetrical, projecting forward on brackets. With its broad eaves, it seems closer to Cutter's chalet.

The most remarkable feature at Fairhaven is the covered piazza, a splendid vantage point offering privacy and protection. Its shingled canopy, standing on four slim columns, sails out from the main roof. At right angles to it, the cross roof with an equally clear-cut form, stands a little higher. In the roof forms, Cutter appears to be exploring, in a rudimentary way, ideas that would be developed brilliantly by Frank Lloyd Wright ten years later in his Prairie Houses.[36]

Cutter and Poetz built another Shingle Style house in Tacoma in 1891 for an attorney named David K. Stevens.[37] Much less complicated in shape, its floor plan was rectangular with only a single turret protruding in one corner (fig. 4.16). Its dominant feature is the shingled roof, which rises steeply from the eaves of the porch on

4.16 D. K. Stevens house, Tacoma, Washington, 1891, described by Cutter as "a quaint cottage in the German style." Photo by the author.

4.17 Sunset Cottage, Short Hills, New Jersey, 1882, by Lamb and Rich. A Shingle Style house composed in a manner similar to the Stevens house. *Sheldon's Artistic Country Seats,* 1886–87.

the first floor, to an immense height covering the second and third stories as well as an attic. The design is reminiscent of McKim, Mead and White's Short Hills Casino in New Jersey (1882–83) as well as Sunset Cottage, by Lamb and Rich, also built in Short Hills in the same year (fig. 4.17). In both houses a cylindrical tower stood against a high-pitched roof with dominant gable ends. Cutter dramatized his version by designing a roof of unusual height and steepness, with its ridge high above the top of the bell-cast turret.[38]

From the slope of the roof, dormer windows stand out to light the upper rooms, each one covered by a little pointed cap similar to that of the turret.[39] Whatever Cutter may have absorbed from the architects of the Shingle Style, his own description of the Stevens house conveyed an entirely different origin for the design. Writing to Stevens in January 1891, he referred to it as "a quaint cottage in the German style of architecture . . . something entirely different from anything ever built in this part of the county."[40] Indeed, the extremely high roof and bell-cast turret and the half-timbered lower walls do have something of the character of certain rural buildings of southern Germany. While it follows no exact type, a Germanic mood pervades the exterior.

However, the open interior, with a living hall, confirms that the Shingle Style was a source of the design. The entire front part of the house is a single room (fig. 4.18). Almost opposite the entry is a large fireplace; to its right a broad staircase rises up to a gallery over-

4.18 Interior of the D. K. Stevens House. The living room and living hall with staircase and fireplace are a single space. Photo by the author.

looking the living space below. In one corner, the hall expands into the base of the turret—an intimate area that is both cozy and well lit. To the left of the entry, the spacious parlor is entirely open to the hall. Cutter was boldly exploring the possibility of the open plan.

One advantage of the unrestricted space, noted in the *Tacoma Daily Ledger* a few years later, was its suitability for "any sort of entertainment, even including dancing." The paper described musicians "concealed in an alcove off the hall," presumably the base of the turret, "so music could be heard distinctly, while the players were hardly visible."[41] At the back of the first floor, the dining room, kitchen, and a study were closed off. Behind the expansive reception area the workings of the household could continue in privacy. The bedrooms above were spacious and well lit, particularly the master bedroom that expanded into the turret.

A letter from Cutter to the contractor shows that he wanted to "give an appearance of age" to the house. He instructed him to apply stain of two colors unevenly to the singles: "You understand we wish to have this building look as weather-beaten as possible and it is therefore very necessary that the work should be done by an artist."[42] Perhaps remembering the public condemnation he had received for the studied effect of age on the Moore house, he wrote to Stevens: "I suppose each day now the natives of Tacoma wonder more and know less about that curious structure, but trust that its appearance will not cause a depreciation of real estate values in the neighborhood."[43]

Cutter and Poetz accepted the challenge of the clean slate offered by Spokane Falls after the fire. At times, overwhelmed by the many options available, they indulged liberally in eclecticism. They were sometimes tempted to look backward to the more exotic ideas of the 1870s, but they were also aware of new forces at work in architecture. In the short period between 1889 and 1891, they progressed from inexperience to maturity and conviction. Some of their work was truly innovative.

Although Cutter had received no formal training in architecture, he had absorbed influences from many sources. From the Arts and Crafts movement he had learned the virtue of simplicity and the beauty inherent in age. From England and Germany, he had acquired an eye for the picturesque. His great-grandfather, Jared Kirtland, had passed on to him a love of nature; the leading American architects of his day provided him with inspiration too. Richardson taught him to enjoy natural materials for their own sake. Shingled houses of the New England coast, with their spacious interiors, generous porches, and simple surfaces, offered models that he could adapt to the Northwest. Cutter's career at this time appears parallel to that of Coxhead in California, who shared some of his sources and his desires. Cutter's designs were a synthesis of many ideas: he emulated the architects he admired, but rarely imitated directly; he preferred to offer his own interpretations of old and new themes. Among his strengths, as a young architect, was the ability to plant a house in the landscape so that it appeared to belong there. Kirtland Cutter exerted a significant influence on the leaders of Spokane that not only benefited his practice but also heightened the awareness of architecture in the community.

CHAPTER FIVE

The Search for a Northwest Architecture (1892–1896)

THE FIRST TWO YEARS OF THE CUTTER AND POETZ partnership were hectic. Frantic letters and telegrams, speeding back and forth between Spokane and suppliers in the East, convey a picture of an office on the verge of crisis.[1] Errors and delays sometimes threatened the progress of building. But although the path from the first sketch to the proud opening of a new building was hazardous, the architects were rewarded with success. Thus Cutter progressed from his role as a banker's nephew, working in his spare time as an amateur architect, to a respected professional with substantial buildings to his credit. By the mid-1990s he had gained a reputation beyond Spokane for buildings that made an important contribution to Northwest architecture.

In 1892 he was ready to take another important step: marriage into high society. His sister Laura had already married a respected member of the community, Cutter's former neighbor and client, the attorney Henry Hoyt. Their wedding the previous Christmas Eve at the Chalet Hohenstein had been a dazzling social occasion. The presence not only of Cutter's mother but also his grandfather Charles Pease, who made the journey from Cleveland for the occasion, enhanced his standing in society.[2] Kirtland had played a major role in the couple's plans by designing a picturesque, half-timbered house (figs. 5.1, 5.2) for them below his own chalet.

Cutter met his future wife through Austin Corbin, his old traveling companion in Europe, who arrived in Spokane in 1892. Austin's father, D. C. Corbin, had come to the Northwest from New Eng-

5.1 Henry and Laura
Hoyt house, 1891–92.
built by Cutter for
his sister and her
husband. This house,
with its ample
porches, embodies
elements of the
chalet and of the
timber-framed
houses he had
seen in Germany.
Demolished. Eastern
Washington State
Historical Society,
L85–174.11.

5.2 An interior of
the Henry and Laura
Hoyt house designed
with Arts and Crafts
simplicity. Eastern
Washington State
Historical Society.

land.[3] As the younger brother of the president of the Long Island Railway, he had been involved in the management of that company, and had come West with entrepreneurial skills and financial backing. He was an astute man with experience in surveying and banking as well as transportation. In the winter of 1883–84, when the gold rush in the Coeur d'Alenes was on, he had reconnoitered the area and recognized that railroads would be the key to extracting the wealth. It was he who selected Spokane as the hub of the operation and "opened the treasure of the Coeur d'Alene to the world" by means of railroads and steamship lines. Austin had returned from Europe to assist his father in his enterprises. While D. C. Corbin was a dour man, totally devoted to business, Austin was more interested in enjoying the pleasures of life. It must have been delightful for Kirtland to renew this old friendship and also to meet, perhaps, Austin's beautiful sister Mary, who had spent even longer in Europe.[4]

Unimpressed by the society of Spokane, Mary found the elegant young architect from a prestigious eastern family much more to her liking than other suitors. Cutter possessed a gentle, charming manner and was always impeccably dressed. They could also share anecdotes of European travel and common experiences on the East Coast. They were married October 5, 1892, at what was described as the "most brilliant wedding of the season." Kirtland must have felt intensely proud as he walked down the aisle to the wedding march from *Lohengrin* with Mary Corbin on his arm. The Glovers and Moores were wealthy members of the community who had come to Spokane Falls on horseback, lived in rough cabins, and made their fortunes through hard work and resourcefulness in this western town. But the Corbins were patricians. Cutter's bride was dressed in the court costume, "decolleté and en traine," in which she had been presented to Queen Victoria a little more than a year before.

After the reception at the Chalet Hohenstein, the bride and groom set off on an extended tour of the Pacific Coast. They were described in the *Spokane Review* as if they could do no wrong: "Mr. Cutter is an architect whose fine genius and profound study are permanently recorded in many of the finest residences in the city. The bride is a charming young lady whose beauty and worth are as well known in London and Paris as in Spokane."[5]

When he and Poetz had opened their practice, the city was full of people eager to spend their fire insurance money on grand new buildings. But Cutter returned to Spokane with his new wife to find the office short of work; new construction was slowing down and more architects were competing for fewer commissions. The slow-down in building was only a prelude to a nationwide depression, for the optimism of the eighties was running out. The day of reckoning was at hand for banks, companies, and individual investors who had staked too much on risky ventures. But Cutter was buoyed by one prestigious commission. Three months before his wedding, he had won a competition for the Idaho Building at the World's Columbian Exposition in Chicago.[6] By the following summer, he would be able to show his talents to the whole nation, indeed to people from all over the world.

In 1851 the British had initiated a trend in international fairs with the Great Exhibition held in the Crystal Palace. New York held a fair in 1853, Paris in 1867, Vienna in 1873, Philadelphia in 1876, and Paris again in 1878. In each case, the host nation built great pavilions to display the products of its arts and industries, and invited other countries to participate. At a third Paris exposition in 1889, the French were able to show their preeminence in engineering in the vast Hall

5.3 The World's Columbian Exposition, Chicago, 1892–93. Court of Honor. Chief Planner, Daniel Burnham. From *The Columbian Exposition Reproduced.* Avery Library, Columbia University.

of Machines and the soaring form of the Eiffel Tower. Then in 1893 it was the turn of a newer city: Chicago. The fair was to commemorate the four hundredth anniversary of the landing of Columbus.

In the 1880s, Chicago had led the world in the steel-framed construction of office buildings. It was here that architects developed a theoretical basis for the design of large commercial structures. Louis Sullivan, expressing verticality to the utmost and subordinating ornament, had rejected imitation of the past. When the fair was announced, progressive architects of what was to become known as the Chicago School assumed that their radically innovative architecture would be displayed for all the world to see. However, the City Fathers decided that the Chicago fair should be a dazzling evocation of Europe's former glory, and therefore a manifestation of America's true culture. The chief architect, Daniel Burnham, coordinated the design of the Court of Honor (fig. 5.3) as a unified ensemble of grand buildings based on Roman originals.

And the public was overwhelmed by the sight of it. As William James remarked: "Everyone says one ought to sell all one has and mortgage one's soul to go there; it is esteemed such a revelation of beauty. People cast away all sin and baseness, burst into tears, and grow religious, etc., under the influence." The American sculptor Augustus Saint-Gaudens, one of the planners of the exposition, described it as "the greatest meeting of artists since the fifteenth century."[7]

Compared with the architectural unity of the Court of Honor, the state pavilions were built in a confusing array of styles. The architecture critic Montgomery Schuyler, scoffing at the lack of architectural coherence, wrote: "A Grecian Temple, a California Mission, an Italian Villa, a Swiss Chalet, a Colonial Mansion—how can anything but higgledy-piggledy result from an aggregation of these, strewn about promiscuously, and without reference to each other, no matter how plausibly each of them may be done."[8]

The Idaho Building, like the California Building, conformed to Burnham's directive that the pavilions of western states should express regional character. Idaho's world's fair commissioner, Captain James M. Wells, recognizing that it would be foolish for Idaho "to compete with older states in the erection of an elaborate building," proposed that the structure should be "somewhat rustic in character" and display "all of the more valuable building materials of the state." Cutter rose admirably to the occasion. His aims, completely in tune with the commissioner's, were "to exemplify some of the chief products of the state, suggest some of Idaho's interesting features, and tangibly express the state's character."[9]

Cutter's strong but rustic design (fig. 5.4) stood in sharp contrast to the eclectic pavilions of other states. He modeled the massive, three-story cabin of cedar logs on the Swiss chalet, but evoked the rugged mountains and pioneer spirit of Idaho more than the neat and orderly settlements of Switzerland. The sheer size of the logs was impressive: some of them ran the full eighty-foot length of the structure. The deeply overhanging eaves of the low-pitched roof were carried on magnificent brackets of corbeled logs, whose round ends stood out against the deep shadows behind. Similarly supported balconies with rustic balustrades projected forward over the base of rough basalt from Idaho. Entering through a huge arch in the foot of a chimney stack, the visitors made their way through a series of spaces to a vast exhibition room at the top, opening onto a roof terrace.

The craggy volcanic rock of the heavily buttressed ground-floor walls and the cavernlike entry (fig. 5.5) gave visitors an impression of the raw geology of the region; other kinds of stone used in the building spoke for the diverse mineral riches of the state. On the roughly stuccoed upper part of the chimney, beneath a giant stag's head, was a shield of magnesia stone from Nez Perce County inscribed with the words: IDAHO GEM OF THE MOUNTAINS.[10] The floor of the entry hall and its fireplace were of lava rock from Logan County; another fireplace was built of rocks from Idaho's mining country that sparkled with precious metals of various types.[11] A third, in the second-floor hallway, was of pure white marble from Cassia County. The wainscoting in this space was covered with 12-by-25-inch sheets of mica "as clear as glass" from the W. J. McConnell mines in Latah County.

Twenty-two types of timber, all from Shoshone County, demonstrated the riches of Idaho's forests; each room was finished in a different species. Doors were made of a single plank of heavy cedar, not sawn but split like the broad shingles of the roof. The mantels over some of the fireplaces were of unplaned lumber and the grand staircase in the center of the building was also of rustic wood. Its newel posts were carved "to represent beavers' work and twining around them . . . imitations of the roots of trees."[12]

Cutter designed many of the fittings to show the resourcefulness of the pioneer and exploited the accoutrements of life on the frontier. At the rear of the second floor in the men's reception room, a

5.4 Idaho State Building, World's Columbian Exposition, Chicago. Built
to evoke the mountains and forests of Idaho. Watercolor by Cutter, ca.
1892. Glen Cloninger Collection.

5.5 Idaho Building, World's Columbian Exposition. Moved to Lake
Geneva, Wisconsin, and later demolished. From *Shepp's World's Fair
Photographed*. Avery Library, Columbia University.

trapper's lodge, the hinges of the doors consisted of "long spear heads while Bowie knives served for handles."[13] The ladies' reception room at the front (fig. 5.6), built like a miner's cabin, had leather straps for hinges and latches, while the hinges of another door were made like picks and shovels (fig. 5.7). Above the fireplace in the entry hall a frying pan served as a clock face, with gold numerals and hands keeping Idaho time. On either side stood miners' candles a foot and a half long, resembling tall coffee pots with wicks emerging from the spouts. In the fireplace of the ladies' room, the andirons represented a miner's pick, shovel, and drill.[14] In another, bear traps served the same purpose. The hearth in the men's reception room had andirons in the form of fish spears, arrows, nets, and bows. The furniture was made of hand-hewn wood and animal skins. The jerked beef, smoked tongues, onion strings, and simple cooking utensils hanging from the beams conveyed a vivid impression of life on the frontier.

The large exhibition room on the third floor displayed the products of Idaho, including sapphires and fire opal, onyx, palladium ("a metal of twice the value of gold"), and petrified wood of amazing size. The crafts of Indian tribes—bows, arrows, baskets, moccasins, spears, fishing tackle—and many rare Indian exhibits were on show, and visitors could see watercolors of Idaho flowers, panoramas of Idaho scenes, and stuffed animals beautifully arranged in natural settings. They could also go out onto a roof garden at the rear of the building to relax and survey the exposition grounds from a lofty vantage point.

Exploiting imagery based on everyday objects, Cutter tried, in the interior, to convey the character of pioneer life in Idaho. The whimsical ingenuity of his designs delighted the public. But in his concept for the massive structure, he aimed higher, attempting to express the heroism of the frontiersman. He drew on folk architecture from Switzerland as his first source, but transformed the chalet in a manner he considered appropriate to the Northwest. Among the pretentious classical architecture of other state pavilions, the Idaho Building symbolized, in a romantic manner, the virtues of nature against the competing forces of civilization.

Visitors flocked to see the Idaho Building and the press gave it enthusiastic reviews. The *American Architect and Building News* wrote: "Idaho's Building is not excelled by that of any State structure in the artistic application of the characteristics and features of the State. . . ." The *San Francisco Argonaut* included it among

5.6 Ladies' Reception Room in the Idaho Building. Designed to resemble a miner's cabin. From *Shepp's World's Fair Photographed*. Avery Library, Columbia University.

5.7 Stair hall in the Idaho Building. Drawing showing hinges made like miners' picks and shovels, and miner's lamp on the newel post. Ink on linen. Easter Washington State Historical Society, L84–207. 275.

the twenty most attractive features of the exhibition. The *Spokane Review* mentioned its "striking originality." The *West Side News* of Cleveland called it "one of the most unique state buildings." To *The Interior,* Chicago, it spoke of the originality and independence of the West. The *American Scandinavian,* under the heading, "Simple Art in Architecture," commented: "It was primitive, signifying undeveloped resources, and at the same time artistic beauty and harmony were reflected in its rustic appearance."[15]

Ten thousand people a day were said to visit the Idaho Building. One of them wrote to a friend in Boise: "The State building is a model of skill, unique in architecture, comprehensive and with all most charming. Built of Idaho logs, filled with a carefully selected collection of the state's most attractive and useful products it becomes at once a speaking object lesson of the state's resources. The Idaho State building is pronounced by all to be the most attractive state building at the fair ground."[16]

The official judges at the exposition echoed the public acclaim and the praise of the journalists. They awarded Cutter and Poetz the prize "for a type of architecture and construction which expresses the character of the state erecting it." The architects received a handsome diploma and a bronze medallion three inches in diameter "bearing the figure of Columbus landing."[17]

The Idaho Building stood for only a few months, yet its significance was very real. During the fifteen years before the exposition, a progressive group of American architects had made a virtue of simplicity. In the work of Richardson and others who contributed to the Shingle Style, dressed stone had given way to rough boulders; historic ornament had been eliminated in favor of plain shingled walls; natural materials and vernacular traditions had been exploited. Now, in the Idaho Building, Cutter had glorified natural materials and rustic construction in a structure of almost heroic scale. While the Shingle Style houses had tended toward complexity of form and emphasized their surface covering, Cutter had built the state pavilion to a design of bold simplicity that stressed its structural organization.

Among the many architects who went to Chicago there were a few who were not impressed by the grandiose classic revival of the White City and to whom the Idaho pavilion may have provided some inspiration. Charles and Henry Greene, who brought the Bungalow Style to its peak in the Gamble house at Pasadena in 1910, went to the exposition in 1893. It is recorded that they were deeply impressed by the Ho-o-den, the Japanese exhibit. It is possible that the Idaho Building also offered some inspiration.[18]

The Idaho Building succeeded with the thousands of visitors because it appealed to their imagination; it conveyed a glorious image of the pioneer West. But there was another aspect of its design for which the architect deserved credit. As one journalist pointed out: "When the various state buildings were erected . . . the question of salvages cut little figure in the plans of the state commissions. . . . The end of the season finds most of the state appropriations exhausted, and several of the commissions are hoping for salvage of the buildings to make ends meet. Most of them will be disappointed. . . . There is but one state building in the entire list of about two score that is eagerly sought by bidders and that is Idaho's unique log house."[19]

Although the building contained 475 tons of timber, Cutter had designed it so that it could be easily dismantled and reconstructed. The logs, some weighing as much as a ton, were virtually held together by their own weight. The individual pieces could be numbered and loaded on freight cars. According to one journalist: "When the building is re-erected with the proper rural surroundings, it will be as handsome a piece of rustic architecture as there is in the country."[20]

There was spirited bidding for the building. Some offers came from "wealthy sportsman's clubs"; Captain Pabst, the Milwaukee brewer, considered erecting it in a suburb of his city; Harry Miner, the New York theatrical manager, hoped to install it on Coney Island; other proposals for its use included a roadhouse, a country resort, and a stock farm. There was also interest from England; a group considered erecting it as a clubhouse on the edge of London.[21] It was finally sold for $4,000 to Celia Wallace of Chicago, who rebuilt it at Lake Geneva, Wisconsin, as a summer home. Unfortunately she neglected it and after a while gave it to a George Thurman in exchange "for a rare black-blue Wisconsin river pearl." The new owner cared for the great log cabin no better; it lay empty and fell into disrepair. There were even rumors in Lake Geneva that it was "haunted by Idaho cowboys." Finally, in 1911 it was dismantled, partly to be sawn up for the planking of a new Lake Geneva pier.[22]

The story of the Idaho Building does not end with its removal to Wisconsin and destruction a few years later. Among its many admirers was an Englishman who was so disappointed not to obtain it that he ordered a replica for his estate in Hampshire. Arthur

Heneage Loyd was an ideal client for Kirtland Cutter: wealthy but unconventional. His family were landed gentry who had amassed a fortune through banking. Although they were not members of the aristocracy, their wives were the daughters of earls, bishops, and admirals. They became justices of the peace, members of parliament, and sheriffs of their counties; they were all educated at Eton. Arthur, following a customary pattern for a younger son, obtained a commission in the army. In 1891 a wealthy uncle died, leaving him £20,000, an enormous sum in those days. Two years later, he was traveling in America and visiting the World's Columbian Exposition.[23]

Loyd fell under the exotic spell of Cutter's Idaho Building. He made arrangements with the architect to rebuild it near Ringwood, at the edge of the New Forest. Cutter, knowing that its construction would be quite beyond the experience of English country builders, put Fred Phair in charge of the enterprise. Phair, who had begun his contracting career, with Cutter's help, as clerk of works of the First National Bank in Spokane, had been responsible for the Idaho Building in Chicago. In June 1896 he set off for England and for Norway, where he hoped to obtain the necessary logs. It turned out that trees that met specifications could not be found in either Sweden or Norway. The contractor returned to Washington for the logs and shipped them "around the horn to Merrie England where it stands today the only building in the British Isles the raw material of which has been supplied Squire Bull by his son Jonathan."[24]

The recreation of the exposition pavilion as a mansion in England named "Idaho" (figs. 5.8–5.10) did justice to Cutter's design. It stood "on an eminence in a pine forest of 550 acres" and commanded "very fine views over the surrounding country."[25] The lower walls and the fireplaces were of local sandstone rather than basalt, but in most details it was faithful to the original. Though the "Idaho Gem of the Mountains" shield was omitted, a fine stag's head graced the chimney as in Chicago. The balconies and corbeled brackets of logs exactly followed the architect's designs, giving the structure the same deep relief. E. W. Charlton, writing in *The International Studio,* commented: "The balcony alcoves . . . set back 15 feet and sheltered by the deeply overhanging eaves, were all adapted to the English climate providing places in which meals could be taken in comfort, even in wet weather."[26] The only major difference from its prototype was the omission of the rear two bays that supported the roof garden.

5.8 "Idaho," Ringwood, England, 1896–97. A replica of the Idaho Building constructed for Arthur Heneage Loyd. Eastern Washington State Historical Society.

The walls of the equally rustic interior were of exposed logs that had been peeled and slightly polished. Each was "squared top and bottom . . . to make the fit more perfect." The ceiling joists of the same lumber, weighing a ton each, were set two feet apart. The most remarkable space was the ballroom at the top of the house—in place of the exhibition room—where roof trusses of highly original construction spanned the full width (fig. 5.10). This room provided an unusual setting for dances and concert parties. Here, Captain and Mrs. Loyd, who were eager organizers of social events for his regiment, regaled their guests with such popular songs of the day as "Mandalay" and "La Serenata."[27]

The forest surrounding the house almost concealing it. Charlton described the setting:

> A backwoodsman coming upon it suddenly (it is so hidden among
> the pines that it is invisible at a distance) might well imagine himself
> in America . . . the trees, the rough growth and fern reach almost up to
> the walls, except where they have been cut away for necessary paths,

5.9 Entrance hall at "Idaho." Eastern Washington State Historical Society.

5.10 The ballroom at "Idaho." A close replica of the upper floor of the
Idaho Building. Eastern Washington State Historical Society,
L84–207.4.119.

or in order to obtain the views . . . ; there are no gardens or fields around it. It is so isolated that there is scarcely a sound to be heard, unless from the many guardian dogs or the keeper's gun in the valley. . . . It is doubtful if the State of Idaho could show a log house as fine as this and for England it is, of course, simply remarkable.[28]

However, Arthur Loyd, having been seduced by a Northwest building, appears to have moved quite soon to British Columbia.[29] By 1903, the estate had changed hands and a new house had been built there.

Cutter must have hoped that the World's Columbian Exposition would bring him a wealth of new commissions. Ironically, his success in 1893 coincided with a "year of gloom and disaster, of crashing banks and crippled industry." On June 5, Anthony Cannon's Bank of Spokane Falls "failed to open its doors for business."[30] Cannon had invested in far-flung and risky ventures; his liabilities stood at $200,000. Other banks called in to help had refused. The strain on the remaining banks proved insuperable, and others followed in suspending payment. By July 25 the First National Bank followed suit, with liabilities of $284,000. Horace Cutter, who had launched his nephew on his architectural career, was doomed, and building projects came almost to a standstill.

The architect was hoping to win a competition for a new county courthouse for which he had submitted drawings in July 1893. He had never designed a public building on such a scale, but his chief competitor, Willis A. Ritchie, had been responsible for the King County Courthouse in Seattle and four other county courthouses in Washington, all since his arrival in the region four years earlier. The *Spokane Review* pronounced Cutter's designs attractive and artistic, but reported that the contest was "wired beforehand" and that the job would go to Ritchie. Three days later, Ritchie's chateauesque design with a tall tower was chosen over Cutter's by a 2 to 1 vote. Cutter's design for this project has not survived to allow a comparison.[31]

That year, Mary Cutter gave birth to a son whom they named Corbin, making Kirtland a father at a time when his prospects were poor. The office survived into 1894 with only a few minor jobs.[32] With little work, there was not much to keep the partnership of Cutter and Poetz together. They had joined forces in the frantic days after the fire. John Poetz had contributed practical skills and experience that Cutter lacked; but it appears that they were not compatible temperamentally and that probably there was more to the dissolution of their partnership than lack of commissions. Malmgren, who had been in the office for over four years, now took over as Cutter's partner.[33] It is hard to establish the exact roles that Kirtland Cutter and Karl Malmgren played in the office over the thirteen years of their partnership. But all the evidence suggests that Cutter continued to meet with the clients, propose designs, and persuade them to accept unusual and imaginative variations from the ordinary. But he needed Malmgren's expertise and thoroughness to bring his ideas to reality.[34] Cutter is reputed to have made trips to Europe to see the vast chalet built for Captain Loyd at Ringwood and to search for materials for other clients. He probably visited some of his usual suppliers in Cleveland, Minneapolis, Chicago, and New York while his partner ran the office.

As Spokane emerged from the depression after the crash of 1893, the firm embarked on several rewarding projects. One of their first was a Shingle Style house on Capitol Hill in Seattle for Charles E. Shepherd, a law partner of Thomas Burke's. This was a more sophisticated variation of the theme Cutter had explored in the Wardner and Stevens houses, with tall gables, dormers, and a bell-cast turret (fig. 5.11).[35] Cutter's major undertaking in 1895 was to design a residence in Kalispell, Montana, for Charles and Alicia Conrad. In this mansion he combined ideas inherent in the Shingle Style with a creative arrangement of the interior spaces that responded to particular needs of the Conrads.

Charles E. Conrad played an outstanding role in the early history of the Northwest. Born in Virginia in 1850, he grew up on his father's fertile plantation and enjoyed the gracious life of the South. But the Civil War brought an end to the family's prosperity and Charles's future as a southern gentleman. Having fought for the South, he returned home with his father and brother to find the plantation in ruins.

In the summer of 1868, lured by stories of fortunes to be made in the West, he set off with his brother William for the Montana Territory. The journey of over three thousand miles up the Missouri River ended at Fort Benton, where they found work at the I. G. Baker Mercantile Company. They made such a good impression on Mr. Baker that they were soon running the business and overseeing its expansion into a vast territory extending north into Canada and as far west as Walla Walla. Charles had a great facility with languages and before long had mastered the Flathead and Blackfeet languages

5.11 Charles E. Shepherd house, Seattle, ca. 1895–98. A further example of the Shingle Style. Demolished. University of Washington Libraries, Special Collections Division, UW14579.

and several other dialects. The Blackfeet, who named him Spotted Cap, regarded him as a friend; indeed he married a woman of their brother tribe, the Bloods. The Conrads profited financially from their prodigious organization skills, courage, and the ability to get on with the Indians.

The brothers opened several new forts, built riverboats to improved designs, and branched out into the cattle business. Their reputation for honesty helped them compete with the Hudson's Bay Company. They gained lucrative contracts with the Canadian government to carry mail and to supply the Northwest Mounted Police as well as the trading posts of Indian agencies. For this purpose they built a large-scale transportation system. The wagon trains that went out with provisions and trade goods returned with furs and hides. Meanwhile the Conrads diversified into banking and invested in mining and real estate. By 1884, when the railroads had superseded river traffic and Fort Benton had lost its economic base, they had secured their future with a fortune in diverse fields.[36]

Conrad's wife, Sings-in-the-Middle, feeling more loyalty to the tribe than to him, left with them when they were moved to a reservation; she married again and died in childbirth. In 1881, Charles Conrad married Alicia Stanford, a well-educated woman of English descent whose adventurous spirit had brought her to teach school in Fort Benton two years before. In 1890, realizing that Fort Benton was finished, they decided to start a new life and intended to go to Spokane. But on the way they stopped for a while in the Flathead Valley. Both fell in love with the area. Fort Benton had been surrounded with "treeless prairie"; in contrast, this lush valley seemed to them like paradise.

Not far from the lake, Conrad chose what he considered a perfect townsite and negotiated with James Hill for the Great Northern Railway, then planning a line through the region, to make a division point there. He also chose the name Kalispell, the original name of the tribe that had been called Flathead by Lewis and Clark. The meeting of the rails on Main Street on the last day of 1891 amid great celebrations ensured the town's success. It was not long before profits from the Kalispell town development increased the Conrad fortune.

A year later, when the Conrads began to plan for a permanent residence in their new city, they traveled to Spokane to look at houses recently built for the Coeur d'Alene mine owners. They found that Kirtland Cutter was the architect of those they liked best. Conrad wanted to recreate the southern plantation house of his youth. Alicia, whose heritage was English, preferred to think of something in the Tudor style. Seeing the wooded seventy-two-acre site with beautiful views of the Flathead range of the Rocky Mountains to the east, Cutter envisioned a romantic rambling mansion such as those he had designed for Glover and Moore. He must have charmed the Conrads as they discussed proposals, for he won them over and left Kalispell with the understanding that he would have "a free hand and no restrictions in cost." Evidently he made the design his own responsibility, for the drawings were done by him personally.[37]

The Conrad residence (fig. 5.12) closely resembled James Glover's mansion in Spokane (fig. 3.18). The most striking change was in the materials. While the earlier house had granite walls below and half-timbering above, shingles covered the Conrad mansion. Only the foundations and the chimneys of roughly coursed stone broke with the texture of the shingles. Compared with Cutter's earlier essays in the Shingle Style, the Conrad mansion appears unaffected and earthbound. If we take seriously Cutter's own statement that he built houses to suit the character of his clients, it is not difficult to

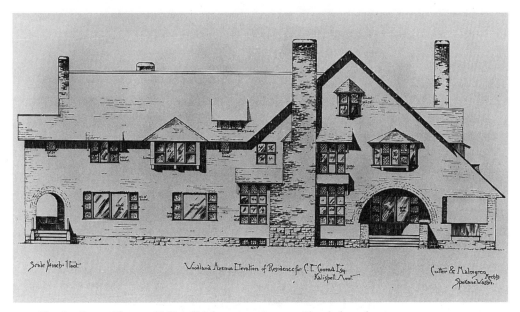

5.12 Charles Conrad house, Kalispell, Montana, 1892–95. Closely based on the Glover house, but entirely shingled. East elevation. This house is open to the public. Eastern Washington State Historical Society, L84–207.4.

imagine him responding to what he had seen in Charles and Alicia Conrad. They were people of their own time, making history in the West; they did not need to be housed in a style that involved any pretense. The architect responded by building in an intrinsically American manner. The result is a mature design in the Shingle Style that appears appropriate to the Northwest.

The living hall is the heart of the house and the principal gathering place. It combines a cozy, low-ceilinged area around the fire and a lofty space where the broad staircase rises. Beneath the dignified oak stair, Cutter placed an arched conversation nook with built-in seats—an area sometimes used as a stage for musicians. From the master bedroom a little balcony hung out over the hall so that Alicia Conrad could observe activities below. While this living hall shared many features with that of the Glover house, details varied and there were major differences on the floor above.

In the Glover residence the upper hall consisted of galleries leading to bedrooms. For the Conrads, the upper hall was an important space in itself. At the head of the stair, the landing broadened into a large room for billiards (fig. 5.13). More typically a billiard room

5.13 Billiard room in the Conrad house, seen across the upper hall. Planned with an unusual openness. Conrad Mansion Collection, Kalispell.

5.14 Library in the Conrad house. Conrad Mansion Collection, Kalispell.

was hidden away in the basement or attic as a purely male preserve, but Cutter placed it in the heart of the house where anyone passing by could stop and watch. A continuous strip of windows ran along the west wall of this space, with a generous built-in seat beneath. On a sunny winter's afternoon, with the low sunlight pouring in, this must have been a delightful place to sit.

For formal hospitality Cutter planned a reception room on the north side of the hall. With its color scheme of rose wallpaper and white paint, an Adamesque frieze, and Louis XV furniture in gilt and rose-colored satin, this space was very elegant. But it was not reserved, like the typical Victorian parlor, for genteel entertaining and solemn occasions. The Conrads called it the music room, and indeed it was well placed to fill the hall with music.[38]

The cozy, oak-paneled library with built-in bookshelves opened directly off the other side of the hall. An arched window on an interior wall was filled with leaded glass roundels (fig. 5.14). Although its main purpose was to provide light to the rear hall that led to the kitchen quarters and the back stair, the window was a positive presence in the room. The leaded roundels of greenish and amber tints reflected light from the window opposite in a changing pattern as the viewers moved around the library. In the rear hall, which might have remained a dismal service corridor, its effect was brilliant. Conrad often worked at the library table, from which he could enjoy splendid views of the Rocky Mountains. This was not a place where he shut himself away from the family; in fact, the library led from the hall to the dining room.

The spacious dining room also offered a prospect of the Rockies. On the inner wall, oak doors opened to the china cupboard and the butler's pantry. Between them at the center of a large built-in sideboard, a barrel, with doors at both ends, served as a hatch through which food could be passed from the kitchen (fig. 5.15). Beside the fine fireplace on the south wall, a glass door opened to the fernery, where a little fountain was to be found amid the green foliage.[39]

The richness of oak and leaded glass was also visible in the spacious bedrooms upstairs. The master bedroom and the rooms of the two girls, Kate and Alicia, were arranged around the hall at the north end of the house; they had communicating doors so that mother and daughters were close to each other. Two of these bedrooms had windows onto the hall that subtly augmented the light coming from the billiard room. From the master bedroom, a pair of Tiffany-style glass doors opened onto the balcony over the hall,

5.15 Dining room in the Conrad house. The fernery is seen beyond; the barrel on the sideboard was a pass-through from the kitchen. Conrad Mansion Collection, Kalispell.

and from Alicia's room a window with similar art glass passed light in either direction according to the time of day. As was characteristic of much of Tiffany's work, the colors were pale and luminous; the rippling surface of the glass gave an impression of shimmering light. The three bedrooms described had box seats under the windows and fireplaces. The room used by the son, Charley, above the library was more austere; it had no fire. But, like Alicia and his parents, he had a view of the mountains. Beyond Charley's room at the southern end of the house were three guest rooms, and by the back stairs a sewing room. There was only one bathroom on the upper floor, but all seven of the bedrooms had marble basins. Both Charles and Alicia had their mothers living with them and they played a vital role in the household. Their rooms, on the first floor, opened through a small rear passage into the hall so that they could easily join in family activities.

Cutter also incorporated some of the latest advances in domestic technology. Not only was the house wired for electricity, but ingenious devices made life more convenient. On both floors, drinking fountains, installed in wall niches, dispensed water chilled by unseen blocks of ice. Behind the scenes, the servants' duties were made easier by laundry chutes and a small service elevator that ran from the basement to the attic.

The architect succeeded in creating an ideal setting for the Conrads' warm family life and their generous hospitality. The living hall showed its full potential at Christmas, when the whole house filled with visitors. With the attic used as a dormitory, twenty-five guests could be accommodated. On Christmas Eve there was always a tall tree rising the full height of the hall. While two men stood guard with firehoses upstairs, and Grandmother Stanford played carols in the music room, the tree was illuminated with beeswax candles.

Their daughter Alicia, who lived in the house until she died, retained memories of visits of Plains Indian chiefs whom her father had known and advised when he lived in Fort Benton. Under the pressure of increased white settlement and the flouting of adverse and fragile treaties, they still sought his advice. She recalled their great courtesy as they dined with the family in their finest regalia, and she gave a vivid description of them gathered together, after dinner, in a semicircle by the fire with her father. As they conversed, in their own languages, using expressive hand gestures, the light of the flames made moving shadows and illuminated their faces.[40]

The rewarding commission in Kalispell helped Cutter weather the period of depression after the panic of 1893. Having begun his professional career in Spokane under the patronage of some of the most influential people in the city, he now faced the disappearance from the scene of his principal supporters. F. Rockwood Moore died in 1895. James Glover, after the collapse of his bank, had done all he could to honor his debts, but had to sell his grand mansion after only three years of occupancy. The architect's uncle, Horace Cutter, who had played a less than honorable role in the winding up of the bank, fled to California in 1894 pursued by sheriff's deputies. His disgrace could hardly have helped Kirtland.[41]

Fortunately, Spokane recovered from the depression more quickly than many other cities. The mining operations that had boosted the economy in the eighties reached their peak during the late nineties. And Spokane's economy benefited also from hydroelectric power, wheat, and lumber. The city gave opportunities to a new generation of capitalists, some of whom began to commission houses from Cutter in 1895.

Cutter designed his first two postdepression houses in Browne's Addition for Henry M. Richards, president of the Washington Water Power Company and vice president of the Spokane and Eastern Trust Companies, and R. L. Rutter, another vice president of the Spokane and Eastern Trust. Rutter was well educated and both were experienced financiers with a strong measure of business acumen.[42] While the opportunists of the eighties, Glover, Moore, and Cannon, had built ostentatiously, these two men were more prudent, displaying simpler tastes at a time when money was scarce.

An attractive pen and ink drawing by Cutter himself (fig. 5.16) presents a house named "The Pines," designed for Henry Richards. Its informal setting and unaffected character provide a further example of Cutter's involvement with the Shingle Style. The broad verandas under the slope of the shingled roof suggest that comfort was considered more important than pretension. The surrounding landscape was equally informal and rural. Although the house was to be built close to downtown Spokane, it was shown as if the pine

5.16 Henry Richards's house, "The Pines," Browne's Addition, Spokane, 1894–95. The last of Cutter's simple Shingle Style houses before he embarked on a series of more pretentious Revival styles. Demolished. Eastern Washington State Historical Society.

trees around it were on the edge of a forest clearing. A winding path between trees meandering around one side of it completed the picturesque scene. The house was built in 1895, unfortunately with reduced veranda space, but nevertheless to an unpretentious shingled design.

A few blocks from the Richards residence, Cutter and Malmgren built a home for R. L. Rutter. The cottagelike simplicity of this house links it to the Arts and Crafts movement. The first-story walls are built of rough basalt; above them a shingled roof is broken by three hipped dormers, the central one larger than the others, making a dominant feature. The picturesque character of the house is heightened by the division of the windows with diamond-shaped leading. A pergola at the west end provides a shady outdoor area. Along the front of the property runs an impressive stone wall of thin, irregular slabs of stone with a jagged coping of similar stone laid on edge. The effect, reminiscent of the dry stone walls of the Cotswolds, is decidedly rustic.

Kirtland Cutter's natural optimism helped to carry him through a depression in his business, but he seems to have been unable to sustain a faltering marriage. Mary Corbin Cutter appears to have been a selfish, impetuous woman who did not share the architect's passion for architecture and could not endure the conditions of life in Spokane after the crash. Hoping that the society of a larger town where he had good connections would be more to her liking, Kirtland took her to Cleveland where Cutter and Malmgren had opened an office.[43] In the fall of 1895, they traveled to England and France together. Mary's sister Louise, following a trend among American heiresses, had married an English nobleman, the earl of Orford, who belonged to the distinguished Walpole family. In October and again in November, Kirtland and Mary visited the country estate in Norfolk, where Louise now presided as countess. Kirtland must have enjoyed his stay at the romantic Mannington Hall, built in 1460 during the Wars of the Roses. Its crenellated walls and mullioned windows may well have provided inspiration for houses he was soon to build in the Old English manner. The Palladian Wolterton Hall, built on the estate by the Walpoles in the 1720s, but later abandoned, provided a classical counterpoint. Awaiting an infusion of Corbin money for restoration, it stood empty when the Cutters were there. On their second visit, Mary spent two weeks with her sister, while her husband stayed only one night. It seems likely that he spent the time traveling and looking at English architecture.[44]

Then the couple went on to Paris, where she told him "that she did not care for him anymore, and that it would be best for him to return to America."[45]

Kirtland had to go back to Spokane to carry on his practice, but on the first of February 1896 he returned to Europe, either to bring Mary and their three-year-old son Corbin home, or to "reach some amicable settlement." But "she received him with insult and abuse, refusing to speak to him, even striking him with a stick, and then surreptitiously stealing the child and fled to Nice, where she was then making her home." In the ensuing divorce proceedings, while she accused him of imperious behavior and constant faultfinding, Kirtland claimed that he had "been a kind and indulgent husband," who had supported her "in a manner befitting their station in life." The divorce became final June 30, 1896, and despite Kirtland's petition for Corbin's custody, the court placed him in Mary's care.[46] Since she lived in England, where she soon remarried, Kirtland had no further contact with his son. Margaret Bean, then a neighbor on Seventh Avenue, described a poignant moment a few years later, when she saw Corbin playing in a nearby garden while visiting his grandparents. Kirtland Cutter, passing by, gazed wistfully at the boy, and walked on, knowing that there was little he could do to establish a relationship.[47]

During the next two years, Cutter appears not to have lived in his own home. At first he listed his address only as Cleveland, Ohio. In 1897, he remodeled the house of his sister, Laura, and her husband, Henry Hoyt, and made himself a studio there.[48] Meanwhile, he applied himself with vigor to his architectural practice.

CHAPTER SIX

Cutter and Malmgren: Mansions for Spokane's New Leaders (1897–1903)

AS SPOKANE RECOVERED FROM THE DEPRESSION OF 1893 and experienced a second economic boom, Cutter and Malmgren were ready to meet the aspirations of the city's new leaders. In their recent domestic work in Kalispell, Spokane, and on the coast, they had explored the potential of simplicity in design and, like many of their contemporaries, had drawn inspiration from vernacular sources. But after 1895 they followed a new wave of architectural developments from the East and indulged in the revival of a wide variety of more pretentious styles. As the architects absorbed new influences, their patrons were ready to exhibit their wealth and good taste in lavish new homes. Cutter and Malmgren created architectural imagery that fulfilled their clients' desire for elegant and stately homes that implied aristocratic lineage. Carroll Meeks characterized nineteenth-century architecture as a period of picturesque eclecticism, and used the term *creative eclecticism* to define its third phase beginning about 1890. Richard Longstreth's alternative term, *academic eclecticism,* is generally accepted as a more fitting description of this phase of American architecture. Longstreth wrote of turn-of-the-century architects "forging links to the creative spirit of past centuries, an urge manifested in the overt use of historical references and reliance on traditional methods of composition."[1]

Although Cutter had no academic training in architecture, he shared such an impulse. He viewed the history of domestic architecture, including recent American designs, as an exciting array of visual ideas from which he felt entitled to draw principles and forms, adapting them liberally to meet the needs of modern life. A few years later in an article entitled "Architecture in the Northwest," he clarified his position on historic sources: "Modern Domestic architecture has sought to assemble the ideals of every age and Nation, and adapt them to the enormously expanded tastes and requirements of modern civilization. . . . From the traditions and customs of all ages, we have claimed the best." There is also evidence that Cutter attempted, by varying the styles of his houses, to express the individuality of their owners. In the same article, writing broadly about human cultures, he stated: "Their arts have told us what they dreamed but their architecture tells us what they did, and into their homes have they written their individuality."[2]

Cutter's travels as a student may have instilled in him another reason for seeking diversity. In Europe he had become accustomed to cities that had developed over many centuries, in which buildings of different eras stood side by side. In Dresden, for example, he must have seen, on a single street, newly built structures standing harmoniously beside Medieval, Renaissance, and Baroque architecture. Such diversity offered not only variety for the eye but evidence of the past. By designing in different styles and giving his houses an appearance of age, he may have been attempting to endow the newly founded city of Spokane with the dimension of time, to convey the impression that it had been there for centuries.[3]

In eighteenth-century New England the social elite were content to live in houses of very similar design, conforming to classic rules of composition and proportion. In Spokane, in the late 1890s, entrepreneurs rejoiced in the opportunity to build exactly as they pleased. Cutter's new clients were from a new generation of capitalists who had understood how the potential of the region could be realized, and had profited enormously. Some, from wealthy East Coast families, were educated, shrewd, and ready to seize opportunities. Others were self-made men, who by hard work, experience, and sound judgment had flourished in a field of heavy competition. Unfettered by convention, they could invoke memories of whatever they had admired in the places they had left to go west; or they could indulge in fantasy about places they had never seen. The parvenu who had traveled the path from rags to riches could display symbols associated with old wealth; he could imply through a time-honored design that his newly built mansion was an ancestral home. And the educated investor backed by old money could bring customary signs of civilization to the frontier. The key to Cutter's success was that he possessed both the familiarity with old traditions and the imagination to give substance to new desires. His years of travel and the many hours he had spent poring over illustrated books had given him roots in the language of architecture; his association with Poetz and Malmgren had made up for his lack of professional experience.

The wives of the high-powered men who commissioned houses from Cutter undoubtedly were influential in decisions reached between client and architect. They had far more time to devote to artistic matters than their husbands, and many of them were active in promoting the arts in Spokane.[4] Cutter was comfortable in the society of women, and they most likely acted as his allies in negotiations for costly or unusual design features.

Between 1897 and 1900, Cutter and Malmgren designed eight mansions in Spokane that represent a peak in the success of the practice. All but one client chose to build in the two most fashionable residential districts: Browne's Addition, on a spur of land west of the downtown overlooking the gorge of the Spokane River, and the South Hill, near the sites under the cliff where Cutter had erected his first architectural works. In both places the architects juxtaposed houses in radically different styles, which a century later still set the character of the neighborhood. At the head of First Avenue stands the Neoclassical house, complete with columned portico, built for mining magnate John A. Finch. Next to it, similar in color but very different in form, is the Mission Revival house of lawyer and capitalist, W. J. C. Wakefield; and beside it, the red brick and half-timbered home of Finch's partner, Amasa B. Campbell, which followed an "Old English" theme. Only two blocks away they created a unique mansion for the most colorful of Spokane's mining millionaires, Patrick Clark. This exotic house, whose architectural vocabulary can be traced in part to early Medieval Spain or Mughal India, defies stylistic classification.

It is clear from an analysis of the plans that Cutter's greatest strength was in the design of picturesque rambling houses rather than formal, classical buildings. On his travels, and through his observations of recent American architecture, he had absorbed principles of composition, construction, and use of materials that enabled him to excel in a romantic type of design. But he had not been educated in the classical language of architecture and showed little interest in its discipline. In his Tudoresque Campbell house he continued to develop the romantic themes he had initiated in the

6.1 Amasa B. Campbell house, Browne's Addition, Spokane, 1897–98. Cutter's first Tudor Revival house. Cutter designed the carriage house in the same style.
This house, recently restored by the Eastern Washington State Historical Society, is open to the public. Eastern Washington State Historical Society, L85–174.15.

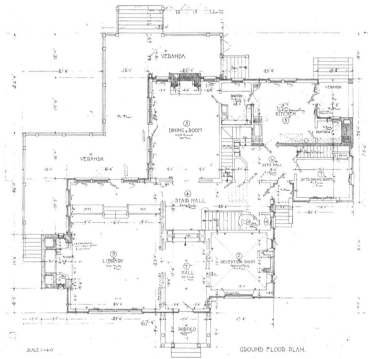

6.2 First-floor plan of the Campbell House. The veranda, zigzagging around the northwest corner of the house, commands a view of the Spokane River Canyon. Eastern Washington State Historical Society, L84–349.1.

114

late 1880s (figs. 6.1, 6.2).[5] With its irregular pattern of gables, dormers, and tall chimneys, it stands as his quintessential turn-of-the-century design.

Cutter consciously composed the Campbell house to avoid symmetry and regularity. He balanced a large half-timbered gable end, which steps slightly forward on the left of the street facade, with two unequal dormers on the right. He placed the porch off-center, but echoed the form of the dormers in its pitched roof. To the right of the main block, he set the service wing back nearly thirty feet behind the front facade, and beyond it placed a freestanding carriage house. But rather than conceal these elements, he included them in the picturesque composition. The dormer window of the sewing room and the gable end of the carriage house reflect similar forms on the main block. Their shingled roofs, half-timbered upper walls and gables, and the red brick lower walls, with stone dressings, provide continuity. The entire building is enlivened by the decorative pattern of the timbers and by effects of light and shade, as overhanging eaves, jettied upper stories, and projecting windows all cast their shadows on walls below.

Without the constraints of a classical ordering system, Cutter placed the veranda of the Campbell house, not as symmetry demanded, but where it could best be enjoyed. It zigzags informally around the northwest corner of the house, providing a variety of sheltered vantage points and linking library and dining room by a pleasant outdoor route. Its position takes advantage of the superb outlook over the gorge of the Spokane River. Not far from the house, the ground falls away steeply into the valley below, dramatizing a distant view of the stone cliffs to the west where the swiftly flowing river turns out of sight in the distance.

The interior of the Campbell house is both inviting and distinctive. Its character comes not merely from the rich diversity of materials and finishes but also from the careful manipulation of space. The architects provided, for those who moved through it, a sequence of spaces of almost theatrical quality. The small entrance hall (fig. 6.3), approached through a heavy oak door, offers a memorable prelude to the rooms beyond. Continuing the pitched roof form of the porch outside, its ceiling, constructed of oak rafters, gives it the appearance of a miniature medieval hall. Broad, curtained doorways on either side, open like prosceniums, reveal sharply contrasting settings. To the right, an elegant little Louis XV reception room (fig. 6.4), decorated in rose moiré silk and gilt, set the scene for the

6.3 Hall in the Campbell house. The Romanesque arch, supported on clusters of colonnettes, makes a powerful transition to the inner staircase hall. The dining room is visible beyond, with light flooding in from the veranda. Eastern Washington State Historical Society, L91–159.12.

6.4 Reception room in the Campbell house, in the Louis XV style, finished with rose moiré silk and gilt. The Rococo plaster frieze represents cherubs carrying garlands. Eastern Washington State Historical Society, L91–120.25.

ceremonious entertaining expected in Spokane society. To the left, the spacious library served as the family living room (fig. 6.5). Its dark oak beams and inglenook fireplace evoke the old world character of an ancestral home. Straight ahead, an arch leads through to an inner hall, framing the view into the stair hall. The deep arch is supported on either side by a row of carved colonnettes. Beneath it four steps lead up to a raised floor, like a stage designed for the perfectly timed appearances of Mrs. Campbell, ready in fine attire to greet her guests. The architects provided light at the end of the vista to lead the eye onward toward a wide opening into the dining room, through which light floods into the hall. In contrast to the dark colors of hardwoods and wall finishes elsewhere, the paneling and ceiling beams of the dining room are painted white and the walls around the fireplace are lined with blue and white Delft tiles. Thus the light of six windows is reflected around the room.

6.5 Library in the Campbell house, with dark oak beams and a Gothic arch over the fireplace. Eastern Washington State Historical Society, L91–159.8.

A change of floor level is also exploited in a raised gallery running across the north end of the library. The main part of this room is focused inward on the huge stone fireplace. Dark paneling, rich hangings, and carved wood in Gothic motifs give a sumptuous sense of enclosure. The gallery, on the other hand, opens through almost continuous windows onto the veranda. With its light, open character, it provides variety within the one large space. For those wanting to find a more intimate place in the room, two seats, each with a minuscule Gothic window, are built into the inglenook fireplace.

Mr. Campbell had his own retreat in the basement, a game room with a poker table carved in black oak. There he could drink, smoke, and play poker in exclusively male company. The five principal bedrooms, opening off a spacious upper hall, were feminine in character, decorated with pretty wallpapers and curtains. Each was given individuality by variations in the design of fireplaces and other details.

The Campbell house is warm and inviting. The architect built for the formal lifestyle of the wealthy, but he also provided for delight as well as decorum. A significant aspect of the design is the consideration given to behind-the-scenes domestic functions. The efficiently planned kitchen quarters were also congenial places for the servants to work. The kitchen itself is a bright room with a fine view across the river valley to the north. It has its own veranda in a secluded position where the cook could relax in the shade. Though the laundry is in the basement, both the sewing room upstairs and the servants' dining room have generous south-facing windows. The scheme by William Otis of Cleveland for the interior decoration included samples of wallpaper and fabrics for the servants room.[6]

The house was both wired for electricity and piped for gas lighting, and it was centrally heated. To integrate the radiators with the decor of the house, some of them were concealed under floor grilles or under built-in seats. In addition to two luxurious bathrooms on the second floor and a simpler one in the attic, water closets were installed in the basement and under the main staircase on the first floor. With the help of such devices as a call bell system with an indicator board in the servants' hall, a dumbwaiter linking all floors, and high quality equipment in the kitchen and laundry, the house was designed to run like a well-tuned machine. In its functional aspects and particularly in the steps taken to improve the lives of the servants, the Campbell house represents a significant advance over the Moore and Glover houses, begun eight years earlier. But as Cutter wrote in his article, there were other ways in which interior design could influence the servants, and perhaps help build loyalty: "The owner of one of the most beautiful homes in Spokane said recently that the servants who came into his home very soon became more quiet, gentle, serious and refined in speech and manner. They could not resist the constant appeal of walls, windows, tapestry, furniture, pictures and even the books into which they had come to live."

The Finch mansion, a close neighbor to the Campbell house, standing at the western end of First Avenue, appears to be its architectural opposite (fig. 6.6). The symmetry of its gleaming white front facade, and its grand Ionic portico, proclaim its classical intentions. However, like the two other classical houses designed the same year, it betrays the architect's inclination toward freedom in design.

6.6 John A. Finch house, 1897–98. The neoclassical design provides a formal counterpoint to the picturesquely composed Campbell house. Photo by Libby. Eastern Washington State Historical Society, L87–1.52314.47.

In the eighteenth and early nineteenth centuries, American architects were guided by pattern books from Europe that not only conveyed the image of Palladian or Neoclassical architecture, but also provided the discipline on which they were based.[7] Several generations of designers, from amateur gentlemen architects of the early Georgian era to the professionals of the Federal period, followed the principles of symmetry, unity, and proportion prescribed in such publications. In Cutter's own time, many architects were educated under the powerful influence of the Parisian École des Beaux Arts, a bastion of Classicism. Cutter, on the other hand, steeped in the romantic tradition of the nineteenth century, conceived even his classical houses in a picturesque manner. While he emphasized the formality of the Finch house by setting it on a broad platform, linking porches on three sides, he broke the symmetry by projecting out unequal balconies to the north and west. Around the central hall he arranged the rooms to give variety, to introduce daylight in different ways, and to suit the rituals of daily life. As in the Campbell house,

6.7 Hall in the Finch house, framed with Ionic columns in the elegant manner of the Adam Style. Eastern Washington State Historical Society, L86–480.

he planned the interior as a sequence of visual experiences for the visitor; but in this case he exploited classical forms to articulate the space and to enhance effects of light and shade. From the entrance he framed the view ahead into the inner staircase hall by means of an elliptical arch supported on Ionic columns (fig.6.7). Beyond the first flight of the elegantly curving stair, light from the fernery at the back of the first floor enters the hall between the columns that carry the broad landing. Above this a large Palladian window floods the hall with light.

The architect provided several alternative ways of moving through the house and onto the surrounding verandas. Guests arriving for dinner could progress from the reception room through an arch flanked by columns to the drawing room and then pass on to admire the plants in the fernery by late afternoon sunlight before being ushered into the dining room. After dinner, the men could join John Finch in the library while the ladies went upstairs to Charlotte Finch's parlor for more intimate conversation.

Cutter also took liberties with his details. Although he tended to describe his classical houses as "Colonial," they combine, in common with other Classical Revival houses of the time, a mixture of Georgian, Federal, and even Greek Revival features. Since he was apparently intent on providing his clients with distinctly different houses, he exploited architectural details from these three historic periods to provide variety of expression. For example, he gave the front windows on the first floor of the Finch house broken, scrolled pediments derived from a design illustrated in James Gibbs's *Book of Architecture* (1728) which was much imitated in Colonial America. On the upper floor, the windows, with shouldered architraves and canted jambs, follow a Greek Revival pattern. Cutter's combination of the two types—sensuously Baroque below and of Grecian purity above—is distinctly eclectic.

John Finch and Amasa B. Campbell, his partner in many mining ventures, had come from different backgrounds. While Finch came from a wealthy family, and had prospered in the iron industry, Campbell was a self-made man. Born in Ohio in 1845, Campbell had worked in the grain and wool business, then for railroad companies in Nebraska and Kansas before turning to mining in Utah in 1871. When he traveled to the Northwest, and discovered the vast potential of the Coeur d'Alenes, he persuaded John Finch, whom he had met in Ohio, to provide the capital for a mining venture. They initiated their partnership in the Coeur d'Alenes in 1887 and were highly successful. The combination of Finch's money and Campbell's experience gave them an edge over many competitors. The partners worked closely in establishing, controlling, and reaping profits from their mines and investments. Although Finch never sought public office, he invested heavily in his city, supporting ventures that fulfilled his beliefs, using his influence to prevent whatever met his disapproval. Owning stock in many of Spokane's enterprises, he held real power. His wife, Charlotte, whom he married "against his associates' advice" was "poor, beautiful, young." Even if eyebrows were raised, the Finches were people who mattered and were accepted.[8]

It would be hard to prove that the Neoclassical and Tudor styles of their neighboring houses actually expressed the personalities of Finch and Campbell. It could be argued that the patrician character of the Finch house reflected the privilege of the owner's ancestry, and that the Tudor style, rooted in vernacular traditions, suited Campbell, who had risen from humbler origins. One can assume, however, that Cutter both influenced and interpreted the desires of the two men and their wives. Their homes stand, above all, for the individualism of the age.

Cutter was quite innovative when, in 1897, he built a house in the Mission Revival Style for the attorney W. J. C. Wakefield, on the site between the Finches and the Campbells (fig. 6.8). This style had emerged a decade earlier in California as a romantic evocation of the decaying Franciscan missions, built in the early eighteenth century. It had been popularized by the construction of Page Brown's California Building at the World's Columbian Exposition in Chicago in 1893. Cutter must have seen that state pavilion, which, like his own Idaho Building, expressed a regional character. While the depression was on, he may have been waiting for an opportunity to design a Mission Revival building. In California, the style was enthusiastically adapted to many different building types, but it was little known in the Northwest until Cutter used it in Browne's Addition. While the original missions were simple, solid structures of adobe or plastered stone with few embellishments, the Mission Revival developed into a decorative style. Architects exploited the domed towers, scalloped gables, and red tiled roofs of Franciscan churches for their exuberant effect on the skyline. It could be argued that a style that had come to California from Mexico, with roots in Spain, was hardly appropriate in the Northwest. Adobe is not suitable for rainy climates, and the low-pitched clay tiled roofs com-

mon in the Mediterranean are inadequate for snow. But in the prevailing mood of eclecticism at the turn of the century, issues of regional integrity were of little concern. Kirtland Cutter joined other architects in many parts of the country in reviving this alternative colonial style that offered fresh architectural interest. To suit a northern climate, he replaced adobe with stucco on wood framing and raised the pitch of the roofs.

Cutter's design for his first Mission house shows that he was familiar with recent work in California.[9] In the Wakefield house he erected a central scalloped gable of white stucco as the principal feature of its facade. He supported this element, not on heavy, earthbound walls like those of the original missions, but on two pairs of columns flanking the front door. Rather than penetrating the walls with small casements, he opened them up with large, double-hung windows with decoratively designed glazing bars. To the west of the Wakefield house he built the carriage house in the Mission Revival manner, enlivening it with a decorative parapet. The total effect of the main house and the outbuilding, with their curvaceous upper walls, is light and playful.

6.8 Wakefield house, Browne's Addition, Spokane, 1897–98. Standing between the classical Finch house and the Tudoresque Campbell house, it is probably the first Mission Revival house in the state of Washington. Photo by the author.

Only two blocks from the Finch, Campbell, and Wakefield houses, Cutter designed an original and exotic residence for Patrick Clark, the most brilliant of Spokane's mining millionaires.[10] Known to his friends and associates as Patsy, Clark came from a poor family in Ireland. He had crossed the Atlantic in 1870, when he was twenty years old, and had gone almost at once to the gold mines in California. Brighter prospects lured him to Virginia City, Nevada, and then to Ophir, Utah, where he was employed by the copper magnate and fellow Irishman, Marcus Daly.[11] They had both labored in the Californian mines and worked their way to success; more important, both men had an instinctive understanding of the art of making successful mines. Clark was not a trained geologist, or a technician, but Daly recognized his extraordinary ability to manage the complex operation of a mine. At Ophir, Daly took him on as foreman and mine superintendent, but he soon moved with his employer to Montana, where at the age of thirty he became superintendent of the Moulton Mine. It was not long before he was managing Butte's famous Anaconda Mine. In the late eighties, at about the time Cutter began his architectural practice, Clark moved his family to Spokane and made the city his center for mining operations. With Marcus Daly he developed the Poorman Gold Mine in the Coeur d'Alenes and as co-owner reaped enormous profits. Then he joined with a Spokane syndicate, including Cutter's clients, Finch, Campbell, Wakefield, and the younger Corbin, to exploit the riches of Slocan and Rossland in British Columbia.

He was now ready to commission Cutter to design him a house without any budget restrictions. According to legend, he asked the architect to create the most impressive house west of the Mississippi. In 1897, as the walls began to rise on Second Avenue in Browne's Addition, he made his best investment ever. He grubstaked two prospectors at a claim in the Eureka Basin of north central Washington and thus started operation of the Republic Mine, the richest in the Washington and British Columbia region.[12] The crux of Clark's wealth was his uncanny genius for buying mines of great potential when the price was low and selling them at the zenith of their value.

The design of a mansion for such a man was a challenging opportunity for the architect. We do not know what specific demands Clark made on him, but Cutter decided to work in an opulent, eclectic style, drawing inspiration from Islamic architecture. The heyday for architectural fantasies based on oriental and Islamic originals had occurred in the middle of the nineteenth century when Samuel Sloan of Philadelphia designed the remarkable "Longwood" at Natchez, Mississippi, and P. T. Barnum had erected for himself a fantastic house named "Iranistan," modeled on the Royal Pavilion at Brighton.[13] Examples of indulgence in that type of dream world were rarer in the later decades of the century. But Cutter, despite his reverence for Arts and Crafts traditions, found it hard to resist the lure of the exotic. His Cyrus Burns house with its onion dome and Islamic arches, and the "Moorish" hall for F. Rockwood Moore, both of 1889, show his fascination with such outlandish styles. The design, in his own house, of a "Turkish Divan," entered through an ogee arch, conjures up images of the Arabian Nights (fig. 3.11).[14] The Patrick Clark mansion may have been a chance for him to respond to a deeply felt desire to realize a complete work of architecture in the intriguing language of fantasy on a Moorish theme.

It appears that Clark wanted to build a residence that stood out from all the others in Browne's Addition. But he can hardly have envisioned the striking originality of Cutter's design (figs. 6.9, 6.10). It was bold in form and extremely rich in color. Built of a warm honey-colored brick with sandstone dressing, it was covered with a hipped roof of brilliant red metal tiles. The colors of the materials were heightened by the use of white paint on the columns and arches around the upper windows and deep red on the balustrades. The front, facing south onto Coeur d'Alene Park, with its central entrance arch and round corner towers, has an appearance of powerful symmetry. Yet Cutter deliberately broke the symmetry by allowing one tower to rise higher than the other and projecting out a veranda on the west side only.

The various elements of the house stand out individually as distinct volumes: the central block, penetrated by a generous arch, commands the center of the main facade; the towers strengthen the corners; between the towers, upper-level balconies thrust forward, casting deep shadows. Above, spacious attic rooms break through the hipped roof as wide dormers. Each of these elements has a separate, low-pitched roof with a very broad overhang, providing excellent shelter from the hot midday sun in summer. Seen from below, the soffits of these roofs read as a series of hovering planes at several different levels, progressing upward from the lowest roofs over the balconies to those of the highest tower and the dormers. Above the solid first-floor walls of smooth brick, the ornamented, white bal-

6.9 Patrick Clark
house, Browne's
Addition, Spokane,
1897–98. Built
in an exotic manner
to convey the wealth
of the owner. Photo
by the author.

6.10 First-floor plan
of the Patrick Clark
house, Eastern Wash-
ington State Histori-
cal Society,
L84.207.109.

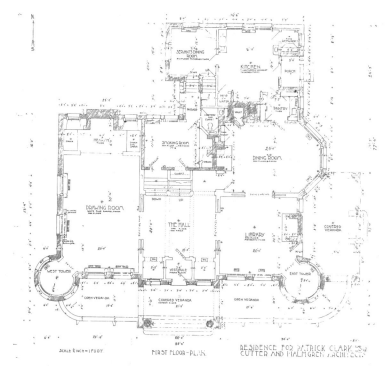

cony fronts and window surrounds run in an arcade across the upper facade, creating a feeling of openness. This arcade, which is also repeated on the front of the dormers, helps to unify the design. Similar white columns at the top of the east tower, level with the dormers, turn the corner gracefully and give further continuity.

One of Cutter's sources for the unique Clark mansion appears to have been the Ponce de Leon Hotel at St. Augustine, Florida, built between 1885 and 1887 (fig. 6.11). This sumptuous resort hotel had been designed by the newly founded firm of Carrère and Hastings with the young Bernard Maybeck as chief assistant. The aim of their client, Henry Flagler, was to create an American Riviera along the east coast of Florida. The Ponce de Leon, which was intended to celebrate the Hispanic colonization of Florida, was loosely based on the Renaissance architecture of Spain and subtly evoked the Moorish influence there.[15]

Cutter could easily have seen drawings of the Florida hotel published in *Architect and Building News* in August 1888. He may even have visited the resort. But just as Carrère and Hastings interpreted

6.11 The Ponce de Leon Hotel, St. Augustine, Florida, 1888, by Carrère and Hastings. A possible source for Cutter's approach to the Patrick Clark house. Flagler College Archives.

freely from their sources, Cutter designed a mansion in his own way, synthesizing several influences. The quality of the design comes as much from the rich play of volumes and of the openings that penetrate them as from the ornament. Indeed, if entirely stripped of embellishment and reduced to simple geometric forms with rectangular windows, it would still present a striking composition. With its strong horizontals and roofs floating one above the other, it would have had something in common with Wright's Prairie Houses that were to emerge in the next decade.

But Cutter did not choose the path of simplicity. He invested the Clark house with an ostentatious character. What it derived from the palaces of Islamic Spain and from the Ponce de Leon Hotel was a mood rather than specific structural forms or ornament. An examination of the details suggests a wider range of sources. The red sandstone arches of the entry and of the veranda, supported on colonnettes with carved capitals, are Richardsonian. The arcades fronting the upper facade like Moorish wall screens are closer to designs from India than from Spain or North Africa. The openings are, in fact, not spanned by arches but by beams supported on bracket capitals. They imitate a system of construction exploited by the sixteenth-century Mughal architects who built the palace at Fatehpur Sikri in India for Akbar the Great. This palace could also have inspired the use of red sandstone, round corner towers, and high pavilions rising above other roofs. However, striking differences from Indian prototypes point to the eclectic nature of the Clark design. For example, the roofs of Mughal buildings tend to swell outward in a convex curve, while those at the Clark house sweep up to their peaks in a manner that appears Chinese. Indeed, from certain angles, Cutter's superimposed roofs appear distinctly pagoda-like.

The experience of entering this house and moving through it fulfills the promise of the facade; the exotic interior confirms the suspicion of a Mughal influence on the design. The entrance hall, finished in dark oak, appears gloomy at first. But out of the darkness, rich colors glow, and mysterious, complex forms create an unforgettable atmosphere. Several cusped arches of Mughal or Mudejar origin enliven the space. Three of these arches separate the hall from the stair; three others, near the front wall, lead to the vestibule and to recessed bays on either side. At right angles to them, springing from the same eight columns, elaborately carved brackets in the form of identical half arches rise to support the ceiling beams. The two freestanding columns opposite the front door dominate the space. Their branching, multifoliate structure, reminiscent of the audience chamber of the Red Fort at Delhi, suggests that Cutter aimed to give his client nothing less than the palace of an oriental potentate. He may, however, have gained inspiration from a source he had actually seen, the East Indian Building at the World's Columbian Exposition (fig. 6.12).

Beyond the arches that spring from these columns, stairways lead up and down. To the left, steps descend to a smoking room; in the center an arch opens, like a proscenium, to the grand staircase (fig. 6.13). Its first flight ascends to a landing, spacious enough to accommodate a sofa and armchair on either side of a fireplace. The climax of the framed vista is a pair of superb Tiffany stained glass windows, whose warm, subtle colors and flamboyant peacock motif proclaim the joys of the Gilded Age.[16] Amber feathers with eyes of lapis lazuli fan out at the base of each window. In the center, a column of red, petal-like forms rises up to a nimbus of pale and dark blues, from which more feathers radiate. On either side, individual feathers drop down, their deep blue eyes making sharp accents against a field of gold. There is a sense of energy flowing up the center, exploding and falling at the edges. These windows represent Art Nouveau at its most sumptuous. Avoiding the floral designs or

6.12 East Indian Building, World's Columbian Exposition, Chicago, 1893. Cutter probably saw this structure, with its cusped arches, when he visited the Exposition. From *The Dream City.* Avery Library, Columbia University.

6.13 Entrance hall of the Patrick Clark house. The cusped arch frames
the stair and the Tiffany stained glass window beyond. Photo by
the author.

fashionably languid female figures common at the time, they show a sophisticated abstraction that combines well with the oriental elements of the hall.

The peacock motif is repeated in brilliant color in the tympanum of a pointed arch over the front door. The walls are covered with a rich golden brown embossed paper simulating tooled leather, and the ceiling panels glow with a deep red. A soft, white light from nine lamps on the stair newels augments the colored light of the windows. Standing high on brass standards, their opalescent glass billows out, gathers in to a narrow waist, and swells again before rising, like an onion dome, to a sharp point. Their design harmonizes with the Tiffany windows and with the intricate balustrade of the stair. The newel posts follow the design of the main columns of the hall, and slim balusters that support the handrail join to form miniature cusped arches. It seems likely that Cutter visited the Tiffany studios in New York to discuss the stained glass windows and light fixtures.

As in the other mansions of the period, the principal rooms open through broad doorways off the hall. Each has its individual character and none but the smoking room follows the Islamic theme of the hall. To the right, Patrick Clark's library conveys a feeling of masculinity. Its beamed ceiling and millwork in fine walnut and mahogany combine with the dark green velvet tapestry on the walls to suggest the quiet luxury of a gentlemen's club. The onyx fireplace and gilt mirror above provide a touch of opulence. From the library a glass door opens out onto the spacious veranda whose brick-built arches were ornamented with sandstone. To the left is the reception room, where Mrs. Clark presided as grand society hostess. This domain of high society ladies, finished elegantly in rose, white, and gold, appears strikingly light compared with the hall. Cutter adapted the Louis XV Style to design this room in an original manner. At the far end of the room toward the back of the house, an elliptical barrel vault supported on Corinthian columns forms a canopy over the fireplace. On either side, under a lowered ceiling, a deep couch fills the space between four columns. Cutter had taken the concept of the humble inglenook and reinterpreted it in the elegant manner of eighteenth-century France. Above the fireplace, a broad mirror gives the illusion of continuing space; in each corner, beside the couch, a stained glass window lights the cozy seating area.

The system of columns and arches continues on the west wall where the two windows are set back in arched aedicules framed by Corinthian columns. A frieze running around the room, above the gilded capitals of the columns, is ornamented with gilt arabesques on a field of white. Both the library and the reception room open, in one corner, into the base of a tower. Thus each offers an intimate circular retreat with sunlight from windows on three sides. The dining room, toward the rear of the house, east of the stair, shares with the library the richness of tapestry wall coverings and dark, polished wood. The handwoven Beauvais tapestry as well as the beams and paneling of gopherwood reveal Cutter's quest for the unusual and the exquisite. He added a medieval touch in the carved monks' heads, each one unique, supporting the ends of the beams and continuing round the top of the other walls. In the arched stone fireplace, andirons in the form of rampant winged dragons present a heraldic quality appropriate to an ancestral home.

More in tune with the realities of life for a mining millionaire, a huge safe was concealed behind the paneling of the dining room wall, beside the entry to the butler's pantry. Behind the north wall of the dining room, Cutter planned the kitchen and servants' quarters to allow for all the needs of the Clark family and their guests. He placed the service wing, as in the Campbell and Finch houses, to one side at the back, so as not to interrupt the light of the window over the staircase. Detached from the house on the west side, but matching it in design, stands the carriage house, where, in addition to horses, carriages, and a sleigh, a cow was kept to provide milk for the table.

The luxury of the main rooms downstairs extends to the bedrooms on the second floor. A comfortable sitting room in the southeast corner connected with Patrick Clark's bedroom in the middle of the south front and that of his wife on the other side. Like the room of their daughter Leah in the southwest corner, the sitting room was finished with exquisite craftsmanship in bird's-eye maple. And much of the furniture of both rooms was specially made of the same wood. They also had the benefit of cozy vantage points in the towers. The three south-facing rooms open onto large roofed balconies; but a decade or two after the house was built, the room in the center was enlarged for Mr. Clark into the space of the balcony. The Clarks had six children: three daughters, whose rooms were on the second floor, and three sons, who slept on the third floor. There was also a large billiard room at this level. The space was originally built as a ballroom, but apparently was never used for that purpose. Reputedly, it was also the scene of poker games, though Patrick Clark himself was said never to gamble.

In 1897, Cutter also began work on houses for his former brother-in-law Austin Corbin and Austin's father, Daniel Chase Corbin. Both chose to build classical houses, on the South Hill, but the older man settled for a far more modest home than his son. While Austin's mansion cost $33,000, Daniel spent only $17,000. More than any other man, D. C. Corbin was responsible for the revival of Spokane after the panic of 1893.[17] However, he was little interested in Spokane society. His wife, Louisa, had become an invalid after the birth of their third child, and now she lived in Europe. Their daughter Mary's estrangement and subsequent divorce from Cutter does not appear to have influenced Daniel Corbin in his choice of an architect. It was without the company of his wife and daughters that D. C. Corbin came to live in Olympian splendor on the hill.

The *Spokesman-Review* of March 7, 1897, described the Austin Corbin house (fig. 6.14) as "an exact duplicate of some old Maine and Vermont houses." Indeed the Ionic portico, approached by a broad flight of steps, and the hipped roof, crowned with a "captain's walk," suggest an influence of the Federal Period. The entrance hall,

6.14 Austin Corbin house, Spokane, 1897–98. Unlike its earlier neighbor, the Moore house, which seems to grow naturally out of the slope, this imposing residence stands aloof from the site. Eastern Washington State Historical Society, L84–325.

in which the view of the grand staircase is framed by Corinthian columns, continues the same first impression. However, the irregular plan shows that Cutter was more interested in offering rooms of varied character than in conforming to Neoclassical principles. It gives the impression that he organized the house from the inside out, allowing rooms to project out where convenient, thus breaking the pristine geometry. The design becomes increasingly asymmetrical toward the rear, where the service quarters stand to one side. Cutter understood how to plan houses for the elaborate rituals of formal entertaining and was clearly successful in the case of the Austin Corbin house. A news report in the *Spokane Chronicle* of May 20, 1899, describes an afternoon tea given by Katherine Corbin that would have enhanced the architect's reputation as well as that of her own family. The *Chronicle* characterized this event, attended by two hundred invited guests, as "the most beautiful of the season." "Mrs. Corbin's home is one of the handsome residences that has been completed in this city in the last few months. Surrounded by lawns, flowers and trees it has a charming location on the hillside. The broad veranda overlooks the entire city and affords a splendid view. The parlors which have been much admired for their richly ornamental furnishings and colorings were made more beautiful on this occasion by large quantities of flowers tastefully arranged."

In the reception room, "finished in green," the flowers were "entirely in pink." Here, supported by a few friends, the hostess graciously received her guests. They could then circulate through the other rooms taking tea in the music room among pink and white roses, or punch in the parlor, where Mrs. Finch had been asked to preside, "surrounded by a bank of palms and potted plants," their foliage contrasting with the red colored walls. Refreshments were in the dining room, whose decorations were in green and white. The musicians performed on the generous landing of the staircase, above the formal, central hall.

This kind of social gathering did not take place at the house of Austin Corbin's father, built a little to the east of his own in 1897. D. C. Corbin's residence (fig. 6.15) lacks the imposing portico of the two other houses, but it is surrounded on three sides by a shady veranda that expands at the front corners into polygonal bays. These elements reinforce the sense of symmetry and give the impression of a larger house. The veranda columns are Tuscan, the plainest of the orders, and the entablature is unadorned. The interior fittings are dignified; columns flank the fireplaces in the principal ground-

6.15 D. C. Corbin house, South Hill, Spokane, 1897–98. The expansive veranda adapts the Colonial Revival type for outdoor living. Photo by the author.

floor rooms, but the character is severe, lacking the gracious and joyful air that Cutter liked to give to his houses. When he furnished it, Corbin set a billiard table near the center of the living room and his rolltop desk in the corner. The Corbin house stood austerely apart from the city, like its owner, who moved from his rooms in the Spokane Hotel into the first house he had owned since his early days in Helena. While the Austin Corbin house was the scene of extravagant parties and costume balls, the only entertainment given by his father was an annual display of fireworks on the Fourth of July.[18] Although offering no personal contact with the host, it was nevertheless splendid, like thunder and lightening emanating from Mount Olympus.

    In 1898, Cutter built another classical house on First Avenue in Browne's Addition for the successful real estate developer, Jay P. Graves. This time he added to the variety of the street by building in red brick, articulated with white pilasters, cornice, and window frames.[19] But in the same year he returned to the Tudor style for his old client, John Sherwood, who chose to build on Summit Boulevard, across the river to the north of Browne's Addition. This house, which has been much altered after a serious fire, represented a further set of variations on Cutter's Old English theme.[20]

Cutter began work in 1899 on a far more significant Tudoresque house on the South Hill immediately to the east of Austin Corbin's property. His client was the flamboyant and often ruthless capitalist F. Lewis Clark, for whom he had built a lodge gate of rough basalt at the entry to the property seven years earlier. In this commission he was able to integrate a house with the landscape more fully than ever before, and to manipulate the volumes for picturesque effect. Poised at a high vantage point to the west of the Moore house, opposite his own chalet, it occupies a broad ledge between two abrupt slopes (fig. 6.16). Under a shingled roof of complex form, the red brick walls, half-timbered gables, and carved barge boards that seem relatively tame on the level ground in Browne's Addition acquire a more dramatic appearance when seen through the trees on this wilder site. The pointed Gothic arches and windows also contribute to the individuality of the F. Lewis Clark house.

Close to its walls, unruly stacks of basalt break out from the slope as reminders of the violent creation of the land thousands of years before. Cutter preserved these outcroppings as dominant features in the gardens, to give a unique, natural character to the outdoor spaces. While he had designed conventional porches for the houses in Browne's Addition, he gave the Clark house a veritable eyrie almost overhanging the steep incline below. He surrounded a large, ten-sided gazebo-like veranda, opening off the dining room, with a superstructure of pointed wooden arches that carried the roof and balcony above. It was supported on uneven walls of basalt as if in imitation of the natural outcroppings of the stone nearby. The *Chronicle* of March 13, 1899, presumably at Cutter's prompting, reported that this "pile of rough stone" would give the veranda the appearance of having been built from a ruined tower. Its position offered superb views over the town and to distant mountains beyond. Combining an agreeable sense of protection and a fine prospect, it could provide shade on hot summer days and catch any cool breezes.

When the weather called for more sheltered conditions, the Clarks were able to use the conservatory at the west end of the first

6.16 F. Lewis Clark house, Spokane, 1899–1900. Romantically sited on
a ledge high on the South Hill, the stone base of its octagonal veranda
echoes the basalt outcroppings on the steep hillside. Eastern Washington
State Historical Society, L84–487.8.

floor, next to the drawing room. This space opened on three sides
through Gothic windows that echoed those of the veranda. Cutter
also repeated the Gothic motif on other ground-floor windows and
the porch outside the kitchen. A few years later, Clark commissioned
him to add an arbor leading west from the outside door of the fernery toward the Austin Corbin house. In this vine-covered structure
he made use, once again, of wooden pointed arches, and carried a
recurring theme of the house out into the garden.

6.17 Outcroppings of basalt and the water tower by the F. Lewis Clark house. Photo by the author.

To the south, close to two large basalt outcroppings, Cutter built a tower (fig. 6.17). Resembling an old windmill that had lost its sails, its wooden top rose from a stone base not unlike the "ruined tower" below the veranda. Although it served as a water tower, its real purpose was surely the same as a romantic folly in an English garden—to create a picturesque effect. The rough piles of basalt, almost as high as the house, and the somewhat similar man-made tower are strange partners in the unusual grounds of the Clark estate. On the north side, lawns swept down the slope toward a little pond surrounded with rocks and flowers, against a background of shrubs. But to the east, as if to seek relief from the native wilderness that dominated the scene, a formal, walled garden offered a more tranquil environment.

Cutter developed the plan differently from the others of the same period. The L-shaped plan called for a hall at the junction of the two wings, but this opened through broad double doors into the principal rooms, allowing space to flow from one room to another. The staircase, with richly modeled balusters, was a major feature of the interior, leading to a ballroom on the top floor. As usual, the interior was sumptuous, conveying the idea of a stately European home. Cutter created diversity in the individual rooms by using a variety of woods and finishes. He paneled the hall and library in oak and the dining room in sycamore. In contrast to these rooms with their exposed hardwood ceiling beams, the reception room, finished in ivory enamel, appears exceptionally light. A delicate frieze of anthemion runs in the cove between wall and ceiling, and the doorway is flanked by Corinthian pilasters. Cutter fitted the house with magnificent fireplaces. In the reception room a plastered hood over the hearth, based on designs in Italian Renaissance palaces, is carried on consoles. In the library the heads of lions, bearing shields, support a similar hood of polished oak. In its hearth the andirons represent a pair of dragons. Clark's wife Wini-fred, who had come from Washington, D.C., was one of Spokane's most brilliant hostesses; their home was the scene of many grand social occasions.

As the last of eight large commissions in Spokane at the turn of the century, Cutter was asked to remodel the old brick residence built at least a decade earlier by J. J. Browne, the original developer of Browne's Addition. When it was bought in 1900 by railroad pioneer Robert Strahorn, it must have seemed out of place beside its new neighbor, the Campbell house. Its vertical massing and heavy mansard roofs evoked the Second Empire Style, which was out of fashion, and it appeared rather plain beside the lavish architecture that had grown up around it. Cutter enlarged it greatly with additions on all four sides, and added a complete roof above its mansard (fig. 6.18). He disguised the old form by breaking the roofline with pointed dormers and adding cross roofs with half-timbered gable ends. To benefit from the view across the river to the north, he built a veranda at the rear, and he added porches at both ends of the house. These elements, whose flat roofs functioned as balconies, extended the building outward, and emphasized the horizontal plane parallel with the flat ground of the neighborhood.

In order to ready the house for the Strahorn family, it is said that sixty carpenters were employed. The carved barge boards and brackets under the eaves, the strikingly patterned half-timbering, and the balustrades as well as the rich wood finishes of the interior required

6.18 Robert Strahorn
house, Browne's
Addition, Spokane,
1900. Demolished.
The Tudoresque
half-timbered walls
and gables encase the
earlier J. J. Browne
house in the Second
Empire Style. Eastern
Washington State
Historical Society,
L87–189.

a highly skilled team of craftsmen. The house was decorated by an artist from France; ceilings were hand painted and a mosaic floor from an old palace in Italy was installed. Its "rare Aubusson rugs, gilded furniture, beautiful upholstery, fabrics of foreign design" and "ornate objets d'art" demonstrated that Spokane did not lack sophistication.[21]

The importance of the eight grand houses that Cutter created between 1897 and 1900 is that they represent both the transformation of Spokane from brash frontior town to sophisticated metropolis, and Cutter's progress from novice to mature professional. The mining boom gave him an extraordinary opportunity to develop his art, and these works demonstrate that he was equal to the task. While in many western towns the millionaires' mansions are, above all, ostentatious, Cutter's homes show sensitivity to the needs of those who lived in them and to the landscape in which they stood. In them he set the pattern for the city which the exacting critic Elbert Hubbard was to recognize as "the model city of America" (see Introduction).

No other Washington city could equal Spokane's building boom in the last three years of the nineteenth century. The mansions built there by Cutter and Malmgren outshone the finest residences in other Washington cities and they began to attract clients from further afield. The commission they received from the Seattle lumber merchant C. D. Stimson provides convincing evidence of the strength of their reputation. Stimson was an educated man who had worked with architects before and knew what he wanted. Having reaped rich profits as a supplier of lumber to the mining towns on the Klondike, he was in a position by 1899 to build a $30,000 house, and to spend a further $16,000 on furnishings.[22] He was willing to put up with the inconvenience of the distance of three hundred miles between Seattle and Spokane to work with the architects he preferred. Stimson may have toured the newly completed houses in Spokane before making any decision. The design he approved (fig. 6.19) was in the Tudor style and based closely on the Campbell house. Although Cutter and Malmgren had created variety in their Tudor projects, they were willing, in this case, to repeat important

6.19 C. D. Stimson house, Capitol Hill, Seattle, 1898–1900. The large porch and porte cochère, which was added later, give this house a horizontal emphasis that distinguishes it from the similar Campbell house. Dorothy Stimson Bullitt Collection.

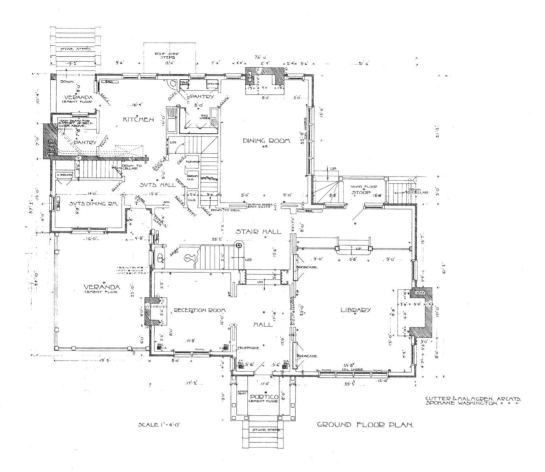

The following labels appear within the floor plan:

STONE STEPS · ROOF OVER STEPS · DOWN · VERANDA CEMENT FLOOR · KITCHEN · PANTRY · PANTRY · DINING ROOM · DOWN TO CELLAR · SVTS. HALL · SVTS DINING RM. · WOOD FLOOR STOOP · DOWN TO CELLAR · DOWN TO DEN. · STAIR HALL · UP · BOOKCASE · VERANDA CEMENT FLOOR · RECEPTION ROOM · HALL · LIBRARY · TELEPHONE · BOOKCASE · PORTICO CEMENT FLOOR · STONE STEPS

CUTTER & MALMGREN, ARCHTS.
SPOKANE WASHINGTON.

SCALE 1"=4'-0"   GROUND FLOOR PLAN.

6.20 First-floor plan of the C. D. Stimson house. Based on a reversal of the Campbell house plan. The veranda has changed position to suit the site. The house is accessible for tours and events. Eastern Washington State Historical Society, L84–207.98.

elements of a successful work. Within the city of Spokane, they had never replicated designs, but they made the Conrad house in Kalispell very similar to the Glover house in Spokane. In both cases, distance seems to have been a factor in making repetition acceptable.

However, true to his principles, Cutter responded to the topography of Seattle's First Hill in a manner that gave individuality to the Stimson house. The first floors of the Stimson and Campbell houses are almost identical, but to take advantage of the hillside site, he reversed the plan (figs. 6.2, 6.20) and allowed the floor to remain high above the sloping ground. Since the front door is approached by a flight of steps, the house is seen from a lower viewpoint and the proportions appear different. A unique feature of the Stimson house is the raised veranda, as large as a room, which projects out parallel to the street on the downhill side. Like F. Lewis Clark's veranda on the South Hill in Spokane, it makes a high vantage point, and similarly it is surrounded by pointed arches. In the urban context of Seattle, not far from the street, the privacy achieved by elevating it above ground is valuable.

The entrance hall, with steps leading up to the inner hall under a Romanesque arch, is almost identical to the Campbell prototype. The reception room recalls the refinement and elegance of the other house, and the library (fig. 6.21) has a heavy beamed ceiling, an impressive fireplace, and a raised gallery at the end farthest from the street. However, Cutter took special care to make the rooms distinctive. He commissioned artists and craftsmen to create works of decorative art, and he traveled in the East to find appropriate furnishings and finishes.[23]

Like many designers of the Arts and Crafts movement in England, he developed a medieval theme in the ornamentation of the house. However, he executed the interiors in an ostentatious and eclectic manner that sometimes strayed from the ethical principles of William Morris. The oak front door is hung on wrought iron hinges whose curvaceous forms celebrate the ancient art of the blacksmith.

6.21 Library of the C. D. Stimson house. The dark oak table was designed to complement the architecture. Dorothy Stimson Bullitt Collection.

In the entrance hall, the capitals of the clustered colonnettes that support the arch are intricately carved. The gold and vermilion background of the walls combines with the carved and polished oak to create a rich effect. Rampant lions in gold on red are emblazoned on the walls among the twisting tendrils of vines, whose arabesques recall the decorations on illuminated manuscripts. The ceiling, in the same colors, is painted with quatrefoils on the flat central part and *fleurs-de-lys* in a complex curvilinear design on the sloping side panels.

Cutter described the glass-fronted bookshelves in the library as "pure, rich, Gothic designs . . . strictly in keeping with the architecture."[24] He had the walls covered in green and yellow tapestry, and designed as the centerpiece of the library a bold and elaborate fireplace, flanked by carved oak lions supporting a massive oak canopy (fig. 6.22). While in other residences Cutter had installed fireplaces that suggested the manor house, this one evokes the cas-

6.22 Library fireplace in the C. D. Stimson house, flanked by carved wood lions. Dorothy Stimson Bullitt Collection.

6.23 Reception room in the C. D. Stimson house, designed in the
Empire style, with yellow silk panels and ornamental plasterwork.
Dorothy Stimson Bullitt Collection.

tle. The royal symbol of the lion and the castellated canopy, decorated with a frieze of quatrefoils, make the hearth positively regal.
In the opening, two elegant but ferocious iron dragons, with twisting tails, served as andirons. Cutter, insisting that there are "no
woodcarvers on the [West] coast who can do justice to this class of
work," persuaded Stimson to pay an East Coast artist $275 to carve
"the two large Gothic lions."[25] The library table was clearly designed
to suit the room. Its legs consisted of clusters of four columns that
almost exactly matched those that flank the steps to the gallery at
the end of the room. The Stimson children discovered a good use
for the gallery by making it into a stage for theatrical performances.

The reception room, though in many respects similar to the one
in the Campbell house, follows the Empire Style of Napoleonic
Paris (fig. 6.23). Panels of yellow fabric, of a shade popular in the
Empire period give the walls a rich glow. Above them, in a frieze

of pale ivory, female figures, draped in a Grecian manner, alternate with swans, the personal insignia of the Empress Josephine, to carry garlands of tiny flowers. Wreaths, palmettes, ribbons, and strings of pearls complete the decoration. The mahogany furniture, conforming to the classical taste of the age of Napoleon, includes an Etruscan chair and the Greek klysmos chair. The gilt bronze inlay of ormolu adds an extra richness. The onyx fireplace, flanked with classical columns, supports a mahogany mantelpiece inlaid with ormolu griffins and a chariot pulled by prancing horses. Cutter personally selected the artisan who executed the "plastic work" on the reception room frieze. He described him as "the best man we have and . . . a fast worker, who would probably be able to finish the room in seven or eight days."[26]

Cutter and Malmgren did not supervise the building of the Stimson house themselves; they made a supervision contract with the Seattle architect Charles Bebb, who had previously worked in Chicago for Adler and Sullivan. The British-born architect, who had been educated in London and Switzerland, was probably congenial to Cutter.[27] However Cutter insisted on maintaining control of the furnishing and even the choice of paintings.[28] Furthermore, determined to avoid "the havoc [made] by that dangerous triumvirate—the housewife, the decorator and the furniture dealer,"[29] he tried to limit the authority of his clients in these important matters. Letters that Cutter wrote to Stimson, many of them in his own flowing hand, give important insights into his views on interior design. When he worked on the Glover house a decade before, he appears to have left it to William Otis of Cleveland to send a freight car load of furniture. In 1900, he was still relying on Otis as his principal supplier, but he played a leading role in the selection and probably designed some of the pieces himself: "After several weeks spent in looking up the best and most artistic things to be found in this country, I have carefully prepared estimates for the decorations, furnishings and fixtures for your residence. A box is being expressed today which contains sketches, photographs and fabrics, showing designs, materials and colorings as in my judgment they should be used to produce the most satisfactory results."[30]

He tried to explain his decisions to the Stimsons. For example, when he sent a sample of the deep blue-green Italian tiles he had chosen for the dining room fireplace, he wrote: "The choice was made from a large number of the best examples of domestic and foreign makes as being in harmony with the decorations of the room." He did his best to deter them from challenging his professional expertise. Concerning the Gothic design for the library bookcases, he commented: "I would strongly recommend the carrying out of work in accordance with the plans submitted, as it, being correct in detail, would always be good no matter how often styles might change." He also tried tactfully to dissuade the Stimsons from selecting furnishings themselves: "While the description of the rug you have recently purchased was good, it is impossible to judge, without seeing it, whether the colors would be in harmony with the colorings of the room." And he reinforced the case for his choice of carpets by arguing the long-term benefits of quality: "I started out on the hunt for rugs and succeeded in finding three beautiful specimens which are in coloring and sizes exactly the things for the rooms. There is nothing better made and they will wear longer than a lifetime."[31]

In some instances, he made Stimson aware of less expensive alternatives, and included suggestions for savings. He believed that furnishings should be "rich and elegant, but never pretentious,"[32] and he urged the Stimsons to avoid excessive ornamentation. Offering them two alternatives for the library wall covering, he suggested that one that was "more subdued in tone would make a finer background for pictures." Showing them a range of designs for bedsteads, he described one as "much showier and very rich in carving, which would probably appeal to most people," but expressed his preference for a less expensive design, on account of its simplicity and graceful lines. However, Cutter sometimes found it hard to resist temptation: "I have just succeeded in getting a very fine and rare suit of Italian armor which is very beautifully etched. It would be very effective and most appropriate in your library. The price is $170. If you should happen to care for it, please let me know at once, as Mr. Clark is talking of buying it."[33]

Cutter considered that the color of stains for the exterior timber and the interior oak paneling was too "important to the success of the work" to be left to Charles Bebb. He traveled to Seattle to supervise their application himself.[34] Inevitably, a few problems arose that delayed the completion of the interiors,[35] but the correspondence suggests that the contract was well planned. Evidently the Stimsons, having followed most of their architect's advice, were pleased with the results. Before the end of 1900, they moved into a house in which Cutter had overseen the design from the structure itself to the smallest detail of the interior design.[36]

In the summer of 1900 while Cutter was working on the furnishing of the C. D. Stimson house, he began on a commission for a large Mission Revival house in Colorado Springs.[37] His client, Philip B. Stewart, was the type of patron who was attracted by Cutter's cultured background and his understanding of the domestic needs of the wealthy. The son of a governor of Vermont, he had received his education at Yale University, and had then profited from mining ventures in Colorado. But he also showed an intense interest in education.[38] Cutter's design was similar in character to the Wakefield house he had built in the same style three years earlier. Its principal, east-facing facade was symmetrically planned around a central Mission gable, but this feature was recessed between two wings of an H-shaped plan. Its upper story opened through three arches to an enclosed balcony. A large veranda, broadening to make an outdoor room in the middle of the south side, greatly expanded the scale of an already large house.

In the interior, Cutter proposed an opulent character evoking the architecture of Islamic Spain (fig. 6.24). The large entrance hall followed the pattern he had established in recent mansions. He carefully framed a view of the staircase and brought in light through large windows above it. But in this design he placed the fireplace, complete with built-in seats, under the stair. Contrasting with the heavy stone fireplace, the balustrade of the stair, consisting of a filigree of carved wood in an Islamic pattern, gave a foretaste of the oriental character of the space above. Five ogee arches on columns with spiral fluting opened the upper hall to the stairwell, and two similar arches gave access to passages leading to bedrooms on either side. The stair was lit by six tall, narrow arched windows, ornamented with leaded glass in a flowing pattern of curvilinear plantlike forms fanning out from a central stem. The effect was almost as exotic as that of Patrick Clark's house.

Cutter traveled to Colorado Springs in August 1900, confident that the house would be built.[39] The opportunity to work for Philip Stewart offered further prospects. Since Stewart was a trustee of Colorado College, the residential commission could have led to important work for the college. Furthermore, Stewart had friends in high places, including Theodore Roosevelt, then the vice president, whom he entertained for a few days after a bear hunting trip in the West while Cutter was working on the drawings. However, the architect's hopes were dashed in 1902 when Stewart decided to buy an existing house instead of building.[40]

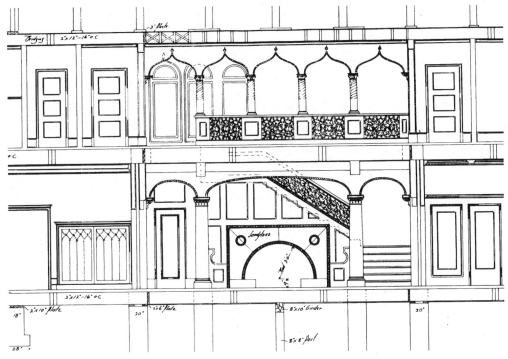

6.24 Philip Stewart project, Colorado Springs. Section through the hall. Eastern Washington State Historical Society, L84–207.117.

A commission in the same year from Louis F. Anderson, professor of Greek at Whitman College in Walla Walla, offered Cutter less scope for his ambitions. In the previous seven years he had designed several large houses for clients who had virtually given him carte blanche to design as he thought fit. Charles Conrad, Patrick Clark, and C. D. Stimson, among others, had placed their trust in their architect and provided ample funds. However, a lengthy correspondence with Anderson shows the other side of the coin. Anderson's letters reveal a client who scrutinized every detail, questioned the architect's judgment, and quibbled over fees.[41]

In Cutter's first letter to Anderson, he gave his credentials as an architect working for important people in many parts of the country. Anderson seemed impressed with "the many fine edifices" and mentioned that he had "seen with pleasure the beautiful church now under construction" (Saint Paul's Church in Walla Walla). However his view of Cutter's 5 percent design fee was far less warm. Cutter rejected his suggestion that they should base fees on a $10,000 house, with no extra charges if the actual cost should increase. They came to an agreement on the design contract, but Anderson opted not to pay an additional 1.5 percent for supervision and chose to use the services of a local architect, Mr. Osterman.[42]

To show the Andersons the range of possibilities, Cutter sent two albums with photographs of buildings designed by the firm. He proposed, at first, to make sketches in "both Colonial and Mission Styles," but it appears that the matter was soon settled in favor of Colonial. The first design submitted seems to have been too ambitious and had to be scaled down. Cutter also suggested replacing the columned portico with pilasters, and warned that "the finish will have to be plain and of native woods in order to come anywhere near the limit of $15,000." Throughout the correspondence it is apparent that Anderson, while wanting to control the cost, was not willing to sacrifice quality or splendor. In any case, the Ionic portico survived and, in addition, pilasters articulated the corners of the house (figs. 6.25, 6.26). During the fall and early winter, the design progressed well; from time to time Cutter reassured Anderson that he was earning his fee. He spoke of "a very good draughtsman constantly at work" and told his client: "You, of course, understand that a house of this class requires a great deal of careful study even after everything has been decided on, which accounts for the time consumed in preparing the work."[43]

Anderson queried some aspects of the design, such as the subdivision of the windows. Cutter pointed out that he was following Colonial precedent, but in late December, Anderson expressed "doubt as to the success of the house." Cutter countered as best he could by stating, "In my opinion both in arrangement and design, it is the best thing I have ever planned in the Colonial Style."[44] The strategy appears to have worked, and the design was accepted by the end of the year.[45] However, Anderson continued to wrangle with him for another year, during which he paid fees only after long delays. Before sending a check on February 10, he asked: "Is it definitely understood that with the payment of the $500 now you will be ready the same as before to make any change we desire in the plans. . . ?" He also inquired under what terms they could terminate their relationship if they decided not to build.[46] On February 27, 1903, Anderson announced: "Every day we have been considering and our decision is now reached. We cannot build at present."[47] Having insisted on the very best, and cutting only the architect's fees, the Andersons now realized that, with the hardwood finishes they wanted, the cost would be well over $15,000.

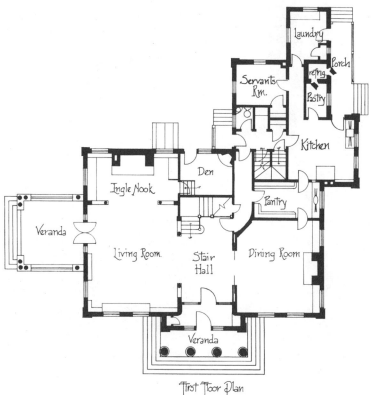

Laundry

Porch

refrig

Servants Rm.

Pastry

Kitchen

Ingle Nook

Den

Pantry

Veranda

Living Room

Stair Hall

Dining Room

Veranda

First Floor Plan

6.25 Louis Anderson house, Walla Walla, 1902–3. The formal, Neoclassical exterior gives little hint of the remarkably open plan within. Now the Baker Faculty Center of Whitman College. Whitman College Archives.

6.26 First-floor plan of the Louis Anderson house. The living room, hall, dining room, and staircase can be seen as a single space. Drawn by Terry Mourning.

Evidently, the Andersons reconsidered; for the next surviving letters in March, April, and May speak of such details as paint colors and the ordering of the "large and small columns for the exterior" from a firm in the East. In late April the architect received a further $250.[48] However, Anderson continued to issue complaints. Misunderstanding Cutter's aesthetic aims, he objected vehemently to imperfections in the tile samples and insisted: "none but perfect ones may be used." In reply, Cutter tried to explain: "Regarding the Grueby Tiles it would be quite impossible to procure them with sharp edges and free of bubbles and other imperfections, as the crude appearance produced is the result of much study and endless experimentation . . . when in a mass the effect is of the charming old hand-made tiles of by-gone days, rather than the perfect machine made tiles of commerce of the present time."[49]

When writing to this client, Cutter was very explicit about important details, as if he feared that the specifications alone would not be sufficient guidance for the contractor: "The brick veneer should be hand made and carefully selected as regards to color. The hand

6.27 Detail of the entablature of the Louis Anderson house, as built under the supervising architect. Photo by the author.

burnt darker shades being preferable for stretchers and the headers varying in shade from half red and half gray, not very black, and do not use any glazed surface. These headers should be placed hit and miss so as not to give a checkerboard effect."[50]

This letter suggests that Anderson, who had moved his old house across the road from the site, was now acting ex-officio as clerk of works and could be prevailed on to educate the builder. Cutter continued to care for matters affecting the appearance of the house, taking endless trouble with questions concerning tiling, paint quality and color, and details of convenience in the servants' quarters. He received additional fees in September and he must have been relieved to hear construction was progressing well. But in the next few months Anderson complained about a "gross blunder" in the design of the staircase and problems with a smoking chimney, both matters that Cutter felt should have been forestalled by the supervising architect. Cutter graciously undertook to pay for putting things right, but could not resist an attack on Osterman's credibility: "If I am not deceived by the photograph of the exterior of your house, a blunder has been made which proves either ignorance or neglect on the part of the architect in charge. A man who has ever studied architecture at all knows that in this classical style the corner pilasters should line with the architrave while in this case they apparently stand forward about 4 inches. This is bound to produce a very unpleasant effect."[51]

Indeed, to this day, the pilasters at the corners of the house stand too far forward of the entablature they carry (fig. 6.27). Although he did not build them according to the drawings, the contractor was never forced to correct his error. The learned professor of Greek and Latin, who was presumably a strict grammarian in his own field, was prepared to overlook a liberty with the classical language of architecture, while grumbling about fees. In late February after the Andersons had moved into the house, the professor conceded: "We enjoy it very much despite all the vexations and delays."[52] The house, whose design and construction had aroused so much acrimony, proved a great success. It was larger than the college president's residence, and designed ideally for receptions. During Anderson's long tenure as vice president and member of the board of trustees, his home became a center for the social and intellectual life at Whitman College. The Andersons were impressive hosts at receptions for distinguished visitors, literary discussions, and other formal occasions. It stands today as the Baker Faculty Center.[53]

The Louis Anderson house succeeded as a social milieu partly because it was revolutionary in terms of interior space. While outwardly conservative, the house has a remarkably open plan in which living room and hall are virtually one (figs. 6.26, 6.28). When sliding doors to the dining room stand open, the entire ground floor, except for the servant's quarters and a small den, is virtually a single space. Pairs of Ionic columns imply a division between hall and living room and define a cozy area around the fire. Light enters the living room from three sides and flows in from both ends of the house. Broad French windows open onto a spacious porch with steps into the garden. Even the staircase, with a built-in seat on the well-lit landing, becomes a sociable space (fig. 6.29). As he did for the Glover house, designed fifteen years earlier, Cutter had used a traditional vocabulary in the development of progressive ideas.

6.28 Interior of the Louis Anderson house. View from the living room across the hall to the dining room. Whitman College Archives.

In 1903, Cutter built another house in Browne's Addition for one of Spokane's influential leaders. In sharp contrast to the pretentious mansions described earlier in this chapter, the home of the newspaper proprietor W. H. Cowles, at the western tip of the elite neighborhood, was surprisingly modest in character. Cowles arrived in Spokane in 1891 to manage the *Spokesman.* He possessed a Yale degree and an inheritance from his father, who, as business manager of the *Chicago Tribune,* had grounded him in the newspaper business. Cowles gradually bought out his partners, and in addition purchased the rival *Review,* combining the two papers under his ownership in 1894. He chose a different way to influence the development of Spokane than the mining, railroad, and real estate magnates, whose elaborate homes Cutter had built: he wielded the power of the press.[54] Cutter built him a large, shingled Craftsman-style house (fig. 6.30), whose plain, steeply pitched roof swept down from a high ridge to the level of the first floor-ceiling. This design revives the spirit of the simpler houses Cutter built in 1895, and predates the Craftsman movement that was to sweep the West in the years that followed. The Cowles house gives further evidence of the individualism of Cutter's clients and his ability to provide them with distinctive homes.

6.29 Half landing of the staircase in the Louis Anderson house, complete with a comfortable built-in seat. Photo by the author.

6.30 W. H. Cowles house, Browne's Addition, Spokane, 1903. A modest bungalow compared with the ostentatious houses of the neighborhood. *Western Architect,* September 1908.

Despite the astonishing range of styles in which Cutter and Malmgren built, their houses possess certain common elements that transcend style. Most were built on a firm platform that allowed the first-floor rooms to open out onto spacious terraces. For example, Patrick Clark's house, for all its exotic character, was planned similarly to the Finch and Austin Corbin houses: a terrace stretched from the entrance, around the corners, to join with the porches at the sides. Sometimes porches thrust out, to become spacious outdoor rooms, and to extend the houses horizontally. In the case of the F. Lewis Clark house, the porch became a dramatic feature, overhanging a steep slope. Typically, the entries of these houses led into finely ornamented halls with framed vistas of stair halls beyond. Staircases, lit by large windows, were sumptuously built with elaborate balustrades; and Cutter usually gave them spacious half landings with built-in seats, or even, as in the case of Patrick Clark's house, a fireplace and loose furniture.

Cutter tended to design rooms in several styles within a single residence. Just as he conceived houses to suit individual clients, he finished the rooms within them to set the mood for different occasions or satisfy the desires of particular family members. He used dark paneling for the library, the male domain, light colors and gilt for the reception rooms where the ladies had their social events, and more exotic finishes in the smoking rooms. Indeed, he sometimes took a similar approach in houses he designed forty years later in California. Another hallmark of the Cutter house at the turn of the century was the creation of small, cozy spaces within rooms. He made seating areas in towers, and recesses with built-in seats in entrance halls, to give a sense of intimacy in the palatial interiors. Above all, he liked to provide inglenooks, "where one may sit in cold nights by the crackling fire and toast his feet to his heart's content."[55]

Cutter followed the architectural trends of his day, but continued to excel in the creation of homes to suit the lives of his clients in the Gilded Age. As his Tudoresque house for F. Lewis Clark suggests, he was most successful when he designed in romantic styles and on challenging sites. His excursion into an exotic world of fantasy for Patrick Clark shows both originality and a successful fusion of disparate elements. While in most cases his plans were fairly conventional, the innovative open plan for the Louis Anderson house was advanced for its time.

7.1 Saint Andrew's Episcopal Church, Chelan, 1897–98. Built of logs to express the pioneer experience. Lake Chelan Historical Society.

CHAPTER SEVEN

Function and Fantasy (1898–1906)

KIRTLAND CUTTER ESTABLISHED HIS REPUTATION AS
an architect mainly by designing homes for the wealthy. During the
first decade of his practice, he exploited a broad repetoire of styles
to enrich the fashionable neighborhoods of Spokane visually. He
offered his patrons choices ranging from quiet elegance to pretentious grandeur. In his commercial and institutional projects in the
first decade of the twentieth century he followed a similar pattern,
designing buildings in a wide variety of expressions. Some clients
wanted simple, practical structures and were not willing to pay for
artistic effects. For those prepared to indulge in fantasy he designed
unique and memorable places.

One example of Cutter's imaginative approach is Saint Andrew's
Episcopal Church at Chelan, Washington (1898).[1] Most Northwest
churches of the late nineteenth century were faced with finished
lumber and displayed at least token features of medieval or classic
ornament. But in Chelan Cutter celebrated the rude character of
pioneer construction by building a church like a log cabin (fig. 7.1).
Since the small town of Chelan possessed a sawmill, it is clear that
Cutter was not responding to primitive conditions but evoking the
romance of the frontier. The church is a simple structure with a
steeply pitched roof whose gable end faces the main street of the
town. Beside it, built in the same fashion, stands the tower with an
open belfry. The architect gave the design strength by emphasizing
the overlapping of the logs at the corners. At the base of the walls
their ends project out, giving the sculptural effect of buttresses on a
medieval church. On the tower, the logs corbel out at the corners to

support the overhanging floor of the belfry, and to carry the hipped roof. Corbeled logs also form archlike openings in the belfry. The sanctuary follows the promise of the exterior by revealing its bare structure. Buttresses stand out from the walls to carry the scissor trusses of the roof. Light entering through high dormers highlights the structure and reflects off the wooden surfaces. Logs for the church were cut from timber growing along the shores of the lake and towed by steamer to a sawmill. There they were milled on two sides before being assembled on the site.[2] The carpenters fitted the joints so accurately that no caulking is visible on the outside. On the interior, they caulked the joints neatly with jute.

Cutter also used his imagination at the turn of the century to create unique buildings in downtown Spokane and Seattle. His most successful commercial buildings of a decade earlier had possessed a massive quality. His Exchange National Bank building (originally First National Bank), with its clearly organized system of piers and arches and its heavily rusticated stone, belonged firmly to the Richardsonian tradition. But in the late 1890s he experimented in several revival styles, adding to the diversity of downtown streets, as he had done in residential districts. In interiors, he borrowed from Tudor traditions to suggest an old-world charm, and from the Italian Renaissance to achieve an urbane elegance. At Davenport's Restaurant in Spokane he created an atmosphere of fantasy in a Venetian Gothic ballroom and an up-to-date stylishness in an Art Nouveau bar.

Louis Davenport was the ideal client for Cutter. Their long collaboration, culminating in the building of the legendary Davenport Hotel, is a fascinating chapter in Spokane's history. To Davenport it was not enough to serve customers excellent meals; with Cutter's help he aimed to transport them into imaginary worlds far from the mundane streets outside. Davenport's own story belongs in the "American dream" tradition. He is said to have arrived in Spokane in March 1889 with only $1.25 in his pocket. After the disastrous fire in August that destroyed most of the downtown area, he joined the clean-up crews and worked hard. He saved his earnings and invested $125 in a tent, a waffle iron, and a large sign announcing "Davenport's Famous Waffle Foundry." On December 8 he opened his first restaurant under canvas on the corner of Post Street and Sprague, and plied a lucrative trade in waffles. From this vantage point, he observed the construction of the Wilson block with three arched openings across the intersection, and considered what he could achieve there. In July 1890, he secured a lease and moved from his makeshift quarters into a comfortable dining room in the new building.[3] In his new premises, he worked hard to expand his menu and offer better services. He operated at a minimum profit to attract patrons and to satisfy their desires. Soon his restaurant became one of the principal eating places of Spokane, and its reputation spread far afield. As his need for space increased, he took over the adjacent spaces and commissioned Cutter to transform them from run-of-the-mill downtown buildings into spectacular architecture.

When Davenport first opened in the Wilson block in the summer of 1890, he had occupied a relatively small room in the center of the block. The next year he added a second room to the west, and in 1893 he expanded into a third on the east side.[4] He now had adequate space, though it lacked the architectural quality appropriate to a fine restaurant. That year the building was damaged by fire, and Davenport used insurance money to rebuild more lavishly. He could now offer seventeen private rooms and a banquet room in addition to the main dining room. By 1895 "the yearly outlay on improvement and repairs" was described as "enough to keep half a dozen restaurants looking new." In 1900, in time for the Spokane Exposition, he enlarged the restaurant again and gave it the form it retained until the 1950s (fig. 7.2).[5]

7.2 The Italian Gardens, Davenport's Restaurant, Spokane, interior. Elegantly remodeled in 1900. Destroyed. Eastern Washington State Historical Society.

7.3 Davenport's Restaurant, Spokane, corner of Post Street and Sprague, ca. 1900. Cutter encased the original modest structure in a playful Mission Revival manner. The Pennington Hotel on Post Street (on the far left) was added in about 1904. Eastern Washington State Historical Society.

Cutter created a dining room that was light, elegant, and spacious. He unified the main interior space with a classical structure of slender Corinthian columns, supporting a grid of beams faced with ornamental plaster work. From each Corinthian capital four consoles spread out linking the columns and beams, and giving energy and lightness to the structural system. The next requirement was an attractive exterior. In about 1900, he clothed the outer walls in white stucco to a design loosely based on the Californian Mission Revival (fig. 7.3).[6] Cutter had first experimented with the Mission Revival Style in the Wakefield house in 1897. But compared with the relatively sober design of the house in Browne's Addition, the mood at Davenport's is exuberant, as if to convey the idea that lunching here is a joyful experience.

The architect added two more broad arches to the three that fronted the Wilson block on Sprague Avenue. The arcade formed in this way has something in common with the arcade of a typical mission, but the jaunty little gables, one rising above each pier to break the roofline, and the short lengths of Spanish tiled roof, jutting out over the walls, elaborate playfully on the Mission vocabulary. The corner tower, based on a church bell tower, but much reduced in scale, is a purely decorative embellishment. The effect on a street of red brick and granite was startling: Cutter's frivolous evocation of the Mission Style stood out flamboyantly from its neighbors.

The wide openings between the piers on the longer Sprague Street facade brought copious daylight to the interior of the dining room. On the Post Street side, and on the corner, Cutter added variety by inserting bay windows of leaded glass. On the upper story, the broad arches springing from floor level gave the rooms a distinctive character. It was, perhaps, the lightness of the interior achieved by the generous provision of daylight and the delicacy of the Corinthian columns that made the restaurant's name, the Italian Gardens, appropriate. Davenport completed the theme by providing a constant supply of flowers.

In November 1903, Davenport acquired both the Wilson block and the Bellevue block to the south, which already contained his kitchens.[7] He had already spent thousands of dollars on improvements with no help from the owners; now he could plan further architectural triumphs entirely for his own benefit. The two upper stories of the Bellevue block had been used by Mrs. Maud Pennington as a boarding house, but Davenport transformed them into the Pennington Hotel.[8] Refacing this addition to match the restaurant presented Cutter with a problem of continuity. The Pennington was three stories high and the floor levels did not match the two stories of Davenport's. But Cutter solved it with a flourish. He accentuated the irregularity by placing a high curvilinear gable at the junction between the two structures, and balancing it with two smaller gables on the third floor. At the corner of Post Street and First Avenue, he built a taller tower skewed 45 degrees and surmounted by a cupola. On the First Avenue facade he picked up the existing window patterns of the upper rooms and elaborated on them. Under three Mission gables, one of which swerves upward to meet the corner tower, pairs of mullion windows alternate with bay windows projecting from pilasters set against the wall. Each has an independent conical roof.

It is typical of Davenport's imaginative approach to his business that he proposed, at the time of acquiring the property, to build a greenhouse on the roof of the restaurant to "raise all the flowers and hot house plants which have been such a feature of the restaurant."[9] This idea developed further into a rooftop cafe with palm trees and other exotic foliage, offering another memorable space for Davenport's guests.

The next major improvement was the construction in 1904 of a ballroom above the restaurant.[10] Known as the Hall of the Doges (fig. 7.4), this ostentatious room offered a new realm of fantasy to Spokane's party-goers. Cutter drew inspiration from the galleries around the Ducal Palace in Venice, and surrounded the dance floor on all four sides with arcaded aisles and galleries above. Thus the walls resemble the nave walls of Gothic cathedrals, but without the

7.4 The Hall of the Doges, above Davenport's Restaurant, Spokane, 1904. Intended to evoke the Doges' palace in Venice. *Western Architect*, September 1908.

7.5 The Peacock Room, Davenport's (date unknown), decorated with peacock motifs in an Art Nouveau manner. *Western Architect*, September 1908.

usual clerestory windows.[11] Since not enough height was available for tall, pointed arches, the openings on both levels are shallow, three-centered arches. However, at the gallery level, each opening is subdivided into five distinctly Venetian arches with interlacing tracery, which also forms quatrefoils above. Cutter designed the ballroom for participation. People at the tables in the low-ceilinged aisles could sit like observers at a theater, watching the drama of the dancers framed by arches. Those in the galleries could look down through the intricate tracery, as if from private boxes at the opera.

Nearby, on the upper floor, Davenport and Cutter continued the medieval theme in the Gothic Room, a small banquet room whose ceiling simulates a late Gothic vault. At about the same time, Cutter remodeled several other spaces. Each was distinctive, but they had in common the use of the avant-garde Art Nouveau style. Just off the main restaurant, he created the Peacock Room (fig. 7.5) for private parties or individual dining. Its vaulted ceiling with a bold and highly stylized peacock feather motif was articulated at intervals by ribs supported on decorative brackets. The entire design implied motion, as of a breeze blowing through feathers and separating the individual strands. The heart-shaped eye of each feather pointed end upward toward the crown of the vault; smaller hearts also decorated the ribs. On the end walls in the tympanum of the

7.6 The Men's Bar at Davenport's, ca. 1904, named the "Orange Bower" because of the miniature carved orange trees behind the bar. A rare example of Art Nouveau in the Northwest. Destroyed. Eastern Washington State Historical Society.

vault, mural paintings took up the peacock theme again. This motif seems to have fascinated Cutter, who had already made it the centerpiece of James Glover's hall ceiling, and the stained glass over Patrick Clark's staircase. He even had a stuffed peacock in his office.[12]

Art Nouveau had clearly appealed to Cutter when he first started to work in architecture, for he exploited the style in a fireplace at his own home. But it barely appeared in his commissioned projects. The solid traditions of long-established styles were more to his clients' taste than anything so new. Louis Davenport, however, was not reluctant to experiment, and Cutter embarked on several essays in Art Nouveau. Close to the Peacock Room, he designed a men's bar (fig. 7.6) in which elaborate wainscoting, decorative panels, and murals enveloped the space with rich surfaces. The tour de force was a back bar fixture ornamented by six tapering fluted shafts spreading out at the top like miniature trees bursting with copious fruit. The architect disguised a heavy beam, already spanning the space, by means of a sinuous wooden casing and a pattern of carved foliage. Only the presence of brass cuspidors on the floor contrasted with the sophistication of the decor. Cutter also used Art Nouveau for Davenport's private suite (fig. 7.7) in the northeast corner, and for the ladies' retiring room (fig. 7.8). In both he exploited the broad arched windows for their curves, which he playfully echoed in the leaded glass. In Davenport's suite, a graceful arch spanned the wide opening between two rooms. Its sturdy oak supports were lightened with decorative patterns combining linear and interlacing elliptical designs. The fireplace of hammered copper stood out as the focus of the room. On either side of the hearth, stylized treelike forms, echoing the decorations just described, branched out and rose to support a high mantelpiece. Cutter ornamented the adjacent walls with tall shafts carrying compact foliage at the top, and designed doors, paneling, and other details in a similar manner. Nowhere did the Art Nouveau ornament seem quirky or excessive: Cutter tempered stylishness with a quiet dignity.[13]

7.7 Louis Davenport's private suite above the restaurant, ca. 1904. Paneled in oak, with a beaten copper fireplace, ornamented with Art Nouveau designs. *Western Architect,* September 1908.

7.8 The Ladies Retiring Room, Davenport's, ca. 1904. *Western Architect,* September 1908.

It was not long before travelers from as far away as the East Coast were singing the praises of Davenport's. Cutter's sumptuous design was matched by Louis Davenport's genius for providing hospitality. The menu offered epicurean delights at reasonable prices, and the staff anticipated any need of the traveler, businessman, or party-goer. One visitor who was thoroughly impressed was Elbert Hubbard, a leading figure in the American Arts and Crafts movement, and editor of *The Philistine.* In March 1906, Hubbard commented enthusiastically on his impressions of Spokane as "The Model City of America" and singled out the restaurant for praise:

> Davenport's is snug, clean and complete as an ocean liner ready to sail. It contains no ratholes, chuck holes, or unsightly corners. The retiring rooms are dreams in marble and tile. Between the serving room and the kitchen are immense plate glass windows, so the customers can get

a look at the kitchen, a place resplendent in copper, nickel and glass, dotted with quick moving men in spotless white. . . . I am told Davenport is a gentleman, low voiced, quiet, tireless, systematic, imaginative, with a patience and persistence like that of Pericles.

The art side of Davenport's restaurant is debtor to Kirk Cutler [*sic*], a designer and architect, who has keyed Spokane in an artistic way. . . . Residences, stores, clubs, banks, proclaim Kirk Cutler's quiet good taste, and his safe, unbizarre lines and color schemes.

Davenport has collaborated with Cutler and the result is Davenport's restaurant, the finest thing of its kind in America. . . . When a man does a thing well beyond compare, though it be but the making of mousetraps, the world will make a pathway to his door, says Emerson. All trails lead to Davenport's.[14]

While Cutter and Malmgren were working on Davenport's establishment they were also busy on other hotels and restaurants. The Chicago Hotel, which they built in 1898, offered simple accommodation for less affluent travelers.[15] The Warwick Restaurant at 825 Riverside Avenue was more elegant. Cutter contrived the dining room in the Empire Style, with mahogany millwork and a yellow silk ceiling. In contrast to such refinement, he had the basement fitted out as a German beer hall.[16] He was perhaps evoking memories of friendly inns where he had refreshed himself while studying in Dresden. The diversity of interior design in the two spaces echoed the difference between the French Rococo reception rooms and the dark paneled libraries of the Browne's Addition mansions; they clearly expressed female and male domains.

The Silver Grill at the Hotel Spokane, which opened triumphantly with a charity ball November 14, 1903, further enhanced Cutter's reputation for restaurant design. This time the inspiration came from Old England. One Spokane newspaper, *Winston's Weekly,* described it enthusiastically as "a complete replica of an old manor house inn," and another likened it to "an ancient English chop room." Cutter and the owner, William S. Norman, "ransacked English inns and London Curio Shops to find models": "From the hand wrought rivets to the wooden pins which hold the hewn timbers in place, all the fixtures . . . are in conformity with the crude, but attractive style of construction prevalent in the days before Shakespeare and Ben Johnson with their boon companions made merry at the Mermaid Inn."[17]

In the "unusually quaint" lobby (fig. 7.9), the architects tried to achieve an authentic old world character by the use of adzed timber framing. Heavy posts divided the wall into panels of rich green, while sturdy rafters supported a straw-colored ceiling. The lobby focused on a fireplace of fire-flashed bricks stepping up to a peak like a Dutch gable. Over the hearth a pointed hood of beaten copper imitated the shape of "an old fashioned candle extinguisher." Heavy oak settles provided cozy seating by the fire, and the room was lit by leaded glass windows.

The half-timbered grill room (fig. 7.10) received a warm glow from red brick on the floor and between the timbers on the walls, as well as from the pumpkin-colored ceiling. The room rose to a high skylight under which lay "a pool surrounded by rustic rock-work—fed by an artificial spring" from which water fell "with a mellow cadence." In a huge brick inglenook with "andirons representing reptiles," chefs broiled the meat over hot coals on "revolving cooking jacks" hanging from "a crane of grotesque serpent design." From "hand-hewn benches" visitors could watch the spitted roast dangle and brown before their eyes." The Hungarian Court Orchestra of Budapest played for the opening ball and regularly performed for patrons at dinner. *Winston's* rejoiced that: "Lovers of music will for the first time in Spokane, have a pleasant Bohemian resort where the best of music and the best of good living may be enjoyed, and where the tastes of the artist and the epicure will alike be satisfied."

To one writer, the Silver Grill represented a special achievement for the city: "The product of Spokane designers, Spokane materials and Spokane workmanship." The reporter of *Winston's Weekly* singled out the architect for praise: "Everything connected with the Silver Grill shows the highest art and nothing that Mr. K. K. Cutter had done will add more to his reputation as an architect and artist."

Indeed, Cutter's reputation was growing. In 1902, he planned an entire resort at Playa del Rey in southern California for the ambitious land developer Henry P. Barbour, president of the Beach Land Company.[18] Barbour had been involved in the development of the town of Hoquiam, Washington, in about 1890. Since then, he had been engaged in mining in Minnesota, Colorado, and Arizona. Now, spurred by the growing population of Los Angeles, and the service of the electric railroads, he was turning to the subdivision of beach property.[19]

Cutter's ambitious design for Playa del Rey included a hundred-room hotel, a restaurant, and a dance pavilion beside the lagoon, as well as a bandstand and a railroad station. The drawings show that his aim was to create an unforgettable atmosphere, evoking the ro-

7.9 The Silver Grill, Spokane, 1903, vestibule. Furnished in an Arts and Crafts manner with simple wooden settles, under a ceiling of adzed beams. Eastern Washington State Historical Society, L84–207.4.35.

7.10 The Grill Room at the Silver Grill. To invoke old world charm, meat was roasted over an open fire. *Western Architect,* September 1908.

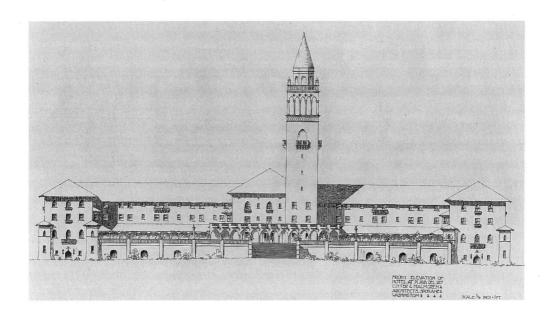

FRONT ELEVATION OF
HOTEL AT PLAYA DEL REY
CUTTER & MALMGREN
ARCHITECTS SPOKANE
WASHINGTON SCALE 1/16 INCH·1FT

7.11 Hotel, Playa del Rey, California. Project 1902–3. Adapting to the southern location, Cutter based his imagery on Italian sources such as the campanile in St. Mark's Square in Venice. Eastern Washington State Historical Society, L84–207.123.

mance of travel to faraway places. They appear to have been inspired by Carrère and Hastings's Ponce de Leon Hotel in St. Augustine, Florida, which had given him ideas for the Patrick Clark mansion in Spokane.[20] The fanciful designs suggest the unique fusion of Italian and Islamic architecture that occurred in Venice. As in the case of the Clark house, Cutter did not attempt to replicate any actual buildings, but employed an eclectic vocabulary alluding to various sources.

The hotel (fig. 7.11) was to be dominated by a slender, pointed tower similar to those at St. Augustine, and also reminiscent of the Campanile of St. Mark's Square in Venice. (It is perhaps no coincidence that 1902 was the year the Venetian Campanile collapsed, creating worldwide concern for the loss of a powerful landmark.) Below the tower the hotel spread out under expansive hipped roofs. Cutter arranged it around two courtyards, one of which, named the Palm Court, had a large fountain at the center. Along the front, a loggia of Gothic arches opened off the principal rooms onto a broad, raised terrace. The restaurant and dancing pavilion, each with a gondola landing, were linked across a canal by a bridge distinctly Venetian in character. Their walls were enriched with Venetian Gothic tracery, and they offered romantic silhouettes enlivened by several towers.

Cutter's proposals at Playa del Rey were not accepted, and he regretfully abandoned his dreams for a romantic California resort.[21]

But his prospects were improved by two prestigious commissions in the East. The first, to design a summer camp in the Adirondacks for a member of the Carnegie family, will be discussed in Chapter 9. The second called for him to design an academic building at Yale University, as a memorial to his great-grandfather Jared Kirtland. The famous naturalist, who had been such a strong influence in Cutter's formative years, had graduated from Yale Medical School in 1815. In 1902 his niece, Mrs. Lucy Boardman, reputedly the wealthiest woman in Connecticut, donated Kirtland Hall to the university in his honor, and chose Kirtland Cutter as the architect.[22] Since she lived only a block away, she probably kept a watchful eye on the construction of Kirtland Hall.[23]

Built at a cost of $110,000, Kirtland Hall is an imposing Neoclassical building with a giant Ionic portico approached by a broad flight of steps. Cutter originally intended to build it of red brick with white stone dressings (fig. 7.12), but it was actually constructed of Long Meadow brownstone, a deep reddish brown sandstone used on several university halls and the nearby Egyptian Revival gate of

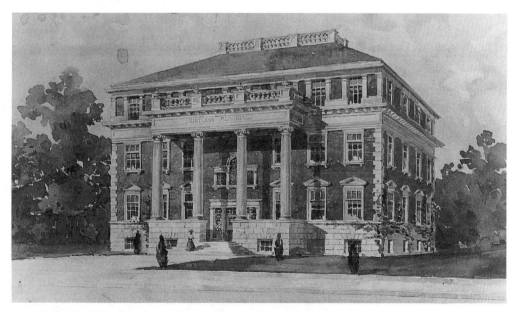

7.12 Kirtland Hall, Yale University, New Haven, Connecticut, 1902–4, built in honor of Cutter's great-grandfather Jared Kirtland. The structure's formal classicism, probably demanded by the patron, seems out of keeping with the famous naturalist's ideals. Watercolor rendering. Eastern Washington State Historical Society.

Grove Street Cemetery.[24] The architect gave the masonry a rough texture and strengthened the base by building it of large, heavily rusticated blocks. Against these rough-hewn wall surfaces, the quoins, cornices, belt courses, and window dressings in artificial stone of a slightly lighter color are smooth and sharply incised. The portico of the same material thrusts forward to provide a generous canopy over the entrance (fig. 7.13). Since the columns stand on a wall over four feet higher than the first floor, the portico lacks the usual openness, but to avoid leaving dead spaces on either side of the entry, Cutter created raised areas at both ends of the portico where students could comfortably gather, sitting on the walls and window sills (fig. 7.14).

Kirtland Hall was occupied by the Department of Geology at Yale from 1904, when it was completed, until 1964. In the entrance hall, a bronze plaque reads: "Kirtland Hall erected by Mrs. William W. Boardman as a memorial of her revered uncle, Jared Potter Kirtland M.D. LLD. an earnest student and investigator in the field of natural history. MDCCCIV. His great-grandson, Kirtland Kelsey Cutter the architect of this building."

The majority of Cutter's buildings had been romantic in conception and irregular in composition; many had a decidedly whimsical quality. The few classically based houses he had done— those for John Finch, the two Corbins, and Professor Anderson— all showed his inclination to rebel against the rules of axial symmetry, spatial ordering, and prescribed proportions. Kirtland Hall stood four square, confident, conformist. It was certainly a far cry from Whippoorwill Farm, Jared Kirtland's own rambling house at East Rockport (fig. 2.5).

While Cutter was at work on Kirtland Hall he appears to have felt confident of his position as a leading Northwest architect. In 1902 he attempted to establish branch offices in both Seattle and Portland. In Portland he formed a partnership with David C. Lewis, an architect trained at Columbia University and in Paris,[25] and early in the same year he sent Edwin Wager, one of his assistants in Spokane, to open a branch office in Seattle.[26] Apparently no significant joint projects materialized in Oregon, and Lewis continued an independent career. However, a commission in Seattle revived Cutter's expectations for a branch office on the Washington coast. On January 10, 1903, the *Seattle Times* announced that the Rainier Club was ready to build a new home designed by Cutter, Malmgren and Wager of Seattle, at a cost of $50,000.

7.13 The Ionic portico of Kirtland Hall, Yale University. Photo by the author.

7.14 Interior of the portico at Kirtland Hall, Yale University. Cutter humanized the grand portico by raising platforms at both ends where students could sit on low surrounding walls. Photo by the author.

The exclusive gentlemen's club, of which C. D. Stimson had been a founding member, had opened in 1888 along the lines of clubs that flourished in England and on the East Coast. The clubhouse, the McNaught mansion on Fourth Avenue, had survived the disasterous fire of 1889 that reduced downtown Seattle to ruins and was used as a center for planning the rebuilding of the city. At the invitation of the club, the leading business and civic leaders of the city met there and agreed on proposals for the reconstruction of Seattle. As reported in the *Seattle Times,* these meetings encouraged some important people who had merely looked on the Rainier Club as "a meeting place for young fellows" to become members.[27] Three years later the membership had grown to the point that a new building was needed. The newspaper announced that the club would be "of the Elizabethan Style and everything will tend toward giving it an appearance of . . . weather beaten age."

While most of Cutter's Tudoresque houses, including the Stimson mansion, were rambling and picturesque, he gave the original scheme for the Rainier Club a solid, dignified appearance by making it a single unified block, with a half-timbered upper story on a rectangular base of fire-flashed clinker brick. The tiled roof with half-timbered gables, and tall chimneys at the two ends, was simple in form, broken only by two tiers of evenly spaced dormer windows. The entry was through a little castellated porch, slightly off center, pierced by three Gothic arches. Between the front of the club and the street Cutter planned "an old fashioned English garden" behind a low brick wall. The Old English theme was to continue in the interior. The Grand Hall, divided into aisles by brick piers, was spanned by "heavy fir joists with adzed surfaces burned and stained to imitate old English oak." Cutter designed the fireplace, eighteen feet wide and eight feet deep, to rival any English inglenook: "Inside the fireplace will be large settles arranged so that persons can sit on three sides of the fire and by looking upward see the sky through the chimney. Some old fashioned fire dogs will also be installed with a crane and a pair of roasting jacks."[28]

Construction of the Rainier Club was well advanced when a fire caused serious damage to the interior. This may have prompted the decision to build the exterior exclusively of masonry. By the time the club opened, the character of the design had changed radically (fig. 7.15). It was as if, in the space of a few months, the Elizabethan era had come to an end and the Jacobean, bringing with it a strong Dutch influence, had begun. The upper walls now burgeoned with

7.15 Rainier Club, 1903–4. Built of red fire-flashed brick with curvilinear Dutch gables. An "English garden" in front created a domestic atmosphere. Photo by E. L. Meyer. Eastern Washington State Historical Society, L84–207.4.48.

curvilinear, stepped gables of red brick with sandstone copings. To avoid the effect of "box-like structures" with "flat, uninteresting and inartistic rooflines,"[29] Cutter had enlivened the club with a rythmic composition of small and large gables.

The new design was said to be "an architectural replica" of Aston Hall, the Warwickshire home of Sir Thomas Holt built between 1618 and 1635 (fig. 7.16).[30] But while the club displayed Dutch gables similar to those at Aston Hall, it differed in materials, layout, and detail. Cutter's brick walls with randomly placed windows do not replicate the stone facades of the Jacobean prototype with their uniformly proportioned, mullioned windows. On the first floor, small, pointed

7.16 Aston Hall, Warwickshire, England, seventeenth century. From
The Baronial Halls and Ancient Picturesque Residences of England (1858),
in Cutter's Library. Eastern Washington State Historical Society. Rare
Books.

Gothic windows alternate with broad bands of leaded casements. As
the walls rise, the windows diminish in size, culminating under the
peaks of the gables with circular openings. The use of clinker brick
laid with an uneven surface would not have been approved in
Jacobean England, but it was to become popular in early twentieth-
century America. The rough, distorted and kiln-blackened bricks,
which would usually have been rejected as unfit for building, were
to become common in California bungalows and other Craftsman
houses.[31] An interesting detail of the design was the system of copper rainwater pipes with ornamental hopper heads to catch water
from the valleys and scrolled brackets on the pipes that twisted to
left or right to avoid windows.

The interior of the club was repaired after the fire with some
alterations. The Grand Hall, originally conceived as "Old English,"
acquired a classical appearance, with Roman Doric columns of
white stucco. To cover their charred surfaces, the adzed ceiling
beams were finished elegantly in plaster. Only the vast inglenook
gave a hint of the original design. The billiard room, which occupied the rest of the first floor at the front, also included a cozy place
around a massive fireplace. The stone hearth, flanked by enclosures

with built-in seats, was separated by screens of heavy timbers from the rest of the room (fig. 7.17). Upstairs were a spacious dining room and a library for the members. The dining room, with exposed, adzed beams, took up the Old English theme again, but in an original manner. A fireplace with a tall hood of wrought iron and beaten copper commanded one end of the room. As in the billiard room, there were built-in seats on either side of the fireplace, screened behind pairs of columns. The lower walls were covered with fir wainscoting (fig. 7.18).

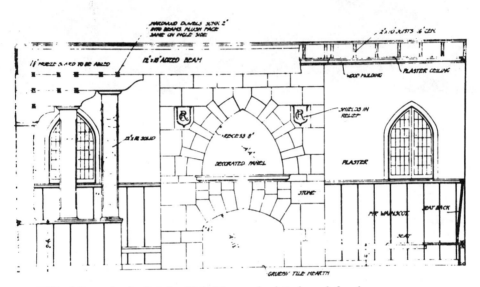

7.17 Billiard Room in the Rainier Club. Heavy adzed timbers defined a huge inglenook lit by Gothic windows. Drawing courtesy of Rainier Club.

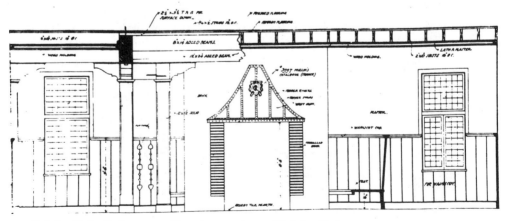

7.18 Rainier Club, dining room. Drawing courtesy of Rainier Club.

FUNCTION AND FANTASY

7.19 The Tacoma
Hotel by McKim,
Mead and White,
1883. The interior
was completely
remodeled by Cutter
in 1905–6 with the
sea as a major theme
of the decor. Photo
Milton Loryea. East-
ern Washington State
Historical Society,
L84–207.4.80.

At the rear of the north side stood a "ladies' annex" to which Cutter and Malmgren made an addition of an extra story in 1907. Here,
in elegant surroundings, the wives of members and female guests
could be entertained in an appropriate manner without invading
the sanctity of the men's clubrooms.[32] In 1927, Cutter provided
plans for expansion that included a tower exactly replicating a
tower at Aston Hall.[33] However, these plans were not executed. The
club was extended by Bebb and Gould the following year in a manner sympathetic to the original design.[34]

In 1905, Cutter received a commission to remodel the principal
hotel in Tacoma at a total cost of $200,000.[35] His clients were
William and Ben Norman, the proprietors of the Spokane hotel
where Cutter had created the popular Silver Grill. The Normans
had already proved their ability to bring the previously bankrupt
Hotel Spokane to profitability.[36] Now they were ready to revive
another hotel. The Tacoma Hotel (fig. 7.19) had been designed by the
important East Coast architects McKim, Mead and White in 1883,
and had enjoyed a short period of success. In the early nineties the
nationwide depression brought the syndicate that built the hotel
into bankruptcy. At the end of the eighties, when Cutter was starting out on his career, he had built several houses influenced by
McKim, Mead and White's innovative work in the Shingle Style (see
Chapter 4). In those days, he was only a fledgling architect emulating the concepts of acclaimed masters. It must have given him satis-

faction only a few years later to remodel a work of theirs that now seemed old-fashioned and in need of a new image. The refurbishment from the roof to the cellar also stimulated local pride and appeared to symbolize good times ahead for the city.

At the Silver Grill in Spokane, Cutter had attempted to recreate the atmosphere of merry old England; in Tacoma he tried to relate the design to its marine environment. The hotel stood on a bluff overlooking Puget Sound; from the porch the guests could watch ships coming and going. The architect chose to take the sea as his theme and to "sing of the sea, the glorious sea." The images he invoked were of mermaids, Vikings, "old sea dogs," and their ships. Each room had its own character; each presented a different marine fantasy. Entering the main lobby (fig. 7.20), the guest was immediately enveloped in sea green: "It is the room of the mermaids. We are under the sea. The ceiling is the ribbed roof of a Spanish Galley

7.20 Main lobby of the Tacoma Hotel, 1905–6. The sturdy wooden columns burgeon into exuberant Art Nouveau capitals of mermaids and sea creatures. Photo by Milton Loryea. Eastern Washington State Historical Society, L84–207.4.81.

decked in gold and green. Superb capitols [*sic*] of the glorious mermaids holding in check the champing seahorses sustain the weight of the great ship's beams."[37] The huge hexagonal columns and beams of Washington fir divided the lobby into three broad aisles. The beams were curved to look like the ribs of a ship, but their curvaceous form also betrayed the influence, once again, of Art Nouveau. The capitals of the columns showed originality, appearing more reminiscent of jewelry designed during the period than of anything architectural.

Throughout the history of architecture, the ornamentation of the capital, however free and organic, has been confined to the space between the astragal and the abacus. Acanthus leaves of classical Greece, the delicate spring foliage of newly opening ferns of Byzantium, and the biblical scenes of Romanesque France, were all confined to their customary space. The mermaids and seahorses submitted to no such limits; their writhing tails overlapped the shafts of the columns with total abandon; thin sinuous forms intertwined around the spreading capitals as if in turbulent motion. Only in Rococo and Art Nouveau was such license possible. Murals in the lobby showed "the old Spanish Galley lying at the bottom of mother ocean with all the flotsam of the ocean around it and the mermaids here and there." The oak newel posts of the main stairway represented "old sea dogs"; the fireplace as "a fisherman's net with the seaweeds clinging to it." The furniture of the room was richly upholstered in Spanish leather.

Another space whose theme was expressed in fanciful capitals was the Room of the Vikings (fig. 7.21):

> . . . we now enter the classic of the house, the home of the Norseman. The handpainted frieze of the Viking ships, a bold massing of color, with its ships of green, its ocean of blue, and the great background of the red sunset is a triumph of the decorator's art. Below the Frieze, the transom line is the gunwale of the Viking ships, and at the door posts old Neptune holds the weight of the portals. The great central posts of which there are two, are the masts of the old Viking ships with the shields of the warriors belted around them, and these in turn sustain the capitols [*sic*] representing the prows of the Viking ship which support and give solidity to the beam structure.

Departing in all but name from the theme of the ocean, one of the bars, following the lead of Spokane's Silver Grill, was designed

like an Old English tavern. The Norman brothers were doubtless eager to repeat their profitable remodeling there with another in the same popular style. The Silver Grill was intended to be pre-Shakespearean. The Tacoma bar, named the Mermaid Inn (fig. 7.22), aimed to evoke the age of the great playwright.

> . . . the quaint old taproom where Beaumont Fletcher, Ben Johnson and Shakespeare, and the great wits of Will's time met and made merry. . . . The walls are the old hewn stones of the cloister, many-colored by the lapse of time. Here and there are the quaint sayings of the master mind done in the rough hew of the stone. "Here's wishing us more friends and less need of them" greets the observer as he enters the portal, and in the main hall, scribbled in the stone, Ben Johnson's couplet greets the visitor: "Here's to a long life and a merry one; a quick death and a happy one; a good girl and a pretty one; a cold bottle and another one." Overhead the great hewn timbers browned by age, hewn by hand and the old-fashioned tap itself with the great barrels where the liquid refreshments are dispersed, all speak eloquently of the harmony of the reproduction.

7.21 Room of the Vikings in the Tacoma Hotel. The capitals of the columns represent Viking ships. Photo Milton Loryea. Eastern Washington State Historical Society, L84.207.4.82.

FUNCTION AND FANTASY

7.22 The Mermaid
Inn in the Tacoma
Hotel. With Roman-
esque stone columns
and adzed timbers,
this is intended to
evoke the old inns of
England. Photo by
Milton Loryea. East-
ern Washington State
Historical Society,
L84–207.4.83.

Throughout the hotel the architect orchestrated the flow of space
from one room to another. From the doorway of the ballroom, there was a
"vista of fully 200 feet in length." An informal dining area provided
a place to "watch the passing throng as it circulates around the
lobby." To the west of the Ben Johnson Dining Hall were several
tastefully decorated private dining rooms, one with a frieze of
champagne glasses by Shandy Kydd on a base of green Hessian
cloth. In the nearby ladies' reception room was a "Viking frieze" by
Walter Crane. Although Cutter's work was mainly restricted to the
interiors, he gave the vast porch special attention:

> . . . a great transformation has been made. The old columns
> which . . . were an incongruous contrast to the classic Queen Anne
> style have disappeared and in their place great hexagonal columns
> sawn from the Western log and left in the rough, heavy corbels of
> rough lumber, sustain the beams of the porch roof. Electric lights
> innumerable, with coloured lanterns, produce a pretty lighting effect,
> and here and there along the beam are hanging baskets loaded with
> ferns and flowers. The balustrade of the porch has been treated in
> the same rough lumber effect and now the whole frontage of the
> house presents a very harmonious picture.

On summer evenings for many years patrons could "idle the evening hours in the glories of the porch." Sitting at the café tables, "listening to the strains of Hugo Schmidt's orchestra," they could "gaze from the ships of the Vikings within the hall to the great ships of commerce on the harbor below."

In addition to the work on the public areas, the staircases, corridors, elevators, and lobbies of the bedroom floors were completely renovated. The contractors laid thousands of yards of new carpets and installed a built-in vacuum system to clean them; every room was given a private bathroom and an outside window, items not considered essential in the eighties. An unusual feature was the option of salt water pumped to the bathtubs.

As the local newspaper pointed out with pride, the work was carried out by Tacoma firms. The Wheeler Osgood Company was responsible for the millwork and the carving of capitals, newels, and other items in the lobby. The Viking ship capitals were also the product of artists working on the spot. Lindstrom and Berg did the "pews of Washington fir which line the approach to the bar." Special light fixtures designed for the bar and the Viking Room were "wrought iron and copper electroliers" made by the Tacoma Ornamental Iron and Wire Works, who also fashioned the hammered ironwork "which adorns the old battered doors and gives the finishing touches to the rooms." Lamps in the bedrooms were of a more delicate design with art glass domes placed over electric lights.

In the Tacoma Hotel, Cutter coordinated the work of many artists and craftsmen. Although his light-hearted decor did not follow the moralistic principles of the Arts and Crafts movement, the creative spirit of the artisans was in tune with William Morris's desires. Such collaboration certainly belonged to the mood of 1906. A year later in Germany, the Deutscher Werkbund was founded to unite "artists, craftsmen, experts and patrons, intent on an improvement of production through the collaboration of art, industry and the crafts,"[38] thus laying the foundation for the Bauhaus School of Design.

In 1906, Cutter found happiness in a second marriage that was to last for twenty-seven years. After Mary Corbin left him in 1895, he had moved from his chalet to share the home of his sister Laura and her husband, Henry Hoyt. With their mother, Caroline Cutter, they made an extended family group in the house at 719 Sixth Avenue which Cutter had enlarged to make room for his own private studio. From 1902 to 1904, he was living in rooms at the Spokane Club

7.23 Kirtland Cutter
with Katharine on
the balcony of their
chalet. Collection
of the author.

7.24 Katharine in the
garden of the chalet.
Collection of the
author.

and the following year at a house at 811 Sprague Avenue.[39] It appears that he moved away from his relatives to gain more privacy at a time of a deepening romance. Meanwhile, he was making extensive alterations and additions to the Chalet Hohenstein.[40]

On February 21, 1906, at the age of forty-five, Kirtland was married to Katharine Phillips Williams at a private ceremony in Spokane.[41] Katharine, who was eight years younger than he, had recently been divorced from Jack Williams of Spokane, with whom she had a daughter, Kathryn.[42] It seems that her attachment to Cutter was the cause of the divorce, and before she married Cutter, Williams dramatized his animosity by kicking the architect off a crowded streetcar, causing him considerable embarrassment, if not physical injury.[43] The wedding took place at the home of Mrs. Harry Glidden, and only a few members of the bride's own family were present. The couple went off by train to California for their honeymoon and returned two weeks later to their newly refurbished chalet, surrounded by beautiful gardens.[44] Over the next fifteen years their home was known in Spokane for its picturesque and artistic character, and was the scene of many social events. Finally Kirtland was able to match his professional success with personal fulfillment.

8.1 C. P. Thomas house, Spokane, 1905–6. Mission Revival. Eastern
Washington State Historical Society, L84–207.92.

CHAPTER EIGHT

Spokane and Seattle (1906–1909)

AFTER THE GREAT BUILDING BOOM AT THE TURN OF THE
century, Cutter and Malmgren's residential commissions in Spokane diminished. Apart from a Tudoresque house for former mayor
David M. Drumheller in 1904, and a large Mission Revival house for
C. P. Thomas in 1905 (fig. 8.1)[1] they had little domestic work in the
city. They suffered the rejection, in 1906, of their design for the Silver Bow Club in Butte, Montana, which would have confirmed their
reputation as the premier designers of gentlemen's clubs in the
region.[2] However, they received more requests for houses. In that
year they designed two substantial residences on the South Hill of
Spokane and one in Lewiston,[3] and they were also responsible for
several more modest homes. Nevertheless, they decided to focus
their efforts on developing an office in Seattle. By working on both
sides of the state they capitalized on previous successes; and like
most architects of their day, they continued to draw freely from
many sources, particularly those that were familiar to them. Partly
under the influence of new draftsmen in the office, they also explored opportunities to use more up-to-date concepts in domestic
and office building.

In the 1906 house for the banker Francis Finucane (fig. 8.2),
which stood by the Glover house on Eighth Avenue, Cutter continued with his favorite Tudor theme. For the first time he dispensed
with the usual half-timbered gables and built the walls entirely of
brick, capping them with cast stone copings. While in the Glover
house, and many others, the pattern of exposed timbers had pro-

8.2 Francis Finucane house, Spokane, 1906–8. Based on typical Tudor manor houses in England. The red-brick walls and stone parapets are a regional variant from the half-timbering of the Campbell and F. Lewis Clark houses. Demolished. Photo by Dennison. *Western Architect,* September 1908.

vided a strong visual effect, the most distinctive elements of the Finucane house were the ascending triangles of the copings above the dark brickwork. Cutter provided a new element of grandeur by combining the stone mullioned dining room windows with those of the bedroom above, in one tall panel. Three heraldic shields ornamented the spandrels between upper and lower windows.

D. W. Twohy, the president of the Old National Bank, gave Cutter the opportunity in 1906 to design a Craftsman-style house that revived the rustic character of some of his earlier work (fig. 8.3). Its walls of craggy basalt rose out of the ground and continued up, above the low-pitched roof, in three massive chimneys. Robust wooden columns carried the roofs of porches and of a porte cochère as well as an arbor along the west side of the house. These skeletal elements, combined with half-timbering on the upper walls, enlivened the exterior volume in a way that recalls the Stick Style of the 1870s. A dominant feature of the design was a horizontal band of cross-braced timber framing above the windows of the first floor, level with the roofs of the porches and the porte cochère. The Twohy house is somewhat reminiscent of the house that Cutter built for his sister and her husband in 1891 (fig. 5.1); however, the greater use of rugged stone, the lower pitch of the roof, and the strength of the timbers give a more robust feeling.

Cutter's hope that he could run a permanent branch office in Seattle with Edwin Wager as partner in charge was frustrated in January 1904, when Wager left to establish his own practice.[4] After his departure, no more work in Seattle materialized for Cutter and Malmgren until 1906, when they received a very desirable commission to design "an Italian park for Samuel Hill, the brother of J. J. Hill, the railroad magnate."[5] They were asked to design a group of at least three houses on a dramatic site in a high position overlooking Lake Union. This particular section of Capitol Hill had not been

8.3 D. W. Twohy house, Sumner Avenue, Spokane, 1906. With its rough stone base and heavy timbering, this house recalls Cutter's rustic designs fifteen years earlier. Demolished. Eastern Washington State Historical Society, L84.207.86.

developed because of its inaccessibility. The steepness of the land and legal objections to access from the established streets had deterred others from building there. Once an entry to this lofty promontory had been secured, it offered an exclusiveness that was ideal for the homes of millionaires. The site was cut off by the waters of the lake on three sides. From a small level area at the top, it plunged down precipitously to the lake. Rich vegetation clung to the slopes of a deep ravine, above which two of the houses were eventually sited.[6]

Sam Hill had joined with J. D. Farrell, former president of the Great Northern Steamship Company, and Hervey Lindley, a California capitalist involved with railroads, and they considered inviting a few others to join them in the development.[7] Since no drawings survive, it is hard to tell how it would have resembled an Italian park, a description probably conjured up in Cutter's romantic imagination. Cutter was in Seattle in May 1906 "perfecting plans" for the houses,[8] and the following month he was back again looking for office space. He had seen the recent growth of Seattle, which had overtaken Spokane as the most prosperous city in the state, and had made up his mind to move his headquarters there. He planned to concentrate on the design of office buildings.[9]

Cutter may have been encouraged to reach this decision because of his engagement in 1906 to design an eleven-story office tower for the Spokane and Eastern Trust Company. For this project, on the site of his Theodore Cushing building of 1889, he attempted Beaux Arts classicism on a grand scale. His rendering shows an eleven-story structure with a tripartite division, perhaps influenced by Stanford White's initial design for the Knickerbocker Trust in New York.[10] To clarify the division, bold cornices projected between the three-story rusticated "base," the seven-story "shaft," and the "capital" or attic story. Cutter treated the three central bays of the base as an Ionic portico, thus emphasizing the entry in a grand manner. This design for the tallest building that he had yet proposed expressed a buoyant verticality; the gridlike elevations showed a logical scheme of planning that was the antithesis of the chaotic building it was to replace.[11]

On December 4 of that year, Cutter and Malmgren hosted a luncheon in the elegant Peacock Room at Davenport's in Spokane to celebrate the opening of their new Seattle office and to bid farewell to the draftsmen who were leaving to run it. Under the barrel vaulted ceiling painted with a design of exotic plumage in deep greens, blues, and purples, the conversation was probably full of optimism about the future of the expanding practice. The departing staff included Clyde Westcott, who had been in the firm for at least a year; Howard Gifford, a more recent arrival; and Carl Nuese, the newly hired head draftsman for the Seattle branch.[12] They established themselves in the Arcade Building, in readiness to take on new work.

Soon after their arrival on the coast, they were joined by Andrew Willatzen, who had recently spent three years in Frank Lloyd Wright's studio in Oak Park. Born in Germany in 1876 and educated both there and in Denmark, Willatzen had emigrated to the United States in 1901. After doing construction work for a few months, he entered Wright's office at the time when the development of the Prairie House reached its peak. While he was there, several key works of Wright's most fertile period were in the process of design and construction. These included the Ward Willitts house, the Larkin building, and the houses for Susan Dana, Daniel D. Martin, and Edwin Cheney. After an enviable apprenticeship as one of Wright's draftsmen in company with George Willis, Cecil Barnes, Walter Burley Griffin, and Barry Byrne, Willatzen left to join the firm of Spencer and Powers. After a short stay there, he moved again, to the office of Pond and Pond.[13] Both firms were doing innovative work at that time. Robert C. Spencer and the Pond brothers had their offices in Steinway Hall, Chicago, when Wright had rented space there. They had all been members of a lunch club named the "Eighteen" at which architectural theories and problems were discussed,[14] and they had attended meetings of the Chicago Architectural Club, which at that time provided a forum for young architects with new ideas. Spencer admired Wright and designed houses strongly influenced by his concept for the Prairie House; he was also inspired by the designs of the English architects C. F. A. Voysey and M. H. Baillie Scott. Although Irving Pond had been doing progressive work in the first decade of the century, he later joined the architectural establishment in condemning Wright.[15] After Willatzen's introduction to the lively world of architecture in Chicago, he moved to Seattle, where he was briefly employed by Harlan Thomas before joining Cutter and Malmgren.[16]

The commission for Sam Hill and his wealthy associates proved, in the end, to be disappointing. Hill's own house, built in a formal manner quite antithetical to Cutter's work, was designed by the successful Washington, D.C., firm of Hornblower and Marshall. Cutter

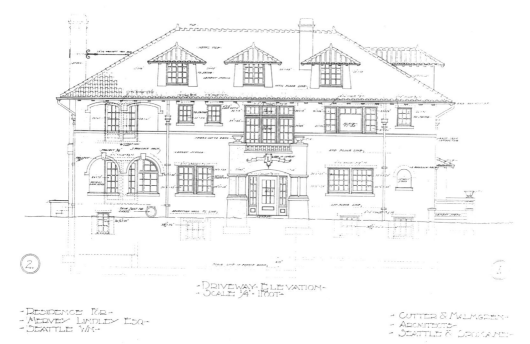

8.4 Hervey Lindley house, Seattle, 1906–8. Reminiscent of the Arts and Crafts manner of C. F. A. Voysey. Eastern Washington State Historical Society, L84–207.152.

only supervised the construction and took responsibility for the layout of the grounds.[17] J. D. Farrell appears to have given up the idea of participating in the venture.[18] The residence for Hervey Lindley (fig. 8.4), built next to Hill's on East Highland Drive, was a rather plain stuccoed block with a hipped roof, sited like the Hill house on the edge of the ravine. Its plain white walls, and small-paned casement windows suggest the influence of Voysey. Since no houses of this type had come out of Cutter's office previously, it is likely that Willatzen was involved in the design. If so, such Chicago architects as Spencer or George W. Maher, who was also associated with the Prairie School, may have provided models.[19]

Since the expected commissions for office buildings in Seattle did not materialize, it seems probable that draftsmen in the new office also worked on projects in Spokane. Houses for C. M. Youle and Clyde Graves, built about 1907 but later demolished, were similar in style to the Lindley house in Seattle.[20] There are strong grounds for suspecting Willatszen's hand in the design of two other houses in Spokane that show a Prairie Style influence. A characteristic hori-

8.5 John Sengfelder house, Ninth Avenue, Spokane, ca. 1908. One of
Cutter's few houses in the Prairie Style. Photo by the author.

zontality is emphasized in the John Sengfelder house (1908) on
Ninth Avenue (fig. 8.5).[21] At ground level it is extended by a terrace
surrounded by a low wall. The roofs of porches on both sides line
up with the heads of the first-floor windows, to create a strong plane,
echoed by the eaves of the main roof and the dormer windows
above. Interior details and cabinets show simplicity in their general
lines, but include unpretentious ornamentation in the spirit of the
later Arts and Crafts movement.

A distinct Prairie flavor also is seen in the Frederick Dewart house
on Sixth Avenue,[22] whose deep porch runs across the front of the
house and round the sides. The porch roof and the main hipped
roof follow the same slope, giving a sense of stability.

Cutter does not seem to have been sufficiently impressed by the
Prairie Style to use it for major commissions. While in the first years
of his practice he had been excited by the indigenously American
Shingle Style, it appears that Wright's rejection of historicism was
too radical for him. Nor did he show much interest in the Craftsman bungalow. Although this type had origins in the Swiss chalet,

a type that Cutter exploited, he never attempted to emulate the brothers Greene, who raised the bungalow to an art form. Cutter and Malmgren were responsible for a few bungalow-like houses, all of them relatively modest.[23]

Cutter was in his element again when he received a commission in 1907 for a large Tudor house on Harvard Avenue, a fashionable tree-lined street on the west slope of Seattle's Capitol Hill (fig. 8.6). His client was C. J. Smith, the president of Washington Securities, for whom Cutter and Malmgren also designed an office building downtown. The romantically conceived residence, for which Carl Nuese took responsibility,[24] carried on the tradition Cutter had begun in Seattle with the Stimson mansion. However, it followed more closely in the manner of the Finucane house. Built in red brick, it displays the irregularity characteristic of Old English houses. Slightly off-center on the street facade, the principal cross gable with stone copings crowns a wall with a two-story bank of stone mullioned windows, like the tall window of a medieval great hall. To its left, as if entering the cross passage of a medieval house, an arched door opens under a crenellated parapet. To complete the theme, a buttress bolsters the corner of the wall beside the door. Because of the slope of the site, the garden front, with three gables, two of them half-timbered, stands a full story higher. The entrance hall, which runs through the house from front to back, leads out onto a brick terrace supported on an arched loggia. A Gothic staircase window provides an accent, and generous bay windows swell out from the hall and the principal bedroom above.

Tudor Gothic arches, formed within the rectangular openings of the library windows, gave the interior a traditional English character, but the paneling was unusually simple, without ornate moldings and decorative features. Furthermore, the staircase, hall, and dining room were paneled in a distinctly modern style that owed more, perhaps, to the Vienna Secession than to Tudor England (fig. 8.7).[25]

The other commission from C. J. Smith, obtained late in 1907, brought Cutter closer to the realization of his plan to specialize in office buildings.[26] This was the headquarters of the Washington Securities Company on the corner of Union Street and Fifth Avenue (fig. 8.8).[27] The design, completed in May the following year,[28] was very different from the Beaux Arts Spokane and Eastern Trust. It possessed the clean lines and simplicity of comparable steel-framed structures built at the time in Chicago by such firms as Holabird

8.6 C. J. Smith house, Capitol Hill, Seattle, 1906–7. A Tudoresque design
by Cutter's chief designer in Seattle, Karl Nuese. Eastern Washington
State Historical Society, L84–207.4.67.

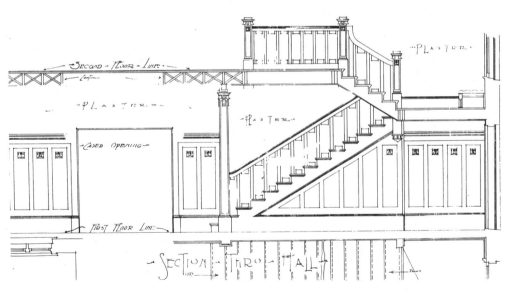

8.7 C. J. Smith house, paneling in the hall designed in a contemporary
manner. Altered. Eastern Washington State Historical Society,
L84–207.154.

8.8 Washington Securities Building, Union Street, Seattle, 1907–8, later known as the Crary Building. Exemplifies the functional approach to office buildings developed in Chicago in the late eighties and nineties. Photo by Asahel Curtis. University of Washington Libraries, Special Collections Division, 13118.

and Roche. Above the storefronts at street level, plain brick piers rose through five stories to terminate in modest capitals of a rectilinear design. Between them the windows and recessed brick spandrels of all ten bays were identical. The general impression was of a simple brick grid with dominant verticals, beneath a strong cornice. The leading architectural critic Herbert Croly praised the facade of the building for its "simplicity and unpretentious propriety" which had "no equal in Seattle."[29] However, since the city was preparing for the Alaska-Yukon-Pacific Exposition of 1909, developers may have been looking for more flamboyant architecture. Despite his work in the city for some prominent clients, Cutter did not receive any more commissions for office buildings in Seattle.

8.9 Competition design for the Old National Bank, Spokane, 1909. An imposing block in the Beaux Arts manner. Glen Cloninger Collection.

In 1909 he reverted to the more conservative Beaux Arts style in his competition design for the Old National Bank Building in Spokane (fig. 8.9). He had a better chance of winning with a design suiting the national taste for classic grandeur than one that would please an avant-garde critic. But the judges selected a design by the famous architect Daniel Burnham of Chicago.

In their main office, Cutter and Malmgren had been diversifying to produce buildings of several types, including college buildings in Lewiston and Spokane,[30] a country club in Spokane,[31] and railroad depots in Palouse and Spirit Lake, Idaho. The two rural stations both drew from the Richardsonian tradition. Like Richardson's station in North Easton, Massachusetts (1881), the Palouse depot was a

8.10 Idaho and Washington Northern Railroad Company, Spirit Lake, Idaho, 1907. Demolished. Eastern Washington State Historical Society, L94–19.43.

compact block of rough masonry with arched openings and a roof that overhung far enough on large brackets to protect waiting passengers from the rain or summer sun.[32] The passenger depot at Spirit Lake (fig. 8.10) was similar in general concept, but larger and more elaborate. It served the dual function of station and company headquarters for the Idaho and Washington Northern Railroad Company. Built of brick, with half-timbered upper walls, it was enlivened by a turret in the center of the side facing the rails. This feature, housing the ticket office at its base, projected conveniently so that the man on duty could look up and down the line for approaching trains. On the upper level, where it rose above the roof, it provided an eyrie for Frederick A. Blackwell, the director of the company.

Blackwell, like several other ambitious pioneers who patronized Kirtland Cutter, was a self-made man who contributed significantly to the opening of the Inland Northwest. Born in Maine in 1852 as the son of a blacksmith, he labored on farms and in lumber camps in the East, before becoming a railroad ticket agent. He then went into business on his own account and gained the respect of wealthy investors in Pennsylvania. He came west in 1902 with financial backing and built the Coeur d'Alene and Spokane Railway electric line. Turning to logging, he founded Blackwell's Panhandle Lumber Company, which acquired huge holdings of forest lands in northern Idaho. When, early in 1907, he incorporated the Idaho and Washington Northern Railroad Company, he combined the hauling of lumber from his mill at Spirit Lake with the management of riverboat lines, and the creation of destinations for pleasure trips, to attract passengers for a first-class railway.

On January 25, 1908, six weeks after Cutter's Spirit Lake Depot was completed, Blackwell carried two hundred invited guests to the end of the line at Newport and entertained them with a luncheon at the depot. Not only had Blackwell employed the leading architect of the region, he had equipped the railroad with Pullman-built passenger cars costing $17,000 each, three times the average cost of such vehicles.[33]

Cutter's most creative project of 1907 was his First Church of Christ Scientist, a striking example of the Mission Revival Style (fig. 8.11).[34] He fronted its broad nave with a surprisingly low Mission gable, which, despite the flowing curves of its parapet,

8.11 First Church of Christ Scientist, Spokane, ca. 1907–8. A striking evocation of the early nineteenth-century California missions of Father Junipero Serra. Demolished. *Western Architect,* September 1908.

8.12 Interior of the First Church of Christ Scientist. This church belongs to a tradition of structural experimentation in Christian Science churches at this time. *Western Architect,* September 1908.

suggested the stability of a pyramid. He broke the symmetry by flanking it with a tower surmounted by a cupola on one side and a low one-story pavilion with a shallow hipped roof on the other. These two volumes stepped forward to enclose a small forecourt, protected by a low wall. Further curvilinear gable ends faced the transepts on either side. Compared with the architect's earlier Mission Revival work, this design went further to exploit the potential of plain stucco surfaces and unadorned geometric openings, an approach that Irving Gill was to develop in a more ascetic manner in a Christian Science Church in San Diego in 1909.[35]

An ingenious structure of diagonal roof trusses spanned the spacious interior (fig. 8.12). At the corners of two large bays, bold corbeled brackets branched out from massive wooden columns to carry this diagonal structure, as well as the longitudinal and transverse beams. In some respects, this design foreshadowed Bernard Maybeck's famous Christian Science Church in Berkeley, California (1909), in which massive piers carried a roof of heavy diagonal trusses.[36]

In Seattle in 1907 the firm extended the ladies' annex of the Rainier Club, and undertook the interior of the College Inn, a more bohemian place of refreshment on the corner of Pike Street and Third Avenue.[37] In this design they created a vaulted, dungeonlike space for male patrons and a lighter, more elegant Art Nouveau style room for women. The rest of Cutter's work in Seattle was residential and mostly based on concepts he had developed earlier in his career.

Cutter had met Judge Thomas Burke, one of Seattle's more dynamic leaders and the future chief justice of the Washington Supreme Court, while working on the Rainier Club commission.[38] Burke asked him to add a garage and an "Indian room" to his home on Madison Street. The judge and his wife were avid collectors, and the new room not only housed part of his collection but also expressed his enthusiasm for Indian art and culture[39] (fig. 8.13). It was

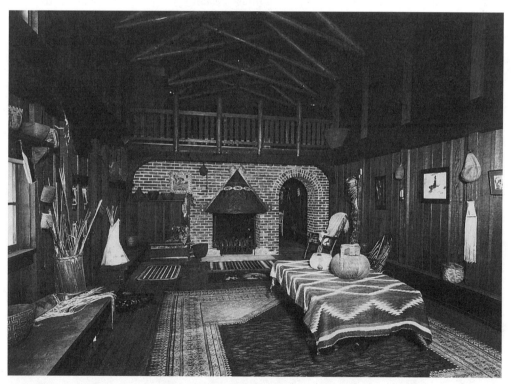

8.13 The Indian Room for Judge Thomas Burke, Seattle, ca. 1908–9. Built to house Judge Burke's collection of Indian artifacts, the foundation of the Burke Museum at the University of Washington. Eastern Washington State Historical Society, L84–207.4.176.

a tall space with a well-lit upper gallery at one end and an open roof of scissor trusses supported on carved heads, similar to typical heads on totem poles. Beneath the gallery in a wall of rough stone, a fireplace is shielded by an enameled copper hood in the form of a tepee. A cauldron hangs over the fire on an iron chain, and nearby a primitive seat made of wood and leather is drawn up close to the hearth. Decorative elements of the gallery balustrade and carvings at the intersections of the roof timbers allude perhaps to Indian crafts.

Cutter did not give Judge Burke's Indian room any clear sense of the spatial character or structural system of an actual Native American dwelling, certainly not of the Northwest Coast. The decorative features convey the white man's romantic view of the indigenous tribesman. Nevertheless, the room gives recognition to the existence of a Native American heritage at a time when almost all historic allusions in architecture were to a European past.

Cutter described a house designed in Spokane in 1908 for the mortgage banker J. M. Corbet as Dutch Colonial (fig. 8.14).[40] Its compact block of dark red brick under a hipped roof suggests the type of seventeenth-century Dutch house that influenced English

8.14 J. M. Corbet house, Seventh Avenue, Spokane, 1907–8. Described by Cutter as Dutch Colonial. Photo by the author.

architecture at the Restoration. Its quoins of a lighter, pinkish brick and a belt course of the same material at second-floor level emphasize a geometrical ordering characteristic of the Renaissance, but the formality is broken in the balanced asymmetry of the windows. The broad overhang of the eaves, casting a shadow on the wall, and the horizontal line of the belt course give a hint of the Prairie School.

Three of the remaining Seattle projects of 1908 and 1909 were inspired, as several of Cutter's earlier works had been, by the Swiss chalet. One of these, drawn up as a weekend retreat in the Highlands for A. S. Kerry, remained unbuilt. The most important commission executed in this style was the Seattle Golf and Country Club (fig. 8.15). It is worth noting that five of the first six presidents of the club were clients of Cutter and Malmgren, among them Judge Burke and C. J. Smith. The club, founded in 1900, first constructed a nine-hole golf course in Laurelhurst, just east of the present site of the University of Washington.[41] Then early in 1907 the club purchased 340 acres of undeveloped land beautifully situated on Puget Sound nine miles north of Seattle, of which 155 acres were to be used for an eighteen-hole golf course and the balance devel-

8.15 Seattle Golf and Country Club, The Highlands, 1908–9. The boldly projecting roof and long sweeps of the roof give a strong horizontality to the chalet type. Photo by Frank H. Nowell. Eastern Washington State Historical Society, L84–207.4.57.

oped for members' houses.[42] The area, which became one of Seattle's most exclusive residential districts, was known as the Highlands. C. D. Stimson, Cutter's first major client in Seattle, the president of the country club, called in famous East Coast landscape architects, the Olmsted Brothers. John C. Olmsted visited in April 1908 and made recommendations for the layout of the site.[43]

In June 1908, Cutter displayed his design for the new clubhouse at the annual exhibition of the Washington State Chapter of the AIA.[44] His perspective rendering shows a bold use of the chalet vocabulary. The long roof, intersected by a cross wing, projects beyond the walls to give an exceptionally broad overhang. The same protection, appropriate to the climate of the Northwest Coast, is also given to the dormer windows. As in Cutter's earlier chalet designs,

8.16 Interior of the Seattle Golf and Country Club. The exposed turned wood trusses enliven the spacious interior. Eastern Washington State Historical Society, L84–207.59.

the roof is weighted down with rocks. But compared with them, the Seattle Golf and Country Club shows a greater sense of horizontality. The first floor, finished in stucco, makes a long white band parallel to the ground, above which the dark upper story seems to float. The windows are also arranged in horizontal bands. It appears as if the eye of Andrew Willatzen, conditioned by his exposure to the Prairie House, had modified the typical Cutter design. Cutter's romanticism comes out, however, in the fretwork on the balcony fronts and in the chimneys that stand high above the roof like dovecotes, each with its little pitched roof. An arbor shown on the rendering with white stucco-covered piers and wooden beams to support vines at one corner of the clubhouse was omitted from the final building. The interiors of the club continued the theme of alpine hospitality suggested by the exterior. But Cutter did not expose the structural timbers on the inner walls, and the roof trusses were finely crafted to suit the sophisticated urban membership (fig. 8.16).

The Swiss chalet also provided the model in 1908 for the L. B. Peeples house on Harvard Avenue on Capitol Hill in Seattle (fig. 8.17). Built on an elevated site at the east side of the road, it presents its gable end to the front above a bank of rhododendrons. Corbeled brackets, molded to an elaborate profile, support the roof overhang.

8.17 L. B. Peeples house, Capitol Hill, Seattle, 1908–9. A simple version of the Swiss chalet shelters the house under a broad roof. Photo by the author.

The projecting ends of solid timbers at the corners and at the intersection of interior partitions articulate the gable front with vertical lines. Bands of sharply cut but restrained ornamentation above the two tiers of upper windows provide a horizontal accent. The windows, like those of the golf club, are grouped together with a sense of continuity.

The dark wood of the outer walls of the Peeples house gives a foreboding of dim spaces inside, but the interiors are surprisingly bright. The bands of windows on two sides of each of the main rooms admit copious light. French windows on either side of the hall allow long views from the living room to the dining room and to the windows beyond. The interior details are relatively delicate, with white painted mullions, glazing bars, and door frames reflecting the light that enters. Window seats expand the spaces into the thickness of the walls. In tune with the Arts and Crafts approach to the house, Cutter decorated the fireplace in the den at the rear of the first floor with handmade Moravian tiles in a series of designs inspired by images of knights, dragons, birds, vines laden with grapes, and Gothic lettering. Colored in earth tones and laid in a seemingly random pattern, the hearth conveys a sense of unpretentious craftsmanship.[45]

Of all the projects initiated in the Seattle office of Cutter and Malmgren, the most original was the house for C. H. Clarke in the Highlands begun in 1908. Clarke, the president of a wholesale grocery company, was a former client in Seattle, for whom they had designed a house on Union Street at the south end of Capitol Hill in 1899.[46] But as one of the leading members of the Seattle Golf Club,[47] he had seen the potential of the Highlands. Clarke also seems to have become a more adventurous client, ready to accept an experimental type of architecture. It is clear from the Prairie School influence that the credit for the design must go to Andrew Willatzen.

The site was a small woodland clearing with a view of the Puget Sound through trees. The Olmsted Brothers were consulted and John Olmsted visited the Highlands in May 1908.[48] He told Clarke: "I think you have selected one of the most interesting house sites at the Highlands." He commented on the "remarkably thick woods" that had never been logged, and "the lace-like view of the Sound and Olympics" through thinner trees on the lower slopes. But he was horrified to find that men employed by Clarke to clear out dead trees and fallen timber had taken little care to protect the smaller trees and undergrowth.[49] In his lengthy report he pleaded with Clarke "to retain to the fullest degree compatible with safety and comfort the remarkably attractive woodland characteristics of the place."

Olmsted obviously feared that the Highlands would be transformed into a typical piece of suburbia unless he intervened. He argued that the planting of lawns and flowerbeds would be entirely out of place with "the wildness of the remaining woods," and suggested that his client should leave the forest intact, except for clearance necessary for the house. He advised Clarke to avoid uniform paths "carefully edged at frequent intervals by the gardener."

"The trouble," Olmsted wrote to Clarke, "is that it requires a rare kind of skill to make and keep a place natural while fitting it to be useful and comfortable. It is a thing which the average gardener usually understands very little about. He has a constant tendency to show his handiwork when every effort should be directly the contrary. It is in this direction that we have given years of study." Olmsted also made detailed recommendations to Clarke about the design of the house, particularly stressing the potential of views toward the Olympic mountains.[50] However, it appears that Clarke put his trust in Cutter, who gave responsibility for the design to Andrew Willatzen. But Clarke took to heart Olmsted's views on preserving the natural woodland and did what he could to preserve the natural site.

The dominant element of the design was the long, low-pitched roof with cross gables, extended on both axes by lower roofs (figs. 8.18, 8.19). As in Wright's houses, a massive chimney rose from the core of the house symbolizing the hearth within. The service wing projected at a 45 degree angle to the main axis of the plan, an arrangement found in a number of late nineteenth-century houses and used by Cutter a few years later in Spokane.[51] The living space, concentrated on either side of the chimney stack, expanded into a broad terrace overlooking the Sound and a shady veranda. The three lower roofs stretched out to protect the veranda opening to the south off the living room, a carriage porch to the east, and a servants' porch to the north. The details throughout showed a consistency characteristic of the Prairie House. Roof slopes were simple planes, unencumbered with dormers. The surfaces of the upper walls were of white stucco, accented with horizontal bands of dark wood; the lower walls of shiplap siding emphasized the plane parallel with the ground. Windows were grouped together in banks of

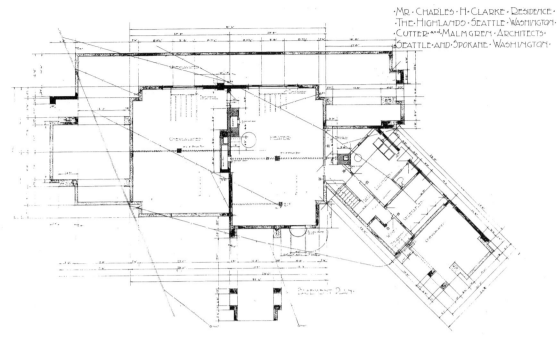

8.18 C. H. Clarke house, The Highlands, 1908. Original plan, Cutter and
Malmgren, designed by Andrew Willatzen, who had previously worked
in Frank Lloyd Wright's Oak Park Studio. Eastern Washington State
Historical Society, L84–207.42.

8.19 C. H. Clarke house, Elevation. Characteristic of the Prairie Style.
Eastern Washington State Historical Society, L84–207.42.

two, three, or four to give continuity and to afford broad views into the trees and on the west side to the water beyond. Interiors were simple, with much use of natural fir, stained silver gray in the hall and living room and rich brown in the dining room.

The skillfully designed Clarke residence showed that the Prairie House, originally conceived in sympathy with prairies of the midwestern states, was in reality as much at home in the Northwest. While, in the region of Chicago, Wright had conceived the long, low roof to echo the forms of the gently rolling land, in the Northwest the broad roof overhangs give umbrella-like protection from the frequent rain. Indeed, the low-pitched, shingled roof has become a vernacular form of the region. In fact the roof pitches and over-hangs of the Clarke house are somewhat similar to those of Cutter's chalet-based houses. Both types were inspired by the tenets of the Arts and Crafts movement, but there was a major difference: Cutter looked romantically back to a European heritage while Willatzen adopted a contemporary American style.

The lack of large commercial commissions may account for the breakup of the Seattle office. Carl Nuese left the firm some time in 1908 and Willatzen took over his responsibility as chief draftsman. However, Willatzen possessed a design philosophy of his own, about which Cutter appears to have had reservations, and was ready to pursue his own career. In February 1909 he formed a partnership with Barry Byrne, with whom he had worked in Wright's office.[52] Willatzen and Byrne not only retained the C. H. Clarke commission as their own; they also designed a Prairie Style house for A. S. Kerry, for whom Cutter and Malmgren had planned a chalet. After Byrne's arrival, the Clarke house underwent revisions, finally achieving a greater consistency.[53] Initially Cutter and Malmgren agreed to give Willatzen and Byrne responsibility for their Seattle work,[54] but this was their last attempt to set up a branch office. Although Cutter continued to receive worthwhile commissions on the coast, he needed to maintain personal control in a relatively small office. The trouble with hiring self-reliant people capable of managing a number of projects was that they acquired a taste for independence. David Lewis in Portland and Edwin Wager in Seattle had not sustained branches of Cutter and Malmgren for long. While Cutter wanted to put his own stamp on the work and to receive viable profits, his associates were interested in developing their own careers.

Another factor in the failure of the Seattle office was the competition from newly arrived architects with excellent credentials from the East and Europe. When Cutter received the commission from C. D. Stimson in 1898, the prevailing style for houses was still Queen Anne, which Cutter had rejected a decade earlier; indeed there were few professionals who could compete with him in residential architecture. The design of public and commercial buildings thrived in Seattle in the late nineteenth century, but three of the most successful architects—Elmer Fisher, Willis Ritchie, and John Parkinson—left the city in 1894 and 1895 to practice elsewhere. Seattle was slow to recover from the depression of 1893, and the ranks of the profession diminished. James Schack arrived from Germany via Chicago in 1901; Ellsworth Story came from Illinois in 1903 after extensive European travels and launched an innovative career; Daniel Huntington moved from New York in 1904. Nevertheless, the field still seemed wide open when Cutter decided to establish his office in Seattle in 1906. But this expansion coincided with a new influx of well-trained and mostly experienced architects, eager to compete for commissions. The same year saw the arrival of Harlan Thomas, from Denver, and two partners from New York, W. Marbury Somervell and Joseph S. Coté, who were well versed in Beaux Arts principles. In the following year several more new architects began to practice in Seattle. These included W. R. B. Willcox, who had spent six years in the prestigious New York office of McKim, Mead and White, the Beezer Brothers from Pittsburgh, and Arthur Loveless from New York, whose particular interest was in Cutter's favorite territory: picturesque English houses.[55] The year 1907 also saw a business depression in Seattle and a consequent reduction in building, mentioned frequently in the pages of *Pacific Builder and Engineer.*

Affirming again that Spokane would be the center for his professional work, Cutter decided to broaden his base in that city by opening an interior design business. Ever since beginning his practice he had attempted to influence his clients in their choice of furnishings and had traveled extensively to select items and develop design schemes that would complement his architecture.[56] In 1909 he went into partnership with Frederick W. Plummer and Louis Davenport to run a showroom on Monroe Street selling furniture, rugs, fabrics, and fixtures and to take on design commissions. The firm had a studio at his sister's house on Sixth Avenue, suggesting that he was personally involved in the creative work; later they moved into offices in Davenport's building. They continued until 1913, when mention of their existence disappears from city directories.[57]

CHAPTER NINE

Summer Camps in the Wilderness (1902–1920)

UP TO THE TIME THAT CUTTER OPENED HIS PRACTICE IN Spokane, much of the effort of the American people had been expended on subduing the wild continent they settled. The architectural styles popular in the eighteenth and early nineteenth centuries reflected their sense of success in this struggle. Houses in the Georgian, Federal, and Greek revival styles, with their formal symmetry, harmonious proportions, and elegant refinements, tended to remain aloof from their natural surroundings, clearly symbolizing the triumph of civilization and the conquest of the wilderness. Even in the last four decades of the nineteenth century, when more picturesque and romantic styles were chosen, their purpose was still to display the superior culture and European origin of the buildings' owners.

Many Americans in the period after the Civil War saw their first vision of the western landscape through the eyes of artists. Albert Bierstadt and Thomas Moran were among those who proclaimed in their canvases the heroic quality of the American landscape. Not content merely to portray the West as beautiful or picturesque, they created images of wild and mountainous scenery that belonged in the realm of the sublime.[1] The settlers who eagerly flocked westward in the last decades of the nineteenth century may have been inspired by such art, but wherever they settled, their aim was to civilize the savage land. As soon as the log cabin phase was over, their buildings responded not to qualities in the landscape but to current architectural fashions.

To the prospector who had toiled with pick and shovel in the goldfields, to the settler seeking a prosperous life on the frontier, the cabin in the wilderness had little appeal; it was certainly not considered architecture. However, once civilized life had been established, and Americans were housed in fashionable residences set in a tamed landscape, they could return to the wilderness and devise primitive buildings for pleasure and inspiration. By the turn of the century, some of the wealthy and successful were ready to build themselves rustic log cabins as summer retreats by remote lakes, in forests, or on mountains. In such places, they could escape the formality of their mansions and play at being backwoodsmen while still enjoying many of the luxuries of the city and avoiding the rigors of the pioneer life. Ironically, tycoons who played a leading role in the industrialization of America were leaders in the fashion of retreating to the wilderness.

Cutter was unusual among architects for his interest in developing a rustic, picturesque style responsive to the mountains and forests of the Northwest. His use of rough basalt in the Fairmont Cemetery Chapel, and massive logs for the church in Chelan, showed his desire to exploit rugged native materials. Above all, in the design of the Idaho Building at the World's Columbian Exposition, he responded architecturally to the romance of the frontier. His first experience with a rustic retreat for a wealthy family came in 1902, when he was given the enviable commission to design a summer camp in the Adirondacks for Mrs. Lucy Carnegie, widow of Andrew Carnegie's brother Thomas.[2]

Interest in the Adirondacks as a picturesque wilderness retreat first arose in the 1830s, when the region attracted adventurous hunters and fishermen as well as a few writers and artists. Ralph Waldo Emerson, who camped there at Follensby Pond in 1858, published a book of verse that helped popularize the idea of camping in the woods and also spread the fame of the Adirondacks. But it was not until after the Civil War that the region began to be developed for summer visitors and that conservation of the forests began to replace their exploitation for lumber.

The individual who led the way in the creation of an Adirondack style of architecture was William West Durant, the son of the president of the Adirondack Railroad Company. Between 1876 and 1900 he designed and built four unique camps and gained a reputation as a popular host, entertaining royally in the woodland surroundings. He used a group of buildings of an appropriately rustic character to convey the magic of the backwoods to wealthy urbanites.[3] Alfred Donaldson describes his camp, Pine Knot, as "a unique blend

of beauty and comfort . . . the showplace of the woods."[4] Camp
Pine Knot brought together elements of the pioneer cabin and the
Swiss chalet, surrounded by ample verandas and balconies and protected by broadly overhanging, low-pitched roofs (fig. 9.1). In the
Recreation Building a delicate web of supporting columns, handrails, and cross bracing of unpeeled branches gave his buildings a
unique, rustic character. Durant's camp, and many of the others it
inspired, take on the role of folk art, seeking to harmonize with the
forest. While appearing to celebrate the simple life, they are, in reality, sophisticated and artful.

9.1 The Recreation
Building at Camp
Pine Knot, Raquette
Lake, New York
ca. 1895–1900, by
William West Durant.
A rustic retreat in
the Adirondacks for
wealthy New Yorkers.
Adirondack Museum.

Durant's cabins show considerable originality and charm, but Cutter could give the Carnegies a mountain dwelling with a European pedigree. He was the first to design an Adirondack cabin based solidly on Swiss prototypes, though others followed. The Carnegie Camp, built like Durant's Camp Pine Knot on the shore of picturesque Raquette Lake, offers southerly views of the lake and the surrounding hills and mountains. Cutter designed two buildings connected by a covered passageway and unified in their architectural character. Both are of the type of log construction that he had employed on his own home and for the Idaho Building in Chicago; both have broad shingled roofs weighted down in the Swiss manner with heavy boulders. The eaves are supported, as before, on corbeled brackets giving the appearance of solid logs (figs. 9.2–9.5).

The larger of the two buildings is T-shaped, with the foot of the T pointed south toward the lake. The principal room, described on the architect's plan as the Assembly Hall, occupies the stem of the T; a cross wing at the north end contains bedrooms. The Assembly Hall, like the great hall of the medieval house, is open to the elaborate roof structure. Forty-five feet long and twenty-seven feet wide, it was designed for large gatherings of family and guests. The south end of this spacious hall opens onto a terrace surrounded by a low wall and shaded by the exceptionally wide overhang of the roof. Above the terrace, and sheltered by the roof canopy, a generous balcony provides a vantage point with a superb view down the lake. The north end of the hall focuses on an inglenook eighteen feet wide. Above this vast fireplace a gallery, like the minstrel's gallery of a medieval hall, runs across the room, giving access to upper bedrooms. This is echoed by another gallery across the south end of the hall that opens through French windows onto the balcony outside.

Built-in settles in the inglenook, and long window seats under continuous bands of casements on the east and west walls, provide ample seating while leaving the center of the room uncluttered. A small writing room opens off one side of the hall. Mrs. Carnegie's chamber, in the north wing, at the head of the T, enjoys light from three sides and views in three directions. It is the only one of nine bedrooms to have a private bathroom.

The second building contained the dining room, kitchen, and a servant's room, above which were eight bedrooms approached by an outside staircase. Since Lucy Carnegie had nine children, the smaller building was probably often used as a young people's dormitory while adult visitors occupied the main structure. The

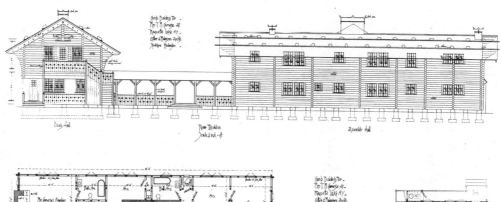

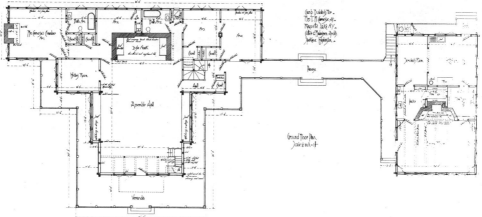

9.2 Carnegie Camp, Raquette Lake, New York, 1902–3, plan and elevation. Cutter expanded on his chalet vocabulary to create a huge interior
space of rustic character. Eastern Washington State Historical Society,
L84–207.159.

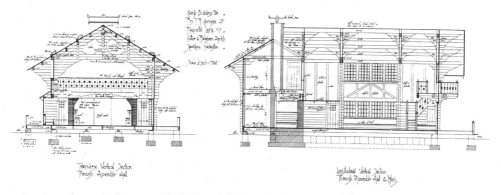

9.3 Sections through the assembly hall at the Carnegie Camp. An elaborate system of huge brackets supports and braces the wooden roof. Eastern Washington State Historical Society, L84–207.159.

SUMMER CAMPS IN THE WILDERNESS

9.4 The Carnegie Camp's assembly hall at the left, where the principal guest rooms are located, is linked by a covered passageway to the building containing the dining room and childrens' bedrooms. Photo by the author.

9.5 The assembly hall roof structure at Carnegie Camp. The massive trusses are adorned with hunting trophies. Photo by the author.

sleeping accommodations were relatively spartan, but the hall was a memorable gathering place, ideal for children's games, theatrical events, and fireside conversation. To add to the rustic character, Cutter designed a windmill on a log base, but this was not built.

Lucy Carnegie was an imposing woman described as having "infectious good humor." Her brother-in-law, Andrew, had married late in life and had only one daughter. He enjoyed the "irrepressible large family of relatives with Lucy the main pillar . . . all revolving around her ample orbit . . . She and Andrew Carnegie would argue over almost any topic, shouting boisterously at each other . . . and laughing uproariously." He called her "The Commodore."[5]

It was only a year after the building of the Carnegie Cabin on Raquette Lake that Cutter built a summer home at Hayden Lake in Idaho for his former client, John A. Finch. The Finch mansion in Browne's Addition of Spokane had been Cutter's first Neoclassical building. Evidently the mining magnate had perceived a portico of white columns as a potent symbol of his status, but he was ready to follow the example of the Carnegies and enjoy rustic simplicity in a summer retreat. Unlike the Carnegies, he did not have to travel far for his wilderness experience. Hayden Lake, only thirty miles east of Spokane, was easily reached when the electric railway link from Spokane to Coeur d'Alene was completed in 1903, the year the Finch chalet was built. Covering the few remaining miles by horse and buggy was simple compared to the long journey into the Adirondacks. Here the Finches could gather their family and entertain their friends lavishly in the lakeside setting.

Their impressive chalet (fig. 9.6) on a low hill overlooking the lake was similar in construction to Cutter's own house and to the Carnegie camp. The walls of squared off logs gave it a more finished look than any pioneer cabin. As the architect preferred, solid corbeled brackets supported the broadly overhanging eaves, and the roof was weighted down with stones. The principal reception room was spacious; the heavily beamed ceiling and huge fireplace of rough local stone combined coziness with grandeur (fig. 9.7). On the gable end of the house and on the adzed beam over the fireplace, inscriptions in Gothic lettering proclaimed a Germanic influence.

The boat house on the lake and the carriage house were constructed of squared logs in the same style and with similar details as the main dwelling. A garden structure of unpeeled logs, described as an "Idaho-grape arbor," carried on the rustic theme.

9.6 "Chalet Laken," the Finch summer home, Hayden Lake, Idaho, 1903. Destroyed by fire. Eastern Washington State Historical Society, L86–488.

9.7 Living room in the Finch Chalet, furnished in the Mission Style. The oak beams and huge inglenook evoke the character of old inns in the alps. Eastern Washington State Historical Society, L.84–207.4.96.

The extension of the railroad from Coeur d'Alene to Hayden Lake in 1906 opened up the possibility of creating a resort there. The directors of the Inland Empire Railroad Company, who had purchased the line while its construction was beginning, included Jay P. Graves, F. Lewis Clark, and F. A. Blackwell, who were eager to exploit the potential of the beauty spot. The formation of the Panhandle Lumber Company and the construction of a sawmill at the south end of the lake ensured some traffic, but they hoped to see hundreds of holiday makers riding the train to enjoy the scenery and the good fishing. Maintaining that the mountains, lakes, and forests of the Inland Northwest offered as much to tourists as some of the popular scenic areas of Europe, they were convinced that the provision of first-class accommodations would lure summer visitors from further afield than Spokane. They also envisaged making Hayden Lake a center for visits by rail to other attractions in the region.

On August 20, 1906, only a week after the railroad opened, the *Couer d'Alene Press* reported that five hundred people had taken the trip, including many campers and fishermen. They described the place as "a mecca for pleasure seekers and lovers of nature." In September a dance was held at the "Wigwam" at Hayden Lake and by December 4 it was announced that the Hayden Lake Improvement Company, headed by Graves, had purchased a property of 163 acres on the west side of the lake to transform it into a summer resort.

The syndicate made ambitious plans for "The Green City in the Pines." They intended to build not only a large hotel but numerous houses for summer lease in a parklike setting. In addition, they proposed a townsite and a racetrack. One of Graves's associates, Aubrey White, had already shown his belief in the conservation of natural resources for the public good by bringing the celebrated landscape architects, the Olmsted Brothers, to Spokane to design the city's park system. His partners had the wisdom to realize that the sensitivity and expertise of the Olmsted Brothers was critical to the success of their project.

In December 1906, in the company of Kirtland Cutter and Aubrey White, John C. Olmsted toured the snow-covered terrain in a sleigh. He noticed a "pretty ravine dense with pine and undergrowth." He suggested a shoreline walk protected with riprap and, with Cutter's approval, proposed a site for the new inn on a bluff commanding a fine view of the lake. To dramatize the position he suggested "a very wide veranda overhanging the top edge of the bluff." Later, when the company, perhaps on the advice of Cutter, sited the inn "close to some tall pines for picturesque effect and shade," he agreed. However, he objected to their idea of a floating boardwalk and a boat landing out in front of the hotel because he felt that it would be "very disturbing to the view of the lake."[6]

Olmsted saw no fundamental conflict between protection of the landscape and profitability; he even proposed several practical ideas to make the plan financially successful. He suggested a shop at the station to sell refreshments to those arriving or meeting people; he advocated the use of earth closets as an economy over a complete sewage system; he proposed vine-covered fences as an inexpensive means of protecting the owners of summer cottages from the gaze of day trippers on their way to the beach. However, he could not accept the profit motive as an excuse for desecrating the land. The conservation of the natural beauty and tranquility of the land was his foremost concern. When pipes for the new irrigation system were run up the ravine without sufficient care, he bemoaned the "destruction of the wild trees and shrubbery." When the builders of the inn threw the earth excavated from the cellar out in front, "spoiling all the wild covering of the slope and burying the trees," he took them to task.[7] Thus, Olmsted not only played the role of landscape designer, he also became the conscience of his clients.

In December 1906, Cutter was at work on the hotel. Once again, he based his design on the Swiss chalet, this time using an H-shaped plan, with two parallel bedroom wings joined by a central block (fig. 9.8). Visitors entered beneath a sheltering balcony into the spacious lobby warmed by inglenook fireplaces at both ends. On the side nearest the lake, French windows opened onto the terrace overhanging the top of the bluff, offering views, framed by a few trees, across the lake. This major social space was used for dancing when balls were held. From here, stairs led up to a balcony stretching the entire width of the hotel and giving access to the upper bedrooms. This and other balconies were fronted with boards ornamented with fretwork in Swiss or German patterns. The kitchen and dining room were placed in a separate adjacent building, connected by a covered passageway.

The interior spaces offered an informality appropriate to the lakeside setting, and a warmth derived, in part, from much use of wood. Since the upper floors were needed for bedrooms, there were no high spaces with elaborate open roof trusses like the assembly

9.8 Bozanta Tavern, Hayden Lake, Idaho, 1906–7. A resort that aimed to recreate in the Northwest the pleasures of Alpine resorts in Europe. Now the Hayden Lake Country Club. *Spokesman Review,* February 10, 1907.

hall at the Carnegie camp or the Seattle Golf Club. However, the public rooms were somewhat rustic in character. Cutter took the theme of the Indians who had once hunted and fished on Hayden Lake as an inspiration for interior details. He designed fireplaces with pointed hoods of beaten copper, embossed with Indian symbols, to represent tepees. The *Spokane Chronicle* went as far as to state that "the general style of architecture is also suggestive of Indian life."

The syndicate, anxious to romanticize their resort, held a competition for a suitable name from an Indian language. Their choice was "Bozanta," a term for "meeting place by the lake." The Bozanta Tavern, as the hotel was called, opened July 20, 1907, with a grand ball. By this time, the railroad company was offering seven trains a day. A golf course superseded the racetrack and, in addition to fishing, many other activities were available. The Bozanta Tavern became a popular destination for weekend visitors; it was occasionally patronized by Cutter himself and was visited by President Taft, who enjoyed a "game dinner" of trout, venison, and bear cub washed down with French champagne.[8] The resort is now the Hayden Lake Country Club.

At about the time Cutter was working on the Bozanta Tavern, he designed a wilderness retreat near Idaho City for Colonel Esta-

9.9 Estabrook log house, Idaho City, 1909. The rustic home of an eccentric soldier. Destroyed by fire. Idaho State Historical Society, Boise.

brook, an eccentric mining engineer from Boise (fig. 9.9).[9] This was simply constructed of solid logs, overlapping at the corners like an American pioneer cabin, and without the carved brackets and fretwork that he had used on the Finch chalet and the Hayden Lake resort. While a monumental chimney at the intersection of the main roof and a cross roof anchored it to the ground, the cabin projected boldly from the mountainside, supported on basement walls of rough-hewn stone. A balcony surrounding it was partly cantilevered and partly supported on pillars of rock.

The interiors had much in common with those at the Idaho Building at the World's Columbian Exposition, featuring fireplaces of rough rock, and interior walls and ceiling beams of whole tree trunks. However, the rugged character of the cabin was accompanied by modern conveniences, including beds that rolled electrically from the bedrooms onto sleeping porches. A bank vault, built into the foundation, was reputed to hold both gold bullion and fine wines. Here Estabrook entertained his friends, particularly members of the Boise Polo Club, with lavish hospitality.[10] The cabin was destroyed by fire in 1918, while Colonel Estabrook was serving overseas.

In 1913, Cutter further enhanced his reputation as a pioneer of rustic architecture by designing a hotel in an early national park. Summer visitors were beginning to flock to the Adirondacks, but the site of Glacier National Park in Montana was still virtually unexplored. In the 1850s, railroad companies searching for an easy way through the Rocky Mountains were thwarted by the wild terrain and its unhelpful natives. It was not until 1891 that the railway magnate James J. Hill, the Empire Builder, was able to lay tracks for the Great Northern Railway over Marias Pass, which now forms the southern boundary of the National Park. By the end of that year, the railway reached Kalispell, and two years later the transcontinental link from coast to coast was complete. In the last two years of the century, mining activity created an interest in the area, but little wealth. The natural beauty of the mountains, glaciers, and lakes was ultimately of far greater importance than any minerals.

9.10 Lake McDonald Lodge, Montana, 1912–13. An early example of rustic architecture in a national park. Photo by Hileman. Collection of the author.

The father of the movement to establish Glacier National Park was George Bird Grinnell, who rode in on horseback in 1887 and discovered the glaciers at the heads of Swift Current and Grinnell Valleys. He quickly made friends with the Blackfeet Indians and was accepted by their tribe. In 1901, Grinnell published "The Crown of the Continent" in the *Century Magazine* and thus helped to arouse popular enthusiasm for the idea of a park. The title of his article alluded to a unique feature of the place: among its peaks was the dividing point between the Pacific Ocean, Hudson Bay, and the Gulf of Mexico. An act of Congress established the park in 1910, and in 1913 Kirtland Cutter was busy designing a hotel on Lake McDonald, in response to the sublime mountain scenery (fig. 9.10).

The first hotel in the park, a very simple structure, had been built on Lake McDonald in 1895 by James Snyder, a furrier who operated a steamboat on the lake. In 1911, John Lewis, who had purchased the hotel, obtained a permit from the National Park Service to build rest cabins at the head of the lake and to operate the hotel. By now the park was attracting many visitors, and in 1912 Lewis asked Cutter to build a larger and more attractive hotel on the same site.[11] Cutter's summer homes for the Carnegies and the Finches had been firmly based on the Swiss chalet, essentially a domestic type of building. The summer camp on Raquette Lake with its large assembly hall and complex form had stretched the chalet type as far as it could go, and now Cutter took the Swiss Alpine resort hotel as his inspiration. While chalets, like classical temples, presented their gable ends to the front, the great hotels from the same region usually had the long slope of the roof facing the front with one or more cross gables at right angles to it. Lake McDonald Lodge, with its hipped cross gables at both ends of a long roof, belongs to this type. Around the exterior walls under the broad overhanging roof, continuous balconies allow the guests to enjoy views across the lake and into the forest. The wooden columns, cross braces, and handrails are reminiscent of the Adirondack style of rustic work.

Visitors first seeing the hotel from the lake would be rewarded with an image of alpine hospitality. However, on entering the hotel lobby (fig. 9.11), they would find an interior space unlike anything in Europe: a great hall rising through three stories to the crown of the roof built of massive tree trunks with their bark still intact. Cutter transformed the rustic tradition of the Adirondacks into architecture on a grander scale. In each corner of the square central space three cedar trunks rise twenty-five feet to support one end

9.11 Lobby of Lake McDonald Lodge. The columns, consisting of tree trunks with their bark intact, rise through three stories to support huge diagonal roof trusses. Glacier National Park Museum.

of a diagonally placed roof truss. Two sturdy trusses intersect at the center, where they share a common crown post. The weight of the roof rests not directly on the columns, but on two tiers of horizontal logs, the lower of which joins two columns together. Below, the same columns support a gallery running around three sides. Heavy cross braces add to the stability of the structure and help to reduce the span of the gallery.

Throughout the tall central space there is a clear hierarchy of structural members, each one scaled to the task it has to perform. They diminish in size from the huge columns to the slenderer beams carrying the galleries and principal members of the trusses. The rafters, braces, and joists carrying the galleries are thinner. Finally, the smallest timbers serve as the handrails of the balcony and stairs. Each element has a distinct role to play and is controlled by a strict grammar. The strength of the corner columns contrasts with the lightness of the handrails. The balconies almost float on

cantilevered joists, yet they appear well supported. In contrast to the awesome structure of the main space, the staircases on either side are more whimsical, with treads made of logs split in two, and balusters and handrails of gnarled and twisted branches (fig. 9.12).

An enormous fireplace, in which great logs from the forest can blaze merrily, completes the hospitable atmosphere of the great hall. On the massive lintel over the opening and on some of the irregular rocks that support it, Indian pictographs are incised as reminders of the region's heritage. The fireplace in the cabin of the western artist Charlie Russell at Apgar, on the same lake, which had sketches of Indians and animals in the concrete, may have suggested the idea to Cutter.[12] Over the hearth, hooks hang from a swiveling iron "crane" to support an iron cauldron. As in the Idaho Building in Chicago twenty years earlier, Cutter gave free reign to his imagination in devising the details.

When Cutter built Lake McDonald Lodge, the rustic tradition in National Park architecture had already been established. In 1902, Robert C. Reamer had designed the Old Faithful Inn at Yellowstone, America's first National Park. The vast central lobby of Reamer's lodge, like Cutter's, was a lofty space surrounded by galleries (fig. 9.13). Following the Adirondack style of William Durant, it makes the most of the natural curve of branches to provide decorative effects.[13] From either side of the many columns supporting the upper balconies and the roof, curved braces reach out like the upstretched arms of standing human figures. In the center, a large stone chimney rises to pass out of sight through the roof, eighty-five feet above the floor. This unique interior makes a splendid response to the landscape of Yellowstone Park.

9.13 Lobby of Old Faithful Lodge, Yellowstone National Park, Wyoming, by Robert C. Reamer, 1902. Photo by the author.

The Forestry Building at the Lewis and Clark Centennial Exposition of 1905 in Portland, Oregon, designed by Ion Lewis of Whidden and Lewis and his young assistant Albert E. Doyle, offered another precedent for rustic architecture on a grand scale. This building, described as the "world's largest log cabin" or the "Parthenon of Oregon" had an interior "nave" of unpeeled logs forty-eight feet high. This veritable cathedral of giant trees was by far the most popular attraction at the exposition and confirmed the public taste for such architecture.[14] Lake McDonald Lodge was not a direct imitation of either of the buildings mentioned, but possessed similar imagery. The rugged tree trunks rising through three stories are as powerful as those of the Forestry Building; the rustic balcony rails and lively detail at Lake McDonald seem closer to the Yellowstone building.

In the same year that Cutter built the hotel, another architect, Thomas McMahon of St. Paul, Minnesota, was building Glacier Park Hotel in the southeastern corner of the park with an interior space remarkably similar to the "nave" of the Forestry Building.[15] As in the exposition structure, the great tree trunks dominate, dwarfing the individual. This lodge may contain one of the grandest spaces ever built of wood, but at Lake McDonald Cutter succeeded in creating a more inviting atmosphere.

Such a building was not easily constructed. The remote location and the sheer size of the main structural members posed a considerable challenge to the builders. All materials except the timber had to be brought in ten miles by barge from Apgar. To preserve the bark intact on the logs, the trees had to be cut in winter when the sap was not running. If they were cut too late in the spring, the sap would form a slippery layer between the bark and the wood, making it susceptible to damage. In time, the inner cambium layer turns to wood, allowing for long-term preservation, but during the entire building operation extreme care had to be exercised in handling the logs. John Lewis himself supervised the construction, and the success of this operation is evident in the fine state of preservation of these tree trunks today. Seventy years later, they are still in almost perfect condition.

In 1919, Cutter had his final opportunity to design a large summer camp, this time on a lake in western Montana. With his understanding of the needs and desires of the wealthy and his ability to design with originality in the rustic tradition, he was the ideal architect for Cornelius Kelley, president of the powerful Anaconda Company. The story of the Kelley camp begins in 1906, when Kelley's friend and associate in the legal department of Anaconda, L.O. Evans, developed a strategy to end the Montana copper wars in Anaconda's favor. Rewarded with a long vacation by the thankful company, Evans spent the entire summer at a peaceful dude ranch on Swan Lake near Kalispell, where he enjoyed the plentiful game in the forests and fish in the lake. When he returned to Butte, he told his friend Kelley that he had found heaven. Over the next few years, Evans and Kelley bought the original dude ranch and some adjoining land to create a 320–acre paradise. For over forty years the two families gathered there in July and August. As they built extra cabins to receive children, grandchildren, and important guests, the accommodations became increasingly luxurious.

Evans turned down an offer of the vice presidency of Anaconda, because he did not want to leave Montana, but in 1918 Kelley became president and moved from Butte to a Georgian mansion set on an eighty-acre estate on Long Island, New York. But he loved Montana and never missed a summer at Swan Lake. For two months each year, the camp became the company headquarters, connected by long-distance phone lines to the outside world. More significant, it was a place to which influential people could be lured and held in joyful captivity. Vital decisions were made and many important people were persuaded to support the Anaconda Company while enjoying the beauty of Swan Lake or fishing in its waters.[16]

In 1919, Cornelius Kelley called on Cutter to design a spacious lodge where he could entertain in style. Like Mrs. Carnegie, Kelley could have chosen any architect in the country; but he put his faith in a man who was little known outside the Northwest. Cutter rose to the occasion and designed a building which seemed to be part of its setting. The Kootenai Lodge "assembly hall" echoes the scale of a medieval great hall, with a roof supported on fine, exposed timber trusses (figs. 9.14, 9.15). But in response to the forest outside, all the main structural members retain their bark. Along one side, above the massive stone fireplace, runs an interior balcony, like a minstrel's gallery. Cutter contrived the structure supporting the gallery and the roof above in an original way. Clusters of four tree trunks, rising through the cantilevered gallery, hold up giant log purlins which in turn help to carry the roof. The handrail of the gallery and the staircase follow the rustic manner of the Glacier Park Hotel. Pairs of columns articulate the long wall opposite while emphasizing the support of each roof truss. The reddish peeled logs

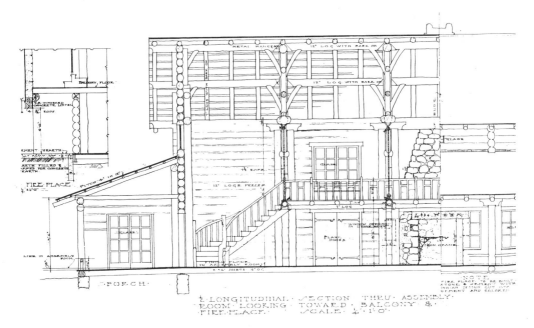

9.14 Swan Lake Camp, 1919–20, section through the great hall. Eastern Washington State Historical Society, L84–207.119.

9.15 Great hall roof structure at Swan Lake Camp. Photo by the author.

of the walls contrast with the grayer tree trunks and branches retaining their bark, which were used for columns, roof trusses, and handrails.

This space is hardly cozy. As the name implies, Kelley built it for large gatherings; and here, summer after summer, members of his elite social circle would gather before and after dinner. But the gallery, divided by the structure into three bays, offered an intimate place for private conversation. Around the assembly hall, on a screened porch furnished with large wicker armchairs, guests could relax and gaze through the trees toward the lake. Six bedrooms and four bathrooms for the Kelley family and their most important guests opened onto a courtyard beside the assembly hall. With exposed log walls, handmade rustic furniture, and large fireplaces of locally quarried stone, these rooms carried on the rustic theme. Other guests were accommodated in separate cabins. The dining hall and kitchen were also in a separate structure.

The finest of the area's log craftsmen, Ward Whitney and Fred Kitzmiller, constructed the Kootenai Lodge. The work, as it had been for Lake McDonald Lodge, was labor intensive. The logs were felled in the winter and seasoned for a year. During that time they were turned every thirty days to ensure even drying. The most arduous part of the process of preparing the logs was the careful stripping away of the outer layer of bark, leaving intact the dark brown cambium layer.

In the early days, the journey from Butte to Swan Lake, by train, stagecoach, steamer, and finally by wagon along the Swan River, took two or three days. By the time Cutter's lodge was built, the railway was bringing visitors to Whitefish, where they were met by chauffeur-driven automobiles. The Kelley family and some of their guests traveled in the "Anaconda," Con Kelley's private railroad car. Even so, the attractions of the Kootenai Lodge and its surroundings must have been unusual to entice them all the way from New York. When they arrived, they could combine the simplicity of the forest scene with the sophistication of high society. In the daytime they could ride, swim, hunt, or fish, or relax in the shade of the trees, watching the shifting light on the water. There were plenty of special events, such as picnics and regattas. Guides were available to lead expeditions and initiate urbanites in the fine points of hunting and fishing. In the evenings there were cocktail parties, barbecues, and formal dinners served as elegantly as they might have been on Long Island.

With gardeners, woodcutters, grooms, chauffeurs, night watchmen, and laundresses, there were about seventy employees on the Kelleys' payroll. The household staff of nine included Thomas Clydesdale, their impeccable Scottish butler, who saw that no luxuries were lacking and made no concessions to the backwoods. Each year he brought the silver chest from New York with fifty place settings. He had tables laid with Wedgwood china, Steuben crystal, and exquisite linen. Dinner was formal and the cuisine outstanding. Even during the 1920s, Con Kelley kept a well-stocked cellar from which he offered fine wines and bourbons, as if Prohibition didn't exist.[17]

Cutter had shown a desire to celebrate the rugged nature of natural materials in some of his earliest designs in Spokane. As opportunities arose to build in wilder places, his rustic imagery responded to the grandeur of the western landscape. His log structures from the Idaho Building to the Kootenai Lodge place him among the masters of a significant American genre.

CHAPTER TEN

The Davenport Hotel and Other Commercial Buildings (1908–1916)

BETWEEN 1908 AND 1914, KIRTLAND CUTTER WAS engaged in the creation of one of America's finest hotels for his long-standing client Louis Davenport. But this was only one of many significant buildings that he contributed to downtown Spokane. While continuing to exploit historic styles in an expressive manner, he experimented both with humanizing the office environment and handling the scale of a vast power station. In 1916 he designed a tall steel-framed office building that combined modern construction and restrained Gothic ornament. Thus he followed a national trend by embracing new technology without abandoning historicism.

Early in the century Cutter had established a reputation for hotel and restaurant design at Davenport's and the Pennington. The Hall of the Doges served as Spokane's most exotic ballroom and banqueting hall, while the Italian Gardens became one of the city's favorite eating places. As the fame of the fanciful and elaborate establishment continued to spread, plans developed to build a first-class hotel next door. On October 9, 1908, the *Spokesman-Review* announced that Spokane was to have a new 550-room, eleven-story hotel, costing $1,750,000. Although the names of the promoters were kept secret, the article disclosed that Louis Davenport, "whose restaurant has been such a big feature in advertising Spokane," was likely to become its active manager. Cutter and Malmgren, "who have made Spokane famous for its distinctive architecture," were named as the designers, and construction was to begin in the spring.

Clearly Cutter and Davenport were still dreaming in an extravagant manner. They planned an "Old Spanish design . . . highly
ornate and complex." At each corner a tower surmounted with a
dome was to rise 185 feet above the street, 35 feet higher than the
tallest building in the city. The architects proposed to focus the
hotel on a spacious central lobby with a mosaic floor, lit by a "high-
arched dome of art glass, shedding floods of multicolored light."
Around the lobby spacious mezzanine galleries supported on stone
or marble columns would connect with the Hall of the Doges, so
that banqueting and dancing could be combined. At the lower level,
patrons could choose between an elaborate new dining room or the
Italian Gardens. Cutter also proposed a large assembly room on the
top two floors with the acoustics of a church or a theater. All bedrooms were to have outside light and private bathrooms. Chilled
drinking water from deep wells under the hotel would be piped to
every guest room and would also be used in an ingenious system
for cooling the interior spaces. The new hotel would be "second to
none in the country" in terms of "service, elegance and convenience";
yet the promoters planned "to have rooms at popular prices."

Two days later, a large drawing of the design (fig. 10.1) appeared
on the front page of the *Spokesman-Review* and floor plans were
printed inside.[1] The richly ornamented central section of the facade
seemed to be based on Spanish Renaissance sources, while massive
corner blocks stepping forward on either side belonged more to
modern America. But the skyline was flamboyantly Baroque. Curving mission gables, in sympathy with the restaurant next door, were
dwarfed by monumental corner pavilions, and the four domed towers rose three stories above the rest like the minarets of a great
mosque. Such opulence would clearly demand enormous investment. On October 20 it was announced that because of the name
and reputation of Louis Davenport, the hotel should be named
after him.[2]

In late December that year Cutter and Davenport set off on a
journey to New York, Chicago, and other eastern cities to look at
the latest developments in hotel design.[3] Several grand hotels had
been constructed recently, and the two men could not have failed
to notice that most of them were compactly built. In such examples
as the Ritz Carlton in Philadelphia and the LaSalle in Chicago, little
expense was squandered on exterior ornament. They were generally
divided like a column into three parts that might be described as a
base, a shaft, and a capital. The base, consisting of two or three sto-

ries, was generally faced in stone and richly decorated in a classical manner. The object was to catch the attention of potential patrons at street level and give an impression of a sumptuous life within. Above this, the walls were built less expensively of brick; the shaft consisted of tiers of identical bedroom windows set in a plain wall. Finally, with a flourish, the upper stories burst forth with architectural ornament again. But this was restricted to the surface of the wall and the cornice; towers, pinnacles, and domes were avoided.

Although Davenport was eager to proceed and the site was available,[4] it seems that he was having difficulties in winning over investors to his lavish plans. In the spring of 1909 two other architects, J. K. Dow and L. L. Rand, were called in to produce alternative plans and estimates.[5] However, by summer Cutter had routed the opposition. On June 24, 1909, it was announced that construction

10.1 Davenport Hotel, Spokane, 1908 project. Ink drawing by F. C. Hutchinson. This design of Spanish Baroque inspiration proved too elaborate to attract practical investors. Eastern Washington State Historical Society, L84–207.433.

would begin that year using a far simpler design by Cutter and Malmgren. They eliminated the towers and other decorative features in favor of interior comforts and the addition of a twelfth floor. They now emphasized such practical matters as enlarging the rooms and giving outside light and ventilation to the bathrooms. They reduced the number of rooms to 270, but allocated the top two floors to display rooms for the many commercial travelers who came to the city. The decision was made to allow for additional rooms in the future without having to add extra stories to the whole block. The sides facing Sprague Avenue and Lincoln Street were to be built to the twelfth floor, but a section facing First Avenue would only go to the third floor. The cost of the project, despite the simplified design, was now estimated at $2,200,000, including site and furnishings.[6]

Although the Davenport Hotel Company was planning to issue bonds both locally and in the East, the response was slow. Hopeful again, Davenport announced early in January 1911 that construction would start in the spring,[7] but more than another year elapsed while complex negotiations and further revisions to the design continued. Finally, on July 25, 1912, a banner headline in the *Spokesman-Review* proclaimed: "DAVENPORT HOTEL COSTING $2,000,000 TO BE STARTED AT ONCE." An impressive new rendering beneath it showed the revised design of the hotel. The years of study and refinement had culminated in a strong, unified composition, very different from the eccentric and overbuilt proposal of 1908 (fig. 10.2). Construction began the following winter.[8]

The design followed the tripartite division typical of modern hotels, but Cutter provided a strong continuity between the base of Boise sandstone and the ornamental "capital" at the top. Above the massive stone supports that carried arches at street level, red brick piers rose the entire height of the building, emphasizing verticality. Between them the lines of identical bedroom windows of eight floors culminated in tall, arched windows uniting two stories with a decorative flourish of white terra cotta. The rusticated stone base of the hotel and the design of its upper windows, modeled on palaces in fifteenth-century Florence, gave a key to the new design theme. Described as Florentine, it was intended to symbolize the progressive nature of Spokane's civic and business leaders. These men were likened to the wealthy burghers of Renaissance Florence, who as inheritors of the culture of Greece, Rome, and Constantinople, employed art as a symbol of strength.[9]

10.2 Davenport Hotel, revised design, July 1912. With its two-story stone base and Florentine windows uniting the top two stories, this became the basis of the final design. Eastern Washington State Historical Society.

Another perspective rendering showed that the interior had also undergone revisions (fig. 10.3). The architects had enlarged the atrium and flooded it with light from the sky. They surrounded it with broad mezzanine galleries supported, like the roof above, on pillars of white Caen stone, the material used in many French Gothic cathedrals. They envisioned the lobby as a social focus and a place to accommodate large gatherings and conventions, and for symbolic reasons chose a Spanish Renaissance style. The patio of the typical Spanish house was considered "wonderfully expressive of the hospitality so characteristic of the Spanish people." In this

10.3 Atrium of the
Davenport Hotel,
revised design, July
1912. Cutter's inten-
tion was to recreate
the welcoming,
vine-covered patio
of a Spanish house.
Watercolor render-
ing. Eastern Washing-
ton State Historical
Society.

open court "the only roof . . . was the vine-covered arbor through
which could be seen the southern skies." Cutter aimed to obtain the
same effect by opening skylights of opalescent glass between transverse beams. He even conceived an ingenious scheme to heighten
the effect with a silver light moving slowly in an arc above the skylight, creating the illusion of the moon moving through the sky.[10]

The new renderings encouraged the investors to finance the construction. However, while the land was being cleared and work on
the foundations began, the architects continued to refine the design.
In the final scheme (fig. 10.4), they increased the base to three stories, permitting taller arches to rise through the first two floors. They
reduced the shaft from eight to six stories and added a further story
above the Florentine windows. With these changes, the total number of stories remained the same, but the proportions improved.
The loftier base looked more gracious at street level and provided
more continuity with the original restaurant; the rooms within now

10.4 Davenport Hotel as built with altered proportions, 1912. A full mezzanine is added to the base, and a story is added above the Florentine
windows, while the central portion is reduced. Davenport's restaurant
and the Pennington are visible at the left. Eastern Washington State
Historical Society, L86–532.

THE DAVENPORT HOTEL AND OTHER COMMERCIAL BUILDINGS 241

10.5 The entablature above the second story of the Davenport Hotel. The white terra cotta device in the center symbolizes the ideals of Spokane by combining the ram's head for determination, Mercury's staff for commerce, and the closed helmet for protection. Photo by Libby. Eastern Washington State Historical Society.

had more generous windows. The enormous upper windows looked less cramped and the cornice stronger. The smaller cornice above the second floor was emblazoned with heraldic devices—a closed helmet symbolizing protection, Mercury's staff with entwined serpents, representing commerce, and most prominently a ram's head for "push and determination" (fig. 10.5).[11]

The design of the atrium also evolved (fig. 10.6). For structural reasons, the columns became sturdier. The transverse beams deepened and the secondary beams were more closely spaced to reduce the size of the glass panels. To reinforce the Spanish influence and convey Davenport's ideals, Cutter developed an elaborate system of iconography. Portrait medallions carved on the beams spanning the huge space evoked the Spanish tradition of honoring ancestors. They were interspersed with national coats of arms, griffins, "symbolic of strength . . . alertness, swiftness and rapidity of execution," and dolphins, "associated in mythology with sociability." The helmet was repeated inside to offer "protection." The friezes on the carved beams of the lobby were painted with a palette of colors taken from the Moorish tradition that had flowered so exquisitely in Spain. The beams, actually of steel and concrete, were painted to simulate oak, but their sides bore carved and painted designs in blue, red, and gold "glazed over with gray to give an antique effect." The beams of the mezzanine echoed those of the atrium (fig. 10.7).[12] Cutter referred to books in his library for examples of Spanish architecture and clearly found inspiration in them, though he copied nothing precisely (fig. 10.8).[13]

10.6 Davenport Hotel, the atrium as built. The "living room of Spokane," as originally furnished. Eastern Washington State Historical Society, L86.87.

10.7 The mezzanine of the atrium, Davenport Hotel. Like the main beams over the atrium, the beams were emblazoned with symbols and painted in deep, rich colors. Eastern Washington State Historical Society, L87–1.10707x.

10.8 Detail of a bracket capital from a book in Cutter's library, *Renaissance Architecture and Onament in Spain.* Eastern Washington State Historical Society. Rare Books.

A monumental fireplace gave the lobby a welcoming atmosphere, and a white Italian marble fountain featured a cherub and a dolphin that spouted water. Finally, an entire pipe organ provided music at the east end. The architects designed special light fixtures appropriate to the opulence of the space: elaborate bronze lanterns, wall sconces like candelabra, and four gigantic bronze columns, spiraling and entwined with vine leaves, produced a soft exotic light. The furnishing colors were generally subtle and subdued.

Surrounding the lobby were several public rooms to suit different moods and occasions and ten shops opening to the street. Davenport's Restaurant became the grill room of the hotel, while a new and grander restaurant, known as the Isabella Room, was built off the south side of the lobby next to the enlarged kitchens. Davenport named it in honor of Queen Isabella of Spain, whose "imagination, confidence and unselfishness" had helped Columbus on his voyage of discovery (fig. 10.9).[14] The impression on entering the new restaurant, decorated in a Spanish Renaissance style, was of white

10.9 The Isabella Dining Room in the Davenport Hotel. Photo by Libby. Eastern Washington State Historical Society, L84–207.4.13.

columns and arches against a background of soft pastel shades. Light from large south-facing windows, draped with rose-colored velvet, played on the eight Corinthian columns that divided the room into three spacious aisles. Many mirrors increased the effect of luminance.

In a frieze on the face of the beams across the room, plantlike forms made arabesques around figures of young boys, rabbits, foxes, and turtles.[15] In contrast to this lyrical theme, the capitals of the columns incorporated grotesque heads as a reminder that "the sculptors of the Middle Ages delighted thus to portray the features of their friends and enemies." This medieval counterpoint to Renaissance serenity was reinforced by gargoyle-like figures with the bodies of lions, human heads, and cloven hoofs on the bolsters supporting the ceiling beams. Chandeliers hung from the mouths of these chimeras (fig. 10.10).

10.10 Capital in the Isabella Dining Room, Davenport Hotel. Eastern Washington State Historical Society. L84–207.4.4.

10.11 The Marie Antoinette Ballroom at the Davenport Hotel, in use for a ball. Eastern Washington State Historical Society, L84–207.159.

The Chinese Buffet between the west end of the lobby and Lincoln Street was intended as "distinctly a man's room," breathing "the spirit of masculinity." But Cutter's design, unlike the typical western saloon, was delicate and sophisticated. He had it finished in dark suki wood with much fretwork and carved capitals picked out in gold, red, and blue. The light entering through the large windows was softened as it passed through screens of latticework and paper. Among ebony furniture, the centerpiece of the decor was a large bronze bowl supported by two sinuous dragons "from the shrine of an old Chinese family of rank."[16]

At mezzanine level, Cutter evoked eighteenth-century France in the Marie Antoinette Ballroom, with its fully sprung dance floor surrounded by upper galleries (fig. 10.11).[17] Honoring the French queen for restoring classic ideals in design after the "vulgar ornateness of the previous era," the architects aimed for a chaste elegance.

They accented decorative moldings on walls, galleries, and ceiling beams with a color scheme of ivory and French gray. To give a festive touch, they ornamented the fascias of the gallery with plaster medallions of court jesters, garlanded with laurel leaves. Three superb crystal chandeliers completed the scene. From the gallery level, French windows opened onto a formally planted roof garden with a promenade between shrubs and flowers and ornate lights that created the effect of a "fairyland."[18]

To allow this ballroom to be used for banquets as well as balls, a large servery was built with stair and elevator connections to the kitchen. It also served the Hall of the Doges and the Elizabethan Room on the north side. This smaller banquet room, divisible into three by folding partitions, added yet another national theme. The dark oak paneling, adorned with heraldic crests, proclaimed that the style was Old English. Ornamental plaster work on the ceiling emulated late Tudor designs, and the furniture, all in oak, was "conscientiously copied after the most famous Elizabethan pieces in existence."[19] Even the solid silver chandeliers were a reminder of the wealth of English country houses.

The cloakroom, the ladies' retiring rooms, and the beauty salon that opened off the mezzanine attained similar standards of luxury; and the men's barbershop in the basement, named the Pompeiian Room, was opulently finished in white marble on a background of Pompeiian red. The motorist who arrived "all dusty and with hands covered with grease" could expect special attention there: in half an hour he could be "turned out by the barber, manicurist and valet a spick-and-span new man with pressed clothes."[20] The male preserve of the basement also included a billiard room with twelve tables and a Turkish bath.

While the public rooms offered the patron an escape into a dream world, the bedrooms were intended to be homelike. The aim was "an utter absence of gaudy trappings." Davenport, arguing that the weary traveler was not very particular whether the bed "was made after the style of Elizabeth or of Louis XIV," installed simple mahogany furniture. He considered the provision of fine mattresses and a restful environment with clean fresh air more important.[21] There were 406 guest rooms, 370 of which had private baths. In the final design, the bathrooms were not placed on the exterior wall, as proposed earlier, but they were separately ventilated. Several opulent suites, including the state suite, were designed for such important guests as presidents of the United States, accompanied by their entire cabinet if necessary, and for senators, governors, movie stars, and tycoons. But room prices started at $1.50. Such a reasonable rate encouraged the less affluent traveler to spend more freely in the dining room.

Louis Davenport stated his own priorities in hotel management: "I consider, first Utility; second, Life; third, Beauty. I place utility first, for the reason that service is the keynote of successful hotel keeping."[22] By "life," he meant the safety and durability of the structure and all the systems within it. Cutter and Malmgren designed the steel frame, encased in concrete, and the hollow tile walls to ensure stability and eliminate the danger of fire spreading through the hotel. As an extra precaution, they installed fireproof doors and sprinklers in the basement. They used materials of the highest quality, and behind the scenes provided elaborate systems to produce, as if by magic, whatever the guests might need. Elevators with silent doors ran smoothly up and down the building; twenty clocks, synchronized by a master, kept perfect time in all parts of the building; a complex lock system allowed staff to know whether rooms were occupied; in the basement a marble switchboard 26 feet long and 10 feet high controlled the electrical system. To keep the hotel clean, they installed a central vacuum system and designed mobile carts for the maids that included even a desk to keep notes. The artesian well, 662 feet deep, produced 400 gallons of water per minute; and twenty miles of pipe delivered it wherever it was required. Iced water, available on tap in every room, was distilled and kept continually circulating, insulated by a layer of cork. The forty-ton refrigeration plant was put in not only to provide ice; it chilled food in the storerooms, cooled countertops on which the chefs worked, and even froze the garbage before it left the hotel. The Davenport was cooled by an ingenious forerunner of air conditioning in which the air was filtered and cooled with chilled water. The kitchen equipment was of the latest and most efficient design available; the kitchens were planned so that four thousand meals a day could be served.[23] In short, the Davenport Hotel and restaurant contained both a dazzling collection of spaces intended to evoke a magical world of fantasy and the latest in American technology.

The citizens of Spokane watched with a sense of excitement as the Davenport Hotel neared completion. The press constantly raised popular expectations with such headlines as "DAVENPORTS IS WONDERLAND."[24] Finally, in the early evening of September 1, 1914, the hotel was "besieged by an admiring crowd." When the moment

10.12 The Crescent, Spokane, 1910–11. With its broad bracketed eaves and decorative tile work, Cutter gave this department store a distinctive character. Altered. Photo by W. O. Reed, Spokane. Eastern Washington State Historical Society, L84–207.4.84.

came for the doors to open, hundreds flooded in. Despite the press of people, "the service that evening was conducted as smoothly as if the hotel had been open for months."[25]

During the next fifty years, the Davenport functioned as the center of Spokane's social and business life. Civic groups, business people, and pleasure-seekers gathered there; it was the venue for all kinds of celebrations, from graduation dances to weddings. Important visitors were feted in the banquet rooms, and Spokane attracted huge conventions only because of the hotel. One patron described it as "a wonderful palace, where rich and poor, old friends and strangers alike can find not a mere shelter, but instantaneous home."[26]

While Cutter and Malmgren were waiting to proceed with the Davenport Hotel, they designed several large, rather plain commercial blocks in Spokane. These included the four-story Sillman Hotel and Store Building of 1908, and the six-story Galax Hotel, built for the newspaper proprietor W. H. Cowles between 1908 and 1910.[27] The Galax Hotel, which displayed stone dressings of a Baroque character on the lower stories, was patronized by actors and vaudeville performers, including Charlie Chaplin, who stayed there when he played at the Empress Theater.[28]

The exterior remodeling of the Crescent store on Riverside Avenue in 1910 made a strong visual impact in downtown Spokane (fig. 10.12). The design, described as "a new departure in storefront construction . . . of a somewhat oriental type,"[29] featured a broad, bracketed roof overhang and a strong use of color. Bands of bright red Moravian tiles, with accents of blue-green and golden buff, surrounded the groups of windows.[30] The structural piers, covered with stucco in a warm shade of light gray, made a neutral background against which the colors glowed. The large expanses of glass, combined with smooth panels of tiling, appeared strikingly modern.

Cutter's design for the Western Union Life Insurance Company building (fig. 10.13) stands out from his other commercial work as an imaginative attempt to humanize the office building. The trend

10.13 Western Union Life Insurance Company, Spokane, 1909–10. Cutter designed this building on a human scale, to resemble the house of a seventeenth-century Dutch merchant, surrounded by a garden. Encased in a larger building by G. A. Pehrson, 1923. Eastern Washington State Historical Society, L84–207.4.50.

in American office buildings during the previous twenty-five years had been toward functional efficiency, the formal organization of large volumes, and the expression of verticality; but in this business office Cutter made a pitch for human scale. He wanted clients to feel that they were being welcomed into the personal domain of a gracious host.

The client for this project, R. L. Rutter, for whom Cutter had designed a somewhat rustic Arts and Crafts cottage in 1895, appreciated the architect's artistic sense and could be persuaded to build something "absolutely distinctive in style." The design was unveiled with considerable fanfare June 8, 1909, at a dinner in the Gothic Room at Davenport's. In the presence of M. E. Hay, the governor of Washington, and the directors of the company, Kirtland Cutter presented his proposal "for a strikingly beautiful Dutch structure . . . of red brick, laid in white cement, with a red tiled roof," standing back from Riverside Avenue "in a Dutch garden with a level lawn, trimmed with quaint formal trees and foliage." A low wall, "in keeping with the Flemish architecture," was to enclose the grounds. The *Spokesman-Review* reported that it would "look for all the world like a medieval Hollandish house, transplanted here from Amsterdam or Rotterdam or some other of the—dam cities."[31] In fact, the design was more like a Dutch house of the early seventeenth century. Although stepped gables of a medieval type surmounted its dormer windows, the regular, symmetrical block with a hipped roof was essentially classical in form.[32]

Avoiding a formal entrance on the principal facade facing Madison Street, Cutter made a more humble entry through a lower wing on the north side facing Riverside. This cottagelike structure (fig. 10.14) evoked the world of Vermeer and Pieter de Hooch; its stepped gable and low roof, sweeping down over the doorway, contrasted with the more classical form of the main block. Visitors were to approach through a wrought iron arch and, after crossing the garden, enter through a simple Dutch Renaissance doorway. They would then find themselves in a comfortable hall with a large inglenook fireplace (fig. 10.15) and French windows, leading to a landscaped courtyard. Above the hearth, a mural decoration in the Art Nouveau Style represented two deer with their young on either side of a stylized tree. The frieze of curling peacock feathers repeated the theme of the Peacock Room at Davenport's. The interior, designed more for public appeal than efficiency, seemed more domestic than commercial.

10.14 Kirtland Cutter beside the entry to the Western Union Life Insurance Company building into which he moved his office in 1911. Eastern Washington State Historical Society, L93–66.234.

10.15 The fireplace in the hall of the Western Union Life Insurance Company continues the domestic theme. The wall decoration is Cutter's last Art Nouveau design. *Architect and Engineer*, June 1921.

An unusual aspect of the project was that the company included future expansion in their planning. Rutter stated that the new headquarters would meet the needs of the company for the next eight or ten years, but "eventually it must give way to a big office building covering all the ground." To solve the problem of increasing the size of a block placed in the middle of its site, the architects generated a daring proposal, "to build the entire structure on steel beams, set on steel rollers, buried in the foundation.[33] True to Rutter's prediction, the insurance company's office was enlarged considerably in 1923, but it was not moved as originally suggested. The Dutch house disappeared within a larger structure that entirely surrounded it. Cutter's plan to set a building of domestic scale in the middle of the site had beguiled the committee, but it did not allow realistically for expansion.

Cutter's design for the insurance company was an immediate success. Within a few months of its completion in the spring of 1910, the University Club, recognizing it as "one of the most attractive of the odd buildings of Spokane," made an offer to buy it. Rutter told the press that they certainly would not sell, or if they did "not for less than $150,000" (three times the cost of construction). He retorted: "It is an artistic building and built to suit our needs."[34]

The building committee, which included Louis Davenport, met with James Dawson of the Olmsted Brothers to develop a landscape plan, and described him as "one of the finest men we have ever met." Committing $2,000 for plants, they implemented a lavish planting program in the fall of 1909, even before the construction was complete.[35] On the north side they planted rhododendrons, cedars, and other evergreens. To the west, facing Madison Street, they selected flowering shrubs for a variety of flowers and foliage. They planted ten thousand crocus bulbs in the courtyard and on the front lawn by the entrance.[36] The following February, in time to enjoy the crocuses in flower, Cutter and Malmgren moved their offices from the Exchange Bank to the spacious attic of the new Western Union Life Insurance Company building.[37]

In 1909, Cutter designed elegant and spacious new premises for the Spokane Club on Riverside Avenue opposite the Western Union Life Insurance Company (fig. 10.16). His recent design for the Silver Bow Club in Butte had been dominated, like the Rainier Club in Seattle, by a curvaceous Dutch gable. This time he chose to work in a Georgian manner. Using red brick with terra cotta dressings, Cutter organized the building symmetrically with a central block stand-

10.16 Spokane Club, Spokane, 1909–11. The central feature of this building in the Georgian Colonial Revival Style incorporates the head of an
Indian warrior and a symbol of the rising sun. Photo by the author.

ing forward from wings on either side. The wings express the quiet
dignity of a pair of Georgian town houses, while the central section
carries more ornament. He emphasized horizontality by means of
a rusticated lower story of white terra cotta, a projecting cornice
above the third floor, and a balustrade concealing the roof. But, on
the center of the facade facing Riverside, the accent is vertical and
the design takes a step toward the Baroque. Coupled Ionic columns
flanking a pedimented window over the entrance carry a bold entablature. Above this feature, the wall is ornamented with a large medallion of an Indian warrior, above which a curved pediment with
jagged profile culminates in a symbol of the rising sun.

  The interior provided the comfort and distinction of a traditional
gentlemen's club. The principal rooms, as was usual in Cutter's
designs, offered variety. The lounge and billiard room, finished in
English oak, were conservatively masculine in character; the dining
room, with white Ionic columns and an elaborate plaster ceiling,
conveyed a classic elegance (fig. 10.17); the card room, decorated

The dining
room at the Spokane
Club conveys a clas-
sic elegance. Eastern
Washington State
Historical Society,
L84–207.4.77.

with an intricate latticework design, appeared like a garden pavilion. The north-facing dining room opened on splendid views, over
sunken gardens, of the falls of the Spokane River.

Cutter also undertook a vast industrial project in 1909. In the
Washington Water Power Post Street Substation, built by the falls
of the Spokane River, he achieved a simple grandeur. The large red-
brick power station (fig. 10.18) stands beside the falls on a base of
rubble-coursed basalt, and bridges one branch of the cascade. The
heroic scale of the pier and arch structure gives an impression of
strength and unity. Between the massively built corners, nine tall,
arched windows open up the centers of the long facades. The graceful system of piers and arches, reminiscent of a Roman aqueduct,
echoes the composition of the Marshall Field Warehouse of H. H.

Richardson, who had provided Cutter and his contemporaries with
architectural models of several types. But Cutter, unable to resist
allusions to past glories of European architecture, placed towers at
the four corners, capped with bulbous domes surmounted by globes
and flagpoles. He formed the cornice of the giant structure of corbeled bricks somewhat like the machicolations of a medieval castle.

The Washington Water Power Substation, completed in 1911, celebrated the success of a company that had contributed enormously
to Spokane's prosperity. F. Rockwood Moore, the first president
of the Washington Water Power Company, had been Cutter's first
client for a mansion. His successor and the current president,
Henry M. Richards, had built a house designed by Cutter in 1895
and was on the building committee of the Western Union Life
Insurance Company.[38] The architect's success still rested on the
trust placed in him by men of influence in the city.

10.18 Washington
Water Power Post
Street Substation,
Spokane, 1909–11.
Built according to
Richardsonian prin-
ciples of composition
to match the heroic
scale of the falls.
*Architect and Engi-
neer,* June 1921.

City Engineer John Chester Ralston designed a bridge to cross the gorge of the Spokane River just below the falls, opposite the power station. Since building intermediate supports was unwise, Ralston spanned the torrent in a single, gigantic reinforced concrete arch complemented with smaller arches at either end. At the time of construction, in 1910, the 281–foot main arch was the largest structure of its type in the United States and the third largest in the world. It was exceeded only by bridges in Aukland, New Zealand, and Rome, Italy. Cutter was commissioned to design handrails and four small lookout pavilions placed over the main structural piers. He aimed to increase the pedestrians' sense of security as they walked over the thundering falls by placing the lookout shelters at intervals along the span. Scaling them carefully to mediate between the grandeur of the bridge and the human pedestrian, he conceived them as integral elements of a great work of engineering. Responding to the dramatic context, he ornamented the sides of the shelters facing the roadway with life-size concrete replicas of bison skulls (fig. 10.19). Cutter's first drawings of 1910 show heads of American Indians in profile, complete with feather headdresses, cast in concrete, and forms like the prows of canoes projecting over the water from each of the structures.[39] In addition, small bison skulls appeared beneath the arched openings. However, by 1911, Cutter had

10.19 Monroe Street Bridge, Spokane, 1910–11. Lookout pavilion with bison skull emblem. Cutter's Washington Water Power Substation is seen in the background. Photo by the author.

10.20 Holy Trinity
Church, Wallace,
Idaho, 1910. The fire-
flashed clinker bricks
give character to the
walls and tower of
this simple church.
Photo by the author.

simplified the design by eliminating the Indians and enlarging the
skulls to symbolize the power of the bridge, while recalling the pre-
history of the region.[40] The massive guardrails were designed with a
chain motif that gave a feeling of strength and continuity. From the
bridge, people could stop and admire not only the spectacular falls
but also Cutter's power station standing confidently beside it.

In the 1910 design for Holy Trinity Episcopal Church in Wallace,
Idaho (fig. 10.20), Cutter gave a rugged strength to a small building
by using hard burnt, fire-flashed bricks like those of the Rainier Club
in Seattle. The principal feature of its gable end was a large Gothic
window with stone tracery. On the surface of its walls, bricks project aggressively in a manner popular in the American Craftsman
movement.

In July 1911, Cutter had the honor of serving on the jury of the competition for the design of a new Washington State Capitol in Olympia. The jury, which consisted of Charles H. Bebb, who had supervised the construction of Cutter's Stimson house in Seattle, Cutter, and the San Francisco architect William F. Faville, met July 31 to begin the selection process (fig. 10.21). They spent the next three days examining the thirty sets of drawings submitted, and on August 3 announced to the State Capitol Commission that they had selected a proposal by Wilder and White of New York City. They had indeed chosen a promising design and one that, with modifications, would prove successful. The essence of the architects' problem, addressed in the final design, was "to create a domed Legislative building in harmony with the other campus structures and yet sufficiently scaled to be the central presence of the group as a whole."[41]

10.21 The Washington State Capitol Commission and Jury of Architects, July 31, 1911. Kirtland Cutter, Charles Bebb, and William Faville. Eastern Washington State Historical Society, L84–207.4.41.

10.22 Camp Lewis Gate, near Tacoma, Washington, 1915. Cutter adapted the vocabulary of his rustic architecture to evoke the imagery of the western fort. Eastern Washington State Historical Society.

Reverting to his rustic manner in 1915, Cutter designed a gateway to Camp Lewis, south of Tacoma (fig. 10.22). Chester Thorne, who was instrumental in having the military camp located on this site near American Lake, may have helped to secure the commission for Cutter. The gateway to the military establishment, built of rough-hewn stone and logs, took its inspiration from the design of forts in the early years of the Washington Territory. Two "fortified" block-houses, similar to those that existed at Fort Nisqually near Tacoma, supported a canopy made of whole tree trunks, spanning the road-way. Stone arches allowed the passage of pedestrians on either side. As in Saint Andrew's Church, Chelan, Cutter evoked the pioneer experience in the Northwest.

10.23 John A. Finch Mausoleum, Riverside Cemetery, Spokane, 1915–16, in the Doric order. A Classical tomb for one who lived in one of Cutter's few Classical houses. Photo by the author.

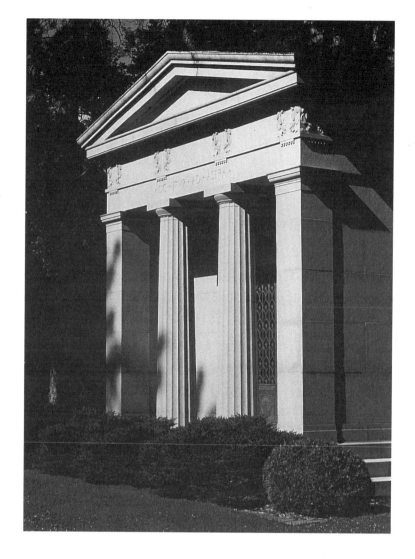

In contrast, Cutter designed a mausoleum for his former client John A. Finch in Riverside Cemetery in 1915 (fig. 10.23). Unlike his Fairmont Cemetery Chapel, built in 1891 of rugged basalt and shingles, this creation is a pristine structure of white granite in the Doric Style, like a classical Greek Treasury at Delphi or Olympia. The strength of this building lies in its simplicity and adherence to classical proportions. Only in the frieze does it depart from the dictates of the Doric order. The frieze consists not of the usual triglyphs and metopes, but is ornamented with garlands of leaves and pinecones, one above each column, bringing a touch of nature to the precise and formal architecture.[42]

In 1916, Cutter and Malmgren designed another industrial building for Spokane, the city steam plant, not far from the Davenport Hotel. This building lacks the conspicuous position of the Washington Water Power Substation by the falls, but the architects attempted a similarly bold form, in which five tall arches, outlined in white stone, stand out against the background of red brick. A heavy white cornice running around the top of the wall makes a strong, horizontal line, echoed on the side elevations by another white band linking the sills of the upper windows. Two tall chimneys rise above the surrounding buildings.

During World War I, Cutter and Malmgren took on several small commissions that demonstrate a change in the character of small commercial structures at this time. Henry Bertelsen could quickly turn out designs for small stores, banks, and automobile dealers, varying the embellishments for variety. These projects, precursors to the Art Deco architecture that was to flourish a decade later, helped to keep the office going at a time when work was short.

Two major office buildings in 1916 marked the new stylistic phase in Cutter's commercial work. His first office buildings in the 1890s had been imposing Richardsonian edifices with huge masonry arches dominating their facades. In the first decade of the twentieth century, he had experimented with various architectural types, ranging from playful versions of the Mission Revival to the Beaux Arts Style. In the Western Union Life Insurance Company building he had deliberately avoided the commercial image, preferring to create something on a domestic scale. In contrast, his Sherwood and Chronicle buildings (figs. 10.24, 10.25) draw from the emerging American tradition of the skyscraper. As business flourished, ambitious corporate directors wanted to display the commercial power of their companies in grandiose towers. Their architects eagerly responded by deploying classical and medieval motifs, often quite indiscriminately, on their facades. Because the Gothic had always been associated with verticality, it tended to predominate over the Classical. Thus many steel-framed buildings were decorated with Gothic tracery and flying buttresses, even sprouting pinnacles and gargoyles. Cass Gilbert, in his soaring 792–foot Woolworth building on Broadway in New York, took inspiration from the Gothic, but in a more forward-looking manner. He allowed piers and mullions to rise sheer through several stories, then balanced them with horizontal bands of Gothic ornament. Finally, he finished the tower with a flourish, terminating it with a distinctly Gothic crown.

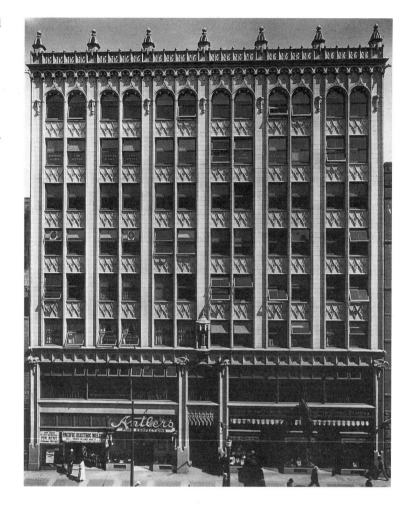

10.24 The Sherwood Building, Spokane, 1915–16. A steel-framed office building with a hint of Gothic ornamentation. Photo by Libby. Eastern Washington State Historical Society, L94–36.70.

In his Sherwood and Chronicle buildings, which were faced in terra cotta, Cutter followed the Sullivanesque tripartite division into base, shaft, and capital. He designed the lower stories to attract the eye, lavishing ornamentation on the doorways. He fronted the office floors with many identical windows; structural piers alternating with slim mullions rise without interruption to the top, where they join in a series of arches. The attics are not as massive as Sullivan's, nor do they overhang the walls as most of his had done; indeed that of the Chronicle is extremely light.

Following the New York precedent, he chose a Gothic ornamentation of the structural frame. In a series of three preliminary studies for the Chronicle he explored the possibilities of different proportions and details. They had in common the division of windows

into three lights—a wide one in the center flanked by narrower
openings on either side. While emphasizing the primacy of the
structural piers, all three designs achieved a more subtle rhythm
of verticals than appeared on the Sherwood building. Two of the
sketches showed elaborate finials above the structural piers; the
third kept the skyline simpler.

10.25 The Chronicle Building, Spokane, 1916–24. The Gothic ornament
is in keeping with the expression of verticality. Eastern Washington State
Historical Society, L87.1.37298.28A.

THE DAVENPORT HOTEL AND OTHER COMMERCIAL BUILDINGS

The design, fully developed in working drawings by Henry Bertelsen,[43] was enlivened with curvilinear tracery. In a band around the attic, the pointed arches of the top-floor windows became part of a system of interlacing ogival tracery in a Venetian manner. Each of the piers was ornamented, at this level, with a little pointed form suggestive of the gable of a medieval buttress pier. Heraldic shields, flanked by lions, adorned the spandrel panels.

As the war affected the economy, W. H. Cowles, the proprietor of the *Chronicle*, decided to delay construction of his building for a few years. In fact, it was not built until 1924, after Cutter had left Spokane. At that time "Gus" Pehrson, who supervised the construction, consulted with Cutter over final changes. The principal difference in the executed structure was the division of the space between the structural piers into two windows, rather than three, an alteration that somewhat diminished the richness of the facade. The ornamentation of the attic was simplified and the structural piers were carried above the roofline like pinnacles. But essentially the Chronicle was built according to the original design, and although Pehrson often claimed that he was really the architect, his role was mainly that of construction supervisor.[44] In its dazzling white terra cotta, the Chronicle building stands as a monument to that period when architects conceived tall office buildings in the Gothic spirit. That movement culminated in Raymond Hood's winning design in the Chicago Tribune Tower Competition of 1923. It is worth noting that W. H. Cowles's father was the business manager at the *Tribune* in the late nineteenth century, and the Cowles family held an interest in the Chicago paper at the time of the competition, as they still do.

CHAPTER ELEVEN

Variations on an Old English Theme (1908–1920)

IN 1911, MRS. EDGAR DE WOLFE, A WELL-KNOWN SOCIETY decorator, described Kirtland Cutter as "a genius in the production of English residences."[1] She was referring to his design for Thornewood near Tacoma, the most authentic of his houses in the Tudor Style (fig. 11.1). But Thornewood, completed that year, was only one of at least twenty-six houses for which Cutter was inspired by Old English architecture during his career. Although these houses had many elements in common, no two were exactly alike. Each was a variation on a well-loved theme. The period between 1908 and 1910 was a particularly fertile time in which Cutter continued to mature in this style of architecture. It was also a time when he intensified his collaboration with the Olmsted Brothers and developed a close relationship with James Dawson, the western representative of that landscape firm. Dawson was a sensitive and skilled professional who was later to play a decisive role in Cutter's career.

Cutter had a far greater affinity for the irregular character of late medieval English houses, with their picturesque gables and dormers, than for more disciplined classical types, and he persuaded some of his most affluent and prestigious clients to share his preference. Many wealthy Americans of the day were attracted to the Old English styles, partly because they originated in a prosperous era that appeared intriguingly romantic. They evoked an aristocratic way of life combined with rural charm; they could be associated with Good Queen Bess, William Shakespeare, and the novels of Sir Walter Scott. Such architecture also allowed the architect a freedom

11.1 Thornewood, home of Chester Thorne, American Lake near Tacoma, 1909–11. Cutter's most faithful interpretation of a Tudor manor house in brick. Collection of the author.

of planning not possible in classical houses, which demanded symmetry and order. Cutter's Old English houses, like those of most American architects, tended to be eclectic. They were based on examples from the reigns of both Tudor and Stuart monarchs, often mixing features of more than one period.[2] Cutter also profited from the wide range of materials, and traditional details, that gave distinctive character to the buildings of different regions. Thus within a single city he offered an astonishing variety of forms.

He had acquired a familiarity with such architecture while traveling in England, and had reinforced his knowledge with the help of illustrated books.[3] But he must also have been influenced by recent houses designed by English architects of the Arts and Crafts movement, such as Shaw, Nesfield, Voysey, and Baillie-Scott, whose works were illustrated in American journals. American architects, like Wilson Eyre, whose designs in the Old English manner were published on both sides of the Atlantic, also provided models for architects of Cutter's time.[4] It is not surprising that Cutter was a good friend of Samuel Maclure, one of the leading architects of British Columbia, who built many Tudoresque houses in Victoria. Unlike Cutter, Maclure did not indulge in a wide variety of stylistic experiments; he adhered closely to the Arts and Crafts principles from which Cutter sometimes strayed. But he admired Cutter's work and enjoyed his company on several visits to Spokane.[5]

Cutter's interest in Tudor houses was first apparent in 1889 in his designs for the Moore and Glover houses. Their rambling assembly of half-timbered gables and dormers certainly suggests English origins, but their design was also inspired by American houses in the Shingle Style. In his next group of houses of Tudor origin between 1897 and 1900, for Campbell, F. Lewis Clark, and Stimson, Cutter was more faithful to sixteenth-century prototypes. The low-pitched roofs of the Glover and Moore houses gave way to steeper roofs more like those in England; and he based details more accurately on the oak-framed houses of the Tudor period. However, Cutter derived some of his details from German types, reflecting his experience in Germany as a student.[6]

Between 1904 and 1908, Cutter designed several Old English houses in Spokane, in which he continued to vary the composition, materials, and details to make each one distinctive. In 1907, he was responsible for the red-brick, many-gabled C. J. Smith house on Capitol Hill in Seattle. This design was the first of a series of impressive houses in the Old English manner which can be counted among his finest works.

Of all Cutter's Old English houses, the one that came closest to historic authenticity was Thornewood (1909–11), built in beautifully landscaped gardens on the east shore of American Lake, thirteen miles south of Tacoma.[7] His client, Chester Thorne, was a shrewd, well-educated, and much traveled man whose sound financial judgment had brought him great wealth. Born in New York in 1863 and trained in civil engineering at Yale, Thorne gained experience in the engineering and transportation department of the Missouri Pacific before coming to Tacoma in 1890. Here he turned to banking and within three years became the president of the National Bank of Commerce. During the panic of 1893 he managed to keep the bank solvent, and over the following years contributed significantly to

Tacoma by supporting ventures that boosted the economic growth of the city and attracted investment from the East Coast. He was associated with cold storage, shipping, gypsum production, and the lumber industry, but his most important role was in the development of the Port of Tacoma. After Thornewood was built, he was instrumental in the creation of Mount Rainier National Park, and the location of Fort Lewis not far from the site of the mansion.[8]

Before appointing Cutter as his architect, Thorne engaged the Olmsted Brothers to lay out his estate and design the gardens. It was to Cutter's credit that Thorne chose him, with the approval of John C. Olmsted, over the many competent architects practicing on the Northwest Coast. Thorne knew exactly what he wanted: a truly convincing Tudor house, set in gardens that would equal those of great English estates.

John C. Olmsted visited the site in June 1908, made his preliminary analysis, and immediately fixed the position of the house. Thorne wanted work on the landscape to begin while the planning for the house and gardens proceeded,[9] and by September of that year he had employed a skilled gardener, Leonard Macomber, to oversee the landscaping under the direction of James Dawson. Within four months twenty men and some teams of horses were at work on the site.[10] They were determined to design a garden appropriate to the topography. In the fall of 1908, on five or six Sundays, Macomber went with packhorses up into the foothills of Mount Rainier to collect plants native to the region that could be used on the Thornewood estate.[11] He took the plants by train and finally by truck to the site. In addition, Macomber sent the Olmsted Brothers a list of thirty-eight species of plants found in the foothills of Mount Rainier. Early in 1909 a permanent gardener, Alex MacDougall, was selected from a list prepared in the Olmsted office to oversee the creation of the gardens. Although he was employed directly by Thorne, he took his orders from Dawson and Olmsted and represented them in various disputes about the work.[12]

The Olmsted Brothers' plan for Thornewood (fig. 11.2), designed primarily by James Dawson,[13] followed principles established by Frederick Law Olmsted in the early days of the firm. The plan was based on respect for the topography but also included more formal elements. The estate was entered by an avenue leading from the lodge gate along the northeast side of the land. After running straight between formally planted trees along the boundary, it curved gently to the left, then to the right through random, more

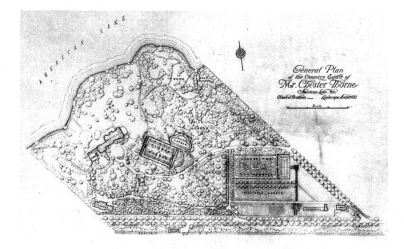

11.2 Landscape plan of Thornewood by the Olmsted Brothers. Frederick Law Olmsted National Historic Site, Brookline, Massachusetts.

11.3 Thornewood, rendering, 1909, by F. C. Hutchinson. *Pacific Builder and Engineer,* December 11, 1909. University of Washington Libraries, Special Collections Division, UW 3074.

natural groupings of trees, terminating in a circular loop in front of the house (fig. 11.3). From the driveway, only glimpses of the lake beyond the house to the north could be caught across flowing lawns between tall trees. Dense trees screened the boundaries of the estate, and where possible the natural woodland was left undisturbed. Between the house and the lake, lawns opened up, but water was visible only through a light screen of trees along its edge. From the two ends of the house, several meandering paths led to other parts of the garden. Some traversed open lawn; others passed through clumps of trees and shrubs. They gradually revealed areas of the garden, each with its own character: the open wood with

11.4 Thornewood, seen obliquely from the formal garden, designed by the Olmsted Brothers. Collection of the author.

11.5 Model of formal garden at Thornewood with Mount Rainier painted in the background. The water garden can be seen on the left. The Olmsted Brothers frequently made elaborate models to study alternative design solutions and to convey their ideas to clients. Frederick Law Olmsted National Historic Site, Brookline, Massachusetts.

grassy clearings, the rock garden close to the edge of the lake, the grotto of rough stone, the wild garden among denser trees.

In contrast to the informality of the general layout, an entirely geometrical, walled flower garden with a wide paved path on its axis lay in the very center of the estate at an oblique angle to the house (fig. 11.4). The focal point of this path was the snow-capped peak of Mount Rainier, framed by two pavilions. The Olmsted Brothers made use of a model to develop the design for this formal garden and to present it to the client. They photographed the model with the mountain painted on a backdrop behind it (fig. 11.5). To one side lay a more intimate water garden with a fountain against a curvilinear wall. Closer to the entrance gate, they placed a second, rectangular, walled garden for growing cut flowers as well as a vegetable garden and tennis court, both screened from the house.

Such was the setting for Thornewood, the most ambitious house of Cutter's career. He chose to build it entirely of dark red brick with dressings of buff Tenino sandstone. Giving the greatest priority to views of the lake, he made the plan long and narrow, organizing it informally on an east-west axis parallel to the shore of the lake (fig. 11.6).[14] Distinct volumes step back and forth, producing, at

11.6 Thornewood first- and second-floor plans. The carefully contrived irregularity creates the impression of a house that has evolved over the years, according to local building traditions. *Pacific Coast Architect,* March 1912.

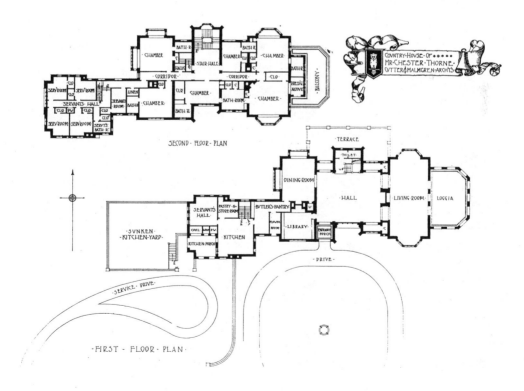

11.7 Hall interior of
Thornewood. The
strapwork on the
ceiling and the panel-
ing are based on
Tudor models. The
staircase was actually
moved from an old
house in England.
Eastern Washington
State Historical Soci-
ety, L84–207.4.172.

roof level, a rhythmic progression of large and small gables sometimes separated by crenelated parapets. Stone mullioned windows
open up the walls where needed; many of them project as bays and
rise through two stories. Tall brick chimneys, directly above fireplaces, contribute to a lively, irregular skyline. But unity prevails
over randomness; by following the logic of old building traditions,
Thornewood achieves a timeless quality. To ensure an authentic
character, Thorne was willing to import materials from England.
The dark red and brown bricks were brought by ship around Cape
Horn from England; the oak staircase and front door came from a
fifteenth-century country house. In Europe he also acquired a collection of old stained glass, some of it medieval, to set in the stone
mullioned windows.[15]

From the curving driveway a Tudor arch leads through a vaulted vestibule into a huge paneled hall from which French windows open onto a broad, brick terrace offering northerly views across lawns to the water. A few tall trees, survivors of the forest that once covered the site, frame the vistas. From the principal rooms, mullioned windows open to the same view as well as to the south and west. At the east end of the house there is access from the living room to a protected loggia with Tudor arches, three to each side, and a castellated parapet. The service wing, at the west end, is set back discreetly from the lakefront, so that the terrace is not overlooked from the servants' rooms. Nearby, a half-timbered carriage house, or garage, echoes the architecture of the mansion.

While the exterior of Thornewood is consistent in style, the rooms are not all of the same period. The interior is reminiscent of many English houses in which different rooms were redecorated in successive eras to keep up with current fashions. The vaulted vestibule and the oak-paneled hall, with its elaborate plaster ceiling (fig. 11.7), are obviously Tudor. The stone fireplace and particularly the staircase with carved newel posts complete the theme with authenticity. The richer plaster work of the library ceiling appears to be a little later in date, and the dining room is based on interiors of the reign of Queen Anne. The drawing room, which traverses the house from north to south, is a relatively simple version of the Adam Style. In this room the dark oak paneling gives way to light-colored plaster, and a molded cornice makes an elegant transition between wall and ceiling. The delicately carved marble mantelpiece is ornamented with Adamesque motifs of urns and garlands.[16]

In 1930, when the gardens had fully matured, the Thornewood estate was visited by members of the Garden Club of America, who named it "one of the most beautiful gardens in America."[17]

While Thornewood was under construction on the coast, Cutter was busy with two other mansions for successful clients in Spokane: one was begun in 1910 for Jay P. Graves, whose mining investments and real estate developments based on City Beautiful ideals had been immensely profitable; the other was begun a year earlier for Louis Davenport.

Davenport selected one of the last remaining sites of any size on the slopes of the South Hill between Seventh and Eighth Avenues, close to the houses Cutter had built in the 1890s. Passed over by others because of the difficulty of building on such precipitous terrain, it offered opportunities that excited Cutter and Olmsted. It provided a relatively level area for the house, from which the ground fell away steeply to the north and west. A stream flowed in a series of cascades through the ravine on the east side of the property, giving life to rich vegetation not able to survive on other parts of the hill. Among pines, alders, and willows, wild syringa and dogwood clung to the rocky incline. Close to the water, ferns, mosses, and rare wildflowers thrived on the perpetual dampness.[18]

To preserve the delicate ecology, Olmsted hired a gardener named William Donald, who could work intuitively without constant supervision. Donald had been employed on Louis Comfort Tiffany's estate on Long Island for six years, executing plans for rock gardens, waterways, bridges, and hanging gardens.[19] He was soon busy in early 1908 on Davenport's challenging site, creating a chain of thirteen pools connected by waterfalls (fig. 11.8). To give the illusion of a natural stream cascading down the hill, Donald concealed a series of strong concrete dams behind moss-covered basalt. Water plants and ferns overhanging the banks helped to soften the edges, and clean pebbles lined the bottoms of the shallow pools, making an ideal habitat for brook trout and goldfish. On the steep inclines he planted 1,400 rhododendrons gathered from the upper slopes of a mountain in Pennsylvania. A system of paths crossed the ravine via four Japanese footbridges and three sets of stepping stones (fig. 11.9). Although the walks appeared to be natural, like old tracks through woods, Donald made sure that they were deeply dug out, filled with stone, covered with cinders, and surfaced in fine gravel. Their edges were defined only by the vegetation on either side.[20]

While Cutter and Olmsted seem to have been in complete agreement on the treatment of the garden, friction developed over the siting of the house. Olmsted and Dawson made the first proposal, but Davenport and Cutter soon changed it, arousing Olmsted's disapproval.[21] He also considered impractical Cutter's original plan for a gate lodge spacious enough for Davenport to live in while the house was under construction. Olmsted felt that there was not room enough for such building on the narrow ledge at the top of the site. And he also objected strongly to Cutter's proposal to build part of the lodge in the form of a windmill. He argued that not only would it appear incongruous, but it would be inefficient as a method of pumping water. The matter was finally settled when he made the case to Davenport that the revolving sails would frighten horses.[22]

John Olmsted proposed instead that a lodge be built "for architectural effect" and also to screen the nearby hospital from view.

11.8 Louis Davenport garden under construction, ca. 1908. "Fishing in the lower pool." The Olmsted Brothers aimed to make the stream, with its thirteen waterfalls, look entirely natural. Eastern Washington State Historical Society, L88–404.19.2.32.

11.9 Louis Davenport garden. A meandering path crosses four rustic bridges and three sets of stepping stones. Eastern Washington State Historical Society, L88–404.19.2.18.

He suggested that "it might be a water tank tower and a playhouse for their little boy and so be smaller than what they had planned." Thus in May 1908 Cutter began to sketch a picturesque design whose tower was capped with a pointed roof like a witches hat. The gate was protected with a shingled canopy in the form of a pitched roof supported between lower towers, also with pointed caps. The effect was more evocative of illustrations for *Grimm's Fairy Tales* than of the lodge gates of English country estates (fig. 11.10). Within a month its rough basalt walls had reached the level of the eaves, and by October it was ready for use as a cottage for Donald.[23] Even before Cutter had begun to develop drawings for the house itself, Olmsted made preliminary proposals for its design. He suggested the position and orientation of the rooms, and even went into detail.[24] Although Cutter followed most of the landscape consultant's suggestions about the lodge, and for a broad terrace north of the house, he rejected his plan for the house and organized the rooms according to his own ideas.

11.10 Louis Davenport, gate lodge, Spokane, 1908. The structure is more evocative of *Grimm's Fairy Tales* than of the lodge gates of English country estates. Eastern Washington State Historical Society, L88–404.19.2.4.

11.11 Louis Davenport house 1908–11. The vocabulary is drawn from German sources; the design shows a fascination with the craft of carpentry. Eastern Washington State Historical Society, L88–404.19.2.1.

As the landscape work got under way the local newspapers regaled their readers with accounts of the "Veritable Fairyland—being planted in the heart of Spokane." It was reported that Thomas Edison visited the estate and exclaimed: "I have seen no place in America with greater opportunities for making a beautiful home near the heart of a city." The *Chronicle* described it as a sanctuary for wildlife, promising that it would be home to "black and white swans, peacocks, deer, gray squirrels, hundreds of tame birds—little lakes full of active trout and many other touches of nature that are generally to be found only at great distances from large cities."[25]

Cutter's design for the house (fig. 11.11) appears English in character, but he also drew from German building traditions. The jerkinhead hipped gables are of a type common in rural buildings in Germany in the area around Dresden where Cutter studied. While the close vertical studding of the gable ends is of a type more common in England than Germany, the brackets under the overhanging upper stories are closer to German examples; indeed, Cutter derived them, and other details, from a book in his library on old timber-framed buildings in Saxony.[26] Yet, taken as a whole, the Davenport house, with its irregular rhythm of dormers and gables, was a product of the Arts and Crafts revival of rural house types. Its lower walls were built of basaltic rock, and its upper walls were shingled in some places, half-timbered in others. The absence of applied ornament conveyed the simplicity of a cottage, although it was as large as a mansion (143 feet long). The sweeping curve of the eaves over a central arched window on the south elevation suggested thatch undulating on an English cottage. The house represented a return to the type Cutter first attempted in the Moore and Glover houses, though executed with far greater maturity.

As at Thornewood, the plan was long and narrow and oriented east-west; but with its many projections, it exhibited a greater freedom (fig. 11.12). The house was centered on a spacious hall from which French windows led out to a north-facing brick terrace with

11.12 First- and second-floor plans of the Louis Davenport house. The plan is similar to Thornewood's, but more freely adapted to modern life. *Architect and Engineer,* June 1921.

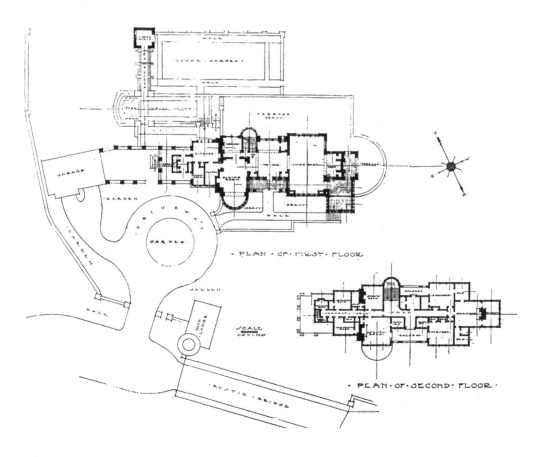

fine views over the garden and the town. To the west of the hall, a ten-foot-wide doorway opened into a huge living room with windows on both sides of the house; to the east was access to the library and the dining room. The staircase rose through a semicircular bay jutting out to the south, while the dining room terminated in a wide bay encircled by ten north-facing windows. The well-organized servants' quarters lay to the west. At the east end of the living room, a huge inglenook offered old-world warmth and hospitality. To one side of it, a secret panel opened to reveal a capacious log store; to the other side, similarly concealed, was a large safe.

Beneath the entire house, Cutter planned the basement to provide for all the needs of a well-run household; in addition, under the terrace he installed an indoor swimming pool and exercise room, probably the only such facility in any house in Spokane. Every bedroom on the second floor had its own bathroom. The master bedroom, which was provided with a fireplace, opened into a sleeping porch, a thoroughly modern element that had recently appeared in a few California houses, notably Greene and Greene's Gamble house in Pasadena (1908).

In 1910, Jay P. Graves decided to move from his rather formal red-brick house that Cutter had built for him in Browne's Addition to a 700–acre estate seven miles north of Spokane, within easy access of the city by automobile. He had already established a model dairy farm with a herd of Jersey cows, but his projects also included a deer park and a series of lakes, made by diverting the Little Spokane River. For his house he chose a site on a high bluff overlooking the river. At the suggestion of his son Clyde, he named the place "Waikiki."[27] An early design for the house shown in a large perspective drawn by Cutter's assistant, F. C. Hutchinson (fig. 11.13), was somewhat similar in character to the Davenport house. Its jerkinhead gables, the pattern of cross bracing in the half-timbering of the upper walls, and the central bell-cast turret suggest a German inspiration, but the studied, picturesque irregularity belongs to the Arts and Crafts style. Graves may have found its random repetition of gable ends and dormers of several different sizes too informal; the house he eventually built is more unified and distinctly English (fig. 11.14). The jerkinheads have disappeared and the half-timbering is of an English pattern.[28]

The front of the house faces south onto a spacious lawn, encircled by a driveway. The two wings of the house meet at an angle to fit the curve of the drive and to give a sense of enclosure, completed

11.13 Early design for Waikiki, Jay P. Graves house, Spokane, 1910.
Rendering by F. C. Hutchinson. Eastern Washington State Historical
Society, L84–207.170.

11.14 Jay P. Graves house, 1910–11, south front as built, with a subtle
rhythm of large and small gables. Eastern Washington State Historical
Society, L84–207.170.

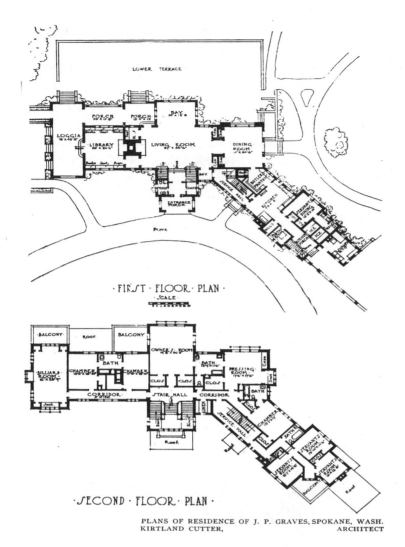

· FIRST · FLOOR · PLAN ·
· SCALE ·

· SECOND · FLOOR · PLAN ·

PLANS OF RESIDENCE OF J. P. GRAVES, SPOKANE, WASH.
KIRTLAND CUTTER,   ARCHITECT

11.15 First- and
second-floor plans
of the Jay P. Graves
house. Spacious,
shady porches and
loggias look into
an enclosed flower
garden to the west
and northward into
the valley. The excep-
tionally large living
room is open to both
the stairs and the
dining room. *Archi-
tect and Engineer,*
June 1921.

around the open space by trees. The main block with the principal
rooms dominates; the slightly lower service wing veers off to the
southeast (fig. 11.15).[29] The linear plan of the house is extended to
the west by a formal brick-paved walled garden with a teahouse at
the far end, and to the east by a large, detached garage with servants'
rooms above. The service yard between the house and the garage
is screened by a low wall surmounted by a vine-covered trellis.

The horizontal expansion of the exterior is echoed inside the
house, where Cutter explored a new spatial arrangement. From the
arched entrance porch the visitor enters under the landing of a divided staircase, up a shallow flight of steps, straight into an enor-

mous living room. The constricted entry emphasizes the effect of spaciousness beyond. The space is almost forty feet wide and extends the same distance ahead into a wide bay whose windows overlook a broad terrace and the valley beyond. To the left a huge fireplace commands one end of the room; to the right a wide opening leads into the dining room, whose mullioned windows on two adjacent sides flood the space with light. As if to compensate for the openness of the plan, Cutter provided a little "nook" with a built-in seat beside the fireplace for intimate conversation. It is balanced on the other side of the hearth by a small vestibule separating the more private library from the living room. With the exception of the living room's ornamental plaster ceiling in a Tudor design, the details of the interior are relatively simple: the oak paneling is plain; ornament is not ostentatious. Indeed, despite its Tudor exterior, there is a modernity about Waikiki that did not appear in Cutter's earlier houses.[30] Throughout the house, built-in window seats that conceal radiators add to the quality of spaciousness, and light falling on the fabric of the cushions brightens the rooms. A detail typical of Cutter is a pair of built-in seats of oak that face each other across the foot of the upper flight of the staircase—an invitation for those who meet on the stairs to stop and converse (fig. 11.16).

11.16 A seat built into the main staircase at the Jay P. Graves house. Photo by the author.

The living room and library both open onto a spacious loggia, which overlooks a formal, enclosed flower garden with a brick teahouse. Thus a variety of covered outdoor rooms and terraces offer shade or sun, distant views or seclusion. As at Thornewood and the Davenport house, the Olmsted Brothers designed the gardens. In the flower garden they attempted to respect the architecture of the house as well as create a natural appearance. When Graves objected to a rough stone wall and some details of the teahouse, James Dawson replied: "[T]he garden, even though it is connected with the house, is a garden, and should be made gardenesque in appearance. We have specially endeavored to have the architecture of the garden harmonize with that of the house, but it need not necessarily be the same as regards details."[31] In the end, the details mostly followed the landscape architects' plans and Graves was "very pleased" with the results.[32] The next few years saw the construction of several smaller Old English houses designed by Cutter and Malmgren—in Lewiston, Idaho, and Spokane. In addition, they were responsible for several houses without obviously Tudoresque elements, whose simple, unaffected qualities are derived from the Arts and Crafts movement.

Cutter's 1910 design for Lewis P. Larson, the founder of Metaline Falls, in northeastern Washington, is a good example (fig. 11.17).[33] In England, at the turn of the century, Ernest Gimson had created new stone cottages that appeared to have been built centuries earlier. His Stonywell Cottage, built in Charnwood Forest near Leicester in 1898, is virtually indistinguishable from a genuine vernacular cottage. Built of stone quarried nearby and originally thatched, it avoided the playful gentrification of cottages popular in the nineteenth century.[34] Cutter attempted to achieve a similar effect in the Larson house. While the Twohy residence of 1906 exuberantly expressed a restless quality with stone and timber, the Larson house conveyed the quiet simplicity of a rustic stone cottage. Its shingled roof rises in two waves over the dormer windows of bedrooms in a manner that recalls the thatching around the upper windows of anonymous rural dwellings. From the front, it appears as a low building containing small rooms. However, perched on the edge of a steep slope, it exploits the change of level. Its rear walls are a full story higher, rising from a steep, tree-covered slope. The interior space is surprising; Cutter created a grander living space inside than might be anticipated from the exterior. The living room is sunk eight feet below the entrance hall and open to it. Thus the hall

11.17 Lewis P. Larson house, Metaline Falls, 1910. Although surprisingly spacious inside, it has the character of a simple cottage. Photo by the author.

becomes the gallery of a high room. The fireplace and chimney breast are of natural river boulders in various colors, emphasizing the character of the material. The living room window on the lower side is extremely high and the space is further extended by a stone-built conservatory, with large windows on three sides, that juts out from the end of the house.

Shingles also sweep in a curve over an upper window on a house that Cutter built in the same year in Spokane for E. H. Knight, secretary-treasurer of the Diamond Drill Company (fig. 11.18).[35] This plain, rectangular house with a hipped roof and columns flanking the recessed front door is more formal than the Larson house, but with its shingled upper walls and simplicity of form, it has much in common.

The formality of the Knight house and the simple rustic quality of the Larson house are both evident in the 1909 residence of Cutter's partner, Karl Gunnar Malmgren, on Sumner Avenue (fig. 11.19).[36]

11.18 E. H. Knight house, West Point Avenue, Spokane, 1910–11. Eastern Washington State Historical Society, L-84.207.49.

11.19 Karl Gunnar Malmgren house, Sumner Avenue, Spokane, 1909. Although he based the design on Arts and Crafts simplicity, Malmgren organized it with a formal symmetry, giving it a central entrance and identical porches at the two ends. Eastern Washington State Historical Society.

Since this is the only building from the large number designed by the firm that can surely be attributed to Malmgren, it sheds valuable light on his personal ideas about design. The front elevation is entirely symmetrical: the stone porch at the center is flanked by the identical sets of windows for the principal rooms; and the windows on the upper floor project out as bays on slender, carved brackets. At the two ends of the house, porches inset on both floors provide equal outdoor spaces for the living and dining rooms, and for the corresponding two bedrooms above. While Cutter used porches to link rooms, Malmgren planned for privacy. The orderliness of the street facade permeates the design, whose rigidity becomes clear as soon as the front door is opened.

Entering the small porch, one is faced with the unusual dilemma of choosing between two identical doors, one leading into the dining room, one into the living room. The two principal rooms are virtually mirror images of each other, except that the living room has windows on two opposite sides. Malmgren eliminated the usual formal stair hall near the front door, and placed the staircase more privately at the back. The interiors were beautifully finished with high quality paneling and glass-fronted cabinets in mahogany. The staircase, with a balustrade of plain boards pierced by simple rectangular cutouts, had the chaste simplicity of a Voysey design. Each of the two principal bedrooms benefited from the large bay window and its built-in seat; but right next to the windows, awkwardly placed corner walk-in closets impeded the light from spreading throughout the room. Malmgren's house makes it clear that his preferences were not the same as Cutter's, but it does not demonstrate that he possessed a great flair for design.

The architects continued to design chalets for clients after the last houses of this type were finished in Seattle. Early in 1910, they designed one for Michael Lang, two blocks to the east of Cutter's own home, on Seventh Avenue.[37] While the Chalet Hohenstein nestled into the slope below the road, the Lang chalet was built on a spur of the hill higher than the road, and was therefore seen from a different angle. Furthermore, its jerkinhead roof with delicately carved bargeboards presented a form unlike the triangular gable end with dominant corbeled brackets of Cutter's residence. Two more chalets, designed by Cutter and Malmgren the following year, remained unbuilt.[38]

In 1912, returning to a Tudoresque style, Cutter developed a new type of plan in a house for Charles Jasper, a successful Spokane

11.20 Charles Jasper house, Spokane, 1912. Profiting from the high ground at the back, the second-floor living room opens onto a terrace level with the garden. Eastern Washington State Historical Society, L84–207.218.

building contractor (fig. 11.20).[39] The site, on Sumner Avenue, a block beyond the steepest slope of the South Hill, steps up to a garden higher than the street. He exploited the change of level to place the principal rooms on the second floor. With no entrance hall occupying valuable space at this level, the living room and library stretch across the entire front. Both the living room and dining room behind it open through French windows to a broad terrace over the garage to one side, from which two steps lead up to the garden. From the library, there is access to a balcony above the front door. Although both the balcony and the terrace are quite close to the street, they are secluded from it by their elevation. The balcony and the rear half of the terrace are shaded by pergolas.

As in the Graves house, the traditional construction in the Old English manner masked a setting for a modern way of life. The spaciousness of the rooms, the openness of the plans, and the easy transition from inside to out belonged to the twentieth century. The

11.21 J. T. Hefferman house, Seattle, 1915–16. Cutter's combination of half-timbered gables with carved bargeboards, and brick gables with stone copings, adds visual variety. Photo by the author.

ballroom in the attic, reached by the elegant main stair with turned balusters, evoked the "good old days"; the large sleeping porch by the master bedroom showed an up-to-date attitude.

In a more conservative vein, Cutter designed in 1915 a large redbrick Tudor house on Lake Washington Boulevard in Seattle for the wealthy engineer and banker J. T. Heffernan (fig. 11.21).[40] For this site, in a fine position overlooking the lake, with views of Mount Rainier, he returned to the architectural language of Thornewood, exploiting tall chimneys, irregular stone coped gables, mullioned windows, and castellated parapets for picturesque effect. The plan, however, was far more compact. The entrance hall was merely a narrow circulation space running through the house from front to back; but, as at Thornewood, one end of the house terminated with a hexagonal loggia. The principal rooms were ornamented with relatively authentic period details. In the oak-paneled hall the tall newel posts of the staircase were Elizabethan in character, and in the drawing room the ornate fireplace with a carved wood overmantel suggested the same style, but the music room was finished in the manner of the late eighteenth century. An Adamesque ceiling and a frieze of urns and festoons set an entirely different tone. In addition to the accommodations on the first floor, a ballroom and billiard room were placed in the basement. Since there was a strong slope on the site, the ballroom was able to receive daylight through large windows on one side.

In 1916, Cutter designed the last of his mansions for a millionaire client in Spokane. By this time Spokane's economy had changed. The mining boom was over and railroad construction had virtually ceased. Those who wanted new homes had less money to spend on building, and tended to go to architects who would lower their fees. Cutter's client Jay P. Graves, who had grown wealthy at the turn of the century, had built Waikiki more on his prospects than on real money in hand.[41] Cutter must have been relieved to receive a commission to design a large house on the crest of the South Hill for the lumber millionaire John A. Humbird,[42] for whom he could once again capture the flavor of Old England in a Northwest context (fig. 11.22). The site, between Sumner and Cliff Avenues, offered fine views over the town; but, rather than placing the house close

11.22 T. J. Humbird house, South Hill, Spokane, 1916–17. The last of Cutter's Tudoresque houses in Spokane. Eastern Washington State Historical Society, L84–487–39.

to the street and building it high to dramatize the view, Cutter set it back among lawns and trees. While the gables of the Heffernan house are clustered energetically around the tallest chimney, Cutter made the Humbird residence long and relatively low with a quiet, more reticent character. The logic of construction, the protection afforded by steep roofs with broad overhangs, and the arrangement of the rooms inside seem to determine its form rather than any self-conscious quest for the picturesque. The main characteristics of the interiors are a spaciousness and a lightness. In this house Cutter did not attempt to vary the styles of individual rooms, and he abandoned dark oak paneling for plain walls and white painted woodwork with Georgian detail.

It was not until around 1920 that Cutter built his next Old English houses. At that time, he designed two stone houses on Puget Sound. The opportunity to build in stone seems to have encouraged him to emulate the rural architecture of the Cotswolds, a region of stone villages, farms, and manors in the west of England. Cutter's houses of this type are characterized by plain walls, pierced by relatively small windows. While gable ends rise to two stories and an attic, the main walls are only a single story high; above them long roof slopes rise to an even ridge. Thus the effect is of a huge expanse of plain roof and the strong horizontals of eaves and ridge. Westwold Manor, the largest of the two, was built north of Seattle on a bluff facing Puget Sound between Richmond Beach and Edmonds, for David Whitcomb, president of the Arcade Building and Realty Company of Seattle.[43] An ink rendering shows the east elevation facing a circular driveway (fig. 11.23). At first sight, the facade appears symmet-

11.23 Westwold Manor, David Whitcomb house, Edmonds, Washington, ca. 1920 (not built). A stone house emulating the traditional architecture of the Cotswold region of southwest England. Eastern Washington State Historical Society, L84–207.171.

11.24 Heather Hill, Ernest Dolge house, Steilacoom Lake, Washington, 1920–21. A further interpretation of Cotswold architecture. Photo by the author.

rical, except for an extra small gable at the right-hand end. A heavily buttressed gable wall with a large oriel window jutting out over the arched entrance door commands the center, but the similar gables at either end of the house are unequal both in height and detail. The taller one to the north is abutted by a short length of castellated wall like the remnant of a medieval fortress; the lower one to the south is pierced by three arched windows separated only by slender columns. This generous opening up of the wall seems like a Renaissance celebration of the fact that fortification is no longer necessary. The Seattle architects Carl Gould and Harlan Thomas also submitted designs to David Whitcomb for stone houses in an Old English style. The version by Thomas was actually built.[44]

The Dolge house (fig. 11.24), named Heather Hill, at Steilacoom Lake south of Tacoma, is much smaller than Westwold Manor, yet with its stone walls it appears more substantial than some larger houses. The house was sited at the top of a steep, heather-covered slope overlooking the lake, and Cutter planned it with the ridge of the roof parallel to the contours and the gables of a cross-roof in the center of each long facade. On the front, facing the entrance drive, he emphasized asymmetry by placing a massive chimney on the right-hand side. Between the central gable and the chimney, an entrance hall with an independent roof stands forward. As usual, the door, covered with a Tudor arch, is hung on wrought iron strap hinges.

Typical of Arts and Crafts design, both houses give the impression that they may have evolved gradually over the years. Their character is the result of well-tried traditional construction, fine craftsmanship, and the absence of applied ornament. Nevertheless, the passage of time from the nineteenth century to 1920 is evident. The interior of Heather Hill approaches the simplicity of modern design. Doors with flush surfaces are set in plain frames, and walls are plastered rather than paneled. The staircase is elegant but not ornate. However, quality was not skimped. The owner, lumber merchant Ernest Dolge, would invite visitors to inspect the attic and offered them one hundred dollars if they could find a single knot in the framing lumber exposed there. The prize was never collected.[45]

Compared with Cutter's highly eclectic mansions at the turn of the century, in which he reveled in the creation of opulence, those he designed after 1907 showed greater consistency and restraint. They represent a second peak in his career, and they signal an evolution in American domestic architecture.

CHAPTER TWELVE

Mediterranean Influence (1913–1921)

DURING CUTTER'S FIRST QUARTER CENTURY IN PRACTICE, the Old English styles of architecture provided ideal models for his domestic work, but his interest in Hispanic types was evident in a few turn-of-the-century Mission Revival designs, and in his Christian Science Church of 1907. In 1913, keeping abreast of new tendencies in American architecture, he designed a large house in Seattle showing a Mediterranean influence, and he followed with several others of a similar type. These commissions were eventually to pave his way to professional success in California. Tudoresque houses appealed to Cutter's romanticism and allowed him a greater freedom in planning than was possible in classical houses, but certain southern European types, particularly those of vernacular origin, offered similar advantages. Furthermore, the simple effect of whitewashed plaster and low-pitched roofs typical of farmhouses in Tuscany or Andalusia, as well as the Spanish missions in the American Southwest, could be employed in a relatively modern manner. Houses of this kind could follow an irregular plan and be fitted informally into the landscape.

Cutter designed the first of a series of Mediterranean houses in Seattle for his former client C. D. Stimson. In 1900, Cutter had provided him with a half-timbered Tudoresque house on Capitol Hill, but soon the neighborhood in which it stood began to lose its peaceful quality and social distinction. Stimson, who had been extremely successful as a developer of commercial buildings, decided to move to the elite and well-protected community of the Highlands and in 1913 commissioned a new design from Cutter.[1]

This new house, known as Norcliffe (figs. 12.1, 12.2), built in a commanding position near the edge of a steep bluff, is large and complex. Irregularly planned around three sides of a south-facing courtyard, its U-shaped main roof maintains a level profile, while lower roofs cluster around it on the southeast corner and a tower rises above it further north. Yet its forms are unified by their white stucco walls and hipped roofs covered with cedar shingles. The effect of the geometrically consistent roofs stepping up is picturesque but disciplined. The only relief from their simple shapes appears in eyebrow dormers and a curvature in the eaves of the tower. A driveway approaching from the southeast leads the visitor to a porte cochère massively constructed with buttressed corners and a hipped roof. Shallow arches open up three of its sides; the fourth leads up a few steps into the cloister, an arcaded and vaulted passage running along one side of the formal courtyard garden to the main door. This covered walk, reminiscent of an early Renaissance loggia, provides a transition between the outside and the spacious staircase hall, allowing the arriving guest to experience the relationship of the house to the court. On the north side of this lavishly planted outdoor space, wide French windows give access to both ends of the vast living room. Opposite the cloister a solarium with large windows on three sides, admitting sunlight throughout the day, occupies the end of the west wing. Dominating the court in the center of the north side, a pair of tall chimney stacks reinforces the symmetry and creates a strong vertical expression. At its base, back to back with the living room fireplace, a garden seat fills a niche between the two stacks. Directly above this recess, the arched window of Mrs. Stimson's boudoir opens onto a balcony which commands the entire scene.

In contrast to the vertical element just described, the half-timbered upper facade on either side of it reads as a horizontal band, an effect emphasized by the fact that it is jettied out and casts a shadow on the wall below. Furthermore, the windows in this band are linked in groups of four, giving a sense of continuity. The half-timbering appears somewhat out of place with the Italian-looking arcade and the white stucco walls; the house displays northern European and Mediterranean elements in an unusual combination. In 1920, the Stimson mansion was described in *House and Garden* as "modernized Mission."[2] Indeed, it has much in common with the Spanish Colonial Revival architecture that was then taking the place of the Mission Revival in California.

12.1 C. D. Stimson house, The Highlands, Seattle, 1913–14. Although the white stucco walls and red tiled roofs suggest a Mediterranean character, the English "Free Style" influence is evident. Eastern Washington State Historical Society, L84–207.7.4.178.

12.2 Courtyard of the C. D. Stimson house. The twin chimneys as a focal point of the facade became a hallmark of Cutter's Mediterranean houses. Dorothy Stimson Bullitt Collection.

The interiors, however, do not borrow much from Hispanic traditions. As in several of Cutter's other houses of the same period, they combine eighteenth- or early nineteenth-century elements of English origin with details more suggestive of the Arts and Crafts. In the living room, the 32–foot width is spanned by steel girders encased in ornamental plasterwork and supported on elaborately profiled brackets, but generally the details convey a simple, classic elegance. The library fireplace is pure Arts and Crafts, with a plain hearth inserted in a field of Batchelder tiles.[3] While the main staircase in the richly paneled hall has turned balusters of a fairly pretentious type, the stair that leads up from the library to the family bedrooms above is simply detailed in a manner that Cutter employed on much smaller houses.

The ballroom in the basement is comparatively grand. Both its huge fireplace, directly under that of the living room, and the stage at one end are flanked by classic columns. The room was planned for a variety of entertainments; small dressing rooms are provided and an organ was built in behind the stage. Next to the ballroom, a "lounging room" appears to be a modern equivalent of the gaming room in the basement of some of Cutter's late nineteenth-century houses, where the men could enjoy themselves away from the watchful eyes of the ladies. This room was finished with light-colored paneled walls and a marble fireplace.

The service quarters of the Stimson mansion were carefully planned to cater to the needs and desires of a wealthy family. Demonstrating a continuing change in the attitude toward domestic servants, they were also designed to give those who worked in the house a comfortable life in agreeable surroundings. On the other side of the blank east wall of the cloister, the principal service rooms occupy as large an area as the living room, hall, and dining room combined. Belowstairs, the furnace and fuel rooms, wine cellars, and storerooms for fruit, vegetables, and other necessities take up as much space as the ballroom and lounging room. The four servants' bedrooms were not relegated to the attic as was usual, but placed like those of the Stimson family on the second floor. Unlike the Spokane houses of the 1890s, in which laundresses were forced to work in dank basements, the laundry room of this house is on the first floor, next to the kitchen, where it receives the morning sun.[4]

The butler's pantry makes the customary transition between the kitchen and the dining room; it also opens conveniently to the breakfast porch. In addition, a dumbwaiter connects the kitchen to a servery in the basement and to the second-floor hall, so that refreshments can be served in the ballroom suite and meals can be delivered to bedrooms. For heavier goods, an elevator links the basement and the first floor. A system of house phones connects various rooms, but in the service areas speaking tubes were installed to allow communication between servants. A bell system, whose indicator board in the servants' hall has twenty-five points, runs throughout the house. In a basement machine room, an icemaker and a central vacuum cleaning plant stand side by side, ensuring that food and drinks can always be cooled and that the house can be cleaned quietly, with minimum dust. The architects provided for all of these functions and many others in as discreet a manner as possible, so that a well-organized staff could perform their duties with minimum disturbance or visibility. The service yard and laundry drying area were carefully planned away from the courtyard, terraces, and pleasure gardens.

Collaborating with the Olmsted Brothers,[5] Cutter extended the house into a series of outdoor spaces that offered varying degrees of intimacy and enclosure. The courtyard is like a huge stage onto which players can enter from various doorways or from the cloister. The central balcony provides an additional platform at an upper level. However, since the courtyard is raised up a little above the driveway, and is protected by a low wall, it offers some privacy. A terrace on the north side of the house is more secluded and quite different in character. Set at a lower level, so that it can be reached by steps from the ballroom in the basement, it overhangs a steep slope. Nevertheless, it was formally planned with a fountain on its main north-south axis, set within a curved wall on its outer edge. In contrast, the breakfast terrace, opening off the dining room in the northeast corner of the house, is an enclosed space designed to catch the morning sun in summer.

Outbuildings harmonize with the house, though they were designed in a more playful manner. The entrance gate to the Stimson estate (fig. 12.3) is similar to the porte cochère, but its wider arch is echoed by a curve in the eaves of its roof like that on the tower of the main house. The garage, visible through the gate, standing beside the driveway, is distinctly picturesque, with an octagonal turret rising up between two gables, but its shingled roof and stucco walls follow the pattern set in the house. Eyebrow dormers, like those on the house, admit light to its attic. In a dominant position on the edge of the bluff, an octagonal gazebo, with a shingled roof

12.3 Entrance to the C. D. Stimson estate, with the garage in the distance. Photo by Richard Cardwell.

rising to a peak like that on the garage turret, takes advantage of the distant views. To the east of the house, connected to it by a long vine-covered pergola, stands the Young Peoples' Cabin. This was actually the first building on the site, possibly designed as early as 1908, when Cutter and Malmgren had their Seattle office.[6] Built with hipped roofs in a U-shape around a little courtyard, with a dominant chimney centered on its inner wall, it may well have suggested the design of the mansion.

While Cutter made some references to the Spanish Colonial Revival in the Stimson house, he made a fuller commitment to it in another house begun in 1913 for W. H. Cowles, the owner of Spokane's leading newspapers. Ten years earlier, Cutter had designed a plain, shingled Bungalow-like house for Cowles in Spokane. It appears that his client had wanted to avoid ostentation in a neighborhood where his equals in wealth and influence were building elaborate mansions.[7] But now that he was planning a winter home in Santa Barbara, California, he felt no such restraint. On a lofty ridge overlooking the Pacific Ocean, Cutter designed Cowles a palatial residence with red tiled roofs and white stucco walls in the Mediterranean manner that was popular in the southern state.[8]

By this time an evolution in California architecture was taking place. While at the turn of the century the mission had provided the chief inspiration for a regional architecture in the state, architects began in the second decade of the twentieth century to abandon the decoratively scalloped mission gables and explore a broader range of traditions from Spain, Italy, and Mexico.[9] Cutter followed this trend, but retained in his design some elements of the mission.

Eucalyptus Hills, the Cowles house at Santa Barbara, was complex and flamboyant (figs. 12.4, 12.5). From many viewpoints it appeared as an irregular, picturesque structure crowning the hill.

12.4 Eucalyptus Hills, Santa Barbara, California, winter home of W. H. Cowles, 1913–14, from the west. The simply constructed arcade around the court provides a serene entry space above which more elaborate forms rise. Eastern Washington State Historical Society, L84–207.4.208.

12.5 Eucalyptus Hills as altered after the earthquake of 1925. The central pavilion has been replaced by twin towers. Partially demolished. Collection of the author.

But seen from the west through the entrance arch on the axis of its huge forecourt, it presented a formal composition. A high wall of elaborately ornamented white stucco, surmounted by a belvedere on the roof, formed the centerpiece of the principal facade. Standing back behind a small inner courtyard, this dominant wall interrupted the low-pitched, hipped roof on either side, rising higher than the ridge and terminating with a scalloped skyline. Plain in the center, it was richly articulated on either side with engaged columns framing three arched windows. The slope of the tall arches was echoed in the openings of the belvedere, which stood at the center of a roof terrace. Although not richly decorated, this feature had the delicacy one might expect in a small pavilion of the Alhambra.

The main living block was T-shaped, with the facade facing the courtyard as the horizontal bar of the T. The courtyard, as large as a mission cloister, was surrounded on all four sides by arcades of unusual simplicity; its piers and arches were unrelieved by capitals or moldings.[10] In this space, a sense of enclosure prevailed. The other side of the house opened out onto terraces with spectacular views to the south and east. The shaft of the T continued the central axis of the court and projected eastward out to the edge of the hill, terminating in a loggia approached by a broad flight of steps. From the sumptuous interiors there was easy access to the gardens, and windows framed a variety of distant views.

Further complicating the plan, an additional block ran down the south side of the courtyard, housing the servants' quarters; beyond this the service yard and laundry yard were tucked away behind walls where they would not interfere with views from the principal rooms. Nevertheless, the servants were able to enjoy a superb outlook to the south with the Pacific Ocean in the background. When the earthquake struck Santa Barbara in 1925, destroying much of the downtown, the belvedere was damaged. The Cowles decided, presumably with Cutter's help, to replace the central pavilion with two sturdier towers, one on each side.[11] The new structures enclosed a more secure roof terrace, but closed off the view to the south.

With the Cowles house, Cutter explored a Mediterranean theme that he was to exploit again in three important houses in the Northwest. Joseph L. Carman, his client for the first of these, came to Tacoma from Iowa in 1890 at the age of twenty-nine, intent on investing his money in a profitable venture. He built a highly successful mattress manufacturing business that catered to the growing population of the state. In 1898 he married Margaret Ann Cootes, and they became active members of the prosperous social elite of the city and developed a reputation as gracious hosts. In 1906 the Carmans obtained a property a few miles south of Tacoma, on Gravelly Lake, where they built a two-story cottage. Here they came each summer for boating, swimming, picnicking, and entertaining their friends in the idyllic setting on the forested banks of the lake.[12]

This delightful retreat was only a short way from Chester Thorne's estate, and the Carmans must have watched with interest the creation of the Thornewood gardens and the building of the rambling Tudor mansion by Kirtland Cutter. They were also familiar with the architect's work at the Tacoma Hotel, which was a center for the social life of the city. Cutter was an obvious choice for this ambitious, pleasure-loving couple, but it was not until August 1919 that he first came to Tacoma to discuss the building of a large house on Gravelly Lake.[13] Like Chester Thorne, the Carmans were discriminating clients who knew what they wanted but also gave freedom to their architect. Margaret Carman's desires developed through reading such books as Herbert Cescinsky's *The Old World House* and Elizabeth Champrey's *The Romance of Italian Villas.* The couple took a trip around the world, and as they traveled they made notes about the architecture and gardens they admired. Their preference was for a villa in the Italian manner surrounded by spacious gardens, including one in the Japanese style. On this journey and subsequent trips, they collected objets d'art and furnishings for the house, even rocks and temple lanterns for their Japanese garden.[14]

Cutter's office accounts show that he made several visits to the coast, usually staying a few days. By early 1920, the design had evolved (figs. 12.6, 12.7). As in the Cowles house, the plan was T-shaped with the living room facing the lake in the shaft of the T, where it could be lit by windows on three sides. To this main part of the house, an L-shaped service wing was added, enclosing in its angle a service court conveniently secluded from the terraces and gardens. The addition of this subsidiary wing and the steep slope of the land effectively countered the inherent symmetry of the design. While from the lake a grand axis leads up steeply by flights of stone steps to the formal south-facing facade, other viewpoints reveal a rambling irregular house growing naturally out of the ground.

The estate is entered from the north on relatively flat ground through an arched gateway of white stucco capped with red tiles. The curving driveway leads to the forecourt of the house. In contrast to the rectangular, arcaded patio and the high central block at

SOUTH ELEVATION
SCALE ¼ INCH 1 FOOT

EAST ELEVATION
SCALE ¼ INCH 1 FOOT

HOUSE FOR J. L. CARMAN ESQ
AT GRAVELLY LAKE WN
KIRTLAND CUTTER ARCHITECT

12.6 Villa Carman, Gravelly Lake, near Tacoma, 1919–20. First-floor plan, east and west elevations. The living block is formally planned with a hall and living room on the central axis; however, the service wing breaks the symmetry. Eastern Washington State Historical Society, L84–207.276.

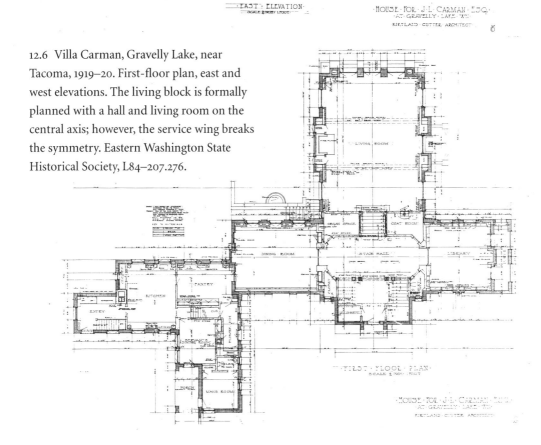

FIRST FLOOR PLAN
SCALE ¼ INCH 1 FOOT

HOUSE FOR J. L. CARMAN ESQ
AT GRAVELLY LAKE WN
KIRTLAND CUTTER ARCHITECT

304

12.7 In the manner of many villas in the northern Italian lake country, Villa Carman steps down toward the lake. The twin chimneys follow the pattern established at the C. D. Stimson house in The Highlands. Eastern Washington State Historical Society, L84.207.4.42.

Eucalyptus Hills, the first view of the Villa Carman is far less imposing. The house appears to be only one and a half stories high. The forecourt is enclosed on one side by the service wing and a low wall connecting it to a picturesquely composed garage with an apartment above; on the other side it is open to the gently sloping lawn. A carved wood front door in the Spanish tradition leads into an entrance hall of unexpected splendor. Passing under the half landing of the staircase and between a pair of classic columns, the visitor enters an elongated octagon. To left and right, double doors lead into the dining room and the library. On the four shorter walls on either side of these openings, narrower, decoratively carved doors, also of a distinctly Spanish type, open into a coat room, a toilet, a corridor to the kitchen, and an organ room providing for music in the living room. Thus practical matters are taken care of in an elegant manner. Straight ahead, a broad flight of steps progresses down a half level to the lofty and spacious living room. Light floods in through arched openings on three sides. French windows open through the end wall onto a broad terrace projecting out high above the paved walk to the lake. Four massive Tuscan columns along the edge of the terrace support a web of carved timbers to which a huge canopy could be attached in hot weather, making the space into a shady outdoor room when desired, without excluding the winter sun as a heavy vine-laden pergola might have done.

In the Villa Carman, Cutter brilliantly exploited the change in level. The steps progressing up from the lake to the terrace are echoed within the house. Inside and out, the alternation of flights of steps on the central axis and stairways leading to the sides is repeated. While the north elevation is low, the south facade, including the terrace wall, appears to rise three full stories. With its low-pitched roof, whose gable end is proportioned like the pediment of a classical temple, the effect is of a grand Italian villa. Yet the details are unpretentious. Plain wall surfaces and the absence of applied ornament give it an underlying simplicity. The many arched openings are made without the articulation of columns or capitals. Nevertheless, the architect could not resist enlivening the design with sculptural forms. Paired chimneys, penetrated by arched windows, similar to those on the Stimson house in The Highlands, rise on either side of the living room block. It must be admitted that three of the four chimneys are false. Only one contains a flue, serving the living room fireplace. A loggia shades the west side of the library; a paved court opens off the east side of the living room, connected by a flight of steps up to a terrace outside the dining room.

As in many Cutter houses, character varies from room to room. But in the Villa Carman there are none of the exaggerated stylistic differences found in his earlier designs. The dining room is light and relatively simple. Its main ornaments are an elegant classical fireplace and a massive marble-topped dining table with high-backed chairs acquired by the Carmans in Italy. The library, with dark wooden bookshelves and a black marble fireplace, provides a contrast. Elsewhere, walls are plain and white. The principal features of the immense living room are the fireplace with a full canopy of a pattern found in Renaissance chateaux in France and a ceiling whose 32-foot beams are richly decorated. These are, in fact, steel I beams, cased and covered with ornamental plasterwork on which an Italian artisan is said to have worked for a year. The arched windows on

three of its four walls offer a variety of views and admit sun throughout the day. This openness, made possible by the mild climate on
the coast, allowed residents the maximum enjoyment of their site.

Domestic convenience was provided for in the most discreet
ways. Firewood was put into the log store next to the living room
fireplace by a servant from the outside without entering the house.
The service wing connected with the rest of the house at only one
corner, and a hidden passage ran from it beside the dining room to
the hall. Joseph and Margaret Carman each had a bedroom with
dressing room and bath, and a breakfast room was situated close by
so that they could take their morning meal privately in their own
wing above the living room.

The gardens, to which Margaret Carman devoted much thought,
combined the classical and the romantic. Classical columns like
those on the terrace were repeated in the formal rose garden and in
a teahouse by the lake. But in the Japanese garden, a teahouse stood
on stilts in the water in an oriental manner.

While Cutter was visiting Tacoma late in 1919 to plan the Villa
Carman, his office accounts show that he also began work on another
house of a Mediterranean type at Gravelly Lake for William Jones
(fig. 12.8). Though similar in some respects, the Joneses' house was

12.8 William Jones
house, Gravelly Lake,
near Tacoma, 1919–20.
The facade almost
attains the simplicity
of an Irving Gill
design. Photo by
the author.

planned very differently. It is a long, narrow, single-story house with a tall central hall rising above the other rooms. Placed in a high position above the lake, it opens onto a wide terrace. But instead of developing a formal axis from the house to the lake as he had done for the Carmans, Cutter designed a romantically winding path descending to the water.

A striking feature of the exterior is the concealment of the roof behind a parapet. Both front and rear elevations present a plain white stucco wall above which are seen only the tall chimney and the hipped, red-tiled roof of the hall. However, the hint of modernity on the exterior is contradicted by the rich and eclectic interior of the hall. While the facade almost attains the simplicity of an Irving Gill design, the lofty central space lit by clerestory windows on all four sides evokes the early Renaissance in Italy and Spain. The vaulted ceiling springs from ornamental corbels, creating a series of arches against the wall, each of which contains a window. Above the arched opening, leading through a small vestibule to the front door, a balcony projects out in a theatrical manner.

On the south wall, looking toward the lake, three tall arched windows open to the terrace and the lake beyond, very much in the style of the Villa Carman living room. Another similar feature is the tall canopied fireplace of Renaissance design. From the east and west sides of the hall, double doors lead to the living room and the dining room. As a variant from previous Cutter dining rooms, this one is square, but with the corners cut off to make an octagon. An unusual element of the plan is the provision of bedrooms at the two ends of the house, creating two private bedroom zones.

Again in 1921, Cutter employed a Mediterranean vocabulary in a house for Leo J. Falk in Boise, Idaho.[15] In this case, he had neither a hilltop, as at Santa Barbara, nor a parklike site overlooking a lake. He planned it to make the most of a corner lot on a suburban street. The result was an informal home with an intimate character opening into a spacious patio (fig. 12.9). The front of the house, facing Warm Springs Road, is set back behind lawn and trees in a conventional way; to the side, facing the other street, a high patio wall of white stucco to match the house provides seclusion and allows an unusual openness between inside and out. The living room in the foot of the L-shaped plan, following Cutter's frequent precedents, enjoys light from three sides. French windows open into the patio on either side of the fireplace. The dining room faces the street, but a breakfast room opening onto a shady porch large enough for out-

12.9 Leo J. Falk house, Warm Springs Road, Boise, Idaho, 1921. Cutter recreates on a smaller scale the character of his previous Mediterranean houses. Photo by the author.

door dining also faces the patio. This courtyard garden, shaded by walnut trees and a pergola of weathered timber, has at its center a wellhead of concrete and wrought iron. With flagstone paved walks and trim box hedges, it possesses a traditional charm; it even includes a small lily pond fed by a spout of water from a lion's head.[16]

On the outer wall of the living room, toward the patio, Cutter repeated the device he had used on the Stimson house and the Villa Carman, the twin chimneys penetrated by an upper-floor window with a wrought iron balcony. This sculptural form, that appears as a Cutter trademark on the design, gives a vertical emphasis to this wall of the patio in contrast to the horizontality of the others. At ground level beneath the balcony is a bench carved of white sandstone.

Cutter also turned to Mediterranean influences for hotel design. After the success of the Davenport, he hoped for a rush of new hotel business. But World War I slowed investment in construction and he received no firm commissions for hotels for several years. The first opportunity came his way in 1916 when he was asked to submit designs for the Broadmoor Hotel on Cheyenne Lake in Colorado Springs. However, he was exploited by an unscrupulous contractor who hoped to secure a contract for the hotel by using Cutter's name and reputation.[17] Cutter himself made a series of freehand sketches showing alternative embellishments, mostly in the churrigueresque manner,[18] but the large colored rendering of the final design showed a more economical arrangement with restrained ornament. Cutter's draftsmen put many weeks of work into the drawings for the Broadmoor Hotel, but their efforts came to nothing; the work went to Warren and Wetmore, the designers of the Biltmore and the Ritz-Carlton hotels in New York.[19]

Cutter had to wait another three years for a successful hotel project, but in 1919 he was rewarded by an opportunity in his own territory, where his experience was appreciated. Business people in Lewiston, Idaho, had for some years entertained the idea of raising capital to build a large hotel that would bring new business and prestige to their city. Such plans had been put to one side as a result of the war, but in the spring of 1919 a committee headed by Eugene M. Ehrhardt revived the project. They retained Cutter at an early stage to advise on the choice of site and the level of investment needed to build a hotel of appropriate size and quality. By mid-March that year, he had selected a site at the west end of Main Street, not far from the bridge leading across the Snake River to Clarkston. The committee accepted his proposal for the location of the hotel, as well as his recommendation that it would be necessary to raise half a million dollars to build the hotel.[20] On October 10, 1919, Cutter confidently sent floor plans to Lewiston that he claimed would "meet conditions naturally and . . . afford ample opportunity for effective treatment, both of the exterior and interior as well as being convenient from the service standpoint."[21]

The design that Cutter developed over the next few months was in some respects similar to his Broadmoor Hotel project. Its white stucco walls and broadly overhanging hipped roofs shared the Mediterranean origin of the earlier design; indeed, they both conformed to the general type that he had exploited in the Cowles house at Santa Barbara. However, the Lewis-Clark Hotel possessed a chaste simplicity: no Baroque motifs complicated its facade, and the skyline was broken only by two square towers. The five-story hotel was arranged in a regular U-shape, whose open side faced east into the town center. The interior of the U was occupied by a spacious lounge and the wings of the U were extended eastward by single-

12.10 Lewis-Clark Hotel, Lewiston, Idaho, 1919–21. In sharp contrast to the opulent, eclectic Davenport Hotel in Spokane, this design is far more modern. Eastern Washington State Historical Society.

story blocks that defined an open garden court. Cutter used these single-story volumes to fit the unevenly shaped site. They could expand to fill the available ground space, while the main roof offered a sense of order and symmetry. Along the main street frontage, several shops were installed behind arched openings in the lower blocks (fig. 12.10).

Contrary to the assumption in Lewiston that the design of the Lewis-Clark Hotel had evolved from Spanish origins, Cutter described it as "Italian Renaissance," explaining that this style was "lighter [and] more ornamental."[22] But since it lacks ornamental features associated with the Italian Renaissance, his perception is hard to understand. The hotel's most striking characteristic is its simplicity; indeed the interior spaces convey a surprising modernity. While only a few years before, Cutter had lavished ornamental detail on the public rooms at the Davenport Hotel, creating spaces that alluded to several distinct European styles, he gave the principal rooms at the Lewis-Clark Hotel plain walls with smooth surfaces. But these spaces are light. Closely spaced arched windows and interior arcades penetrate the plain walls without the elaboration of moldings or flanking pilasters. The austere effect is similar to that in designs by Irving Gill and some of his contemporaries in southern California. Both the main dining room and the lounge are spanned by massive beams, spaced to rest on the piers between the arches. To complement the harmonious simplicity of the structure, Cutter collaborated with an artist, Carl R. Berg of Seattle, who was brought in to execute a series of mural decorations. The objective was to "put into them the distinctive character of the hotel and some of the history and legend of the north Idaho country."

In the murals for the lobby, Berg focused particularly on the Indian tribes of the region and tried in his work to create an "Indian Renaissance":

> The scrolls, representing the rolling hills, start from the figures of oxen instead of the grotesque or hideous monsters that appear in many ancient pieces of architecture. And there are animals, coyotes and bears that were many years ago worshipped by the Indians.
>
> On one of the crests stands an Indian, his eyes shaded, looking back into the distance, where are the hieroglyphs of the signal fire. . . .
>
> There too is the canoe flowing smoothly by, and Sacajawea with Lewis and Clark, whom she piloted to a winter place of safety.[23]

In contrast, the decoration for the ballroom was described by Berg as belonging to the "futuristic renaissance or secessionist school." Here he aimed for an effect of freedom and lightness. In the lounge (fig. 12.11), a tall room lit by clerestory windows above the arched openings to surrounding corridors, the iconography was more confused. In honor of the allied victory in World War I, it was named the Victory Room. The deep structural beams that supported its roof were painted with the conventional acanthus leaf "intertwined with devices carrying the coats of arms of the Allied Nations and the insignia of several army corps engaged in the World War; all embellished with Indian symbols and drawings suggestive of local history, with particular reference to the Lewis and Clark party and early pioneers."[24] The fireplace, the only element that can be identified as Italian Renaissance, was surmounted with a replica of the Winged Victory of Samothrace, thrusting forth aggressively from the hood over the hearth.

The last few commissions discussed in this chapter were executed without the participation of Karl Malmgren, who, after associating

12.11 The lounge, or Victory Room, of the Lewis-Clark Hotel. The plain arches devoid of capitals and moldings exhibit a chaste simplicity. Brochure for the formal opening of the Lewis-Clark Hotel, 1922.

with Cutter for thirty-two years, left the firm in 1917. There is little documentation of the professional relationship between Cutter and Malmgren, but the office accounts suggest that there were financial reasons for the breakup of their partnership. Over the years as the economy changed, the work load in the office fluctuated; the fees received in good years were substantial, but not enough to sustain the office through leaner times. The practice earned almost $35,000 in 1910, an exceptionally profitable year. But the following year brought in only $20,000, and the partners had to reduce the number of draftsmen in the office from ten to five. In 1912 the fees from the Davenport Hotel boosted receipts to more than $42,000, but over the next four years the annual income averaged less than $7,000. Early in 1914, the drafting room staff was down to two.

During their partnership, Cutter always drew considerably more money than Malmgren did from the firm's profits; indeed the figures suggest that their incomes were tied to the commissions they attracted. Since Cutter was an active member of Spokane society and Malmgren lived a simpler life centered on his family, it was Cutter who brought in the majority of the commissions. The depression that began in 1913 was enough to negate the security that

Malmgren had found in association with the favorite architect of Spokane's elite. He was successful in starting his own practice and is best known for his work at Central Washington State College in Ellensburg. Cancer intervened in his career, however, allowing him only four years more to live.[25]

The capable and genial Henry Bertelsen, who had worked with Cutter and Malmgren since 1909, took over the running of the drafting room and produced many of the excellent drawings; but Cutter did not offer him a partnership.

CHAPTER THIRTEEN

Casting a Lot in Wonderland (1921–1923)

CUTTER ENJOYED EXPENSIVE TASTES. HE LIKED TO DRESS well, to entertain generously, and to dine in style; he traveled widely and preferred to do so in luxury. Although he received many prestigious commissions, he was usually short of money. By the time of World War I, the economic climate of Spokane had changed. His clients were far less lavish than during the building boom at the turn of the century; but he failed to adjust by reducing his fees or cutting corners to compete with other architects. In 1911 he borrowed $7,000, and in 1913, even after receiving the fees for the Davenport Hotel, he was deeper in debt and chose to mortgage his beloved chalet to his client, Charles Corbet, for $16,000. This loan came due in 1918, but he repaid nothing until the next year, when he parted with a meager $2,000.

In 1921 the firm survived on fees from commissions completed in Tacoma the year before, but Cutter was able to pay Corbet only a further $1,000.[1] Cutter's desperate need for work is demonstrated by his willingness to design a single-story rooming house for laborers for the Hurley Mason Company in Tacoma.[2] The year 1921 also saw the death of Karl Gunnar Malmgren after a long struggle with throat cancer.[3]

However, in the summer of 1921, Cutter received an accolade from respected professionals. The June issue of *Architect and Engineer* focused on the buildings and landscape of Spokane and announced the selection by a jury of the ten most notable examples of architecture in the city. In 1919 the journal had sent jurors to Portland, Oregon; in 1920, they had done the same in Los Angeles. In each case, the jury had commented on the standard of design and picked what they considered the ten best buildings. The Spokane jury consisted of two leading Seattle architects, Carl F. Gould and Arthur Loveless; Albert E. Doyle, the preeminent architect of Portland; George W. Fuller; and Charles H. Cheney, who was both an architect and a city planner. Cheney had been particularly vocal during the previous four years, expressing his disgust with the general standards of American architecture. He had appealed to city authorities to eliminate ugliness from the urban scene by instituting design review programs. Applying well-defined criteria, the jury spent three days in October 1920 visiting the buildings, and responded in a complimentary manner:

> It is evident from the photographs reproduced in this number that Spokane's buildings and gardens measure up very well with the standards set in Portland and Los Angeles and yet with a character of design that is very distinctive from that shown by the typical buildings of the other two cities.
>
> When we consider that Spokane is an inland city of only 100,000 population, while Portland has nearly three times as many people and there are ten times that many in Los Angeles County, it is distinctly to the credit of the smaller city that so many fine things have been produced. Why haven't the larger cities given more in proportion?

Of the ten examples selected, six were by Cutter. These were the Davenport Hotel, the Jay P. Graves residence (Waikiki), the Monroe Street Bridge, the R. B. Porter house (formerly the Louis Davenport residence), the Washington Water Power Company Substation, and the Western Union Life building. Also included was the Elks Temple by E. J. Baume, for which Cutter had been the associate architect. In addition, they gave an honorable mention to Cutter's own house, the Humbird and Finucane houses, and Saint Augustine's church and school. In their explanation for the awards, they spoke of "the rare architectural force and genius for design of Mr. Kirtland Cutter. . . . For years, the strength and yet exquisitely finished character of Mr. Cutter's work has been well known throughout the northwest at least." They singled out the interior of the Davenport Hotel, particularly the "livable quality of the lobby," which "extends throughout the hotel" and the "crisp and sparkling detail" of the Isabella Dining Room. They characterized the R. B. Porter residence (originally the Davenport house) as "a remarkably attractive house of distinctly domestic character, yet with a bigness and boldness of treatment that is very pleasing."[4]

With this feature in a prominent professional journal, Cutter must have hoped that new commissions would come in. He felt confident that his fine reputation for hotel work would be his salvation and hoped to secure at least one of three possible hotel jobs in Seattle, Tacoma, and Sandpoint, Idaho.[5] Unfortunately, Cutter failed to recognize that other competent architects were practicing in an atmosphere of cutthroat competition. He continued to believe that the quality of service that he provided would eventually win him work, and he was not willing to cut his fees to compete against newcomers. In fact, he lost all three opportunities for hotel commissions, and 1922 became another bleak year.

His draftsman, Robert Turner, left the firm at the end of March, leaving only Henry Bertelsen to do the drafting. In the entire year, only $6,572 came in, and Bertelsen was not paid for his work after the end of July. Cutter owed money to many Spokane businesses, not least Davenport's Restaurant, where he had continued to entertain prospective clients. But these debts were trifling compared to the amount he still owed to the impatient Charles Corbet. Unwilling to listen to optimistic promises, Corbet resorted to the courts. On December 8, 1922, Cutter's chalet on Seventh Avenue and all its contents were seized by order of the Superior Court of Washington.[6] The house that had been the scene of so many social occasions was snatched away, leaving Kirtland Cutter and his beloved Katharine as outcasts.

Early in 1923, Cutter saw a prospect of some school work. In May, he developed plans for a $33,000 addition to Otis Orchards School, for which he had already designed an extension in 1918.[7] But the plans came to nothing and he received no fees for the design. The only projects his firm had that summer were a top-floor extension to the Galax Hotel, where vaudeville performers boarded, and an interior renovation of Whitehead's Dancing Palace.[8] While the high society of Spokane no longer provided patronage, the only gleam of hope came from the world of popular entertainment. Charles Whitehead, a member of an old theatrical family, was said to have been "born backstage."[9] He was known as an exceptional drummer and succeeded in drawing large crowds, but the pleasures he offered were hardly those of Spokane society in the glittering age.

To add insult to injury, "Gus" Pehrson, who had spent ten years in the office, was now in competition. Cutter was proud of his design for the Western Union Life Insurance Company on Riverside Avenue, but Pehrson was building a substantial addition that encased the original red brick structure in a larger mass of white terra cotta in a style described in the *Spokesman Review* as Grecian.[10] This ostentatious addition, eclipsing the gentle Dutch character of Cutter's building, proclaimed the end of an era.

Although Cutter had often been in debt, he had always kept up appearances. Now, at the age of sixty-three, he was in desperate straits. But he was not alone in worrying about his future; evidently some of his friends were concerned too. Harry Wraight, for whom he had designed a small house on Summit Boulevard in about 1908, had the idea of writing to James Dawson, the western agent for the Olmsted Brothers. Dawson, who had worked on the landscape for thirty of Cutter's commissions, was now assistant director of design for a remarkable development project at Palos Verdes, California. In this project he was associated with Jay Lawyer, who also knew Cutter, and Charles H. Cheney, a member of the jury for *Architect and Engineer*. Exactly what Wraight said is unknown, but Dawson's warm reply on January 30, 1923, must have been deeply reassuring to him:

Dear M. Wraight,

It certainly is a distressing piece of news that you send to me about Cutter. I can't express to you my sorrow for Cutter—a man who has done the vast amount of work, and good work, that he has done for the Northwest, going broke at this stage of the game, with this lack of ability to "come back", is certainly a sad thing to think about. You must realize that Mr. Cutter has done more than anyone else for the architectural attractiveness of Spokane, Tacoma, Portland, Seattle, and now he gets his answer. . . .

The particular information I should like to have concerning Cutter is whether he can make sketches, in the way of elevations and perspective views of proposed buildings and groupings of buildings. I have already talked to Jay Lawyer, who is likely to be one of the most, if not the most, important factor of this big undertaking. Lawyer often speaks of Cutter and often refers to him with great admiration for the work that he has done. Only a few weeks ago Mr. Lawyer said to me that he wished some of these architects in Los Angeles could have associated with them a man of Cutter's artistic ability. Therefore I think that Mr. Lawyer would endeavor to help Cutter find something to do. I think that he would try to arrange it to have Cutter design the houses of some of his, Mr. Lawyer's, friends, which might be built on the Project within the next year; but as Lawyer stated, the difficulty is to find something to earn food and clothes for Cutter at once.

That being the case, will you let me know if Cutter is still in a position to make perspective drawings, and would he be willing to take a salaried job temporarily until he could run across some real work in designing houses? If he would take a salaried job, how large a salary would he want?

Of course it is very difficult indeed to try to get something for a person when he most needs it, and I must say that I have been unsuccessful when I have tried it. But in spite of that, I shall certainly make every effort I possibly can, because it is at just such a time that a person needs his friends.

James F. Dawson[11]

The praise that Dawson lavished on Cutter was a genuine tribute to the architect's achievements. Dawson was a sensitive and highly professional man who had worked with most of the major architects of the Northwest and watched the development of its principal cities over many years. His concern for quality in design and his ability to judge architectural work can hardly be questioned. Jay Lawyer, considering Cutter's work from the investor's point of view, seemed equally complimentary. On March 1, Kirtland Cutter sent the following touching letter to Dawson at Palos Verdes:

Dear Dawson

Harry Wraight recently handed me a beautiful letter from you which so characteristically expressed your warm friendship and sympathy for me, together with your high regard for my work, the profound appreciation of which I am quite unable to convey to you, but be assured your words of sincere concern did me a world of good, for in the span of life mutual attachment, amounting to friendship, is to few confined, and, with the clearer understanding of maturing years, these ties bind closer such treasures to the recipient heart.

As friend Wraight has written you, after climbing to a comparative eminence over the toilsome trail to success with ever alluring prospects just beyond, I have unsuspectingly wandered into the desert, and with humiliation am now appealing for guidance out of this land of promises unfulfilled.

Misfortune has not yet broken my spirit or modified my enthusiasm, and with the advantages of long experience, I feel better equipped for good work today than ever before, and am told by qualified critics that my late creations testify to the belief.

During the past few years I have been most interested in Architecture of the Italian and Spanish renaissance, and have designed a number of houses and small hotels in these styles which have been very successful.

My work in designing is confined to small scale, usually free hand, sketch plans, elevations and perspectives, which are developed by a clever all around man that I have had with me for the past fourteen years. Together we are able to turn out the preliminary work quickly and in an attractive way, which includes studies of groupings done in perspective.

I am trying to pick up enough work in the northwest to keep us busy until autumn, when we hope to go south to remain, and I shall certainly appreciate anything that you and Mr. Lawyer are able to do towards getting me in on any small part of the work coming up in connection with the great Palos Verdes Project.

Again assuring you of my regard for you and for the sincere interest in my welfare, expressed in your letter, I am always

Kirtland Cutter[12]

On March 4 Dawson telegraphed Cutter:

Do you plan to come to Los Angeles Please send me immediately some photographs of your work especially Italian and Spanish houses and including Thorne and Cowles houses.[13]

On the 17th, Cutter telegraphed Dawson to say that photographs, plans, and sketches were on the way and that he would probably be ready to leave for California by June 1.[14] Dawson's reply on the 19th was guarded, but contained a hint of optimism:

Wire received only Cowles photographs have arrived Unable to make any promises or predictions After you were located here believe you could get considerable work as boom seems to be on.[15]

The boom in southern California was indeed on. While Spokane plunged into depression, the Los Angeles area was thriving; the discovery on June 23, 1921, of oil in Long Beach contributed to its prosperity. However, there was still reason to be cautious; the project at Palos Verdes had been initiated ten years earlier, but had faltered.

The First World War and problems with financing had delayed development, which was only just getting under way (see Chapter 14). Cutter needed assurance of work, but when the drawings of the Cowles house finally reached Palos Verdes, Dawson was leaving for Seattle and Tacoma. Cutter did not meet him while he was traveling in the Northwest, and several weeks passed without any decision being made. But early in June he received a letter from his old friend Lane Gilliam, who was now involved with Henry B. Barbour in large-scale real estate ventures in southern California. Barbour, for whom Cutter had designed the unbuilt hotel at Playa Del Rey, had been involved in real estate ventures on the Washington coast, but he had moved to Los Angeles in 1902 and become one of the most successful real estate promoters in the area, laying out subdivisions in Long Beach, Los Angeles, and San Pedro.[16] Gilliam wrote as follows:

> Dear Kirt:
>
> I have recently associated myself with the Henry P. Barbour Company of Long Beach and just now we are taking over an addition at Laguna Beach about twenty-five miles south of here. It is a beautiful location, I think one of the most beautiful on the Southern Pacific coast.
>
> It is going to require a great deal of landscape and architectural work and Mr. Barbour, knowing of your prowess along those lines, has asked me to get in correspondence with you to see if inducements could be made for you to come down here and take up this particular line of work, of which there will be a vast amount.
>
> He contemplates many improvements in building houses, lodges, and in a general way having you as his chief architect to pass upon all plans as well as make plans for the many houses that they expect will be built there. I want to say to you personally that this is a new and very broad field in which you could so far outshine anyone that is now on the ground that you could establish yourself here in what I think would be a wonderful business. The field is wide open and can be had for the asking. . . .
>
> There is a vast amount of building going on in this part of the country and I certainly think that you will make no mistake by casting your lot with us. At the present time there is a colony of some sixty celebrated artists located at the town of Laguna and it is the intention of Mr. Barbour to make this the most artistic place in California. Mr. Barbour owns 148 acres of land with many of the most beautiful situ-

ations of any piece of land of like size that I know of in any part of the West and it will be a field in which you could elaborate to your heart's content.

Aside from this particular place, Long Beach is growing by leaps and bounds and there are many buildings being built here and the field for you would be the whole southwest coast which is alive and teeming with all kinds of industries and building operation.

Weigh this thing carefully and if you feel that you would like to cast your lot with us write me at your earliest convenience.

With kindest regards to both Katie and yourself, I beg to remain

Yours most truly, Lane[17]

At the top of the letter Cutter had scribbled: "This sounds good. Am writing Lane today." His reply to Gilliam on June 13 conveys both gratitude and enthusiasm.

Dear Lane:

Your letter of the 5th was awaiting me on my return to the old burg today and it was a real joy to hear from one of my oldest and dearest friends and to learn that both you and Mr. Barbour hold so high a regard for my professional ability.

Many years have passed since you and I with light and hopeful hearts traveled those flowery trails together which teemed with adventure and promise.

In the interim I have endeavored to keep in step with the rapid march of progress and it pleases me greatly to be assured so sincerely of my maintained position in the ever enlarging profession, and to be urged so heartily to cast my lot with you in a field of unprecedented activity and unlimited possibilities. . . .

During the past few years I have been most interested in architecture of the Italian and Spanish renaissance and have designed a number of important houses and hotels in these styles which have proven very successful. In connection with the country homes I have had charge of the laying out of extensive estates and with the benefit of this experience I feel better qualified to undertake the interesting problems which the Laguna Beach addition presents, and am keen to don my old thinking cap in an environment of inspiration. . . .

Very sincerely yours, Kirt[18]

The wait for a reply must have been interminable. Five long weeks passed before Cutter telegraphed Gilliam: "When may I expect to

hear from Mr. Barbour. Kirt." This telegram produced an immediate reply from Henry Barbour.[19]

My dear Mr. Cutter:

I was very glad to read a letter from you the other day handed to
me by our mutual friend Mr. Lane C. Gilliam. It seemed like old
times.

I have, after very carefully investigating the Laguna project, been
obliged to turn it down. It was especially tempting to me from a
beauty point of view but on account of expense in platting and
putting in the necessary improvements, I finally abandoned the idea.

This need not be especially disappointing to you. Long Beach, now
a city of one hundred and twenty thousand people, is assured by
developments of the past week in the practical establishment of a
great steel industry of becoming a city of three hundred thousand
people. I do not want you to show this letter to anyone but as far as
I know there is not a real architect here and there is a great deal of
work to be done.

If you will come down here and look the field over, I shall be glad
to introduce you to the Directors of the Chamber of Commerce,
some twenty strong men, and to the Board of Realtors, two hundred
and fifty strong, of which Board I am unfortunate enough to be serving my fifth term as President, as well as to many other good strong
people here in order to get you started. . . .

Come down and look the situation over anyway. Awaiting your
reply, I beg to remain,

Yours very truly, Henry P. Barbour

On July 23, Cutter sent a wire to Barbour that suggests some reservation and anxiety: "In your opinion would I be likely to miss anything important by delaying arrival at Long Beach until September
Fifteenth. Please wire reply collect." The same day Barbour replied:
"There being nothing definite at present to offer think you would
lose nothing by delay however the sooner you get on the ground I
think the quicker and surer your start."[20]

Cutter wrote immediately to Gilliam announcing his decision,
but expressing concern about living costs.

Dear Lane:

Since the receipt of Mr. Barbour's very kind letter I have decided to
cast my lot with you in "Wonderland" and expect to reach Long

Beach by the middle of September, if nothing unforeseen further delays our making the break. In the meantime there is much to be done in order to get my affairs here in shape.

After a long period of small and unprofitable work my exchequer has become depleted in spite of rigid economy practiced, and which we have learned so thoroughly through that austere teacher "Necessity". Hence, with but a small surplus for tiding over an indefinite period of waiting, it will be prudent to do a little figuring before making the leap. I am, therefore, going to ask your assistance in the way of information as to the cost of living in some convenient and pleasant, but not fashionable, district.

For the present a combination living and bedroom with bath and good plain food would fill our requirements, not forgetting shelter for the car.

Later, if things come my way, a tiny cottage on the installment plan would insure Kate's contentment. Until that time our furniture will be stored in Spokane. It was my idea to secure a very small office until work is assured and then expand accordingly. I have a man of exceptional ability who has been with me for many years. He would close this office and come south to take charge when the time for organizing arrives. . . .

Sincerely yours, [Kirt][21]

Gilliam's reply on August 11 closed as follows:

Activity in building in Long Beach is the liveliest of any place I have ever seen and with the influence of Mr. Barbour and other friends I have no fears that you will be most successful. I am certainly living in hopes of seeing you as soon as it is convenient for you to arrive for I believe the time is now ripe for you to cast your lot here.

With my very kindest regards to Kate, I am, Yours sincerely, Lane[22]

Cutter was determined not to be lured to California by unrealistic promises. While Dawson and Barbour had painted glowing pictures of prospects there, neither had been able to offer anything tangible. However, since he had lost both home and office, he had little alternative. On September 10 he wired Gilliam that he expected to be in Long Beach on the 18th, but his able assistant Henry Bertelsen was not willing to leave Spokane. Indeed, Cutter owed him several months' salary when the practice had wound up, a score he settled by selling him and his secretary, Dana Agergaard, the entire contents of his office for the sum of one dollar "and other valuable considerations."[23]

Ironically, Cutter's sad departure from Spokane occurred at the time of his greatest professional triumph, his election as a Fellow of the American Institute of Architects in March 1923.[24] The coveted rank of Fellow had been awarded to only 140 out of 2,700 members nationwide and only two Northwest architects had been so honored. While there was undoubtedly a certain amount of jealousy among his rivals in the profession, he could not have been elected to a fellowship without their support. Letters of recommendation for the honor included the following comments:

> Mr. Cutter was a pioneer in the Pacific Northwest, beginning at a time when aesthetic appreciation was particularly lacking. Mr. Cutter has consistently contributed to the community the work of an artist.
>
> I know of no individual in this district who has so uniformly raised the standard of architecture above the general level of the community's taste.
>
> Many times he has sacrificed financial profit to himself in order to produce these results. Among the fellows and non-fellows of the region, I know of none who is more deserving of this honor than Mr. Cutter.
>
> We . . . feel it a privilege to endorse the name of a man whose progress we have watched through many years, who has contributed to the profession the splendid gifts of his genius, and who has striven to elevate in the public mind a greater respect for and a deeper understanding and a finer appreciation of Architecture.[25]

The news of Cutter's honor, reported in the Spokane papers, brought a congratulatory letter from Frederick Phair, one of the city's leading contractors whom Cutter had started on his career as the clerk of works on the Exchange National Bank after the fire in 1889. Phair had been responsible for the construction of the Idaho Building in Chicago and its replica in Ringwood, England. He wrote: "While the honor is a signal one, it is, I think, only a small testimonial, in comparison to what you deserve. I hope that you who have done so much to beautify the city of your adoption may be given many further opportunities to give us more examples of your artistic skill and ability."[26]

A warm tribute from a satisfied client may have been the most touching. Helen Falk, responding to reports of his honor, wrote from Boise in July 1923: "We have always known that you were one of the greatest architects in the country—but it is nice to have people who are acknowledged critics agree with me. . . . We regret you leaving for California—as I had hoped you would build some more houses in Idaho—but I still contend you can do more from a distance than most people can do on the ground. . . . "[27]

Professional recognition in Washington, D.C., did not help to bring in the commissions, still less to pay the bills, but it must have raised Cutter's spirits as he left for his new life in the south. Nor did he slip out of Spokane entirely unnoticed. On August 26, Hannah Hinsdale wrote in the *Spokesman-Review*:

> Architecture is the geology of civilization, and by it you may discover what periods people lived in and what were their standards of taste. Spokane from such a standpoint would rank high and any scientist judging us architecturally would be surprised by our artistic cubic content of number of square feet of beauty. And the reason is that Kirtland K. Cutter lived here and built here, often much better than we ourselves knew. . . .
>
> And all through the town may be traced the trail of Mr. Cutter's idealism, his visions come true in stone and brick, in wood and plaster. If ever one man set his seal on a place, Mr. Cutter has on Spokane.

As soon as Cutter arrived in California in September 1923, he decided, on the advice of Henry Barbour, to set up his office in Long Beach. The discovery of oil there had brought prosperity and with it potential clients to whom Barbour had promised introductions (see Chapter 15). However, he came without his office staff or even the furnishings and equipment necessary to launch a convincing architectural practice. Fortunately, Dana Agergaard, his devoted secretary for over twenty years, followed him and resumed her work as office manager, typist, and accountant. He was also lucky to find Jess J. Jones, a thirty-five-year-old draftsman who could produce his working drawings and specifications, and supervise construction.[28]

Like many of Cutter's partners and assistants, Jones was in many respects his opposite; yet each needed the other. Cutter had come to architecture through academic study, travel, and experience with wealthy clients; he was steeped in the history of architecture and the artistic side of his profession. He moved easily among the rich and beguiled them with his charm; to convey his ideas he produced little freehand sketches from which designs could be developed. Jess Jones was a practical man, experienced as a carpenter, bricklayer, and shingler; he understood the business of contracting and was also an able draftsman, but he had never enjoyed the benefit of travel or higher education. He felt no rapport with the wealthy and was more comfortable with working people. Among craftsman in the building trades he showed a confidence born of experience. Once, when Jones overheard a bricklayer complaining about the demanding instructions he was expected to follow, he put the man to shame by quietly laying the bricks himself.

Cutter, in the tradition of his scientifically minded ancestors, was an atheist, while Jones was a deeply religious member of the Calvary Presbyterian Church. He went through life "with a bible in one hand and a hammer in the other," his bible well worn through daily use. When, during Prohibition, he had to design fold-away bars to conceal liquor, he would "draw a line and ask for forgiveness." But Jones respected Cutter as a teacher for whom it was a privilege to work. When, as sometimes happened, Cutter was unable to raise the money for his salary, he accepted the delay as a small price to pay for his introduction to the profession of architecture. The office in the Farmers' and Merchants' Bank in downtown Long Beach was small and quite austere. Dana Agergaard worked in a cramped space in the entrance lobby from which a door led into a small drafting room. Cutter occupied a private room with glass-fronted bookshelves where he could receive clients.[29]

Early in 1924, after a period of anxious waiting, it was announced that Cutter had been engaged for a period of ten years as consulting architect for the new city of Palos Verdes.[30]

CHAPTER FOURTEEN

Palos Verdes and the California Style (1923–1934)

KIRTLAND CUTTER'S CARMAN AND FALK RESIDENCES, completed shortly before he left the Northwest for California, confirm his growing interest in the Mediterranean Style developing there. In his Mission Revival buildings at the turn of the century, he had emulated early attempts in California to revive Hispanic traditions. Like his contemporaries in many parts of the country, he had exploited decorative elements of the missions for dramatic effect. Two decades later, he recognized a changing architectural vocabulary on the southern Pacific Coast and gave it his own interpretation. His arrival in California in 1923 came at an opportune time when debate was taking place on the nature of Californian architecture.

A group of architects practicing in the Los Angeles area in the twenties and thirties, including George Washington Smith, Wallace Neff, Roland Coates, and Gordon Kaufman, concentrated not on exterior embellishments but on interior space and the relationship of the house to the site. Their buildings were conceived as "sculptural volumes closely attached to the land."[1] It was to these designers that Cutter showed the greatest affinity. He had begun his long career in Spokane designing houses in an Arts and Crafts manner that seemed to grow out of the rocky hillsides. Although in the course of his career he had often been seduced by opulent eclecticism, he was ready to embark on a series of designs for the new development at Palos Verdes that called for a simple, unified language appropriate to the terrain and to the ideals of the project's promoters.

The high Palos Verdes Peninsula that juts out into the ocean between Long Beach and Santa Monica Bay served in the late nineteenth century as a range for cattle and sheep. As the population of nearby Los Angeles grew, it offered a new potential. In 1913, a New York banker, Frank E. Vanderlip, purchased 16,000 acres there—unseen—for a financial syndicate he headed. Their plan was to create "the most fashionable and exclusive residence colony" in the nation. They retained the distinguished architects Howard Van Doren Shaw of Chicago and Myron Hunt of Los Angeles, as well as the Olmsted Brothers of Brookline, Massachusetts, to carry out preliminary designs.

The concept that they produced was a series of "model villages" as social and commercial nuclei of the residential communities. They aimed to create "towns having all the charm of some places that so delight tourists traveling in rural districts of Germany and England." Insisting on a system of design review, they stated: "In each village the architecture of every building from the business blocks to the humblest cottages will be regulated." Frank Vanderlip built himself a cottage at Palos Verdes, but with the advent of World War I the syndicate lost interest in the project. In 1921 they sold the land to Edward G. Lewis, a real estate promoter from St. Louis. However, when his scheme faltered for lack of financial support, Vanderlip took control again and refinanced it with capital from Los Angeles banks. The eminent city planning consultant Charles H. Cheney joined Frederick Law Olmsted, Jr., in refining the original plans for immediate implementation.[2]

While the first idea in 1913 had been to create a millionaires' colony, the development was now opened to a broader middle-class public.[3] Unlike the Garden Cities conceived by Ebenezer Howard in England, in which the inclusion of industry and other opportunities for employment was considered essential, this was to be purely a residential suburb. Carefully fitting roads to the contours of the land and profiting from the series of terraces on its slopes, the designers platted neighborhoods to encourage picturesque arrangements of houses on lots of diverse character. An unusual element of the design was that one-quarter of the total acreage was given over to parks, beaches, and the golf course. Shopping centers, surrounded by a limited number of apartment buildings, were proposed about two miles apart.[4]

The developers used extraordinary means to ensure that the principles of the City Beautiful movement were maintained. It is clear that they regarded the profit motive as a potentially dangerous force capable of undermining their idealistic vision. Although the project was financed by investors, they were to have no say in the direction of the development. Control was vested in the Palos Verdes Trust, which was governed by the Palos Verdes Homes Association, in which every lot owner had a share. This was a nonprofit, non-stock organization, representing the residents and responsible for the management of the entire community.

The ultimate power in making decisions about the physical form, or affecting the appearance of the Palos Verdes Estates, was in the hands of the Art Jury. The Homes Association was obliged to submit all proposals for buildings, roads, landscape improvements, walls, fountains, and so forth, to the Jury, as were the individual property owners.[5] But the members of the Jury were bound primarily by their professional standards and ethics. They were paid for their services. The Palos Verdes development succeeded because the Art Jury consisted of highly qualified experts who were independent of the company selling the land and entirely above influence peddling or other forms of self-interest.[6] They were responsible for developing the criteria by which designs were judged. Furthermore, they did not merely respond to drawings submitted but actually commissioned designs for shopping centers, parks, schools, libraries, recreational buildings, and landscaping.

The Jury carefully described the "types" of architecture that would be permitted in the development. These varied according to the topography and over the years were slightly modified. The three districts they defined were the Ocean Slopes, the Mesas Crowning the Hills, and the Northern Slopes of the Palos Verdes Hills. In the first, a Mediterranean or "Latin type" was required with a tiled roof not exceeding 35 degrees and walls of light-colored material. Both Spanish and Italian influences were encouraged. On the mesas, roof pitches could be increased to 40 degrees. English Colonial and Southern French types were permitted, but the Mediterranean types were favored, and in fact prevailed. Darker colors and steeper roof pitches up to 60 degrees were allowed on the northern slopes. In this area, designs of Elizabethan, Norman French, and Flemish were accepted in addition to the Latin, increasing the range of architectural expression.[7] Frederick Law Olmsted, Jr., stressed the goal of unity, but also made it clear that there was no desire to stifle the creativity of individual designers:

The great distinction of Palos Verdes as a residential community is the consistent emphasis on the two-fold principle: first, that the success of a great whole depends on the harmony of all the parts, that there is no class of physical changes which can be made in disregard of the rest without danger of impairing the whole. . . ; and second that the inventiveness and imagination of many individuals must be given scope—so as to avoid a monotonous and stereotyped quality. . . . [8]

When Cutter reached southern California in late September 1923, the Art Jury was already in place. It consisted of four architects, Myron Hunt, John Galen Howard, Robert Farquhar, and David Allison, as well as landscape architect James Dawson of the Olmsted Brothers' firm, city planner Charles H. Cheney, and the general manager of the project, Jay Lawyer.[9] Six districts of the Palos Verdes Estates had been mapped and one planned in detail; work had begun on the construction of roads. To encourage buyers, the comfortable La Venta Inn, designed by Pierpoint and Walter S. Davis, had been built to accommodate visitors and give them a foretaste of life in a suburb where good design could be taken for granted.

Dawson and Cheney were ready to support Cutter when the opportunity arose, and he only had to wait for two months before the Art Jury awarded him an important commission to design Lunada Bay Plaza, an entire village center, serving two of the six residential districts.[10] After his last two years in Spokane, barely surviving on small, unrewarding jobs, the scope of this project must have thrilled him. He was in sympathy with the Jury's aims and quickly embarked on a design modeled on the piazza of a picturesque Italian town (fig. 14.1). Following Italian precedent, he surrounded the open space with arcaded walks so that shoppers could enjoy complete protection from sun and rain, while going about their errands, or lingering to talk with friends. Although the piazza he designed was rectangular in plan and the buildings around it were similar in height, Cutter broke up the masses by stepping some structures forward a little and added drama to the skyline with a few taller blocks and towers. The general impression was of a group of buildings that had evolved over many years without any preconceived idea of symmetry. In one corner, a tall gatehouse made a picturesque accent; elsewhere a broad arch opened up a lower block. One tower rose sheer like an Italian campanile or watchtower and another, based on a mission bell tower, stepped up in three stages.[11]

14.1 Lunada Bay Plaza, Palos Verdes, 1923–24. Cutter's romantic evocation of an Italian town was never built. An economic depression prevented its construction. *Landscape Architecture*, July 1927.

Early in January 1924, Cutter presented his design to the Jury, who made some suggestions for revisions; he returned in mid-March for further discussions with the Jury, but no immediate action was taken to implement the plan.[12] There is no doubt that Cutter's design was highly regarded, because it was illustrated in articles by Frederick Law Olmsted, Jr., Myron Hunt, and James Dawson.[13] However, the development of Palos Verdes did not proceed as fast as had been intended and Cutter had to wait while one of the other village centers, Malaga Cove Plaza, was built. This scheme by Webber and Spaulding, begun in 1925, was slightly less ambitious than Cutter's design for Lunada Bay Plaza, but it followed the same pattern of arcaded walks around a central square. It was built incrementally, each building owner constructing his section according to the master plan. As the years passed with no progress on his plaza, Cutter must have felt a deep frustration, but he was soon busy with domestic commissions.

His first house, begun in 1924, was for Mr. and Mrs. Adrian E. Cameron, who had chosen a lofty site commanding a fine view over Santa Monica Bay to the north (figs. 14.2–14.4). Working with the Olmsted Brothers, who designed the gardens, he planned a house that profited from the view but also offered protection from the

14.2 Cameron house, Palos Verdes, 1924, from the south, looking toward Santa Monica Bay. This picturesque cluster of low-pitched, red-tiled roofs surrounds a secluded patio. Malaga Cove Library, Palos Verdes.

14.3 The patio of the Cameron house combines the serenity of a mission cloister and the luxury provided by an outdoor fireplace. Photo by the author.

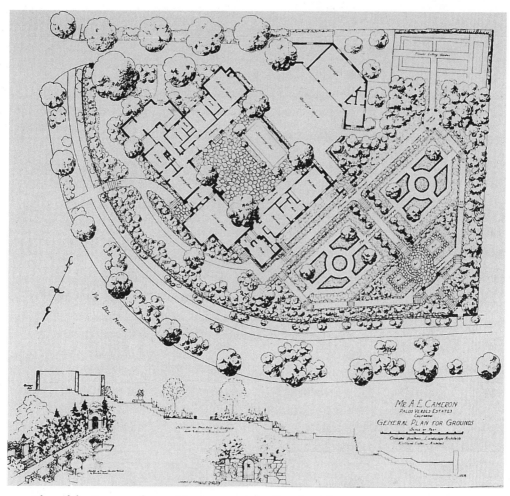

14.4 Plan of the Cameron house. Most rooms open directly to the open air or into a shady arcade. The garden, laid out by the Olmsted Brothers, combines formal and informal areas. *Pacific Coast Architect,* April 1927.

wind.[14] He took advantage of the mild climate to create a home for informal living. He arranged it on three sides of an almost square patio that serves as a generous outdoor room as well as a means of circulating between the interior spaces. On the east and west sides, bedrooms open onto arcades constructed in the simple, massive style of the missions. Rising a little above the long, low roofs of these two wings, the gable end of the living room stands higher, dominating the court as a simple church might dominate a cloister. But beside the living room an open-air fireplace, within an arch of rough stone, proclaims that this is no place of monastic asceticism.

Even on a winter evening, the residents and their guests can enjoy the outdoors around a blazing fire. The south side of the patio, beyond a rectangular swimming pool, is closed by a high wall screening the service yard and garage.

Although this is essentially a U-shaped house around a court, various projections and changes of roof level as well as slope of the ground around it create visual variety. The northern end of the living room, emphasizing its dominance, stands forward to protect the front door from the westerly wind. In the Northwest corner, a square tower with a hipped roof rises up as a romantic gesture. From the owner's study beneath the tower a passage leads out onto a long terrace of rugged stone overlooking a formal garden at a lower level and the distant view over the Pacific. At the southern end of the terrace, curving walls articulate the corner. Even the kitchen court in the northeast corner is walled in a sculptural manner. The front door, framed in stone in a style typical of old Mexican houses, is more dignified than ornate. But many intriguing details catch the eye: a quatrefoil window in the gable end of the living room, iron grilles similar to those found in Mexico over some of the smaller windows, and, in the heavy wooden doors opening to the ambulatories from the garage court, ornamental ironwork representing peacocks with elegantly curling tail feathers (fig. 14.5). Once again, Cutter returned to a motif he had first used at the Glover mansion and Davenport's restaurant.

The interiors avoid ostentation; details are simple. The wooden ceiling of the living room, supported on exposed rafters and heavy wooden trusses bound by iron straps, shows an Arts and Crafts delight in the expression of structure. The dining room ceiling, also of wood, is divided into small squares by intersecting beams. The living room fireplace, flanked by columns and covered by a canopy, is less ornate than those in Cutter's recent Northwest houses. The character of the interiors depends on the play of light, the gentle transitions from indoors to out, and the definition of the spaces by solid structure. Moving from the enclosed rooms into the arcaded ambulatories where the light constantly changes and out to the open patio, one discovers how sensual such plain, unaffected architecture can be.

The low-pitched, red-tiled roofs, thick walls, and arcades of the Cameron house present imagery from the mission, but without the scalloped gables and bell towers that characterized the Mission Revival in a decorative way. In many respects, this house is closer to

14.5 Ornamental ironwork in a door leading into one of the arcades at the Cameron house. Photo by the author.

14.6 John Wehrman house, Palos Verdes, 1924. Like Cutter's earliest
houses in Spokane, this one seems to grow organically out of the
landscape. *Palos Verdes Bulletin,* August 1925. Malaga Cove Library,
Palos Verdes.

an Andalusian or Tuscan farmhouse than to any of the missions.
Designed for the site and climate, it possesses the timeless qualities
that the Palos Verdes Art Jury hoped to see. Indeed, the Jury initiated its awards program in 1924 by giving the design the Certificate
of Honor for the best architecture of the year.[15] Thus Cutter established the vocabulary he was to use on sixteen houses at Palos
Verdes.[16] Each one was built on a site of individual character,
offering diverse problems and opportunities; the clients expressed
their own particular desires and needs and the architect played variations on his new theme.

Cutter's second Palos Verdes house was for John Wehrman. Also
designed in 1924, it responded to a very different site in the Miraleste
district on the southern slope of the peninsula overlooking San
Pedro Harbor (fig. 14.6).[17] The architect composed it of three volumes, one of which rises above the others as a low tower. Lying
below Via Colonita, it is entered from the street by a bridge above
a sunken garden. From the upper level, an entrance hall and garage
steps lead down into the living space below and out into a walled
garden beyond. Since the house effectively screens the garden from
public gaze, privacy is easily achieved, but views from the living
room into the sunken garden on the north side add diversity of

outlook. A balcony, shaded by an overhanging roof, makes an upper-level vantage point; below, a terrace and a more intimate paved court in the corner offer a variety of places to relax in sun or shade.

Three years later, on a steep site with access from above, Cutter went further with the idea of entry at the top of the house. In the Sisson house on Via Montemar,[18] he made no attempt to present the conventional image of a house facing the street. Nothing is seen but the garage, beside which a discreet entry leads down into a surprisingly large residence concealed below.

As the Palos Verdes project progressed from paper plans to a real community with a village center at Malaga Cove, and enticing homes on the surrounding slopes, contractors became interested in building houses speculatively on the estate. Two such men turned to Cutter; he built three homes for F. F. Schellenberg and two for W. M. Sutherland.

The Schellenberg houses, built on flatter ground east of Malaga Cove near the golf course, are smaller than the Cameron and Wehrman houses; but expanded by patios and shaded ambulatories or porches, they offer similar opportunities for informal outdoor living. The first, on Paseo del Campo, sold by the builder to Robert G. Paull, was the most conventional; however, in Cutter's usual manner, it is broken into a series of separate volumes, one of which steps forward toward the street under a low-pitched roof. At the back, in the angle of the L-shaped plan, an inset, two-story porch provides shady indoor space overlooking a small patio. This house expressed the role of the automobile in suburban life by including a wide garage opening in the front facade.

In the second, which Schellenberg occupied himself, Cutter developed the patio, with an ambulatory of four broad arches on solid piers (fig. 14.7) as the principal focus of the house.[19] The house is set well back from the street, almost concealed behind the garage; a flagstone-paved path beside the garage leads to a door and down steps into the ambulatory. Entering this court is like going into the cloister of a small monastery. It is a peaceful place in which the play of light and shade is the essence of the architecture. Passing the kitchen and the dining room, one reaches another door, which opens into the hall and the living room beyond. The living room, profiting from its position in the foot of the L-shaped plan, has French windows on all four sides, opening onto small balconies and into the patio. The most striking feature of this room is its lightness

14.7 Schellenberg house, Palos Verdes, 1926. The arcade, opening to the patio, leads from the entry arch to the main door. Malaga Cove Library, Palos Verdes.

and the simplicity of the decor. The doors and windows are set directly in the plaster without the embellishment of moldings. A plain arch leads into the hall. The staircase, as in all the Palos Verdes houses, has tiled risers and a light, wrought iron balustrade. The compactly planned bedrooms above cover only the living room and dining room, allowing light to enter the patio over the lower roof of the kitchen.

The third Schellenberg house (1927), sold to Edgar S. Gilmore, on Paseo del Campo facing the golf course (figs. 14.8, 14.9),[20] gets its character from a long balcony cantilevered out below an overhang-

14.8 Schellenberg/Gilmore house, Palos Verdes, 1927. The balcony, shaded by the roof, evokes Mexican traditions. Malaga Cove Library, Palos Verdes.

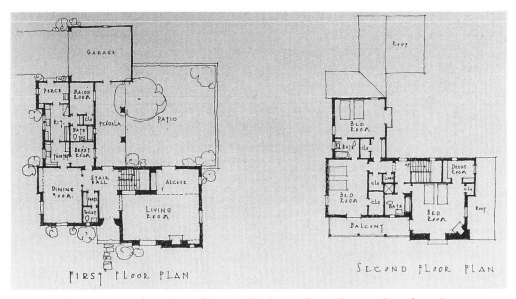

14.9 Plans of the Schellenberg/Gilmore house. The informal arrangement around the patio creates privacy and shade. *Architect and Engineer,* January 1930.

340

ing roof over more than half of the upper facade. Although window openings are fairly large, plain wall surfaces predominate. To simplify the facades, the small windows of bathrooms are covered with stone grilles, whitewashed in continuity with the walls. This was a device the architect used on most of his Palos Verdes houses. As in the other Schellenberg houses, a patio was enclosed in the angle of the L-shaped plan. The garage, placed discreetly at the back, in this case, partly sheltered a third side. Rather than build an arcaded ambulatory, as in the previous house, Cutter placed a pergola on solid piers along one side between the hall and the garage.

Sutherland, the other contractor for whom Cutter worked in 1926, put up two large and complex houses side by side on a natural terrace between two steep slopes (fig. 14.10).[21] Their site on Via

14.10 Two houses for W. M. Sutherland, Palos Verdes. Cutter placed the houses, separated by a terraced garden, picturesquely on the brow of a hill. Poper Collection.

Horquilla looked northwest beyond Malaga Cove to Santa Monica Bay and across a great sweep of country inland. From the road on the upper side, each house appeared as a unified, solid block, but from the slope of the hill they grew in a series of steps out of the steep terrain. Between the two houses and on the slopes around them, white walls defined a series of intimate garden spaces. To enjoy the view, almost every room opened onto a balcony or stone terrace. Some of these were shaded by roofs, some by vine-covered pergolas or trees; others were open to the sun. The rooms within offered a similar variety of size and shape and echoed the Mediterranean character of the exteriors.

As in the Cameron house, the front door of the first of this pair is framed in stone in the manner of old Mexican houses. Flanked by pilasters, the arch over the door is ornamented with an elegant scalloped design. Otherwise, the only decorative work is in the turned balusters of balconies and the molded brackets that support them. The first of the two houses was sold to Mr. W. White Cotton, the second to Mrs. Fannie Wilkins.

Below the two houses just described, Cutter built his largest Palos Verdes home for Earle W. Gard, a successful engineer who at the time of the commission was assistant manager of the Pan American Petroleum Company Oil Refinery. This house of about 10,000 square feet occupies another natural terrace from which, despite its lower position, there is still a good view. Following the contours of the land, it is long and fairly narrow, but broadens out at each end (figs. 14.11–14.13). While the general massing is simple, Cutter enlivened the surface by detail. At one end of the north facade, a low, round tower makes a bulge in the wall.[22] At the other end, from the master bedroom and dressing room, balconies of two different types project out, and at the back of the master suite an inset balcony of more solid construction adds further variety. Cutter used the Mediterranean and Mission vocabularies for picturesque effect, much as he employed the architectural language of Old England in previous years.

On the north side of the Gard house, between the projections at the two ends, lies a huge, level terrace, but a more attractive outdoor space is a stone-paved patio at the back, opening off a long ambulatory defined by massive stone arches. Paved with red clay tiles, handmade to give an aged appearance, and roofed with heavy wooden beams, the ambulatory creates an impression of antiquity. The forty-foot living room conveys a sense of privilege, resembling,

14.11 Earle W. Gard house, Palos Verdes, 1927, south side, seen from the Sutherland houses. From this side it seems as simple as a Tuscan or Andalusian farmhouse. The Otto Stein house can be seen beyond. Malaga Cove Library, Palos Verdes.

perhaps, the home of a Spanish nobleman or merchant of colonial Mexico. It is not so much the richness of the ornament as the solidity of the structure that exerts power. Two huge beams a foot and a half deep and more than a foot thick span the room and support sturdy joists, creating a lively pattern overhead. A small library opens off the corner opposite the door from the ambulatory. In the basement below, other needs were satisfied in a billiard room and a playroom.

In the Gard house Cutter offered the oil magnate of the 1920s the same sense of an ancestral home that he gave the Spokane mining millionaires thirty years earlier, but in a simpler and more unified

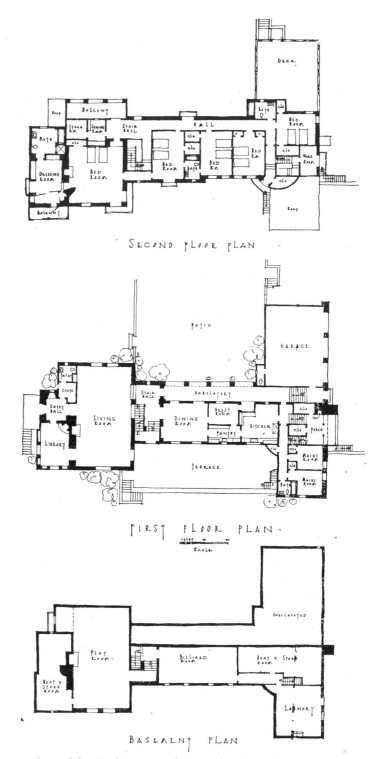

SECOND FLOOR PLAN

FIRST FLOOR PLAN.

BASEMENT PLAN

14.12 Plans of the Gard house. *Architect and Engineer,* January 1930.

14.13 North side of the Gard House. The two projecting wings enclose a raised terrace facing Santa Monica Bay. Poper Collection.

manner. Its careful planning for a complex of subtly intertwined functions demonstrates that the architect understood how the home of a wealthy family was run. From the kitchen quarters to the master bedroom suite, he considered every detail.

In the Buchanan house (1927),[23] Cutter once again designed an introverted living environment in which the barriers between indoors and outdoors are broken down. He enhanced the sense of privacy by creating a carefully controlled entry sequence, leading gradually from the public domain outside the gate to the inner sanctum of the living room (figs. 14.14–14.17). The house stands two stories high on the edge of a steep bank above Via del Monte, the road that winds up the northern slope of Palos Verdes from Malaga Cove Plaza to the high vantage point of the Cameron house. A rough stone wall and dense shrubbery, interspersed with a few palm trees, protect the house from this side. Turning left, into Via Somonte, level with the upper story, the visitor is confronted with a gate house in a high whitewashed wall as simple as the wall of a farmhouse. A stone-flagged path approaches its broad arch, and, if the gate is open, the path can be seen continuing through a walled garden to a second arch beyond. This leads into an arcaded ambulatory which opens to the right into a secluded inner patio. To the

14.14 James E. Buchanan house, Palos Verdes, 1927. Appearing to be only one story high, this house makes use of the steep slope to accommodate a full story below. Malaga Cove Library, Palos Verdes.

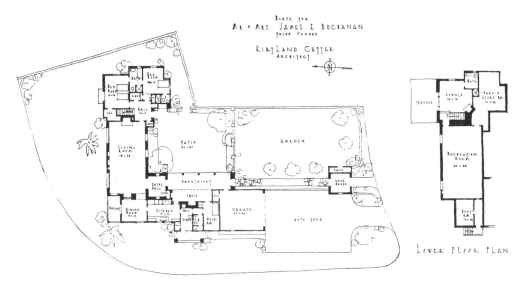

14.15 Plan of the Buchanan house. The visitor, passing from the gatehouse through a walled garden and by a second arch into the ambulatory, continuing into the entrance hall, and finally reaching the living room, experiences realms of increasing privacy. *Architect and Engineer,* January 1930.

14.16 Buchanan house from the street below. Poper Collection.

14.17 The living room of the Buchanan house. Massive beams on corbel blocks resting on the thick walls create a sense of permanence.
 Poper Collection.

left, the ambulatory broadens into a covered outdoor room with built-in seats around a fireplace, offering a comfortable transitional zone between inside and out.

The long living room (fig. 14.17), entered through a third doorway straight ahead, has an open wooden roof reminiscent of a medieval hall. Its massive tie beams, resting on corbel blocks set in the thick walls, give a sense of stability. The room receives light from the south through glass doors onto the patio; to the north large windows look over rooftops toward Santa Monica Bay. The elevated position gives a fine prospect, but discourages anyone on the road below from seeing in. The two bedrooms and a bathroom clustered at one end, and a dining room at the other, are comparatively modest in size. From a small hall by the bedrooms, which also opens to the patio, steps lead down to a recreation room and study on the floor below. The kitchen is carefully planned so that it can

14.18 Dr. Otto Stein house, Palos Verdes, 1928. The architect continues to play variations on the Mediterranean theme. Poper Collection.

14.19 The patio of the Stein house. The outdoor fireplace is sheltered by an overhanging roof. Malaga Cove Library, Palos Verdes.

serve both the dining room and the ambulatory. It shares a porch with the maid's room, from which the service court by the garage can be reached. Like the Cameron house, the Buchanan house responds to the site and to the informal lifestyle of California in the twenties.

The year 1928 saw the construction, on the slope below the Gard home, of a house for the distinguished brain surgeon, Dr. Otto Stein (fig. 14.18) and his wife Evelyn, who had come from Chicago to retire at Palos Verdes.[24] Dr. Stein was very active in the management of the community, devoting energy to the library board and presiding over the Arts Association. The Steins wanted to make their home a place where artists and musicians, invited to show their work or perform at Palos Verdes, could be graciously entertained.[25]

Cutter arranged the house on three sides of a patio focusing on an outdoor fireplace under a low roof (fig. 14.19). From this informal area, colorful with Mexican tiles, French windows open into a lofty, well-lit living room. Although many details followed old Mexican traditions, the emphasis was not on the replication of antiquity, but on the creation of a light, open home for contemporary use. Across one side of the double-height living room, a large gallery provides an elevated stage where musicians could perform for family and guests below. The interior of the hipped roof above their heads was inventively designed as an acoustic reflector, amplifying sound. Built to an intriguing geometric design (fig. 14.20) with exposed rafters, it gives the room a unique character. The doubling of rafters at the angles and the introduction of purely decorative elements add richness to the structure. High up on a wall, a small rectangular window of amber glass roundels, similar to those Cutter used in some of his earliest houses, admits a shaft of amber light. This detail, like many others in his California houses, evokes Arts and Crafts traditions. Since Mrs. Stein was not interested in cooking, the kitchen was a low priority; food discreetly prepared by the servants in a small kitchen below was raised by a dumbwaiter to the main floor, where it could be served to guests.

In 1928, on Via Anita, close to the Schellenberg houses, Cutter also built his two smallest houses in Palos Verdes, for W. H. Monroe and Grace Snelgrove.[26] Although both appear quite modest from the street, they possess the sense of spaciousness he achieved in other houses on the estate. Once again, he exploited an L-shaped plan to light the living room from three sides and to expand the interior space into a secluded patio. In the Monroe house, he scaled down the type of open, wooden roof he had designed for the Camerons and Buchanans; its slender tie beams, turned on a lathe, were appropriate to the size of the room (fig. 14.21). While in the Buchanan house a formal fountain with two prancing horses within an arch appears quite pretentious, a small bronze head in the Monroe patio directs a jet of water into a stone basin on a vine-covered wall. The coming of the depression slowed down Cutter's Palos Verdes practice and put an end to the hope of realizing the Lunada Bay Plaza. No new work came to him in 1929;[27] but he produced one house in 1930 for Dr. Hugo Jones,[28] not far from the Gard residence, a compact block with a three-car garage projecting out in front at a lower level, and a shady court with an outdoor fireplace to one side (fig. 14.22).

In 1931, as if in defiance of the depression, Cutter designed his grandest Palos Verdes house for Norman Phillips in a high position on Via Panorama.[29] Although not as large as the Gard house, it is

14.20 Living room roof of the Otto Stein house. This ingenious wooden roof enhances the acoustics of the music room on an upper gallery at one end of the room. Photo by the author.

14.21 W. H. Monroe house, Palos Verdes. Living room roof, 1928. Turned wooden tie beams fit the scale of this small house. Photo by the author.

more ornate, borrowing decorative forms from the Italian Renaissance. From the end of the cul-de-sac on which it stands, it appears as a formal rectangular block to which unequal wings enclosing a forecourt have been added; from the other side, as it rises from the slope of the hill, it is less regular. The front entrance, surmounted by a broken pediment and a coat of arms, is an obvious symbol of wealth and power borrowed from the days when aristocrats displayed

14.22 Dr. Hugo Jones house, Palos Verdes, 1930. Informally placed on the hillside, this house conceals a patio with an outside fireplace to the rear. Pencil sketch. Poper Collection.

their pedigrees for all to see. The door opens into a vestibule leading past a reception room into a central hall divided by three elegant arches on slender classical columns. Large windows ahead open to an elevated terrace, a high vantage point facing inland toward Los Angeles. This is enclosed on one side by an open loggia whose roof is carried on slender composite columns, and on the other by the more solid living room. From this terrace, steps lead down in a grand, formal manner to further terraces and gardens at lower levels. In many of Cutter's earlier mansions, rooms are decorated in different styles; in the Phillips house, the theme is Mediterranean throughout, but ornamental details are stressed and play distinctive roles in the various rooms. The richness of the detail is in sharp contrast to the plain, massive elements of the Cameron, Buchanan, and Gard houses.

Apart from a small house for Major V. E. Miltenberger, built in 1934,[30] not far from the Wehrman house in Miraleste, this was Cutter's last house on the Palos Verdes Estates. However, he was given a commission for a beach house (fig. 14.23) for the swimming club.[31] He sited it picturesquely at the foot of a cliff in a rocky cove, with changing rooms and a cafe behind a broad terrace overlooking the water. A small Italianate tower, red-tiled roofs, and thick looking stucco walls combine to give the impression of a villa on one of the northern Italian lakes. Although the cancellation of the Lunada Bay Plaza must have been a bitter blow to Cutter, he had the satisfaction of contributing significantly to a progressive development that was gaining national recognition. He continued to receive design awards, from both the Art Jury and the American Institute of Architects.[32] Furthermore, he played a role in giving the state of California its own distinctive architecture.

In 1929, the Palos Verdes Art Jury passed a resolution in which they declared that the terms "Mission Style," "Spanish Style," and "Mediterranean Style" were unfortunate misnomers for "an art which has progressed to a degree in which we all may justly take pride." They resolved, therefore, "that this type of architecture shall hereafter be designated as 'Californian Style.'" Myron Hunt summed up the view of the Jury:

The time is now ripe for us in California to recognize that we have arrived at a distinctive style of architecture which is our own, and which is a real expression of our culture and civilization. Whether it

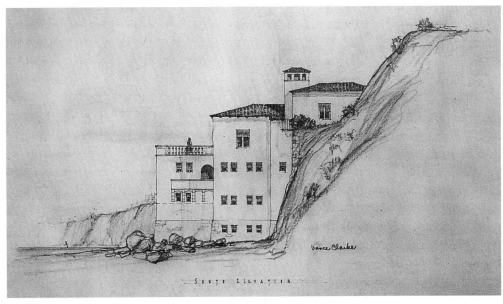

14.23 Palos Verdes Beach House, 1929. Poper Collection.

has been arrived at through the rich Colonial heritage of the Spanish fathers who used forms that they knew and loved from their earlier days on the Mediterranean, or through the fortunate blending of the New England Colonial with the Spanish Colonial at Monterey which gave us the pleasant galleried type of house with its tile, shake or shingle roof, or through our better trained architects of recent years who have wider knowledge and understanding of the architecture that preceded us, all that we have done here is, after all, of a new time, in a new spirit, and the product of our western thought and progress in expression.[33]

The jury sent out their resolution to chambers of commerce, school boards, civic societies, city planning authorities, and regional offices of the AIA. They also issued a press release to all California newspapers asking them to assist in the "patriotic movement to adopt the term 'Californian Architecture'" by publicizing the initiative. Many newspapers responded with editorials and feature articles; by December 7, 1929, the resolution had been adopted by fifty-seven public authorities in the state.[34]

While many other architects contributed to the development of the Californian Style, it is clear that the leaders of the Palos Verdes enterprise held Cutter's work in high esteem. Several articles on the Palos Verdes Estates were published by them in professional journals between 1927 and 1931. In a series of articles written by Frederick Law Olmsted, Jr., Myron Hunt, Charles Cheney, David Allison, James Dawson, and Jay Lawyer, the works of twenty architects were illustrated, but forty percent of the illustrations represented the work of Kirtland Cutter. Ten of his sixteen houses and his design for Lunada Bay Plaza were shown.[35]

Out of respect for his work, the directors of the Palos Verdes project rescued Cutter's career from ruin and provided a vital focus for his revived architectural practice. In his houses on the high terraced peninsula he exploited, in a new regional style, the principles of picturesque design that he had developed over the course of thirty years in the Northwest. Freed from the temptations of an eclectic age, he now achieved a consistency that had often eluded him in the past. Cutter's work in California also represented a national trend in the architecture of the twenties and thirties, toward the expression of regional character and ideals.

CHAPTER FIFTEEN

Long Beach: The Last Years
(1925–1939)

DURING THE MIDDLE 1920S, CUTTER'S OFFICE IN LONG Beach was generally busy. Cutter was the "Captain" of the enterprise, while Jess Jones took the role of "chief engineer." Cutter "lived the houses" they designed; Jones interpreted his rough sketches, and, with dialogue between the two, the designs evolved until every detail was settled.[1] When there was too much work in the office for one draftsman, Cutter hired others. In the summer of 1924, while Jones was busy with the Cameron house, Albert Ford, a very able draftsman and perspective artist, joined them to work on the Tudoresque C. C. Anderson house in Boise.[2] In 1928, Vance Clarke joined the office staff and remained there for about eight years, although Cutter sometimes shared him with Hugh Davies, another architect in the same building. Clarke drew many small, lively sketches in colored pencil on flimsy yellow paper to explore ideas and to show the clients. Over the years, Ford continued to work for Cutter as a freelance designer when needed. Despite the introduction he had been given by Henry Barbour, and his award in 1924 from the Palos Verdes Art Jury, Cutter received no commissions in Long Beach until his office there had been open for four years. He refused either to compromise his standards or to reduce his fees below ten to twelve percent; he simply waited for clients ready to pay for a full professional service.[3] Apart from his early houses at Palos Verdes, Cutter's only commissions came from Northwest clients. He had been asked to design the Anderson House in Boise before he left Spokane.[4] Thomas Autzen, a pioneer in the production of plywood,

15.1 C. B. Peeples house, Lombardy Avenue, San Marino, 1925. Photo by the author.

knew of Cutter through his work in Seattle and Tacoma. The house that Cutter designed for him in Portland in 1926 was the last of the architect's Tudoresque houses.[5] C. B. Peeples, who commissioned a house in San Marino, California, in 1925, was related to L. B. Peeples, for whom Cutter had designed a chalet in Seattle in 1908.

The Peeples house (fig. 15.1) stands on Lombardy Avenue in the elite suburb of San Marino. Sited among grandiose mansions, it retains the simplicity of a large farmhouse. Its character, like that of the Palos Verdes houses, comes not from applied ornament but through the subtle play of volumes. Its mass is broken down by slight changes in roof level and by the stepping forward of an asymmetrical central block. Except for the lightly rusticated stone arch surrounding the front door, and a tall upper window opening onto a balcony, it conveys the simple, solid character of rural houses in Italy. At the back an ambulatory, fronting a single-story wing, opens onto a secluded patio.

In 1928 and 1930, Cutter designed two more houses on Orlando Avenue, Pasadena, both of which draw inspiration from the Monterey Style.[6] The first was for Karl Von Platen, a lumber man from the Midwest who had found the Peeples house to his taste and approached Cutter. In a preliminary sketch, Cutter had shown a balcony of the Monterey type on the front facade. Von Platen liked this feature and asked him to lengthen it.[7] The result (fig. 15.2) was a house entirely different from the one he had first admired. Like Monterey Style houses, the Von Platen house combines Hispanic and New England elements. The double-hung windows and the moldings belong to the early nineteenth-century architecture derived from English patterns. The horizontality of the entire design under a single, low-pitched roof with level eaves produces a regularity that Cutter avoided at Palos Verdes.

In the second, designed for Walden Shaw, the owner of the Yellow Taxi Company of Chicago, also on Orlando Avenue, Cutter utilized the same vocabulary to produce a more imposing effect.[8] While the Peeples house was composed asymmetrically, the long balcony of

15.2 Karl Von Platen house, Orlando Avenue, San Marino, 1927. Combining both English and Spanish Colonial features, this house has elements of the Monterey Style. Poper Collection.

15.3 Walden Shaw house, Orlando Avenue, San Marino, 1930. Stylistically similar to the Von Platen house, but symmetrical. Photo by the author.

the Shaw house runs between two equal flanking wings (fig. 15.3). In both houses, the balcony with its overhanging roof protects the south-facing rooms behind it from the summer sun, while allowing it to penetrate in the winter. Secluded patios behind the two houses are in keeping with the informal lifestyle of California.

Finally, in 1928, Cutter received his first commission in Long Beach, a house of modest size for Irwin Marr. From then on he built one or two houses there every year until his death in 1939. In addition, he completed at least eight more in the region and executed some school buildings. Thus the practice was just busy enough to support him and his employees through the depression, after the opportunities at Palos Verdes ceased. The Marr house, overlooking the Pacific, rose from the edge of the ocean bluff on an arcaded gallery which provided a sheltered place to enjoy the marine view. Above this space, a tall living room with an open wooden roof followed the precedent of the Cameron and Buchanan houses.

In Cutter's next two Long Beach houses, he played variations on the theme he had explored in San Marino. The homes of L. T. Edwards on Country Club Drive (fig. 15.4) and D. P. Condit on Pacific Avenue in Los Cerritos, both stretched out horizontally on level ground with long balconies sheltered by roof overhangs.[9] The large expanses of plain stucco, the low-pitched gables, the relatively small windows, and the heavy doors with many small panels sug-

15.4 L. T. Edwards house, Country Club Drive, Long Beach, 1929.
Poper Collection.

gest a Mexican inspiration, but the double-hung windows remain
English. In the Condit house, Cutter gave the living room an open
wooden roof, but this time, instead of making the structure heavy,
he designed trusses with lightweight turned tie beams.

The house Cutter designed for the Long Beach attorney Henry
Clock on Pine Avenue, Los Cerritos, in 1932,[10] followed similar
lines, but without the long, covered balcony facing the street. Instead, a shady loggia at ground level and a balcony off the master
bedroom opened into the garden at the back. He gave some relief
to the front facade by projecting the upper story beyond the first-
floor walls, as he had often done at Palos Verdes (figs. 15.5, 15.6).

While Hispanic character dominated Cutter's first Long Beach
residences, his house for the oil magnate A. T. Jergins (1930), and
that of Robert Peyton in Beverly Hills (1932) (figs. 15.7, 15.8) evoke
another Mediterranean type. Their hipped roofs, as well as the
proportions and details, suggest an Italian source.[11] The formal
two-story block of the Peyton house is supported by lower wings,
irregularly planned around a large courtyard. The interiors of the
Peyton house, illustrated in *Architectural Digest,* show that Cutter
returned to the practice of designing individual rooms in the
manner of different historic periods.[12] The character is mostly
classical, conveying eighteenth-century elegance. The living room
is decorated in a restrained version of the Adam Style, light colored

15.5 Henry Clock house, Long Beach, 1932. Photo by the author.

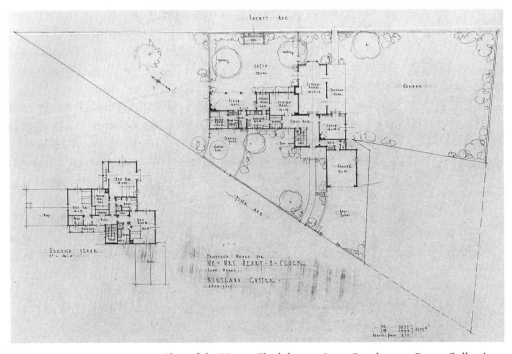

15.6 Plan of the Henry Clock house, Long Beach, 1932. Poper Collection.

15.7 Robert Peyton house, Beverly Hills, 1932. Cutter broke this large house down into small-scale elements. Poper Collection.

15.8 Plan of the Robert Peyton house. The house is carefully zoned into separate areas for the owners, their children, and service functions. Drawn by Terry Mourning.

FIRST · FLOOR · PLAN

15.9 Chinese room in the Robert Peyton house. Poper Collection.

with delicate Adamesque carving on the marble fireplace. The oak-paneled library follows a Georgian scheme, and French Rococo is introduced in the master bedroom. The breakfast room, jutting out under its own roof into the garden, picks up the late eighteenth-century fascination with the Orient. Chinese paintings framed in delicate fretwork adorn the walls, and the rafters of the hipped roof hint at the exposed structure of traditional Chinese houses (fig. 15.9).

In the late 1920s and during the 1930s, Cutter also designed some houses of a less formal type. He built the first of these in 1929 for his nephew John D. Hoyt, the son of his sister Laura. John, who had followed his father in the legal profession, practiced as an attorney in Los Angeles and chose to live in Beverly Hills. Cutter designed a rambling house in keeping with John's relaxed lifestyle (fig. 15.10). He took advantage of an ancient pepper tree of prodigious size to

15.10 Hoyt house, Beverly Hills. The home of Cutter's nephew John Hoyt. Built around a patio with an enormous pepper tree. Poper Collection.

define one side of a patio enclosed in the angle of an L-shaped plan. The principal rooms, including the master bedroom, opened onto the patio; further bedrooms upstairs shared a long shady balcony. Compared with his other recent houses, this one, though similarly planned, was more modern with less emphasis on historically inspired details. While Cutter finished the hall and dining room with delicate millwork in a simple eighteenth-century style, he gave the living room a more contemporary look with a plain fireplace and knotty pine paneling.[13] When this house was later purchased by Robert Montgomery, a Hollywood movie star, it was described as an ideal place for a "wise young man" in the film industry "to escape the Hollywood razzle-dazzle."[14]

Informal planning and simple interiors were also the key to two beach cottages designed by Cutter in about 1933 on Balboa Island, about twenty miles south of Long Beach. One for Robert Honey-

15.11 Honeyman house, Balboa Island, ca. 1933. Entered through a walled patio. Photo by the author.

man, with the Hispanic character of Cutter's more typical Californian houses, appears like a family home. A balcony of the Monterey type overlooked the intimate courtyard contained on three sides by two-story walls (fig. 15.11). The other, for Victor Fleming, who a few years later became famous as the director of *The Wizard of Oz* and *Gone with the Wind,* was probably conceived as a hideaway from the pressured life of Culver City Studios. Built after the film director's marriage in 1933,[15] it was a place where he could entertain and work on scripts (figs. 15.12, 15.13). The living room and porch overlooking the narrow bay connected the two long wings of a U-shaped plan. The central court focused on an outdoor fireplace, back to back with that of the living room. The master bedroom, complete with dressing room, bath, sleeping porch, and two balconies, occupied the upper floor, while at ground level four double bedrooms, each with a private bath, allowed for easy entertaining of guests. Walls of plain brick or board and batten and plain porch posts conveyed the same desire for simplicity as the knotty pine wall coverings on the bar in the dining room and on living room walls. Common to both houses was an Arts and Crafts approach to carpentry. Cutter gave character to the fireplaces by framing the bare wall to either side

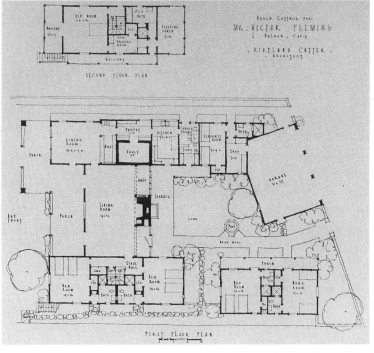

15.12 Victor Fleming beach house, Balboa Island, the patio. The house was designed for weekend entertaining and for work sessions on movie scripts. Like the family house that Cutter designed for him in Bel Air, it is unpretentious and informal. Demolished. Poper Collection.

15.13 Plan of the Victor Fleming beach house. Two bedrooms for guests are isolated from the main house. Poper Collection.

15.14 Living room of the Honeyman house, Balboa Island. The ingle-nook recalls Cutter's Arts and Crafts designs of the late nineteenth century. Poper Collection.

with massive timber posts heavily braced to the beam above in an Old English manner. In the case of the Honeyman living room, he set the hearth in an inglenook with the built-in seats as he had often done in the Northwest (fig. 15.14).

In 1937, Fleming returned to Cutter for a permanent residence in Bel Air. Clark Gable, wanting to build in a remote place where he could escape from autograph hunters, had bought some property in Hog Canyon in the upper Moraga Valley, but he had lost interest in it and sold it to Fleming.[16] Having approved the design for his home, Fleming showed enough confidence in Cutter to leave him money to construct it and carte blanche to work out the details.[17] The simply built and unpretentious Fleming house, now much altered, spread out under low-pitched roofs onto the large site, its rooms opening wide to shady porches. The only touch of fantasy was in a low tower rising above the other roofs like the watchtower of a western fort. In a basement workshop, Fleming liked to tinker with his tools and to carve toys for his daughters.[18]

Cutter's Long Beach clients of the thirties were neither as wealthy as Peyton nor as colorful as Fleming. He designed homes there for doctors, lawyers, businessmen, and people working in the oil industry. Colonial was the most popular style in America at this time, and in his last years he tended to build more Colonial houses or to combine English, Spanish, and Colonial elements. His Long Beach houses for D. E. Humphreys (1932), attorney John Clock (1935), Clarence Mills, a supplier of electrical equipment (1936), pediatrician Dr. J. R. Jimmerson (1936), Thomas Rowan, an oil driller (1930), Eldridge Combs (1938), and the three Ware sisters, all teachers (1939),[19] possessed interiors detailed so as to convey eighteenth-century character in a quiet, understated manner. Cutter gave them gracious living rooms, lit in his usual way from three sides. French windows opened first-floor rooms onto patios and bedrooms onto balconies. He framed doors and windows with delicate and precise moldings of Georgian or Federal types. Staircases in spacious halls had slender, turned balusters and mahogany handrails. Ivory-colored millwork against pale walls encouraged the reflection and modulation of light. The character of the exteriors varied. In the John Clock house (fig. 15.15), board and batten siding covered the walls. Clapboard enclosed the Mills house, and dormer windows broke its

15.15 John Clock house, Long Beach, 1935. Photo by the author.

15.16 Rowan house, Long Beach, 1930. Photo by the author.

eaves line. The Rowan house, with a long, covered balcony facing the street, was built of red brick and white stucco (fig. 15.16). The Humphreys, Combs, and Ware sisters' houses were all faced with stucco but in different styles. While the first was Hispanic in design with an entry arch, a dominant Federal Style doorway gave character to the second; the third featured a wide bow window to the dining room and a small balcony from one of the bedrooms. Despite their Colonial character, all of these houses, with the exception of the Mills house, were planned with asymmetrical facades. Among them the Clock and Rowan houses stand out for the beautiful proportions of their living rooms and halls.

One of Cutter's last houses, for the respected pediatrician Dr. J. R. Jimmerson (fig. 15.17),[20] shows the same attention to detail that he lavished on his wealthy clients. Although the fees for this modest home cannot have justified a large expenditure of the architect's time, he passed many hours with the Jimmersons planning the details of the design. Jimmerson was a well-traveled man with a passion for the study of nature. He had no desire to build a grand house; instead Cutter designed him a cottage. The architect may

15.17 Jimmerson house, Long Beach, 1936. In this design Cutter reverts to a cottagelike version of the Shingle Style. Photo by the author.

have recalled visiting old cottages in England with thick walls and small windows that had been remodeled in the eighteenth century with surprisingly elegant interiors. The Jimmerson house gives such an impression. The roof and upper walls were shingled like New England houses of the seventeenth century, but more in the manner of cottages in Kent or Sussex, whose less regular roofs and walls were often hung with clay tiles. Windows break the eaves line, providing light where needed, without thought to the formality of the elevations. Inside, the rooms are surprisingly spacious; they are miniature versions of those in Cutter's larger houses. The windows are set in deep paneled reveals, painted white to reflect the light. Arched niches recessed in the walls provide space for the Jimmersons' china collection. At the back of the house the doctor's study is paneled in polished mahogany. While bookcases full of rich leather-bound volumes cover the inner walls, the sides of the projecting window are fitted with shelves to display a collection of colorful antique syrup jars and Stafforshire china figures that shine in the daylight. It appears that Cutter gained the same satisfaction from this simple but finely detailed house as from his mansions.

As Dr. Jimmerson expressed in a letter to his architect, he and his wife were entirely satisfied:

> My dear Cutter, the enclosed check is but partial payment for value received. Nothing of a material nature could possibly pay you in full for the happiness you have brought us. The Chinese say that "a house is the counterpart of the inhabitants within"—I hope we may be able to uphold the standard.[21]

Although most of Cutter's work in California was residential, he was responsible for two elementary schools in Long Beach and for the master plan of Long Beach City College. His eclectic design for the John Russell Lowell Elementary School (ca. 1926) spread horizontally from an octagonal central tower which rose above the neighborhood. This structure did not survive the 1933 Long Beach earthquake, providing good reason for Cutter to keep the Abraham Lincoln School of 1934 (fig. 15.18) to a single story.[22] With this design Cutter returned to the Hispanic tradition of stucco and red-tiled roofs on an almost domestic scale. A central gable end with an arched entrance provides the focal element of a low, symmetrical structure that spreads horizontally to surround a spacious forecourt.

The danger of a further earthquake also explains the low, heavily buttressed walls at Long Beach Junior College, where Cutter planned the campus and designed the first buildings. These became the nucleus of the present Long Beach City College, whose later additions have generally followed the example of Cutter's unpretentious, low-lying architecture, if not the entire master plan. As at Lincoln School, Cutter laid out the college on an axial plan, in this case, arranging it around a formal quadrangle (fig. 15.19). The buildings he proposed varied between one and two stories; while the majority

15.18 Abraham Lincoln School, Long Beach, 1934. Poper Collection.

15.19 Long Beach Junior College, campus plan, bird's-eye perspective.
Cutter executed several buildings on the campus; Jess Jones and later
Richard Poper continued to add others. Poper Collection.

were extremely simple, the principal hall opposite the arcaded
entrance loggia conveyed the character of a small mission church.
Arcades fronting some of the other blocks continued the same
theme. The construction completed before Cutter's death, which
included the student union building and the buildings for the
English and social sciences departments, demonstrates that Cutter
could adapt the architectural legacy of the missions to modern use
in an unaffected manner.

The depression slowed down the building industry during the
thirties, and many of Cutter's projects remained unbuilt, but the
large collection of sketches he left behind suggests that he continued to hope for better times. Some may be preliminary schemes for
houses that were actually built; others were drawn speculatively to
entice potential clients.[23] They include houses at Palos Verdes, Beverly Hills, and Montecito, a church in Burbank, a bakery in Santa
Ana, a golf club at San Pedro; but the majority are not identified

by place. Potential clients included millionaire C. M. Cotton and movie actress Laura Hope Crews;[24] however, many drawings do not show the patrons' names and very few are dated. Collectively, they represent the continuing dreams of a confirmed romantic. The houses, predominantly in the Californian Style, range from Italian to Mexican with a hint of English Colonial here and there. Of the larger houses, a few examples are grand and formal. One colored sketch, for example, shows a vista through an arcade carried on slender Tuscan columns toward a distant wing of the same building (fig. 15.20). The majority are designed in an irregular fashion, rambling over their site in a series of blocks of different heights or stepping down hillsides in the manner he employed at Palos Verdes (fig. 15.21).

The typical elements of Cutter's Californian Style vocabulary appear in these sketches. They show heavy Mission Style arcades as well as light arches supported on elegant classical columns. Stairs

15.20 Unidentified house, colored pencil drawing. This is one of many undated sketches of unexecuted projects in California. Poper Collection.

15.21 Unidentified house, possibly a preliminary sketch for the Cameron house, Palos Verdes. Colored pencil drawing. Poper Collection.

and balconies find many expressions: outside staircases with solid stuccoed balustrades rise in a series of steps, providing surfaces for boxes of cascading flowers. Thick stuccoed walls in front of balconies are penetrated by openwork screens of red clay tiles; in contrast, wrought iron and turned wood offer lighter alternatives for porch posts and balcony or stair rails. Imposing pedimented doorways proclaim the patrician status of the owner, and simple unframed entrances in white-plastered walls convey an Arts and Crafts simplicity; heavy wooden doors and gates show the architect's fascination with Spanish craftsmanship. Almost universally the drawings represent buildings with low-pitched roofs, either hipped or gabled, covered in red clay tiles.

An exception to Cutter's use of the Californian Style can be seen in the unbuilt project for Mr. and Mrs. E. A. Parkford at Montecito, in which he reverted for the last time to an English Medieval Style (fig. 15.22). Drawings by Albert Ford show the attempt to recreate the great hall of an English manor house of the Tudor era. Massive king post trusses support an open roof over a large living room. The braced and pegged wooden frame gives form to the end walls as well as to the roof structure. A deep bay window on one side is echoed by a huge inglenook fireplace on the other.

Living Room

House of
Mr & Mrs
E. A Parkford.
Montecito Calif

Kirtland Cutter
Architect.

15.22 Mrs. E A. Parkford house, Montecito, interior. In this design Cutter returns to the vocabulary of Old English architecture. Pencil sketch by Albert Ford. Poper Collection.

15.23 Unidentified resort hotel, California. Perhaps Cutter's last attempt to realize a hotel commission in the grand manner. Pencil sketch. Poper Collection.

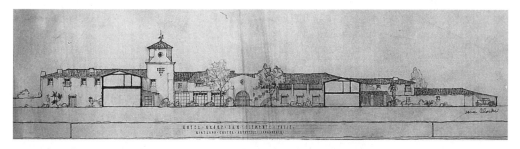

15.24 San Clemente Hotel Project, 1930. Pencil sketch. Poper Collection.

A series of pencil sketches show what appears to be a grand resort hotel standing behind a high ocean wall (fig. 15.23). This flamboyant design, with an elaborately ornamented tower and tall arcade of eleven arches opening onto an esplanade, recalls the confident mood of the 1915 San Diego Exposition. However, it was never realized; nor was a hotel at San Clemente (fig. 15.24), which he designed in 1930 for Ole Hanson, a former mayor of Seattle.[25] Cutter conceived the San Clemente hotel in an equally romantic manner, but he returned to the simpler style of architecture in which he had built so successfully at Palos Verdes. Arranged around three courtyards, the design conveys the harmony and human scale that can be found in the missions, while avoiding decorative clichés. The plain square tower with a subtly faceted upper stage rises informally from the corner of the central court to enliven the skyline. Cutter's sense of the exotic remained with him; a sketch he made for the Pacific Coast Club at Long Beach recalls the Bohemian decor in the entrance hall of his own home in Spokane, where oriental rugs hung from the ceiling. His proposal was to transform a vast, perhaps gloomy, hall into a huge and luxurious tent by hanging fabrics from the ceiling (fig. 15.25).

Although Cutter was sixty-three years old when he opened his practice in Long Beach, he continued to work for another sixteen years. With his reputation for quality and the reliable assistance of Jess Jones, he was able to weather the depression. He was respected by his employees, who felt that it was a privilege to work for him. He always appeared as a perfect gentleman of the old school. Eccen-

15.25 Pacific Coast Club, Long Beach, interior remodeling project, designed to give an exotic and festive character to a vast space. Pencil sketch. Poper Collection.

trically dressed in formal, old-fashioned suits and a high collar, he must have looked out of place in the rapidly changing world of the thirties. Though he still wore the unconvincing wig of a younger man, he impressed people with his dignity.[26] Kirtland Cutter and his wife Katharine had been active in Spokane society; the Chalet Hohenstein had been renowned for its artistic character and unusual parties. In Long Beach, separated from their old friends, they lived very quietly in a small apartment off East Ocean Boulevard, where they did not attempt to entertain much. Kirtland made use of the Pacific Coast Club as a place to meet a few acquaintances and cultivate clients, but he was anxious not to get into debt again and was very careful with his expenditures.[27]

Katharine's daughter from her previous marriage, Kathryn, lived with her husband in Honolulu. Kirtland reestablished a clandestine relationship with his estranged son, Corbin Corbin. In 1898 his first wife, Mary Corbin, had married Charles Balguy, a member of an aristocratic family in Derbyshire, England. But the mariage did not last and she returned to the United States to live in California. Corbin graduated from the Naval Academy at Annapolis and later worked in banking in California. As a young naval officer, he had fallen in love with a vivacious Broadway actress and Vogue model named Genevieve Wilmot, who became his wife. They appeared to be an ill-matched couple. He became cold and aloof, disdaining the show-business people she entertained. During the thirties, Corbin would occasionally meet his father and stepmother at the Huntington Beach Hotel for lunch and tour some of Cutter's new houses. He took his own son, also named Corbin Corbin, with him but never revealed the identities of the elderly couple they were visiting.[28]

Corbin's pleasure in seeing his own grandson must have been tempered by the secretive nature of the relationship, no doubt the result of conditions in Mary Corbin's will. However, Kirtland and Katherine were devoted to each other: it appears that they passed some happy years together in the benign climate of Southern California.

Early in 1933, Katharine became ill. After an operation she began to make an encouraging recovery, but on March 10 of that year a severe earthquake struck the city, causing extensive damage. The Ocean Boulevard apartment survived, but Katharine was badly shaken and suffered a relapse. Over the next few months, Kirtland was deeply worried about her health; then in October the doctor told him confidentially that she would live only two more weeks. He summoned her daughter from Hawaii, but not wanting his wife to know the truth, disguised the true purpose of the visit. As predicted, Katharine died that month; Kirtland was now alone, grieving her loss, and short of commissions to distract him.[29]

To assuage his loneliness he indulged the love of nature he had acquired as a child from his great-grandfather, Jared Kirtland, and played host to a large collection of birds. He built an aviary at his apartment and at one time he is said to have accepted fifty parakeets in part payment of fees.[30] A visitor in 1935 called at his office and found him "literally festooned with birds":

> If anybody has a lingering doubt as to the miracle of St. Francis of Assisi . . . he should have seen Cutter in his private office. Beginning with friendship of a pair of linnets that lit on his window sill on that high spot in the heart of the roaring traffic, he acquired in two years no less than 60 birds, mostly linnets and canaries. They flew through the open window after a breakfast and bath on the sill, perched on his hair, his shoulders and even on his open hand—they even attempted to nest among his drawings and papers.

The same reporter visited Cutter again in the summer of 1937 and found him sitting "desolate" with the window shut and entirely without birds, because the neighbors had objected; he was "consoling himself with occasional visits to San Juan Capistrano to frolic with Father Hutchinson's white pigeons in the lovely mission garden."[31]

Birds were not the only creatures he befriended; for example, on a visit to a building site, while talking to the client he picked up a snake he found and carried it around as if it were a familiar friend.[32] His love of nature went hand in hand with his sensitivity to the landscape as he designed buildings to fit their sites.

Cutter's last surviving writing, entitled "Vernal Vibrations of a Victorian Virtuoso," confirms his feelings about nature in a rapidly changing world:

> With budding spring comes the urge to all nature lovers for the great untrammeled open spaces, and being one of the dwindling old guard I wander forth in search of a bit of what is left of Mother Earth's natural face, pausing in wonderment that the lark still sings and the

cricket wings his lay surrounded by a blatant, synthetic mob going—
where? in this discordant age of fearful progress. . . .

Nature loving should be included in the all embracing command-
ment "Love thy neighbor as thyself"—which, if from early childhood
were universally taught as the prime daily necessity, would finally become a habit natural to civilized man, ever leading back to the sweet
paths of earthly peace and happiness. K. C.[33]

In his old age, Cutter never lost his pleasure in designing houses,
working with clients, fitting the building to their needs and resolv-
ing aesthetic problems. He took pride in his work and liked to celebrate its completion with suitable ceremony. He is remembered
arriving in a chauffeur-driven car, dressed in a frock coat and
striped trousers, to present the keys of a new house to the waiting
family. He then consecrated the home by personally lighting a fire
in its hearth.[34]

During his years in Long Beach, Cutter had tended to remain
aloof and had not given Jess Jones credit for his role in the architecture they produced.[35] However, in 1939, as Cutter approached the
age of seventy-nine, he was growing weaker and finally made the
decision to offer a partnership to his assistant so that he could take
responsibility for the completion of the work in hand.[36] By this
time Cutter's sister Laura, now a widow, had come to live with
him,[37] but he was afraid of being a burden to anyone and determined to keep his independence.[38] He continued to go into the
office for a short time almost every day and is remembered by a
young assistant, Hugh Gibbs, who worked there for a few months.
Gibbs recalled spending many enthralling hours with him talking
about architecture, and later regarded him as a mentor who had
set him on a favorable path in his chosen profession. The young
draftsman could hardly believe it when, on September 26, 1939,
he learned that Kirtland Cutter, after an absence of a few days,
was dead.[39]

Jess Jones, now an architect in his own right,[40] carried out his
partner's final request. Although state law prohibited the sprinkling
of the ashes of the dead on land or sea, he walked out to the end
of a pier, accompanied by his young son Richard, and released the
mortal remains of Kirtland Cutter over the waters of the Pacific
Ocean.[41]

Conclusion

WHILE MANY OF HIS CONTEMPORARIES HAVE BEEN
relegated to the sidelines of history, Kirtland Cutter survives as a
quintessential architect of his era. His long and multifaceted career
began in the late 1880s and continued until the brink of World War
II. His first architectural designs were rooted in the late nineteenth
century, but his ideas evolved with the passing decades, expressing
the desires and preoccupations of a rapidly changing world. Like
most American architects of the early twentieth century, he never
accepted the central doctrines of modernism, or embraced the
International Style. He was an avowed eclectic who saw no conflict
in drawing inspiration from diverse traditions and adapting them
to modern life.

It may seem contradictory that he evoked both Arts and Crafts
simplicity and high style revivalism; that he designed rustic structures nestling into their natural surroundings and at the same time
exotic, artificial environments rich in imagery. One may ask how
an architect who strove to develop regional expression in both the
Northwest and California could also have appropriated styles from
many different geographic and cultural origins. The answer lies in
his openness and versatility as he met a variety of opportunities.
Just as one individual, within a single day, can honestly appreciate
the stillness of a rural scene and the clamor of a theatrical perfor-
mance, he was able to respond spontaneously to a host of different
circumstances. Drawing from a wide range of historical precedents,
and making a variety of allusions, he maintained a freedom that has

scarcely existed in any other time or place. His strength was his understanding of the life of his era and his consummate skill in providing for his clients' needs.

Cutter constantly looked back to the architecture of the past and remained unimpressed by modernist design. He showed little interest in the expression of new building technology, a *leitmotiv* of the International Style. Nevertheless he independently explored other concepts that belonged to the new tradition in architecture. Although he arrived in Spokane as a young man without any formal professional training, his very first projects showed progressive tendencies. Most architecture in the Northwest at this time, including the work of his chief rival Herman Preusse, was somewhat old-fashioned, still conforming to High Victorian modes, but he began immediately to experiment with ideas that were new to the region. In some of his earliest projects he took advantage of natural materials that more conservative architects would have rejected as inferior. For example, his use of rough basalt for the Fairmont Cemetery Chapel departs, in a refreshing manner, from the historicist and ornamental traditions of ecclesiastical architecture. In his Moore house and many that followed he attempted to develop an organic relationship between building and site, both through the building materials and the irregular form. In the Glover and Wardner houses he extended the principal volumes into the landscape by allowing low-pitched roofs to sail out over porches. Equally, in the Stevens Conrad and Anderson houses, he opened up interior space in a daring manner.

It is true that he did not always follow such experiments to their conclusion, or use them to formulate a progressive architectural theory, but he repeated them throughout his life. At Palos Verdes, in the mid-1920s, he continued to explore similar ideas. His Buchanan house of 1927 shows him as a master in the art of relating building to site. Those who move through its sequence of courtyard gardens, shady porches, and interior spaces experience subtle transitions between inside and out. While stylistically it does not convey the impression of a modern house, it addresses many of the same issues pursued by the pioneers of modernism. Cutter conceived the design as a response to both the pace and the character of twentieth-century life.

Although Cutter found his greatest inspiration in nature, he could not resist the temptation to design in an exotic manner. Patrick Clark's house of 1897, with its strange fusion of Islamic, oriental, and European elements, stands as the perfect example of architecture expressing the desires of a western millionaire. The architect produced many such fantasies, some built, others remaining on paper. The *fin de siècle* exoticism of Cutter's early years is manifested also in his hotel and restaurant designs for Louis Davenport between 1900 and the outbreak of World War I. Their very purpose was to transport the public into magical places far from their everyday life. It is a sign of changing times that his later designs became less ornamental, but, while such extravagent features as cusped ogee arches disappeared from his vocabulary, his fertile imagination continued to indulge in fantasy. The transition to simpler forms can be seen as he progressed from the Cowles house at Santa Barbara in 1913 to the Villa Carman at Tacoma in 1919 and to the Cameron house at Palos Verdes in the mid-1920s, but in all of these he evoked the romance of Mediterranean and Mexican architecture, much as he had called forth more exotic styles before.

While Cutter was greatly influenced by the latest developments in architecture, which he experienced on his frequent travels and through illustrated articles in professional journals, he was selective. After the World's Columbian Exposition of 1893 the strongest trend in America was toward Beaux Arts Classicism, but he remained true to his love of medieval irregularity and the simplicity of vernacular traditions. Indeed his picturesque and romantic structures far outnumbered his classical designs. It seems likely that he encouraged his clients to accept less formal types. He designed a few Colonial Revival houses, and some commercial buildings in a neoclassical style, but they are clearly not among his most characteristic works. Furthermore they show little discipline, reflecting his lack of Beaux Arts training, and also suggesting that his desires were focused elsewhere.

Other talented architects made significant contributions to the architecture of Spokane in Cutter's time. Willis Ritchie designed the stately county courthouse in 1893 at a stage when Cutter probably could not have handled a building on that scale. Preusse and Zittel received far more commissions for large office buildings than Cutter did, and Albert Held and C. Ferriss White created comfortable eclectic houses that contribute to the pleasant character of their neighborhoods. Furthermore, several of Cutter's assistants became successful architects in their own right, not least G. A. Pehrson and Henry Bertelsen, who thrived after his departure for California. But Cutter remains Spokane's architect, widely known and celebrated for his creations. When he moved on to California, though he had to compete with established architects such as George Washington Smith and Roland Coates who were in the forefront of new developments, he held his own and won professional honor for his contributions to the regional style.

There can be little doubt that, from his vast and diverse body of work, Cutter's most significant contributions to American architecture are his rustic structures that evoke the wilderness and his designs that express the escapism to which his countrymen are prone. The celebration of the primeval forest in Lake McDonald Lodge and the enthusiasm for the exotic in the Hall of the Doges, speak eloquently of opposing forces of nature and artifice tugging at the American psyche.

Appendix 1:
Cutter's Draftsmen and Partners

Few of the drawings in the EWSHS or other collections are dated or include the names of draftsmen. The list prior to 1991 is based mainly on the Letterbook but may be incomplete. Between 1991, when the Letterbook ended, and 1906, when the available office accounts begin, information is sparse; some comes from city directories. No office records have survived from the Long Beach period. Hugh Gibbs and Vance Clark provided some information.

John C. Poetz (partner)	1889–94
Karl Gunnar Malmgren	1889–1917
(partner)	1894–1917
Arthur Pearman	1890
E. B. Brown	1890
Edwin Wager	1901–4
(partner, Seattle)	1902–4
David C. Lewis (partner, Portland)	1902
Clyde Westcott (Spokane)	1904–6
(Seattle)	1906–7
G. Albin Pehrson	1905–6, 1907–17
Frederick A. G. Rigg	1905
Howard L. Gifford (Seattle)	1906–9
(Spokane)	1916*, 1917*
Frederick E. Westcott	1906–7
Carl Nuese (head draftsman, Seattle)	1906–8
Andrew Willatzen (Seattle)	1907–8

V. P. von Ehrlich	?
Charles Hayes	?
Chester H. Houghteling (structural engineer)	1907–9
Fred W. Plummer (partner, Cutter and Plummer)	1909–
Henry Bertelsen	1909–23
Ray L. Amos	1910–12
Paul Jagow	1910*
H. P. Sharpe	1910*, 1914*
F. G. Hutchinson	1910–12, 1919*, 1920*
R. R. Christian	1910*
L. M. Starr	1910–12, 1916*, 1917*
Arthur Sanders	1910*
E. J. Baum	1910*, 1916*, 1917*, 1918*, 1919*
Curtis Richardson	1910*, 1915*
Arthur Malmgren	1910*
Howard Gates	1910*
Clarence Anderson	1914–17
Kenneth Mills	1916*, 1917*
H. C. Parry	1917*
Jack Rideout	1917–18
John Graham	1918*, 1919*
W. T. Thomas	1919*
Robert Turner	1919–22
Jess Jones (partner 1939)	1923–39
Albert Ford (employed intermittently)	
Vance Clarke (employed intermittently)	
Hugh Gibbs	1938–39

*Denotes a period of less than a year.

Appendix 2:
Cutter's Buildings and Projects

This list includes all buildings from Cutter's office for which documentary evidence exists. Sources include drawings, office accounts, and correspondence. All buildings were believed to be standing at the time of publication except where indicated by symbols in parentheses. (See key below)

For each year, houses are listed first, followed by buildings of all other types. Both groups are in alphabetical order. Dates given are the years in which each project was initiated in the office. All buildings are located in Washington State unless otherwise noted. The location of drawings is shown in parentheses.

Location of drawings

EW   Cutter Collection, Eastern Washington State Historical
      Society Archives, Spokane

IH   Idaho Historical Society, Boise

PV   Palos Verdes Home Owners' Association, Malaga Cove,
      Palos Verdes, California

P   Poper Collection, Long Beach, California. At the time of
      publication these drawings had been offered to the Architectural Drawings Collection, University of California,
      Santa Barbara.

UW   University of Washington Archives, Seattle

Wh   Whitman College Archives, Walla Walla

Status of building

Unbuilt
project   *Italics*

There is evidence
that it was built   b

Location and
status unknown   ?

Demolished   d

Destroyed by fire   df

Date uncertain   *

Kirtland Cutter

1887   Horace Cutter house, Seventh Avenue, head of Stevens
Street, Spokane (d)

K. K. Cutter "Swiss Cottage," Seventh Avenue, Spokane (d)

Cutter and Poetz

1889   Cyrus Burns house, head of Washington Street, Spokane (d)

Chalet Hohenstein (Swiss Cottage enlarged), Seventh Avenue,
Spokane (d; EW)

James Glover house, W. 321 Eighth Avenue, Spokane (now a
restaurant; EW)

F. Rockwood Moore house, Seventh Avenue, Spokane (d; EW)

James Wardner house, Fairhaven (1103 Fifteenth, Bellingham)

Augustine Bean and Hoyt Building, Howard Street, Spokane
(d; EW)

Theodore Cushing Building, northwest corner of Sprague
and Howard, Spokane (d)

First National Bank, northwest corner of Riverside and
Howard, Spokane (d)

Rookery Building, southeast corner of Riverside and
Howard, Spokane (d; EW)

*Washington State College, Pullman** (EW)

White House Store, Riverside Avenue, Spokane (d; EW)

1890   Dr. Burne house, Lidgerwood Park, Spokane (b)

*F. Lewis Clark house, Spokane** (EW)

F. Lewis Clark lodge gate, 705 W. Seventh Avenue, Spokane
(EW)

Thomas F. Griffiths residence, Spokane (b?)

B. Norman semidetached cottages, Adar Street, Spokane (b?)

Sherwood Building, 508 Riverside, Spokane (d)

T. Cushing semidetached cottages, Spokane (?)

*Daniels Building, corner of Front and Stevens, Spokane** (EW)

Fairmont Cemetery Chapel, Spokane

Portland City Hall Competition

E. L. Powell Building, Riverside, Spokane (d)

William Quirin Building, corner of Riverside and Browne,
Spokane (d)

W. H. Taylor Building, Spokane (?)
Wardner Miners' Union Building, Wardner, Idaho

1891　Henry Hoyt house, 719 Sixth Avenue, Spokane (d; EW)
Hughson house, Spokane (?)
Waldo Payne house, 2509 Summit Boulevard, Spokane
(d; EW)
D. K. Stevens house, 802 N. Yakima, Tacoma
Three sketches for shingled houses (EW)
Business premises for F. L. Clark, Riverside near Bernard,
Spokane (EW)
Traders National Bank, and F. Rockwood Moore Building,
Spokane (EW)

1892　Columbia School, 3817 E. Sanson, Spokane (EW)
Idaho Building, World's Columbian Exposition, Chicago
(d; EW)
Pedicord Hotel, 209 W. Riverside, Spokane (EW)

1893　*Spokane County Courthouse Competition*

1894　Pioneer Building, Corner of Eighth and Main, Boise, Idaho (d)
Sketch for a stable (EW)
Arlington School, Hillyard, Spokane* (?; EW)

Cutter and Malmgren

1895　Charles Conrad house, Woodland Ave., Kalispell, Montana
(now a historic house museum; EW)
Farmhouse for John A. Finch (?; EW)
Henry M. Richards house, 2136 W. Riverside, Spokane (d; EW)
R. L. Rutter house, 1725 W. Pacific, Spokane
Charles E. Shepherd (Harry Krutz) house, 602 Boylston,
Seattle (d)

1896　"Idaho" Mansion, Ringwood, Hampshire, England (d)
Alterations to Moore house, Spokane, for Judge Turner (d)

1897　Amasa B. Campbell house, W. 2316 First Avenue, Spokane
(now a historic house museum; EW)

Patrick Clark house, W. 2208 Second Avenue, Spokane (now
    a restaurant; EW)
Austin Corbin house, W. 815 Seventh Avenue, Spokane (EW)
D. C. Corbin house, W. 507 Seventh Avenue, Spokane
John A. Finch house, W. 2340 First Avenue, Spokane (EW)
Thomas Herrick house, W. 726 Seventh Avenue, Spokane (d)
Herbert Moore cottage, southeast corner of Eighth and
    Bernard, Spokane (d)
W. J. C. Wakefield house, W. 2328 1st Avenue, Spokane (EW)

1898   Additions to Hoyt house for K. K. Cutter Studio (d; EW)
Saint Andrew's Episcopal Church, Wooden Street, Chelan
    (EW)
Ridpath Block, between Howard and Stevens, Spokane (?)
Spokane Country Club, near Fort Wright and Greenwood
    Cemetery (?)
Warwick Restaurant, 520 Riverside, Spokane (d)

1899   H. C. Brown house, 1106 Nora, Spokane (?)
F. Lewis Clark house, Seventh Avenue, Spokane (EW)
C. H. Clark house, 1121 Union Street, Seattle (d; UW)
Jay P. Graves house, 2123 First Avenue, Spokane
Cottage for Hypotheek Bank, corner of Third and Spokane
    Street, Spokane (d)
Dr. Luhn cottage, W. 2236 Pacific, Spokane (EW)
R. O. McClintock house, 2103 Fourth Avenue, Spokane
J. D. Sherwood house, W. 2941 Summit Boulevard, Spokane
    (df)
C. D. Stimson house, 1204 Minor Avenue, Seattle (now open
    for tours and events; EW)
H. D. Trunke house, 2109 Fourth Avenue, Spokane
Mrs. Wilson house, 2115 Fourth Avenue, Spokane (d)
Chemical Building alterations, southwest corner of Sprague
    and Howard, Spokane (?)
Chicago Hotel (Norden Hotel), northeast corner Main &
    Washington, Spokane (d; EW)
Emerson School, 1116 W. Alice, Spokane (d; EW)
Squire Building, renovation for the Spokane Club (?)

1900   Louis F. Anderson house, Whitman College, Walla Walla (Wh)

Philip Stewart house, Colorado Springs, Colorado (EW)

Robert Strahorn house (remodel), W. 2216 First Avenue,
    Spokane (d; EW)

Davenport's Restaurant, Italian Gardens, Spokane (interior d;
    EW)

Grape Arbor, Liberty Park, Spokane (d)

Saint Paul's Church, Walla Walla

1901   John W. Graham Building, Sprague between Post and Wall
       (formerly Mill), Spokane (d)

       White Palmerston Building, corner of Post and First,
           Spokane (?)

1902   Carnegie Camp, Raquette Lake, New York (EW)

       E. O. Graves house, corner of Mercer and Harvard, Seattle
       (d)

       Hotel, Playa del Rey, California (EW)

       Kirtland Hall, Yale University, New Haven, Connecticut (EW)

1903   John A. Finch caretaker's house, Hayden Lake, Idaho

       John A. Finch chalet, Hayden Lake, Idaho (df; EW)

       W. H. Cowles house, W. 2602 Second Avenue, Spokane (d)

       Idaho Building, St. Louis Exhibition, St. Louis, Missouri (d)

       Insinger Apartments, Spokane* (?)

       Lange Building, Railroad Addition, Spokane (?)

       Rainier Club, 810 Fourth Avenue, Seattle (EW)

       Riblet Building, Sprague and Washington, Spokane (d; EW)

       Saint Paul's School, Walla Walla (d; EW)

       Silver Grill, Hotel Spokane, W. 500 First Avenue, Spokane (d)

       Tidball Block, Riverside, Spokane (d; EW)

1904   D. M. Drumheller house, Sixth and Cedar, Spokane (EW)

       Improvements for Louis Davenport:

           Hall of the Doges, Davenport's, Spokane (EW)

           Orange Bower, Davenport's* (d; EW)

           Peacock Room, Davenport's* (d)

           Pennington Hotel, Spokane, alterations (interior d; EW)

       Adams Block, Lewiston, Idaho (b?)

       Butler Hotel, Seattle, alterations (?)

       Coeur d'Alene Boat Club (?)

Hazlewood Dairy, Browne and Pacific, Spokane (d; EW)

Lyceum Theater, Browne near Riverside, Spokane (d; EW)

O.K. Stable, south side of First below Post and Lincoln, Spokane (d; EW)

Tidbay Block, additions, Riverside, Spokane (?)

Weisgerber Building, 142 Fifth, Lewiston, Idaho (EW)

1905   Brokaw house (perhaps at Fourteenth and Klamath, Spokane)* (?; EW)

Frank Graves house, Spokane (EW)

D. L. Huntington house, 2515 Second Avenue, Spokane (d; EW)

C. P. Thomas house, 1212 N. Summit Boulevard, Spokane (EW)

Adams Block, Lewiston, Idaho (b?)

Bollinger Hotel annex, Lewiston, Idaho (?; EW)

Exchange Bank (five story addition), Spokane (EW)

Hotel and Sanitorium, Medical Lake (?)

Idaho Trust Company Building, Lewiston, Idaho (EW)

Tacoma Hotel, interior remodel (df)

Training School, Idaho State Normal School, Lewiston, Idaho (d)

Olympia Brewing Company warehouse (?)

C. P. Thomas warehouse, Railroad Addition, Spokane (?)

Vaudeville Theater, Spokane (?)

Vollmer Block, Lewiston, Idaho

Washington Theater, Spokane

Weisgerber Brewery addition, Lewiston, Idaho (EW)

1906   Francis Finucane house, Spokane (d; EW)

John W. Graham house, Spokane (EW)

Samuel Hill "Italian Park," E. Highland Drive, Capitol Hill, Seattle

    J. D. Farrell house

    Samuel Hill house (supervision only), 814 E. Highland Drive

    Hervey Lindley house, 904 E. Highland Drive (d; EW)

W. P. Hurlbut house, Lewiston, Idaho (d; EW)

W. G. Parks house, corner of Second and Adams, Spokane (?)

James Smyth house, S. 428 Hemlock, Spokane (EW)

Samuel Stern house, 211 Eighth Avenue, Spokane (EW)

Dr. James Sutherland house, Spokane (EW)

D. W. Twohy house, Cliff Avenue, Spokane (d; EW)

Chicago Hotel addition, northeast corner of Main and
Washington, Spokane (d; EW)

Grandstand for Washington Water Power, Natatorium Park,
Spokane (?; EW)

Col. E. H. Morrison, business block, Spokane (?)

Silver Bow Club, Butte, Montana (EW)

Spokane College, Twenty-ninth Avenue and Grand, Spokane
(d; EW)

*Spokane and Eastern Trust Building, northwest corner of
Howard and Sprague, Spokane* (EW)

Washington Water Power Office Building, W. 825 Trent,
Spokane (df; EW)

*Whitman College Chapel, Walla Walla (plans donated by
Cutter and Malmgren)*

1907 F. A. Blackwell house, Spirit Lake, Idaho (EW)

Albert Burch house, Berkeley, California (EW)

Frederick Dewart house, W. 201 Sixth Avenue, Spokane (EW)

Clyde Graves house, E. 127 Twelfth Street, Spokane (d; EW)

Dr. W. H. Hare house, W. 1123 Fourteenth Avenue, Spokane
(EW)

W. M. O. Seligman house, S. 2203 Manito Boulevard, Spokane
(EW)

C. J. Smith house, 1147 Harvard Avenue, Seattle (EW)

Alterations to former James Glover house for Mrs. Charles
Sweeny (EW)

C. M. Youle house, Twelfth Avenue, Spokane (d; EW)

Bozanta Tavern, Hayden Lake, Idaho

Station for F. A. Blackwell, Spirit Lake, Idaho (d; EW)

College Inn, Jaffe Building, 311 Pike Street, Seattle (d; EW)

BPOE Elks Monument, Greenwood Cemetery, Spokane (EW)

First Church of Christ Scientist, Spokane (d)

Graves Building, Spokane* (EW)

Gardener and Engedahl Apartments, 1304-12 Broadway,
Spokane (EW)

Idaho State Normal School, women's dormitory, Lewiston,
Idaho (d; EW)

Jasper Apartments, corner of Division and Liberty, Spokane

Moore Building, alterations for Alexander Pantages, Spokane
(?; EW)

Pedicord Hotel additions, Spokane

Rainier Club, ladies' annex, Seattle (EW)

Palouse Station, Spokane and Inland Railway Company,
Palouse* (d; EW)

Washington Securities Company Building, northwest corner
of Fifth and Union, Seattle (d; EW)

Woodward Apartments* (?; EW)

Hotel Yakima alterations* (?)

1908   A. M. Anderson house, 2926 East Oval, Corbin Park, Spokane
(EW)

Manson F. Backus house, 1110 University Street, Seattle (d)

Thomas Burke, garage and Indian Room, Madison Street,
Seattle (d; EW)

C. H. Clarke, country home (EW)

C. H. Clarke house, The Highlands (completed by Willatzen
and Byrne; EW)

J. M. Corbet house, 820 W. Seventh Avenue, Spokane (EW)

Man's cottage for H. C. Henry, The Highlands, Seattle (EW)

Chester D. Gibbs house, 1718 W. Ninth, Spokane (EW)

J. B. Jordan house, alterations and extensions (EW)

C. H. Jones house, W. 312 Sumner, Spokane (d)

A. S. Kerry house, The Highlands, Seattle (EW)

L. B. Peeples house, 948 Harvard Avenue, Seattle

John Sengfelder house, W. 1321 Ninth Avenue, Spokane (EW)

Patrick Welch, alterations to former James Glover House,
Spokane (EW)

Harry Wraight house, W. 2711 Summit Boulevard, Spokane
(EW)

Bank of Colville (EW)

Carman Manufacturing Company warehouse, Spokane (EW)

*Station building for W. H. Cowles, Spokane** (EW)

Davenport Hotel, First Design, Spokane (EW)

Dutton Block, Spokane (EW)

Galax Hotel, corner of Main and Bernard, Spokane (d; EW)

Idaho State Normal School Gymnasium, Lewiston, Idaho
(d; EW)

Mulcahy Apartment House, Spokane (?; EW)

Old National Bank, Spokane, competition design
Seattle Golf and Country Club, The Highlands, Seattle
    (EW)
Sillman Store and Hotel, Spokane (d; EW)
Stokes Tea Room, Seattle (EW)
Yale Hotel, Chewelah (EW)

1909   E. T. Coman house, southwest corner of Seventh and Monroe,
            Spokane (?)
        Louis M. Davenport house, Spokane (d; EW)
        Estabrook log house, Idaho City, Idaho (df)
        James Glover house, 1408 N. Summit, Spokane (EW)
        Karl Gunnar Malmgren house, 709 Sumner Avenue, Spokane
            (EW)
        Lucius G. Nash house, Spokane (EW)
        Chester Thorne house, "Thornewood," American Lake (UW)
        Asotin Power Station, for Lewiston Clarkston Company,
            Asotin (EW)
        BPOE Memorial Tablet, Moscow, Idaho
        Idaho State Normal School Domestic Science Building
            addition, Lewiston, Idaho (d; EW)
        Spokane Club, 1002 W. Riverside, Spokane (EW)
        Spokane Country Club, near Fort Wright, Spokane (?)
        Spokane Humane Society, Broadway between Mill and Post,
            Spokane (?)
        Mercantile Building, Bank of Colville, Colville (EW)
        Washington Liquor Company Building, 706 or 766 Main
            Avenue, Spokane (EW)
        Washington Water Power Post Street Substation, Spokane (EW)
        Western Union Life Insurance Company, W. 1023 Riverside,
            Spokane (d; EW)

1910   Jay P. Graves house, "Waikiki," Spokane (EW)
        F. W. Kettenbach house, 819 Sixth Avenue, Lewiston, Idaho (EW)
        E. H. Knight house, N. 1715 West Point Road, Spokane (EW)
        Michael Lang chalet, 1034 W. Seventh Avenue, Spokane
        Lewis P. Larson house, Metalline Falls (EW)
        The Crescent Store, Riverside and Wall, Spokane (d)
        Eiler Music Building, southeast corner of Sprague and Post,
            Spokane (d)

J. W. Green Building, Monroe and Maxwell, Spokane (EW)
Holy Trinity Episcopal Church, Wallace, Idaho
Portland Hotel addition, Portland, Oregon
Ryan and Newton Cold Storage Building, Post Street,
    Spokane (EW)
Security National Bank, Cheney (EW)
Street lights, Spokane
United Cigar Stores Building, Spokane (?)
Warwick Building, Spokane (?)

1911   *Isaac Anderson house, American Lake, Tacoma* (EW)
Jay P. Graves garage, "Waikiki," Spokane (EW)
C. P. Lindsley house, Spokane (?)
Lang house, W. 1034 Seventh Avenue, Spokane (EW)
Fred H. Mason house, 214 Eighth Avenue, Spokane (EW)
James Smythe Building, Spokane (?; EW)
Bolster Memorial, Spokane (?; EW)
Chicago Hotel alterations to bar room, Spokane (d; EW)
Georgian Room remodel, Davenport's, Spokane
James Smythe Hotel Building, Spokane (?; EW)
Monroe Street Bridge, Spokane
Nott Atwater Warehouse, Monroe and N.P. tracks, Spokane
    (?; EW)
Simon Piano House (remodel), Cascade Bldg, W. 911-15
    Riverside, Spokane (d; EW)
Stock Barn, University of Idaho, Moscow, Idaho (?; EW)
Stock Judging Pavilion, University of Idaho, Moscow, Idaho
    (?; EW)

1912   Dr. Coburn house (?; EW)
Charles Jasper house, 503 Sumner, Spokane (EW)
Jasper house, 919 S. Adams (d)
Weisgerber house, 811 Sixth Avenue, Lewiston, Idaho (EW)
Davenport Hotel, Sprague Avenue between Post and Lincoln,
    Spokane (EW)
Cyrus Happy Building, Spokane (EW)
Bank of Fairfield, Fairfield
Metaline Falls School, Metaline Falls (now the Cutter
    Theater; EW)

Statler Hotel, Cleveland, Ohio (EW)
Camp for D. W. Twohy, Hayden Lake, Idaho (EW)
Woldson Apartment House, 1214 W. Sprague, Spokane (EW)

1913   W. H. Cowles house, Santa Barbara, California
J. E. Lewis house, Montana (EW)
C. D Stimson house, The Highlands, Seattle (EW)
D. W. Twohy house, near 104 Sumner, Spokane (d)
Lake McDonald Lodge, Glacier National Park, Montana (EW)
Sons of Norway Hall (Robertson Building), 305 W. Riverside,
   Spokane (EW)
C. D. Stimson mill office, 2116 Vernon Place, Seattle
C. D. Stimson garage, The Highlands, Seattle
C. D. Stimson Young People's Cabin, The Highlands, Seattle
   (EW)

1914   *Many Glaciers Hotel, Glacier National Park, Montana* (EW)
Church and School for Saint Augustine's Parish, W. 420
   Eighteenth Avenue, Spokane (EW)
Spokane and Eastern Trust Co., Sprague and Howard,
   Spokane (?; EW)

1915   John F. Clark house, alterations (?)
W. H. Cowles gardener's cottage, Santa Barbara, California
   (EW)
Heffernan house, 408 Lake Washington Boulevard, Seattle
   (EW)
Kilroy house, Sandpoint, Idaho (?; EW)
Mrs. John G. Moroney house, Great Falls, Montana (?; EW)
J. D. Porter residence
William Schaeffer Apartment House, Kellogg, Idaho (?; EW)
W. H. Wright house, Newport
Armory Building, interior remodeling, Spokane
Exchange National Bank, alterations, northwest corner of
   Riverside and Howard, Spokane (d; EW)
*President's house, Boston Okanogan Apple Company** (EW)
Seven Seven Company Building, Spokane (?; EW)
Symons Building, S. 7 Howard and First Avenue, Spokane (d)
Theis Garage, Spokane (d; EW)

Extrance to Riverside Park Cemetery, Spokane (EW)
Church of the Immaculate Conception, Garfield (d; EW)
Finch Mausoleum, Riverside Cemetery, Spokane (EW)

1916   T. J. Humbird house, W. 612 Sumner Ave., Spokane (EW)
O. G. Labaree country house, Spokane (?; EW)
Norton Morrison house, Fairfield (?; EW)
Ralston Wilbur house (?)
Theodore Wilcox house, Tulatin Valley, Oregon (EW)
Camp Lewis gate, near Tacoma (EW)
Chronicle Building, 929 W. Sprague, Spokane (EW)
First National Bank, Cle Elum (d EW)
Fraternity House, Moscow, Idaho (EW)
St. John Bank, Main Street, St. John (EW)
Sherwood Building, 510 W. Riverside, Spokane (EW)
Steam Plant, 151-65 S. Post, Spokane
Tacoma Hotel alterations, Tacoma
Theater in Walker Building, remodeling and completion (?)

1917   *Mrs. Leonard house, Spokane*
H. F. Samuels house, Samuels, Idaho
Hefferman Building (?)
Gearhart Hotel, Gearhart, Oregon (EW)
B. C. Riblet Building (proposed home for YWCA)
Spokane Heat Light and Power Building (EW)

Kirtland Cutter

1918   Sweeney house (remodeling), 109 Sumner, Spokane
Westwold Manor, Woodway Park, Edmonds (EW)
Weyerhaeuser House, near Tacoma (EW)
The Crescent, 719 W. Main, Spokane (d)
Elks Lodge, Spokane (associate architect with E. J. Baume)
Post Office, Cheney (EW)
Otis Orchards School addition, Spokane (d EW)
Riverside Park Cemetery, Spokane

1919   Mrs. J. M. Bonner house, alterations, Lewiston, Idaho
       (?; EW)
Villa Carman, 11211 Gravelly Lake Drive, near Tacoma (EW)

B. L. Gordon log cabin, Penrith (?; EW)

Dr. Murray house, Wenatchee (associate architect with E. J.
Baume) (?)

H. S. Rand house, Yakima (?)

Alexander Hotel, Tacoma (EW)

Deaconess Hospital (associate architect with E. J. Baume),
731-37 W. Fourth, Spokane

B. L. Gordon Ballroom (?)

Hurley-Mason Co. Hotel, Hoquiam (EW)

Swan Lake Camp for Cornelius Kelley, near Kalispell,
Montana (EW)

Visitation Academy, proposed school (EW)

1920   Ernest Dolge house, 11430 Gravelly Lake Drive, Steilacoom
Lake, Tacoma (EW)

William Jones house, 12718 Gravelly Lake Drive (EW)

Floyd T. McCroskey house, W. 414 Sumner, Spokane (EW)

John P. Gray house, 521 S. Thirteenth Street, Coeur d'Alene,
Idaho (EW)

Walla Walla Hotel, Walla Walla

B. L. Gordon, alterations to store, Spokane (EW)

Madison Hotel, remodeling lobby and entrance, Spokane

National Bank of Tacoma, Tacoma

A. L. Porter Movie House, Lewiston, Idaho

*Chapel, mausoleum, and crematory, Riverside Park Cemetery,
Spokane* (EW)

Spokane Hotel, alterations, Spokane

Remodeling of building, 823 First Avenue, Spokane (EW)

1921   Davenport cottage, headwater of Little Spokane River,
Spokane

Leo J. Falk house, 1320 Warm Springs Road, Boise, Idaho (EW)

Mrs. Charlotte Finch house (EW)

Ralph Gordon house, ballroom, and cottage, Spokane

C. T. Kipp house (?; EW)

Harry Turner house (?)

Coeur d'Alene School, Coeur d'Alene, Idaho

Halleine Hall (?)

Apartments for Hurley Mason, Tacoma (EW)

Madison Hotel, remodel first floor, Spokane

Manito ME Church and parsonage, S. 3220 Grand, Spokane
L. T. Murray, Tacoma (?)
Sandpoint Hotel, Sandpoint, Idaho

1923   Roy Gill house, Spokane (?)
Galax Hotel, alterations and additions, Main and Bernard,
    Spokane (d; EW)
Otis Orchards High School addition, Spokane (EW)
Whitehead's Dancing Palace, interior, Sprague Avenue,
Spokane (EW)

California

All projects below are in California unless otherwise stated

1923   *Lunada Bay Plaza, Palos Verdes*
Palos Verdes Project, rendering* (Malaga Cove Library, Palos
    Verdes)

1924   C. C. Anderson house, 927 Warm Springs Avenue, Boise,
    Idaho (IH)
Thomas Autzen house, 2425 NE Alameda, Portland, Oregon
A. E. Cameron house, 881 Via del Monte, Palos Verdes (P; PV)
John Wehrman house, 6325 Via Colonita, Palos Verdes (PV)
C. B. Peeples house, 2075 Lombardy, San Marino (P)

1926   F. F. Schellenberg house, 3604 Via Palomino, Palos Verdes
    (PV)
Schellenberg / Paull house, 3621 Via Colonita, Palos Verdes
Schellenberg / Gilmore house, 3825 Paseo del Campo, Palos
    Verdes (PV)
Sutherland / Cotton house, 633 Hoquilla, Palos Verdes (PV)
Sutherland / Wilkins house, 637 Hoquilla, Palos Verdes (PV)
Vanderlip guest house, Portuguese Bend (P)
John Russell Lowell Elementary School, Long Beach* (d
    earthquake)

1927   James E. Buchanan house, 700 Via Somonte, Palos Verdes (P;
    PV)

Earle W. Gard house, 2728 Via Elevado, Palos Verdes (P; PV)
Katherine Sisson house, 1705 Via Montemar, Palos Verdes (PV)

1928   Grace Snellgrove/Omar Holliday house, 2709 Via Anita, Palos Verdes
Irwin Marr house, 21 Thirty-seventh Place, Ocean Bluff, Long Beach (P)
W. H. Monroe house, 2705 Via Anita, Palos Verdes (PV)
Dr. Otto Stein house, 2733 Elevado Lane, Palos Verdes (P; PV)
Karl Von Platen house, 1465 Orlando, San Marino

1929   D. P. Condit house, 4282 Pacific Avenue, Long Beach
L.T. Edwards house, 4286 Country Club Drive, Los Cerritos, Long Beach
John Hoyt house, 1718 Ambassador Avenue, Beverly Hills (d)
Palos Verdes Swimming Club, 389 Paseo del Mar, Palos Verdes (P)

1930   Dr. Hugo Jones house, 2800 Via Campesina, Palos Verdes (P; PV)
A. T. Jergins house, 2925 E. Ocean, Long Beach (d earthquake; P)
Walden Shaw house, 1585 Orlando, Pasadena
San Clemente Hotel, San Clemente (P)

1931   Norman Phillips house, 900 Via Panorama, Palos Verdes (PV)

1932   Henry Clock house, 4242 Pine Avenue, Los Cerritos, Long Beach (P)
D. E. Humphreys house, 4120 Locust Avenue, Los Cerritos, Long Beach
Robert Peyton house, 190 Foothills Road, Beverly Hills (P)

1933   Honeyman house, 2009 East Bay Front, Balboa Island (P)
Victor Fleming beach cottage, Balboa Island (d; P)

1934   Major V. E Miltenberger house, 4324 Via Frascati, Palos
        Verdes (PV)
        Abraham Lincoln School, Long Beach (P)
        Long Beach Junior College* (P)

1935   John Clock house, 525 Devon Place, Long Beach (P)

1936   Dr. J. R. Jimmerson house, 4181 Country Club Drive, Los
        Cerritos, Long Beach (P)
        Irwin Marr beachhouse, 1212 Temple Terrace, Laguna Beach
        (P)
        Clarence B. Mills house, 4100 Locust Avenue, Long Beach.

1937   Victor Fleming house, 1050 Moraga Drive, Bel Air

1938   Eldridge Combs house, 4120 Cedar Avenue, Palos Verdes
        Lewis house, 3851 Linden Avenue, Bixby Knolls, Long Beach*
        Thomas M. Rowan house, Bixby Knolls, Long Beach
        Ware sisters' house, 206 Bennett Avenue, Long Beach (P)

Undated projects 1923-39 include the following. Drawings of others
are unidentified.

        W. P. Anderson house, Palos Verdes* (P)
        C. M. Cotton house, Bel Air* (P)
        Laura Hope Crews house* (P)
        Kingsley house, Palos Verdes (P)
        John E. Marshland house, Portuguese Bend* (P)
        Mrs. E. A. Parkford house Montecito* (P)
        Dr. and Mrs. Thornbury guest cottage* (P)
        Maurice Von Platen house* (P)
        Episcopal Church, Benmar Hills* (P)
        Golf Club* (P)
        Kilpatrick's Bakery, Santa Ana* (P)
        Pacific Coast Club, Long Beach, interior remodeling* (P)
        Resort hotel and yacht club* (P)

NOTES

Introduction

1. Isaac C. Jolles, quoted in John Fahey, "When the Dutch Owned Spokane," *Pacific Northwest Quarterly* 72, no. 1 (1981): 3.

2. *Spokane Spokesman-Review*, September 28, 1905.

3. *The Philistine* (East Aurora, New York), March 1906, 122.

4. Frederick Jennings, "The Most Notable Architecture and Landscape Architecture of Spokane, Washington," *Architect and Engineer* (San Francisco) 65, no. 3 (June 1921): 47–91.

5. *The Philistine*, 126; *Architect and Engineer*, 49.

6. Richard Longstreth, in his article "Academic Eclecticism in American Architecture," states that architects of the Academic Movement wanted to "reestablish a sense of continuity with the past," and they believed that architecture should once again become an art based on a deep knowledge of historic precedent. They also believed, however, in the role of intuition: "The overriding interest was practice, not theory." *Winterthur Portfolio*, Spring 1982, 55–57.

Chapter 1   Whippoorwill Farm

1. William Ganson Rose, *Cleveland: The Making of a City* (Cleveland, 1950), 26–33.

2. Allene B. Duty, *The Pease and Risley Families* (Cleveland, 1979), 13.

3. "History of Wallingford," handwritten manuscript, Cutter Collection, Eastern Washington State Historical Society (hereafter EWSHS).

4. J. S. Newberry, *Memoir of Jared Potter Kirtland* (Washington, D.C., 1879), 129–32. EWSHS.

5. Jared Potter Kirtland obituary, *Cleveland Herald*, December 10, 1877.

6. Unidentified newspaper clipping. EWSHS.

7. Jared Potter Kirtland obituary.

8. Jared Kirtland to Caroline Cutter, April 12, 1871. EWSHS.

9. *Spokesman-Review*, April 8, 1917.

10. *Cleveland Daily Ledger*, December 3, 1859, 212. Newberry, *Memoir*, 137–38.

11. Jared Potter Kirtland obituary.

12. Duty, *Pease and Risley Families*, 13.

13. Benjamin Cutter and William R. Cutter, *A History of the Cutter Family of New England* (Boston, 1871), 211–12.

14. *Cleveland Daily Ledger*, advertisements, December 1 and 6, 1859, and October 5, 1866.

15. Cutter and Cutter, *History of the Cutter Family*, 212.

16. *Annals of Cleveland* (indexes of Cleveland newspapers) lead only to references to the bank.

17. *Cleveland Daily Ledger*, April 27, 1875.

18. Newberry, *Memoir*, 135.

Chapter 2   The Education of an Artist

1. The "Roll of Brooks School, 1876" (Western Reserve Historical Society, Cleveland, Ohio) shows Kirtland Cutter as a member of Second Company of the School Battalion. On the school's curriculum see William G. Rose, *Cleveland: The Making of a City* (Cleveland, 1950), 398. See also the *Cleveland Daily Ledger*, January 5 and March 8, 1875, and *Cleveland Evening Herald*, December 10, 1887. The school was founded as a memorial to the Reverend Frederick Brooks, whose plan to start a preparatory school for boys had been cut short by his tragic drowning. Quotations on parades and drills are from the *Cleveland Daily Ledger*, March 7, 18, and 20, and December 20, 1876.

2. See Vincent Scully, *The Shingle Style* (New Haven: Yale University Press, 1971), 2.

3. Rose, *Cleveland*, 298.

4. Richard N. Campen, *Architecture of the Western Reserve, 1800–1900* (Cleveland: Press of Case Western Reserve University, 1971), 115, 117.

5. Ibid., 240.

6. Carl Wittke, *The First Fifty Years: The Cleveland Museum of Art, 1916–1966* (Cleveland, 1966), 11–12.

7. Josephine W. Duveneck, *Frank Duveneck* (San Francisco: John Howell-Books, 1970), 18, 35–48, 57, 89–90. Richard J. Boyle, *John Twachtman* (New York: Watson Guptill, 1979), 7. Richard H. Love, *Theodore Earl Butler* (Chicago: Haase-Momm Publishing Co., 1985), 415.

8. *Dictionary of American Biography* (New York: Scribner's Sons, 1928), 4:478.

9. Wittke, *The First Fifty Years*, 14–17. Otto Bacher, "With Whistler in Venice" [1880–86], *Century Magazine*, 1908. See also *Dictionary of American Biography* (1928), 1:465.

10. *Spokesman-Review*, April 8, 1917.

11. Rosina A. Florio, Executive Director, Art Students League of New York, interviewed by the author April 10, 1987.

12. The introduction to the *Spokesman-Review* interview (see note 10) stated that Cutter came straight from Europe to Spokane. This tends to eliminate the theory of a second period at the League.

13. Marchal E. Landgren, *Years of Art: The Story of the Art Students League of New York* (New York: R. M. McBride and Company, 1940), 18–19.

14. Allen Tucker, *Fiftieth Anniversary of the Art Students' League of New York* (New York, 1925), 9, 11, 50.

15. Richard J. Boyle, *American Impressionism* (Boston: New York Graphic Society, 1974), 116. Beckwith was one of the organizers of the successful exhibition of French paintings in New York in 1883 to raise money for the base of the Statue of Liberty. Barbizon School and Impressionist painters were well represented.

16. *Dictionary of American Biography* (1928), 4:478. Kenyon Cox, *The Classic Point of View* (New York: Scribner's Sons, 1911), 3–4.

17. Kenyon Cox, *Artist and Public* (London: Allen and Unwin, 1914), 15, 21–22.

18. Michael Quick, *American Expatriot Painters of the Late Nineteenth Century* (Dayton, 1976), 36.

19. Bacher, "With Whistler in Venice," 207–10.

20. Unidentified newspaper report, Necrology Files, Western Reserve Historical Society, Cleveland.

21. Her passport, taken out in 1880, is in the EWSHS Collection.

22. Peggy Bayless, her granddaughter, interviewed by the author January 15, 1985.

23. The picture was reproduced years later in an unidentified newspaper under the title "Do You Remember?" Its caption states that the scene took place on a walking party in Switzerland (n.d., EWSHS).

24. Cutter to M. E. George, Portland, January 26, 1891, in the Letterbook, Private Collection.

25. Mary Alden Hopkins, in an article on Cutter's work, in *House Beautiful*, September 1921, 190–91, mentions that Kirtland Cutter and his client, Austin Corbin, were students in Paris together.

26. Charles Dickens, *American Notes and Pictures from Italy* (Oxford, 1957), 26, 28.

27. See Wolfgang Herrmann, *Gottfried Semper: In Search of Architecture* (Cambridge: MIT Press, 1984).

28. *Spokesman-Review*, April 8, 1917, interview with Cutter.

29. Cutter's library included thirteen volumes of Ruskin's works, a biography of William Morris, and several portfolios, including Arts and Crafts designs. His library list and some of his books are in the EWSHS Collection. For information on the Aesthetic movement, see *In Pursuit of Beauty: Americans and the Aesthetic Movement* (New York: Metropolitan Museum of Art; Rizzoli, 1986).

30. The entry for Cutter in *Men of the Pacific Coast* (San Francisco: Pacific Coast Art Company, 1902–3) gives the time of his arrival in Spokane as October 1886. While other directories, such as *Who's Who in California* (1928), state that he arrived there in 1885, the later date appears more likely.

31. *Spokesman-Review*, April 8, 1917.

32. The painting is in the collection of the Washington Trust Bank, Spokane.

33. *Spokesman-Review*, April 8, 1917.

34. H. H. Hook and F. J. McGuire, *Spokane Falls Illustrated* (Minneapolis: Frank L. Thresher, 1889).

35. *Spokesman-Review*, April 8, 1917.

Chapter 3 Spokane Falls: Architecture on the Frontier (1886–1889)

1. *Men of the Pacific Coast* (San Francisco, 1902–3), 536

2. N. W. Durham, *History of the City of Spokane and Spokane County* (Chicago, 1912), 1:372, 374, 366, 386. In 1881 the railroad provided only partial access for settlers: the Northern Pacific Railroad's transcontinental route was not completed until 1883.

3. Ibid., 412. Glover's brick bank building was constructed in 1883.

4. *Spokesman-Review*, April 8, 1917. Cutter recalled his reactions when interviewed thirty years later.

5. Various views in the EWSHS Museum collection contribute to this description.

6. Rowland Bond, *Early Birds in the Northwest* (Nine Mile Falls, Wash.: Spokane House Enterprises, [1973]), 214–18.

7. The topography is effectively portrayed in the panorama engraved by Henry Wellge in 1884. EWSHS Collection.

8. The conditions described can still be observed today.

9. *Historic Landmarks Survey* (Spokane: City Commission, 1979), 36.

10. H. H. Hook and Francis J. McGuire, *Spokane Falls Illustrated* (Minneapolis, 1889), 44, 55. The 1887 panorama published by Lewis & Dryden of Portland shows the house already in place (EWSHS).

11. Napoleon III's empire lost its allure when, in 1871, the French suffered defeat in the Franco-Prussian War.

12. Durham, *History of the City of Spokane and Spokane County*, 1:366, 573; 2:170. *Spokane Falls Illustrated*, 40.

13. *Spokane Falls and Its Exposition* (Buffalo: Matthews, Northrup and Co., 1890).

14. *Spokesman-Review*, April 8, 1917.

15. *Spokane Falls Review*, reports on January 6, 9, 10, 12, 15, and 16, 1887.

16. See *Spokane Falls Illustrated*, 12–14, 41, 44–45. Having urged Kirtland to come to Spokane and to live in his own home, it is unthinkable that Horace Cutter would have had someone else design the house, particularly since Horace's partners, Glover and Moore, both commissioned Cutter to design their mansions within a year.

17. *Spokane Falls Review*, January 1, 1887, and Polk's *Spokane City Directory*, 1887.

18. *Spokane Falls Illustrated*, 44, 57. Roofed balconies opening off bedrooms were common in Shingle Style houses. Lamb and Rich designed several such features. Cutter might well have known the John H. Ammon residence on Euclid Avenue in Cleveland, built by Julius Schweinfurth in 1881. That house had a jutting upper-story balcony with curiously turned posts.

19. *Oregonian*, July 30, 1888, Spokane Falls Supplement. The William H. Vanderbilt house in New York (1879) had a Japanese room.

20. Agreements and warranty deeds in the Spokane County Assessor's Office confirm the transactions.

21. It is likely that Cutter was introduced to the writings of Downing by his great-grandfather. Jared Kirtland had conducted experiments to produce improved varieties of fruit trees even before Downing was born, and was a leading authority on horticulture. The publication of Downing's *Fruits and Fruit Trees of America* in 1845 must have been of great interest to Jared Kirtland, and the picturesque quality of Whippoorwill Farm suggests that he also had read Downing's architectural works.

22. Andrew Jackson Downing, *The Architecture of Country Houses* (New York, 1850), 28, 271.

23. Ibid., 123.

24. P. F. Robinson, *Rural Architecture* (London, 1823), plate 10.

25. Design 26 in Palliser and Palliser's *American Cottage Homes* (Bridgeport, Conn., 1878) shows a relatively plain chalet incongruously built by the sea. Bicknell and Comstock's *Speci-*

men *Book of One Hundred Architectural Designs* (New York, 1880) illustrated a fanciful house in "Modified Swiss Style," 15. In designing a more authentic chalet, Cutter was following a national trend toward faithful study of the prototype.

26. A discussion of American chalets and their European origins is to be found in Sarah Bradford Landau's paper "Richard Morris Hunt, the Continental Picturesque, and the 'Stick Style,'" *Journal of the Society of Architectural Historians* 42, no. 13 (October 1983): 272–89.

27. Cutter stated in a letter to M. E. George, Portland, January 26, 1891, in the Letterbook, that he had "made a careful study of the architecture" in Switzerland.

28. The characters in the photograph of the chalet and its neighborhood were identified by John B. Fiskin. EWSHS Photograph Collection.

29. *Spokane Falls Review*, February 15, 1888. The place of burial is confirmed in the Necrology files of the Western Reserve Historical Society, Cleveland.

30. The picture of the house in *Spokane Falls Illustrated*, published in August 1889, shows the house with its first extension on the west side, but the architect may have supplied a drawing representing hopes rather than realities.

31. Drawings in the EWSHS Collection.

32. *The Oregonian*, July 30, 1888, Spokane Falls Supplement. This issue, with four pages of illustrations, gives an excellent idea of the city in that year. The only pictures of Cutter's work are two interiors. The same engravings appeared in *Spokane Falls Illustrated*, 47. There is no proof that the Turkish Divan was ever executed.

33. On Moore see Durham, *History of the City of Spokane and Spokane County*, 1:90; *Spokane Falls Illustrated*; and Edward J. Crosby, *The Story of the Washington Water Power Company and Its Part in the History of Electric Service in the Inland Empire, 1889–1930* (n.p., n.d.).

34. *Spokane Falls Review*, January 1, 1887, and photographs in the EWSHS Collection.

35. Many contemporary pictures of Spokane convey this impression, and Preusse was certainly the architect of several in the Second Empire Style.

36. In 1905, in a newspaper interview, Cutter stated: "The old Colonial style in this country and its equivalent style, the Georgian, in England which had flourished upto the beginning of the 19th Century, fell into decadence and there came a mixed style known as the Queen Anne, which included everything atrocious in the line of architecture." *Spokesman-Review*, September 29, 1905, 7:4.

37. Leland Roth, in *McKim, Mead and White, Architects* (New York: Harper and Row, 1983), described the Dunn house as their "most Shavian project" (p. 47). He points out that McKim admired English architects such as Richard Norman Shaw for their true understanding of this historic building.

38. A full discussion of the work of the architects mentioned and the development of the Shingle Style is in Vincent Scully, *The Shingle Style* (New Haven: Yale University Press, 1971).

39. *Home and Garden* (1901), quoted by Gavin Stamp and André Goulancourt in *The English House, 1860–1914* (London: Faber and Faber, 1986).

40. Letterbook (1899–91); the color scheme was discussed in a letter to Brooks Otis of Cleveland, January 30, 1890.

41. The living hall, with grand staircase, was a feature of houses of the new Shingle Style initiated by H. H. Richardson. In one example, Shingleside, in Swampscott, Massachusetts, by W. R. Emerson (1881) a balcony overlooks the hall. This was illustrated in *Building News*, April 28, 1882.

42. *Moderne Bauformen* (Stuttgart), 1905 and 1906. These portfolios also illustrated works by Lutyens, Voysey, Baillie Scott, and others.

43. A similar feature appeared in the M. M. English house, New Westminster, British Columbia, by Samuel Maclure (1891). See Martin Segger, *The Buildings of Samuel Maclure* (Victoria, B.C., 1986).

44. Dr. William Seward Webb was the son-in-law of W. H. Vanderbilt, "a big man in the Vanderbilt Railroad system and director of nearly all

its companies" (*Pacific Builder and Engineer*, April 8, 1905). At the time of his visit to Spokane, Webb was involved with Thomas C. Durant in the opening of the Adirondacks in northern New York State to vacationers. It seems likely, therefore, that he appreciated picturesque qualities in architecture.

45. *Spokesman-Review*, April 8, 1917.

Chapter 4 Cutter and Poetz: Rebuilding Downtown Spokane (1889–1891)

1. *Spokane Falls and Its Exposition* (Buffalo and New York, 1890). Biographical sketch of J. C. Poetz.

2. The roles of the two partners are made clear in the pages of the office Letterbook (1889–91).

3. Drawings of the Cushing building and the Burns house were shown in *Spokane Falls Illustrated* (Spokane, 1889; ready for printing by August 1889), 15 and 44. Neither had been constructed at the time of publication.

4. The Burns house seems to hark back to a period of exotic revival more than twenty years earlier, exemplified by the designs of Samuel Sloan in *The Model Architect* (Philadelphia, 1852), and revived in the 1870s and 1880s by Louis Comfort Tiffany, the Herter Brothers, and other major designers. The house survived only until 1899, when it was purchased by J. P. Graves for the value of its site. *Spokane Chronicle*, May 4, 1899.

5. Durham, *History of the City of Spokane and Spokane County*, 1:416, 417.

6. John Hoyt was part owner of the Rookery. The southernmost section of the Rookery is identified on a drawing as the Augustine, Bean and Hoyt Building. EWSHS, Drawing L84–207.177.

7. A photograph shows the half-constructed block among the debris after the fire. EWSHS Museum Collection L86–586.

8. Letterbook. Correspondence with the suppliers makes it clear that the First National Bank was the last of the three to be constructed.

9. Letterbook, Cutter to Tiffany Pressed Brick Co. of Chicago, November 26, 1889; order for bricks for additional story. The Spokane National Bank occupied one corner of the Rookery block designed by Cutter and Poetz at the same time. It was presumably named after Burnham and Root's Rookery Building in Chicago. The facades of the Rookery, flanking those of the bank, were designed in a version of the Chicago commercial style.

10. Letterbook, Cutter to Quimby and Ormis, Duluth, March 17, 1890. On March 12, Cutter and Poetz had written to the same firm asking them to ship the stone "very bold and rough."

11. Letterbook, Cutter to Houston and Harris, Minneapolis, March 13, 1890; approval of estimate for brick.

12. Letterbook, Cutter to Houston and Harris, July 1, 1890; order for quarter round bricks.

13. There is evidence in two letters that he made substantial changes to the design on his return from Chicago; Letterbook, March 7, 1890, and March 17, 1890.

14. Letter from Marie Malmgren Theis, Malmgren's daughter, to Willard Robinson, February 18, 1965.

15. Ernst Skarstedt, "Washington och dess svenska Befolkning" (1908), 465. I am grateful to Dennis Andersen for providing me with a translation of this article.

16. Theis to Robinson, February 18, 1965.

17. *Spokane Review*, January 1, 1892. Fred Phair's role is described in Robert B. Hyslop, *Spokane's Building Blocks* (Spokane, 1983), 97. Later he was the contractor for several of Cutter's major buildings.

18. The Letterbook contains many letters from Cutter to Brown and Haywood in Minneapolis. Concerning windows for the First National Bank, see letters dated December 5, 1890, and June 10, 1890. The frames were made by Johnson and Hurd of the same city.

19. The location of Cutter and Poetz's office is first mentioned in a letter to Brown and Haywood on November 19, 1890; see also Cutter to G. T. Oliver, November 9, 1890, Letterbook.

20. John Fahey, *The Inland Empire: Unfolding Years, 1879–1929* (Seattle: University of Washing-

ton Press, 1986), 215. Jolles is quoted in Fahey, "When the Dutch Owned Spokane," *Pacific Northwest Quarterly* 72, no. 1 (1981): 2–10.

21. Hyslop, *Spokane's Building Blocks*, 269. Cutter's role as Sherwood's architect is confirmed in the Letterbook. Polk's *Spokane City Directory*, 1889.

22. Durham, *History of the City of Spokane and Spokane County*, 1:405, quotes Sherwood's account, but gives the year as 1891. The Letterbook shows that excavations were complete in April 1890 (Letterbook, April 26). The building was ready for glazing by September of that year (Letterbook, August 19).

23. Hyslop, *Spokane's Building Blocks*, 269. It was fifteen years later that Hendrik Berlage, hailed as a pioneer of modernism, wrote: "Above all we should show the naked wall in all its sleek beauty. . . . Pillars and columns should have no projecting capitals: the joint should be fused with the flat surface of the wall." Quoted by Sigfried Giedion in *Space, Time and Architecture*, 5th ed. (Cambridge: Harvard University Press, 1967), 313.

24. Powell Grocery Company: Letterbook, four letters written between July 12 and September 2, 1890, deal with construction. A letter of February 7, 1891, mentions completion. The building was demolished in 1908 and no good photograph of it exists (see Hyslop, *Spokane's Building Blocks*, 237). Quirin building: thirteen letters between October 15, 1890, and July 6, 1891, deal with its construction and the difficulties that arose when the contractor defaulted.

25. The drawing submitted by Cutter and Poetz is undated, but it can be presumed that it belongs to the year when the college was founded; the drawing has lettering by Poetz. On the winning entry see *Pullman Herald*, May 16, 1891. See also Task Force for Historic Preservation, *Historic Resource Survey and Analysis* (Pullman: Washington State University, 1985).

26. Dating of the chapel is confirmed in the Letterbook, between March 1890 and February 1891.

27. See Vincent Scully, *The Shingle Style* (New Haven: Yale University Press, 1971), 92–93.

28. The lodge was illustrated in *American Architect*, December 26, 1885, 304.

29. Jeffrey Karl Ochsner, *H. H. Richardson: Complete Architectural Works* (Cambridge: MIT Press, 1982), 339.

30. See Richard Longstreth, *On the Edge of the World* (Cambridge: MIT Press, 1983), 104.

31. The dating is confirmed by correspondence in the Letterbook, July to December 1890, dealing mainly with the payment for a man and team hauling stone.

32. One of these drawings, labeled Cutter and Poetz, must have been done no later than 1894, the year the partnership dissolved. The others are stylistically very similar.

33. Daniel E. Turbeville, *An Illustrated Inventory of Historic Bellingham Buildings* (Bellingham, 1977), not paginated.

34. Letterbook. Letters from Cutter to Wardner written between December 9, 1889, and March 16, 1890, confirm that Cutter was the architect. Turbeville attributes the house to Longstaff and Black, but *Fairhaven Illustrated* (Chicago, 1890) states that they were not the architects.

35. See Scully, *Shingle Style*, 99–100.

36. The Warren Hickox house (1900) at Kankakee, Illinois, exemplifies Wright's clear expression of intersecting roofs. The Ward Willets house (1902) at Highland Park, Illinois, included a fine example of a covered porch like an outdoor room.

37. Letterbook. Correspondence between January and August 1891.

38. Sunset Cottage was illustrated in George W. Sheldon, *Artistic Country-Seats* (New York, 1886–87), 86. Cutter's Stevens house predates the E. Wiler Churchill house at Napa, California, by Coxhead and Coxhead, which is composed in a somewhat similar manner. See Longstreth, *On the Edge of the World*, 151.

39. The pointed roofs of these dormers are very similar to those on the Samuel Colman residence, Newport, Rhode Island, by McKim, Mead and White (1883).

40. Letterbook, Cutter to D. K. Stevens, February 21, 1891.

41. *Tacoma Daily Ledger*, February 16, 1896.

42. Letterbook, to Jas. D. Horrocks, Contractor, August 31, 1891.

43. Letterbook, to D. K. Stevens, August 6, 1891.

Chapter 5 The Search for a Northwest Architecture (1892–1896)

1. Many of the letters in the Letterbook contain urgent pleas to suppliers to hurry with shipments.

2. *Spokane Review*, October 9, 1892.

3. Durham, *History of the City of Spokane and Spokane County*, 2:550–51.

4. John Fahey, *Inland Empire: D. C. Corbin and Spokane* (Seattle: University of Washington Press, 1965), 4, 17, 20.

5. *Spokane Review*, October 9, 1892.

6. Don Hibbard, "Chicago, 1893: Idaho at the World's Columbian Exposition," *Idaho Yesterdays*, Summer 1980, 23.

7. William James, quoted by Sigfried Giedion in *Space, Time and Architecture*, 5th edition (Cambridge: Harvard University Press, 1967), 394. Louise Hall Tharp, *Saint-Gaudens and the Gilded Era* (Boston: Little, Brown and Company, 1969), 250.

8. Montgomery Schuyler, "State Buildings at the World's Fair," *Architectural Record* 3 (1893–94): 55–71.

9. J. R. DeLamar, Idaho World's Fair Commissioner, to Norman Willey [*sic*], Governor of Idaho, February 23, 1892, Norman Wiley Files, Idaho State Archives, Boise, quoted by Hibbard, "Chicago, 1893," 25. Cutter's explanation was reported in a letter of March 14, 1893, Norman Wiley Files. For information on Daniel Burnham's philosophy, see Jeffrey Karl Ochsner, "In Search of Regional Expression: The Washington State Building at the World's Columbian Exposition, Chicago 1893," *Pacific Northwest Quarterly* 86, no. 4 (1995): 165–77.

10. This stone, carved by Dick Beale of Lewiston, could be cut easily with a knife when fresh from the quarry, but became hard when exposed to the air. See Hibbard, "Chicago, 1893," 25.

11. Ibid., 26. James W. and Daniel B. Shepp, *Shepp's World's Fair Photographed* (Chicago, ca. 1893), 372.

12. *American Scandinavian*, July 1909.

13. Ibid., quoting *American Architect and Building News* (date not given).

14. *Spokesman-Review*, May 24, 1893.

15. *American Architect and Building News*, quoted in the *American Scandinavian*, July 1909; *San Francisco Argonaut*, January 22, 1894; *Spokane Review*, May 24, 1893; *West Side News* (Cleveland, Ohio), November 10, 1894 (this paper refers to Cutter as "a well known Cleveland artist now living in Spokane"); *The Interior* (Chicago), October 12, 1893; *American Scandinavian*, July 1909.

16. Hibbard, "Chicago, 1893," 28.

17. *Spokane Review*, May 24, 1893.

18. Randell L. Makinson, *Greene and Greene* (Santa Barbara, 1977).

19. Unidentified news cutting headed "Idaho in Luck," among Cutter materials in the Peggy Hoyt Bayless Family Papers, EWSHS.

20. *Lewiston Morning Tribune*, January 10, 1922.

21. "Idaho in Luck" news cutting and "Lines from My Notebook," in the Bayless collection, EWSHS.

22. Hibbard, "Chicago, 1893," 29.

23. Information on the Loyd family was obtained from *Burke's Landed Gentry* (London, 1898) and through correspondence with Peter Loyd of London. Arthur Loyd's unconventional nature is suggested by the fact that in 1894 he married the daughter of a master butcher. "That sort of thing would have been frowned on by the Loyd family." Peter Loyd to the author, January 29, 1986.

24. *Spokane Review*, June 22, 1896, and *Scandinavian American*, July 1909.

25. *Kelly's Directory* (London, 1899).

26. E. W. Charlton, "Studio Talk," *The International Studio* (London), November 1898, 53. The omission of the rear bays is clearly shown in a drawing by Charlton.

27. *The Bournemouth Visitors Directory*, February 20, 1897, describes a concert to raise funds

for C Company of the Hampshire Volunteers, commanded by Captain Loyd, at which they sang the songs mentioned.

28. Charlton, "Studio Talk," 54.

29. Mrs. Loyd's will in Somerset House, London, shows that she was living in Vancouver, B.C., when she died in 1913. Her husband died in Las Palmas in 1911.

30. Durham, *History of the City of Spokane and Spokane County*, 1:449–50.

31. *Spokane Review*, July 14 and 26, 1893. For information on Willis Ritchie, see Jeffrey Karl Ochsner, ed., *Shaping Seattle Architecture* (Seattle: University of Washington Press, 1994), 40–45 and 305–6.

32. These included a new school in Hillyard, announced in the *Spokane Review*, January 7, 1894. Drawings for the school are in the EWSHS Collection.

33. Malmgren first appears as Cutter's partner in Polk's *Spokane City Directory* of 1894.

34. Interview of Dana Agergaard by Phyllis Poper, Long Beach, California. "He [Malmgren] was the working end of the business and Mr. Cutter was the artistic end." Malmgren's obituary in the *Spokesman-Review*, May 24, 1921, describes him as "of a retiring disposition." Financial accounts available from 1910 until the end of the partnership do not show Malmgren making any journeys to see clients, as Cutter frequently did.

35. See Frank Calvert, ed., *Homes and Gardens of the Pacific Coast, Volume 1: Seattle* (Beaux Arts Village, Lake Washington: Beaux Arts Society, 1913), 77. The house appears as the Harry Krutz house. It is attributed to Cutter and Malmgren. King County tax rolls show that it was built by 1894 and owned by Charles E. Shepherd. Dennis Andersen has pointed out that this house was not on the 1895 Sanborn map and that tax records are often inaccurate. However, the Seattle Blue Book for 1898–99 shows that the house was occupied by Henry Kyer in 1898.

36. James E. Murphy, *Half Interest in a Silver Dollar: The Saga of Charles E. Conrad* (Missoula: Mountain Press Publishing Co., 1983), 5–22, 24–27, 39, 45, 57, 69, 108, 115–17. Subsequent information about the Conrads is from this source. James Willard Schultz, *Blackfoot and Buffalo: Memories of Life among the Indians* (Norman: University of Oklahoma Press, 1962), 84, 173, 295, confirms Conrad's friendly relations with the tribe and mentions his large donation of cattle during the 1885 famine.

37. The drawings in the EWSHS Collection show Cutter's distinctive drafting style.

38. Cutter's plan shows this room labeled Reception Room. Murphy, whose information came from the Conrad family, refers to it as the Music Room.

39. The fernery was not shown on the original drawing, nor was the pass-through barrel.

40. Murphy, *Half Interest*, 182.

41. Durham, *History of the City of Spokane and Spokane County*, 1:461, 475.

42. Ibid., 2:237–38.

43. *Spokesman-Review*, undated article headed "Called to a Broader Field," states that K. K. Cutter and his wife would leave for Cleveland to remain at least a year. It reports that he had lived eight years in Spokane (thus it was probably printed in 1894).

44. Mannington Hall Visitors' Book, October 2 and November 4, 1895. The houses are illustrated in *The Mannington and Wolterton Estate* (Cambridge: Jarrold Publishing, 1992).

45. Superior Court of Spokane, March 20, 1896, complaint by Kirtland Cutter.

46. Ibid., and decree of divorce, June 30, 1896.

47. Author's interview with Margaret Bean, October 15, 1987.

48. Polk's *Spokane City Directory*, 1897–98.

Chapter 6 Cutter and Malmgren: Mansions for Spokane's New Leaders (1897–1903)

1. Carroll L. V. Meeks, *The Railroad Station: An Architectural History* (New Haven: Yale University Press, 1956). Richard Longstreth, "Academic Eclecticism in American Architecture," *Winterthur Portfolio* 17 (Spring 1982): 55–82. Longstreth broadened his discussion of academic eclecticism in *On the Edge of the World* (Cambridge: MIT Press, 1983). In this book he

applies his theory to a study of four San Francisco architects, all contemporaries of Cutter: Ernest Coxhead, Willis Polk, A. C. Schweinfurth, and Bernard Maybeck.

2. The article, "Architecture in the Northwest: Modern Architecture and Its Relation to the American Home," first appeared in *Opportunity Magazine* (Spokane, n.d.) and was reprinted in *Pacific Builder and Engineer*, December 11, 1909, 484. The statement seems consistent with a remark Cutter is reported to have made when interviewed by the *Spokesman-Review*, April 8, 1917: "French women are renowned the world over, not only for their artistic gowns, but also for the peculiar manner in which their costumes fit their personalities." In this instance he was discussing the siting of houses. Mary Alden Hopkins reported in her article, "Building on a Spokane Hillside" (*House Beautiful*, September 1921), that Cutter insisted that every house should be fitted to "the needs and individuality of the owner."

3. Cutter specifically mentioned his desire to make buildings appear old (for example, the F. Rockwood Moore house, the D. K. Stevens house, and the Rainier Club).

4. Society pages in the Spokane newspapers record countless meetings of women's societies dealing with the arts. These convey a picture of a thirst for knowledge in a city that was culturally still on the frontier.

5. *Spokesman-Review*, June 27, 1897; report that the plans of the Campbell house were ready, at a cost of $20,000.

6. EWSHS Collection.

7. Among the pattern books that were very influential in eighteenth-century America was James Gibbs's *Book of Architecture* (London, 1728).

8. John Fahey, *The Inland Empire: Unfolding Years, 1879–1929* (Seattle: University of Washington Press, 1986), 217–18.

9. The Wakefield house bears a resemblance to Crocker Row, Santa Barbara, a group of houses in the Mission Style designed in 1894 by Page Brown.

10. The commission for the Patrick Clark house is reputed to have been as early as 1895. But it seems unlikely that Clark would have waited so long for completion. It has been suggested that when Cutter was in England in 1897 for the construction of the replica of the World's Columbian Exposition building for A. H. Loyd, he was also seeking material in Europe for the Clark house. The first known news report in the *Spokesman-Review* on April 10, 1898, announces a "handsome residence to be built for Patrick Clark."

11. Durham, *History of the City of Spokane and Spokane County*, 2:295.

12. "Patsy Clark's History Manual" (Spokane), 1–4. Patsy Clark's Restaurant, which now occupies the mansion, produced the manual to inform the staff about its history.

13. The design of "Longwood" was based on an illustration in Samuel Sloan, *The Model Architect*, vol. 2 (Philadelphia, 1852), plate LXIII. On Barnum's house, see Patrick Conner, *Oriental Architecture in the West* (London: Thames and Hudson, 1979), 39, plate XIII, and 174–75.

14. The translation of *The Arabian Nights Entertainments* by Sir Richard Burton, 1885–88, sparked a new interest in oriental imagery.

15. Meredith L. Clausen makes the case for the Ponce de Leon Hotel being a source for the Patrick Clark house in *Landmarks* (Seattle) 3, no. 1 (1983): 15–17. On the Moorish influence in architecture, see Kenneth H. Cardwell, *Bernard Maybeck: Artisan, Architect, Artist* (Santa Barbara: Peregrine Smith, 1977), 21–23.

16. The attribution of the window to Louis Comfort Tiffany has not been proved. However, Cutter's New York education, his presence at the 1893 World's Columbia Exposition where Tiffany had a spectacular exhibit, Clark's budget, and the character of the work make it almost certain that the windows came from the Tiffany studios. The peacock as a decorative motif seems to have fascinated Cutter. It appeared, among other places, on the hall ceiling of the Glover house (1889), in the Peacock Room at Davenport's Restaurant (ca. 1905), and on a fireplace in his own house.

17. John Fahey, *Inland Empire: D. C. Corbin*

and Spokane (Seattle: University of Washington Press, 1965), 3–4.

18. Fahey, *Inland Empire: D. C. Corbin and Spokane*, 193.

19. The Graves house is discussed in Lucile McDonald and Werner Lenggenhager, *Where the Washingtonians Lived* (Seattle: Superior Publishing Co., 1969), 201. See also *Spokesman-Review*, March 31, 1940.

20. *Spokesman-Review*, March 13, 1899; the house is fully described and the completion date is given as May 1899.

21. *Spokesman-Review*, June 20, 1948, and March 31, 1940.

22. John R. Ross and Margaret Byrd Adams, *The Builder's Spirit: The History of the Stimson Lumber Company* (Portland: John Ross and Associates, 1983), 26.

23. An extensive correspondence in the Dorothy Stimson Bullitt Archives gives many details of the process of building and furnishing the house (hereafter DSB Archives). Cutter to Stimson, January 24, 1900. For additional information, see Lawrence Kreisman, *The Stimson Legacy* (Seattle: Willows Press and University of Washington Press, 1992).

24. Cutter to Stimson, January 24, 1900, DSB Archives.

25. Cutter to Stimson, December 18, 1899, DSB Archives.

26. Cutter to Stimson, DSB Archives. July 6, 1900, DSB Archives. The craftsman's price was "$8.00 a day and traveling expenses."

27. Bebb, who had come to Seattle in 1890 to superintend the construction of Louis Sullivan's Opera House project, became one of the leading architects of the city. See David A. Rash and Dennis A. Andersen, "Bebb and Mendel," and T. William Booth and William H. Wilson, "Bebb and Gould," in Jeffrey Karl Ochsner, ed., *Shaping Seattle Architecture* (Seattle: University of Washington Press, 1994), 72–77, 174–79.

28. Cutter introduced William Morris, an art dealer, to Stimson, describing him as "a buyer of unusual talent and taste." See Kreisman, *Stimson Legacy*, 70–71.

29. Cutter used these words in his article, "Architecture in the Northwest," in 1909.

30. Cutter to Stimson, January 29, 1900, DSB Archives. See Chapter 5 for details of furnishings for the Glover house.

31. Cutter to Stimson, March 30, 1900, and January 29, 1900, DSB Archives.

32. Cutter, "Architecture in the Northwest," 1909.

33. Cutter to Stimson, January 29, June 19, and June 16, 1900, DSB Archives.

34. Cutter to Stimson, May 3, 1900, DSB Archives.

35. For example, "bungling errors" by the carpet suppliers and faulty switching of the electric chandeliers. Cutter to Stimson, October 16 and November 5, 1900, DSB Archives.

36. Cutter, writing to Stimson, November 20, 1900, left it up to his client to determine the "matter of commissions on extra work on the house." Stimson replied with a generous payment. DSB Archives.

37. The commission is referred to in a letter from Cutter to Stimson, July 20, 1900, DSB Archives. The *Colorado Springs Gazette*, August 15, 1900, reported: "The probability that Mr. Stewart will build on the site at an early date gains color from the fact that architect Cutter, of Spokane, Washington, one of the leading architects of the Pacific Slope, has been in the city for some time on business in which Mr. Stewart is interested."

38. *Gazette Telegraph*, Colorado Springs, July 22, 1959.

39. *Colorado Springs Gazette*, August 15, 1900.

40. *Facts*, Colorado Springs, February 16, 1901 (p.15), and March 8, 1902.

41. The letters are in the Whitman College Archives, Walla Walla, Washington.

42. Cutter to Louis Anderson, July 21, 1902; Anderson to Cutter, July 25, 1902. Osterman, a Walla Walla architect, is mentioned in several letters. He was responsible for many buildings in Walla Walla, including the county courthouse.

43. Cutter to Anderson, October 10, October 4, and December 11, 1902.

44. Cutter to Anderson in reply to a missing letter, December 29, 1902.

45. Anderson to Cutter, January 6, 1903, deals with the settlement of the final account.

46. Anderson to Cutter, February 2, 1903.

47. Cutter to Anderson, April 22 and May 6, 1903.

48. Fee account, April 21, 1903.

49. Anderson to Cutter, June 22, 1903; Cutter to Anderson, June 25, 1903. William Grueby, who displayed his tiles at the World's Columbian Exposition, experimented with new formulas for glazes, producing yellows, ochers, browns, and a dark watermelon green for which he became famous.

50. Cutter to Anderson, July 11, 1903.

51. Cutter to Anderson, September 30, 1903; Anderson to Cutter, November 20, 1903; Cutter to Anderson, December 20, 1903; Anderson to Cutter, February 26, 1904.

52. Cutter to Anderson, March 11, 1904.

53. Susan H. Skillman, "Baker Faculty Center," typescript in Eells' Northwest Collection, Penrose Library, Whitman College, Walla Walla, Washington.

54. Fahey, *The Inland Empire: Unfolding Years*, 217–18.

55. Cutter, "Architecture in the Northwest," 1909.

Chapter 7 Function and Fantasy
(1898–1906)

1. Richard H. Steele, *An Illustrated History of Stevens, Ferry, Okanogan, and Chelan Counties, State of Washington* (Spokane: Western Historical Publishing Co., 1904), 724–25. A persistent myth in Chelan that Stanford White was the architect of the church is untrue.

2. *Spokesman-Review*, November 25, 1956.

3. In the *Testimonial Album* consisting of letters written on the thirty-second anniversary of Davenport's first restaurant on February 14, 1922, the story of Davenport clearing burnt mortar from bricks is told in a letter from W. C. Ufford. W. S. Hayford recalled going to work for Davenport "in your waffle foundry, located in a tent"

(EWSHS). The beginning of Davenport's is described in the *Spokesman-Review* of December 8, 1895, on the sixth anniversary of its opening: "a beardless boy" opened "a little restaurant in a tent." Ralph Dyar, in *News for an Empire: The Story of the Spokesman-Review* (Caldwell, Idaho: Caxton Printers, 1952), 59, attributes the design of the Wilson block to Cutter. The *Spokesman-Review* of July 16, 1890, reports the opening of the restaurant in the Wilson block.

4. Jonathan Edwards, *History of Spokane County, Washington* (San Francisco: W. H. Lever, 1900), 440.

5. *Spokesman-Review*, December 8, 1895; September 13, 1900.

6. Robert B. Hyslop, *Spokane's Building Blocks* (Spokane, 1983), 80.

7. *Spokesman-Review*, November 9 and 15, 1903, reports the sale at a price of $120,000.

8. *Spokesman-Review*, November 9, 1903, reports that the two blocks would look like one.

9. *Spokesman-Review*, November 9, 1903.

10. *Spokesman-Review*, June 8, 1904. "Davenport to spend $30,000 on an elaborate ball, reception room above his restaurant."

11. Cutter compared the Hall of the Doges to a cathedral in his article, "Architecture in the Northwest," 1909.

12. James McNeill Whistler may have provided inspiration for the peacock motif through the design of his Peacock Room in London. A book in Cutter's library, *Das farbige Malerbuch* (Leipzig, 1900), provided examples of a bold style of wall painting in sinuous curves, similar to that in the Peacock Room. The peacock in his office is mentioned in the *Spokesman-Review* interview, April 8, 1917.

13. Undated sketches of the rooms described exist in the EWSHS Collection. The Peacock Room, destroyed during remodeling, is illustrated in *Western Architect*, 1908. The plan of the Davenport Hotel in the *Hotel Monthly* (Chicago), September 1915, 44, shows that the Peacock Room still existed at that time.

14. Elbert Hubbard, article in *The Philistine*, March 1906.

15. Drawing L84–207.25, EWSHS. Construction announced in the *Chronicle*, June 2, 1899. See also Durham, *History of the City of Spokane and Spokane County*, 2:156, and Dorothy Powers, "Chicago a Hit in Old Spokane," *Spokesman-Review*, November 15, 1987.

16. *Spokesman-Review*, May 11, 1898.

17. *Winston's Weekly*, November 14, 1903; *Spokesman-Review*, or *Chronicle*, November 15 or 16, 1903.

18. The site just south of Santa Monica had been proposed sixteen years earlier by a group of investors as a tidewater terminal for the Santa Fe Railroad. The Ballona Harbor and Improvement Company began dredging for a harbor to "float the fleets of the world." But tides and shifting sands prevailed and the harbor was never realized. See W. W. Robinson, "Playa del Rey: Ranchos Become Cities," undated typescript, Playa del Rey Public Library.

19. Walter Case, *History of Long Beach and Vicinity*, vol. 2 (Chicago: S. J. Clarke Publishing, 1927), 378–80. Henry Bertelsen's undated list of Cutter's projects includes a Hoquiam Hotel.

20. The hotel is illustrated in *Historic Preservation*, December 1987, 38–43.

21. The drawings were not developed to completion. While most are in ink on linen, some are only roughed out in pencil. A hotel and pavilion at a combined cost of $300,000 were built by another architect and Playa del Rey became a popular destination for excursions. Later, the resort attracted large crowds for automobile and boat races. But the hotel and pavilion burned down and the place declined.

22. See *New Haven Evening Register*, May 29, 1902, and the *Yale Alumni Weekly* 12, no. 16 (January 21, 1903), for details of the project. Lucy Boardman is described as the wealthiest woman in Connecticut and the greatest philanthropist in the state in the *Cleveland Leader*, March 30, 1906. In 1890, Mrs. Boardman advanced her nephew, Kirtland Cutter, $2,000 to help buy some property in which she was to own a half share. See Letterbook, Cutter to W. F. Fields, New Haven, January 10, 1890.

23. Letter to the author from Judith A. Schiff, Chief Research Archivist, Yale University, January 7, 1986.

24. The original design is shown in a colored rendering in the EWSHS Collection. It includes a stone balustrade above the portico, which was omitted from the final design. Otherwise, there is little change, except for the choice of materials. The construction is reported in the *Yale Alumni Weekly* article.

25. David Chambers Lewis (1867–1918) came from a wealthy Portland family and studied architecture both at Columbia University and in Paris. Between 1901 and 1911 he designed several fine houses and four major downtown buildings. See Richard E. Ritz, "Conversations on Architecture," *Architalk* (Portland, Oregon), August 1988, 11. This series of articles by Ritz has been published under the title *An Architect Looks at Downtown Portland* (Portland: Greenhills Press, 1991).

26. Cutter had been dissatisfied with the arrangement he had made with Charles Bebb as the supervising architect for the Stimson house. On July 6, 1900, he wrote to Stimson that he intended "having his own force of men on the spot" and spoke of a "capable man" he expected to put in charge. He did not implement this plan immediately. Wager is listed in Polk's *Spokane City Directory* for 1900 as an architect, and in 1901 "with Cutter and Malmgren." The *Seattle Times* of March 22, 1902, reports on a large house in the Mission Style for E. O. Graves to be built on the corner of Mercer and Harvard by Cutter, Malmgren and Wager. The *Seattle City Directory* for 1903 lists Wager as a partner in Cutter, Malmgren and Wager. The following year he is listed as an independent architect.

27. *Seattle Times*, October 30, 1927.

28. *Seattle Post-Intelligencer*, January 10, 1903.

29. In an interview in the *Spokesman-Review*, April 8, 1917, Cutter characterized "our larger cities" in this way.

30. Aston Hall is illustrated in S. C. Hall, *The Baronial Halls and Ancient Picturesque Edifices of England*, vol. 1 (London: Willis and Sotheran, 1858), which was in Cutter's library (now in the EWSHS Museum). The Rainier Club was

described as a replica in the *Seattle Times*, October 30, 1927.

31. Greene and Greene first used clinker bricks on the Tichenor house in Long Beach in 1904. Cutter's brickwork at the Rainier Club predated this.

32. National Register nomination for the Rainier Club, Seattle.

33. *Seattle Times*, October 30, 1927.

34. For information on Bebb and Gould, see Ochsner, ed., *Shaping Seattle Architecture*, 174–79.

35. *Tacoma Daily Ledger*, July 29, 1906.

36. Durham, *History of the City of Spokane and Spokane County*, 2:361–66. The five-page entry on W. S. Norman shows the versatility of this Spokane entrepreneur. He graduated from court stenographer to railroad provisioner, shipbuilder and operator, and developer of water power for electricity and of street railways before he entered the hotel business.

37. *Tacoma Daily Ledger*, July 29, 1906, for this and all subsequent quotations concerning the Tacoma Hotel.

38. Statutes of the Deutscher Werkbund quoted by Gillian Naylor in *The Bauhaus* (London, 1968).

39. Polk's *Spokane City Directory*, 1895–1905.

40. *Chronicle*, February 18, 1906.

41. *Spokesman-Review*, February 21, 1906.

42. Information supplied in an undated letter from Mrs. Kenneth F. Brown (Katharine's granddaughter) to Mrs. Wentz, Spokane. EWSHS.

43. *Spokesman-Review*, September 4, 1907.

44. *Spokesman-Review*, February 21, 1906.

Chapter 8 Spokane and Seattle (1906–1909)

1. The drawings of the Thomas house in the EWSHS collection suggest that they were adapted from those for the unexecuted Stewart house in Colorado Springs.

2. Drawings in the EWSHS Collection (L84–207.241) show a compact four-story block, surmounted by a Dutch gable. *Pacific Builder and Engineer*, June 30, 1906, 3, states: "Cutter and Malmgren are the architects of the new Silver

Bow Club in Butte." The more pedestrian design that was built is illustrated in Don James, *Butte's Memory Book* (Caldwell, Idaho: Caxton Printers, 1975), 245.

3. Cutter and Malmgren began work on a Neoclassical house for J. P. Hurlbut in Lewiston at a cost of $20,000 immediately after his previous residence was destroyed by fire January 16, 1906. See Don Hibbard, *Normal Hill: An Historic and Pictorial Guide* (Lewiston: Luna House Historical Society, 1978).

4. *Seattle Daily Bulletin*, December 2, 1903.

5. *Pacific Builder and Engineer,* December 8, 1906, 3.

6. The Interstate 5 freeway now runs between the high promontory and Lake Union. Building has also encroached on the shores of the lake.

7. *Seattle News*, May 13, 1906 (unidentified news clipping dated in Cutter's hand).

8. *Pacific Builder and Engineer*, May 19, 1906, 3.

9. *Pacific Builder and Engineer*, June 30, 1906, 3.

10. The Knickerbocker Trust Company was illustrated in *Architecture*, March 15, 1904. See also Leland M. Roth, *McKim, Mead and White, Architects* (New York: Harper and Row, 1983), 301–2. Cutter's design for the Spokane and Eastern Trust was illustrated in the AIA Exhibition Catalogue (Seattle, 1908).

11. In 1907 the decision was made to reduce the Spokane and Eastern Trust building to four stories; and in the end, only one bay of the smaller version was built. A rendering of the reduced design was reproduced in *Western Architect*, September 1908. The drawings are in the EWSHS Collection. A photograph in the collection shows the one bay squeezed between the still standing Cushing building and its neighbor.

12. *Pacific Builder and Engineer*, December 8, 1906, 3. All three draftsmen appear as Cutter employees in Polk's *Spokane City Directory*, 1906.

13. H. Allen Brooks, *The Prairie School: Frank Lloyd Wright and His Midwest Contemporaries* (New York: W. W. Norton, 1976), 82 and 85. *Pacific Builder and Engineer*, February 6, 1909, 42. See also Ochsner, ed., *Shaping Seattle Architecture*, 168–73, 313, and Sylvia L. Gillis, "Andrew

C. P. Willatsen, Architect, A.I.A. (1876–1974)," master's thesis, University of Washington, 1980.

14. Brooks, *The Prairie School*, 31, 91.

15. Ibid., 30. Irving K. Pond expressed his opposition to the principles of the Prairie School in *The Meaning of Architecture* (Boston, 1918).

16. *Pacific Builder and Engineer*, February 6, 1909, 42.

17. Sally Woodbridge and Roger Montgomery, *A Guide to Architecture in Washington State* (Seattle: University of Washington Press, 1980), 195 and 363. Hornblower and Marshall were also the architects of Maryhill, Sam Hill's palatial house on the Columbia River near The Dalles, built in 1914–26 in the same style.

18. J. D. Farrell is not shown living near Hill and Lindley in Polk's *Seattle City Directory*. They are first listed at 814 and 904 East Highland Drive in 1909. In that year, Farrell moved to a farm in Renton. Only a preliminary sketch for his house exists, while complete drawings for Lindley's have survived. EWSHS.

19. Brooks, *The Prairie School*, 93 and 106. Spencer's own home in River Forest and Maher's C. R. Erwin house in Oak Park, both built in 1905, had white stucco walls beneath broadly overhanging hipped roofs. The Ervine house had an inset porch behind an arch at one corner and a dominant projecting entrance porch, also of stucco, near the center, both features of the Lindley house. An element of the Spencer house, typical of the Prairie School, was a band beneath the sills of the second floor windows that emphasized the horizontal plane; this feature also appeared on the facade of the Lindley house. In addition to Willatzen, V. P. von Ehrlich and Charles Hayes, who both worked in Cutter's office, designed in the Prairie idiom. Both had houses illustrated in *Homes and Gardens of the Pacific Coast* (1913).

20. The Youle house was apparently designed in 1907 or 1908; a photograph is included in an album of work by the Spokane photographer, Charles Libby in the EWSHS Collection. Polk shows Youle living at E. 108 Short Court, now part of Twelfth Avenue, in 1909. The job number 107 for the Graves house suggests the year 1907,

the same year as the Bozanta Tavern (job no. 108), which was initiated in 1907. Clyde Graves was living at E. 127 Short Court in 1908.

21. Polk shows Sengfelder living at 1321 Ninth in 1909.

22. Polk shows Dewart living at W. 201 Sixth by 1907. Though considerably less ponderous, the Dewart house bears a strong similarity to the John Farson house at Oak Park, Illinois, by George W. Maher, who was associated with the Prairie School. See Brooks, *The Prairie School*, 35–36.

23. Houses for Samuel Stern (1906), James Smyth (ca. 1906), W. H. Hare (ca. 1906), W. D. Seligman (ca. 1907), and the contractor Harry Brokaw (date unknown) all embody some aspects of the Craftsman Bungalow. The most interesting example is the summer home of F. A. Blackwell at Spirit Lake, Idaho (1907).

24. Design is attributed to Carl Nuese in Frank Calvert, ed., *Homes and Gardens of the Pacific Coast, Volume 1: Seattle* (Beaux Arts Village, Lake Washington: Beaux Arts Society, 1913).

25. Volumes of the work by Joseph Maria Olbrich, published by Wasmuth, and editions of *Moderne Bauformen* (Dresden, 1905 and 1906) in Cutter's library may have offered precedents for his experimentation with interior forms. A later owner stripped out much of the interior paneling and millwork and replaced it with authentic material salvaged from a English house.

26. *Pacific Builder and Engineer*, November 2, 1907, 6.

27. Although it was designed as an office building, the client intended to use it first as a hotel to receive visitors to the Alaska-Yukon-Pacific Exposition of 1909. See *Pacific Builder and Engineer*, March 7, 1908, 10.

28. Ibid.

29. Herbert Croly, "The Building of Seattle," *Architectural Record* 32 (July 1912): 10–11.

30. Their first building at the Lewiston campus was the Training School (1905). See *Lewiston Tribune*, May 28 and December 10, 1905. Their 1907 commission was for a Tudoresque girls' dormitory (EWSHS drawings L84–207.240). See *Pacific Builder and Engineer*, April 6, 1907, 10;

Lewiston Tribune, March 24, 1907, 6. The following year they designed a gymnasium there (EWSHS drawings L84–207.241). See *Lewiston Tribune*, May 22, 1909. The classical Spokane College was a scaled-down version of Kirtland Hall at Yale University. See *Pacific Builder and Engineer*, July 28, 1906, 7, "excavations for foundations begin, new Spokane College"; EWSHS drawings L84–207.163, labeled Spokane and Seattle, therefore 1907–9. The $300 fees were received in January 1910. Illustrated in Polk, 1910.

31. The country club was a simple framed building of fir on the Little Spokane River. See *Pacific Builder and Engineer*, January 23, 1909, 13. Cutter had been on the board of directors and participated in social events. See *Chronicle*, March 21, May 5, and May 15, 1899.

32. EWSHS drawings L84–207.162; *Pacific Builder and Engineer*, December 1, 1906, 7, and January 5, 1907, 12.

33. John M. Finney, "The Idaho and Washington Northern Railroad: The Pend Oreille River Route," in *The Big Smoke* (journal of the Pend Oreille County Historical Society, Newport, Washington), 1986, 3–7. See also *Spirit Lake Herald*, April 3, 1908.

34. EWSHS drawings L84–349.2. The church was illustrated in *Western Architect*, September 1908.

35. See Esther McCoy, *Five California Architects* (New York: Praeger Publishers, 1975).

36. Ibid., 24–35.

37. *Pacific Builder and Engineer*, May 18, 1907, 12, and September 14, 1907, 24. The College Inn is shown in Polk's *Seattle City Directory*, 1909, at 311 Pike Street, A. L. Jaffé, President.

38. Burke was an active member of the club. Cutter also made preliminary studies for a multistory addition to the Burke Building in downtown Seattle, designed in 1890 by Elmer Fisher. The drawings are in the EWSHS.

39. Burke's collection is now the nucleus of the Burke Museum Collection at the University of Washington.

40. *Pacific Builder and Engineer*, January 11, 1908, 30, reports beginning of construction of the Corbet house at a cost of $15,000. *Spokane*

Historic Landmark Survey refers to Cutter's description of the house as Dutch Colonial; no citation is given.

41. The original clubhouse was a converted residence. It appears that Cutter's associate, Edwin Wager, was consulted about an addition to it in 1904, consisting of an assembly hall with a huge fireplace.

42. H. A. Fleager, *History of the Seattle Golf Club* (Seattle: Seattle Golf Club, 1959), and *Pacific Builder and Engineer*, November 12, 1904.

43. Visits by J. C. Olmsted, April 1 to 21, 1907, and January 23, 1908, Olmsted Papers.

44. *Pacific Builder and Engineer*, June 13, 1908, 229.

45. Moravian tiles were manufactured to his own designs by the eccentric Henry Chapman Mercer (1856–1930) in Doylestown, Pennsylvania, as a revival of Pennsylvania-German redware pottery.

46. This house is mentioned in Cutter's correspondence with C. D. Stimson. Drawings are in the Manuscripts and University Archives Division at the University of Washington Libraries.

47. Clark is shown in Fleager, *History of the Seattle Golf Club*, as a founding member and president in 1913.

48. Visit of John C. Olmsted, May 25 and 28, 1908, Olmsted Papers.

49. J. C. Olmsted Site Notes, May 28, 1908, Olmsted Papers, Job 3641.

50. J. C. Olmsted to Chas. H. Clarke, June 1, 1908.

51. The service wing set off at a 45 degree angle appears in a number of houses in George William Sheldon, *Artistic Country-Seats* (New York: D. Appleton, 1886). Cutter employed the same device at the Jay P. Graves house, Spokane, in 1910.

52. *Pacific Builder and Engineer*, November 17, 1908, 378, reports that Nuese opened his own office in Seattle in November 1908. See *Pacific Builder and Engineer*, January 16, 1909, 23, for the announcement of Willatsen's partnership with Byrne.

53. The drawings in the Cutter Collection can

be compared with final plans published in *Country Life in America*, January 25, 1914, 63, 64.

54. Willatzen and Byrne's partnership was dissolved in 1913 when Byrne departed for California. The breakup is attributed to artistic and temperamental differences. See Brooks, *The Prairie School*, 176–77. In 1918 Willatzen changed his name to Willatsen. For Willatzen's subsequent career, see Jess M. Giessel and Grant Hildebrand, "Andrew Willatsen," in Ochsner, ed., *Shaping Seattle Architecture*, 168–73.

55. For articles on all the architects mentioned, see Ochsner, ed., *Shaping Seattle Architecture*.

56. Documentation exists in the EWSHS Collection for the furnishing of the Campbell house and for the first C. D. Stimson house.

57. A photograph in the EWSHS Collection shows their sign on the corner tower of the Pennington Hotel. The principal source of information on Cutter and Plummer has been advertisements in the Spokane press (EWSHS).

Chapter 9 Summer Camps in the Wilderness (1902–1920)

1. The distinction between the beautiful or picturesque and the conception of the sublime was made by Edmund Burke in *A Philosophical Inquiry into the Origin of Our Ideas on the Sublime and the Beautiful* (1756). The work of Bierstadt, Moran, and their contemporaries was rooted in European traditions in which Burke's theories played a role.

2. Harvey H. Kaiser, *Great Camps of the Adirondacks* (Boston: D. R. Godine, 1982), 109. Thomas Carnegie was Andrew's partner. After Thomas's death, Andrew bought up his interests over a long period, making Lucy very wealthy. See Joseph Frazier Wall, *Andrew Carnegie* (New York: Oxford University Press, 1970), 491.

3. Kaiser, *Great Camps*, chaps. 2 and 5.

4. Alfred L. Donaldson, *A History of the Adirondacks*, 2 vols. (New York: Century Co., 1921), quoted by Kaiser.

5. Wall, *Andrew Carnegie*, 954.

6. J. C. Olmsted Site Notes, December 17, 1906, Job 3108, Olmsted Papers.

7. Ibid., December 17, 1906, March 28 and 30, and June 17 and 18, 1907.

8. *Spokesman-Review*, February 10, 1907, and historical information comes from Bozanta Tavern, *The Hayden Lake Country Club 75th Anniversary, 1907–1982* (Hayden Lake, 1982), which quotes the *Coeur d'Alene Press*, December 16, 1905, August 15, December 4 and 21, 1906, and January 9, April 4 and 12, 1907; and the *Spokane Chronicle*, July 20, 1907; and other, undated references.

9. The Estabrook cabin is dated 1905 by the Idaho Historical Society. The job number (131) suggests that it was not designed until about 1909.

10. Arthur Hart, "Colonel's Dream Cabin Built in Popular Rustic Architecture," *Idaho Statesman* (Boise), January 8, 1979.

11. Donald H. Robinson, *Through the Years in Glacier National Park* (Glacier Natural History Association, 1960), 12–36, 61–63.

12. See *Hungry Horse News: Glacier Park 75th Anniversary Edition* (Columbia Falls, Montana), July 17, 1985, 20.

13. See Robert A. M. Stern, *Pride of Place* (Boston: Houghton Mifflin, 1986), 180–83.

14. Thomas Vaughan and Virginia G. Ferriday, eds., *Space, Style and Structure: Building in Northwest America* (Portland: Oregon Historical Society, 1974), 315–18. Doyle became one of Portland's most successful architects.

15. Stern, *Pride of Place*, 184.

16. Bett Wetzel, "Kootenai Lodge: Wilderness Waldorf for Copper Magnates," *Montana Magazine* (Helena), 1980. Robert G. Mahrt, "National Register Nomination: Kootenai Lodge Historic District" (Helena, 1983). Further information was gained in an interview with Dennis Thomkins, president of the Kootenai Lodge Association, October 1986. It is said that guests included royalty, ambassadors, politicians, bankers, corporate moghuls, stage and screen entertainers, adventurers, authors, and artists. Names logged in the guest books included Will Rogers,

Mary Roberts Rinehart, Irvin S. Cobb, Charles M. Russell, John D. Rockefeller, and Charles Lindbergh.

17. See Judy Clayton Cornell, "Kootenai Lodge," *Big Sky Journal* (Bozeman) 1, no. 2 (Summer 1994): 56–59.

Chapter 10 The Davenport Hotel and Other Commercial Buildings (1908–1916)

1. *Spokesman-Review*, October 11, 1908. The plan was also to appear in *Western Architect* (Minneapolis) and *Pacific Builder and Engineer*.

2. *Spokesman-Review*, October 20, 1908. *Pacific Builder and Engineer*, December 12, 1908, 434, announced that it would be named the Empire Hotel.

3. *Pacific Builder and Engineer*, December 26, 1908.

4. *Spokesman-Review*, October 14, 1908.

5. *Pacific Builder and Engineer*, March 6, 1909, 73.

6. *Spokesman-Review*, June 24, 1909; Davenport Hotel to be twelve stories.

7. *Spokesman-Review*, January 15, 1911.

8. The plans were finished by October (*Spokesman-Review*, October 9, 1912). The contract for excavation was awarded late the same month (*Spokesman-Review*, October 31, 1912) and the project went out for bids when specifications were complete in early November (*Spokesman-Review*, November 3, 1912). The main contract was awarded to Brayton Engineering Company of Portland, Oregon.

9. The Florentine description was given in *Spokesman-Review*, July 25, 1915.

10. William K. Shissler, *Davenport Hotel, Spokane, U.S.A.* (Spokane, 1915), 9, 15, 17, 18. This booklet, which regales the reader with lessons in the history of architecture, appears to have been written with many promptings from Kirtland Cutter.

11. *Spokane Chronicle*, undated clipping.

12. Shissler, *Davenport Hotel*, 21, 22.

13. Several plates from *Renaissance Architecture and Ornament in Spain* by Andrew N. Pren-

tice in Cutter's library suggest that he used the book extensively while designing the Davenport Hotel.

14. Shissler, *Davenport Hotel*, 27.

15. In *Spokesman-Review*, November 3, 1912, an article on the dining room states that the ceiling between the beams "will be decorated to represent a canopy, through the edges of which the blue sky apparently is visible." It appears that this was not carried out.

16. Shissler, *Davenport Hotel*, 27–29, 44.

17. The use of springs to give a floor buoyancy was a new idea which, according to *Spokesman-Review*, August 22, 1913, had been "used slightly in the east in private ballrooms, but so far is known never on so large a scale."

18. *Spokesman-Review*, August 22, 1912.

19. Shissler, *Davenport Hotel*, 37.

20. *Spokesman-Review*, July 21, 1914.

21. Shissler, *Davenport Hotel*, 46, 66.

22. *Hotel Monthly* (Chicago), September 1915, 44.

23. The most complete description of the hotel's facilities and services is given in *Spokesman-Review*, August 30, 1914, two days before the hotel was to open.

24. *Spokane Chronicle*, July 21, 1914.

25. *Spokesman-Review*, September 4, 1914.

26. *Testimonial Album*, Thomas Hooker, editor of the *Spokane Chronicle*.

27. Correspondence in the EWSHS Collection, October 21, 1908, to January 31, 1910.

28. *Spokane Chronicle*, July 1, 1959.

29. *Pacific Builder and Engineer*, December 31, 1910, 268.

30. Correspondence with Moravian Tile Company on estimate, November 23, 1910. EWSHS.

31. *Spokesman-Review*, June 9 and 13, 1909.

32. In some respects it resembled Rubens's house (1610) in Antwerp.

33. *Spokesman-Review*, June 13, 1909.

34. *Spokesman-Review*, September 18, 1910.

35. Rutter to Olmsted Brothers, n.d. (early 1910), Olmsted Collection.

36. Olmsted Brothers to Alex Cummings (the gardener they appointed), November 22, 1909.

37. *Pacific Builder and Engineer*, December 31, 1910, 268.

38. Edward J. Crosby, *The Story of the Washington Water Power Company, 1889–1930* (n.p., n.d.).

39. Craig Holstine, "Nomination of Monroe Street Bridge" (to Spokane Register of Historic Places), April 1990, quoting *American City*, January 1912, 420–21. See also *Spokesman-Review*, November 12, 1911, and *Engineering Record*, April 29, 1911, 478–79.

40. *Chronicle*, October 29, 1971, 10.

41. Norman J. Johnston, *Washington's Audacious State Capitol and Its Builders* (Seattle: University of Washington Press, 1987), 20–24.

42. The contract was awarded to the P. N. Peterson Granite Company, September 9, 1916. Correspondence, EWSHS Collection.

43. Office accounts show Bertelsen as the principal designer/draftsman on this contract.

44. The roles of Cutter and Pehrson are clearly stated in an article in the *Chronicle*, September 29, 1939.

Chapter 11 Variations on an Old English Theme (1908–1920)

1. Mrs. Edgar de Wolfe's comment in an unidentified architectural magazine is referred to in the *Spokesman-Review*, May 21, 1911, under the heading: "Kirk [*sic*] Cutter is a Genius."

2. American houses based on these traditions have been described, not always accurately, as either Tudor, Elizabethan, Jacobean, or Queen Anne. To overcome difficulties of exact identification, some of these terms have been combined to produce such hybrid descriptions as Jacobethan, Tudoresque, and Tudor Gothic. Such confusion results partly from the fact that the English building traditions that developed in the fifteenth century and earlier persisted in most areas for two hundred years or more. Differences in regional character were often more marked than stylistic changes, and many builders were unaffected by fashionable developments. Some of the most innovative designs were produced on estates far from London, whose wealthy owners vied with each other in architectural display.

3. Cutter owned several books of this type, some of which are in the EWSHS Collection.

4. Wilson Eyre turned to English architecture as an inspiration after a sketching tour of England in 1895. He was editor of *House and Garden* and his work was illustrated in both American and European journals. Cutter's Glover house of 1889 possessed qualities that Eyre was to develop in his work.

5. See Martin Segger, *The Buildings of Samuel Maclure: In Search of Appropriate Form* (Victoria, B.C.: Sono Nis Press, 1986).

6. Books in Cutter's library may have been sources for his work, including S. C. Hall, *The Baronial Halls and Ancient Picturesque Edifices of England* (1858); *English Country Houses* (Boston: Bates and Guild Co., 1898); and O. Döring, *Alte Fachwerkbauten der Provinz Sachsen* (Magdeburg, 1903). If this is the case, they contributed to Cutter's understanding of the traditions, but did not provide exact prototypes. It is not known when Cutter acquired these books.

7. See *Pacific Coast Architect* (Portland) 2, no. 6 (March 1912): 266, followed by six pages of pictures.

8. *Tacoma News Tribune* and *Tacoma Daily Ledger* obituaries, October 17, 1927.

9. J. C. Olmsted Notes, June 7, 1908.

10. J. C. Olmsted to J. F. Dawson, September 30, 1908, and J. C. Olmsted Site Notes, January 29–31, 1909.

11. L. Macomber to Olmsted Brothers, September 12 and 21, 1908.

12. J. C. Olmsted to L. Macomber, February 8, 1909, and J. C. Olmsted Notes, June 10, 1909.

13. The design was attributed to Dawson in a memoir written about him on his death in 1941, by F. L. Olmsted, Jr., Olmsted Papers.

14. After trees on the estate were cut, revealing the view toward Mount Rainier, Olmsted wanted to reposition the house, but Mrs. Thorne was so pleased with Cutter's perspective that she did not want any changes. See J. C. Olmsted Notes, June 10, 1909.

15. Author's interview with Mrs. Connie Palmer, the owner of Thornewood, February 2, 1985.

16. Drawings in the EWSHS collection show preliminary designs of the principal Thornewood interiors in a considerably more ornate manner. The hall paneling was shown as linenfold; spandrels had carved patterns of oak leaves. The ceiling was to be a grid of oak beams with Tudor roses at the intersections, and the same motif was repeated on brackets under the beam ends. The Adam Style decoration of the living room was far more elaborate. The walls were articulated with Corinthian pilasters and the ceiling was richly ornamented. The drawings, executed with an artistic flair, are stamped "John F. Bradstreet & Co. Minneapolis." The design for the dining room fireplace was Mannerist in character with atlantes supporting the heavy mantelpiece.

17. *Horticulture*, March 1931. Such an achievement was not easily attained: between 1908 and 1912 the Olmsted Brothers produced 116 sheets of drawings, from layouts of the entire estate to constructional details and planting plans. The drawings are in the inventory of the Frederick Law Olmsted National Historic Site at Brookline, Massachusetts.

18. J. C. Olmsted Notes, February 2, 1908.

19. Dawson to Davenport, April 2, 1908.

20. Dawson to Davenport, April 1 and May 8, 1908.

21. Dawson to Olmsted, October 19, 1908.

22. Olmsted to Davenport, April 4, 1908.

23. J. C. Olmsted Site Notes, May 12 and 13, and June 13, 1908.

24. Olmsted to Davenport, March 25, 1908.

25. *Chronicle*, November 6, 1908.

26. *Alte Fachwerkbauten der Provinz Sachsen* (Magdeburg, 1903) shows a number of structures with hipped gables. Plate 114 shows cross bracing to an elaborate design exactly like that on the shutters of the Davenport house. A pencil sketch on plate 115 follows a detail of a jetty on the same page which is reproduced on a section through a wall of the Davenport house (sheet 16). A *Spokesman-Review* article of November 22, 1908, describes the house as "an American adaptation of a German type."

27. Author's interview with John Fahey, October 22, 1987.

28. In a preliminary version of the final design, the dominant gable over the main entrance was of brick with stone copings. It included a rather unusual element, a Gothic version of a Palladian window.

29. This type of plan with a subsidiary wing at an angle of 45 degrees from the main block appears in several houses illustrated in G. W. Sheldon, *Artistic Country-Seats* (New York, 1886).

30. Margaret Bean, in "Mansions of Yesteryear: Waikiki Beauty Spot on Little Spokane," *Spokesman-Review*, December 18, 1956, states that Waikiki was decorated by Elsie de Wolf.

31. Graves to Dawson, September 19, 1911, Olmsted Papers, Job 3879, and Dawson to Graves, September 28, 1911.

32. Graves's satisfaction was reported by the contractor, P. L. Peterson, to the Olmsted Brothers, July 11, 1912.

33. Durham, *History of the City of Spokane and Spokane County*, 2:316.

34. See Lionel Lambourne, *Utopian Craftsmen* (New York, 1980), 168–76.

35. Polk's *Spokane City Directory* shows Knight living at N. 1715 West Point Road in 1911.

36. *Spokesman-Review*, August 1, 1909; Some fine residences built this year. Polk shows Malmgren living at 709 Sumner in 1910.

37. *Pacific Builder and Engineer*, May 7, 1910, 12.

38. One was for Fred Mason on a dramatic site off Cliff Avenue in Spokane (Drawings, EWSHS). See *Pacific Builder and Engineer*, September 23, 1911, 152. The other was for Isaac Anderson, near Thornewood, south of Tacoma (Drawings, EWSHS). Date deduced from Job No. 145.

39. *Pacific Builder and Engineer*, March 23, 1912, 250.

40. Entries in the office account books show fourteen visits to Seattle by G. A. Pehrson or Cutter between June 1915 and December 1916.

Fees of $5,382 were received in January 1917. Correspondence in the Olmsted Collection L. C. file 5787 sheds more light on the commission.

41. Author's interview with John Fahey, October 22, 1987.

42. Office accounts. Fees of $9,024 were received from Humbird in October 1917. EWSHS.

43. Cutter's Seattle office was also located in the Arcade Building in 1908. Whitcomb began planning for the home in 1916, and commissioned the Olmsted Brothers to advise on the development of the estate. But he delayed because of his wartime activities with the Red Cross. Cutter may have been consulted as early as 1918. See correspondence between Whitcomb and the Olmsted Brothers, April 24, 1918. Olmsted Collection L.C. Job 6344.

44. T. Williams Booth and William H. Wilson, *Carl F. Gould: A Life in Architecture and the Arts* (Seattle: University of Washington Press, 1995), 124–25.

45. Author's interview with Mrs. Wardie Day at Heather Hill, 1986.

Chapter 12 Mediterranean Influence (1913–1921)

1. The drawings are dated 1913 (EWSHS). For a detailed study of C. D. Stimson's patronage of architecture, including the house in the Highlands, see Lawrence Kreisman, *The Stimson Legacy* (Seattle: Willows Press and the University of Washington Press, 1992).

2. *House and Garden*, January 1920, 22–24.

3. Ernest Batchelder, inspired by Grueby and Moravian tiles, both of which Cutter used, opened a pottery for the production of tiles in Pasadena in 1910. His tiles were much used by the Greene Brothers in their Craftsman houses.

4. The Campbell house of 1897 had an attractive kitchen and servants' hall, but the laundry was in the basement and the servants' bedrooms were in the attic.

5. Olmsted Correspondence, Library of Congress and Brookline, Massachusetts.

6. In a site report of May 28, 1908, J. C. Olmsted refers to Stimson's son's cabin on the site.

The "Young peoples' cabin" is shown as an existing building in the first site drawings by the Olmsted Brothers.

7. The Cowles house was illustrated in *Western Architect*, September 1908.

8. W. H. Cowles to James Dawson of Olmsted Brothers, March 29, 1913, asks Dawson's advice on giving the commission to Cutter. The correspondence in the Olmsted archives, Library of Congress, outlines the roles of architect and landscape architect.

9. See David Gebhard, "Architectural Imagery, the Mission and California," *Harvard Architecture Review* 1 (Spring 1980): 336–45.

10. The Cowles patio may have been inspired by the Mission Inn at Riverside, California, designed by Arthur B. Benton in 1921. Only two years before Cutter designed the Cowles house, Benton had published a lengthy article in which a discussion of the virtues of the mission buildings was accompanied by many pictures of the Riverside hotel. See Arthur B. Benton, "The California Mission and Its Influence on Pacific Coast Architecture," *Architect and Engineer of California* 24, no. 1 (February 1911): 36–75.

11. Information supplied by Santa Barbara Historic Preservation Office. By then Cutter was practicing in Long Beach. A negative and print of the rebuilt single tower were among the papers remaining in his office there (Poper Collection).

12. Lee Eliot, "Madera" (Tacoma: Madera Development Corporation, 1980), no pagination.

13. Office accounts (EWSHS).

14. Eliot, "Madera."

15. The drawings are dated 1920. Fees were received in April 1921.

16. *Idaho Sunday Statesman*, August 5, 1923.

17. John C. Olmsted site meeting notes, September 23 and 24, 1916.

18. The churrigueresque manner had been popularized by the San Diego Exposition of 1916.

19. Office accounts. This project, for which Cutter received no fees, was very costly for him. In September and October 1916, the chief draftsman, Henry Bertelsen, worked for 183 hours, 23 of them overtime, while the assistants, Gifford and Perry, worked for 236 hours.

20. Unidentified news clipping dated March 16 (presumably 1919), "Begin Campaign for New Hotel."

21. Cutter to J. M. Bonner, October 10, 1919. Nez Perce County Historical Society Archives.

22. *Lewiston Morning Tribune*, June 10, 1922.

23. *Lewiston Morning Tribune*, July 23, 1922.

24. Souvenir program of the formal opening of the Lewis-Clark Hotel, September 28–29, 1922.

25. Frances M. Hannaford (K. G. Malmgren's daughter) to Robert and Laurel Maudlin, June 11, 1992: "I never remember socializing with Mr Cutter. He was society, my dad said. He knew where money was and designed their homes. My dad was a structural designer. . . . Why the partnership broke up was a 15 year period of depression. No one was building. That was when my father went to Mayo Brothers, but they couldn't do anything at that late date."

Chapter 13 Casting a Lot in Wonderland (1921–1923)

1. Fees received in the years after Malmgren's departure are as follows: $10,287 in 1918; $21,435 in 1919; $6,463 in 1920; $22,245 in 1921, including $14,250 from Joseph Carman in February and $6,239 from William Jones; $6,572 in 1922. In 1923, there are no entries in the office accounts for fees received. A copy of the mortgage note dated October 17, 1913, and details of repayments are attached as Exhibit A to a complaint by Charles Corbett to the Superior Court of the State of Washington in the County of Spokane, March 31, 1922, Case No. 68675. A chattel mortgage to Charles Corbett for $17,835, dated October 24, 1918, is also attached. EWSHS.

2. Drawings in the EWSHS Collection demonstrate little interest in the potential of low-income housing.

3. Obituary, *Spokesman-Review*, May 24, 1921.

4. Frederick Jennings, "The Most Notable Architecture and Landscape Architecture of Spokane, Washington," *Architect and Engineer* (San Francisco) 65, no. 3 (June 1921): 47–91.

5. The Tacoma and Seattle hotels are mentioned in a letter from James Dawson to Harry Wraight, January 20, 1923. Drawings of the Tacoma and Sandpoint hotels are in the EWSHS Collection.

6. Suit brought by Charles Corbett against Caroline A. P. Cutter, Kirtland K. Cutter, and Katharine P. Cutter (see note 1 above).

7. *Chronicle*, May 12, 1923; plans under way to construct $33,000 Otis Orchards School.

8. *Spokesman-Review*, May 20, 1923.

9. *Spokesman-Review*, June 8, 1949.

10. *Spokesman-Review*, May 21, 1923.

11. Dawson to Wraight, January 30, 1923. EWSHS.

12. Cutter to Dawson, March 1, 1923. EWSHS.

13. Telegram, Dawson to Cutter, March 4, 1923. EWSHS.

14. Telegram, Cutter to Dawson, March 17, 1923. EWSHS.

15. Telegram, Dawson to Cutter, March 19, 1923. EWSHS.

16. Walter Case, *History of Long Beach and Vicinity,* vol. 2 (Chicago: S. J. Clarke Publishing Co., 1927, 378–79).

17. Gilliam to Cutter, June 5, 1923. EWSHS.

18. Cutter to Gilliam, June 13, 1923. EWSHS.

19. Telegram, Cutter to Gilliam, July 18, 1923. Barbour to Cutter, July 19, 1923. EWSHS.

20. Cutter to Barbour, July 23, 1923. Barbour to Cutter, July 23, 1923. EWSHS.

21. Cutter to Gilliam, July 25, 1923. EWSHS.

22. Gilliam to Cutter, August 11, 1923. EWSHS.

23. EWSHS.

24. Confirmed in a letter from Florence H. Gervais, Head, Membership Department, AIA, to Willard B. Robinson, May 31, 1961.

25. Extracts from nine such letters were supplied by Gervais. See note 24.

26. Phair to Cutter, June 24, 1923. EWSHS.

27. Falk to Cutter, July 5, 1923. By permission of Jane Oppenheimer.

28. Jess Jones was responsible for the drawings of the Cameron house, completed by June 1924.

29. Author's interview with Richard Jones, son of Jess Jones, January 18, 1985.

30. *Spokesman-Review*, or *Chronicle*, January 29, 1924.

Chapter 14 Palos Verdes and the California Style (1923–1934)

1. David Gebhard, "The Spanish Colonial Revival in Southern California (1895–1930)," *Journal of the Society of Architectural Historians* 26, no. 2 (May 1967): 131–47.

2. Augusta Fink, *Time and the Terraced Land* (Berkeley: Howell-North Books, 1966), 105–11.

3. According to Fink (p. 116), many homes were no more than 1,000 square feet.

4. Charles H. Cheney, "Palos Verdes: Eight Years of Development," *Architect and Engineer* vol. C, no. 1 (January 1930): 39.

5. F. L. Olmsted, Jr., "Palos Verdes Estates," *Landscape Architecture*, July 1927; reprint, 12–15.

6. Myron Hunt, "Palos Verdes, Where Bad Architecture Is Eliminated," *Pacific Coast Architect* (Los Angeles) 31, no. 4 (April 1927): 3–4.

7. Charles H. Cheney, "Palos Verdes: A Model Residential Suburb," *Pacific Coast Architect* 31, no. 4 (1927): 14–15.

8. Olmsted, "Palos Verdes Estates," 10–12.

9. Thomas P. Gates, "Palos Verdes Estates: The City Beautiful," *SAH SCC Review*, 1984, no. 2, 2.

10. Minutes of the Palos Verdes Art Jury, November 22, 1923 (Palos Verdes Home Owners Association).

11. Valmonte Plaza, designed by Marston and Mayberry, was similar in character. See *Pacific Coast Architect*, January 1930.

12. Minutes of the Palos Verdes Art Jury, January 3 and March 21, 1924.

13. Olmsted, "Palos Verdes Estates"; Hunt, "Palos Verdes," 4. James Dawson, "The Placing of Houses in Relation to One Another," *Architect and Engineer*, 100, no. 1 (January 1930): 75–83.

14. A letter from the Olmsted Brothers to Cutter, May 26, 1924, indicates that foundation plans were complete by that time. The building permit was issued June 10, 1924.

15. *Palos Verdes Bulletin* 1, no. 9 (August 1925): 1.

16. The number of houses was established by looking at all the building permits issued at Palos Verdes between 1923 and 1939. The architect's name is always entered on the permits of houses. Drawings for most houses are on file at City Hall, Palos Verdes.

17. The John Wehrman house was shown in the *Palos Verdes Bulletin,* August 1925, 1, 6, 7.

18. The permit for the Sisson house was issued February 2, 1927.

19. The permit for the F. F. Schellenberg house was issued July 26, 1926.

20. The permit for the Schellenberg/Gilmore house was issued April 26, 1927.

21. The permit for the Sutherland/Cotton house was issued September 30, 1926. That for the Sutherland/Wilkins house was issued October 4, 1926.

22. This tower is purely for exterior appearance and is not exploited as an interior space.

23. The permit for the Buchanan house was issued September 13, 1927.

24. The permit for the Stein house was issued May 10, 1928.

25. Information supplied in a letter to the author from Mrs. Kathy Farrell, December 13, 1985.

26. The permits for the Grace Snelgrove and W. H. Monroe houses were issued June 28 and September 26, 1928.

27. The Palos Verdes Estates were hit hard by the depression. Only 20 percent of the assessments from owners were collected in 1931. Fink, *Time and the Terraced Land*, 122.

28. The permit for the Hugo Jones house was issued July 10, 1930.

29. The permit for the Norman Phillips house was issued April 20, 1931.

30. The permit for the Miltenberger house was issued November 10, 1934.

31. The permit for the Swimming Club Beach House was issued July 1, 1929.

32. The Buchanan house was given Honor Awards by the Art Jury in 1929 and by the Southern California Chapter of the AIA in February 1930 (*Los Angeles Times*, March 19, 1930).

33. Palos Verdes Art Jury press release, February 5, 1929, Malaga Cove Library.

34. A list of fifty-seven authorities adopting the resolution and a number of news clippings are filed in the Malaga Cove Library.

35. The articles are those cited in notes 4, 5, and 6; one by Jay Lawyer in *Architect and Engi-*

neer, January 1930, 49–52; and one by Charles Cheney in the same issue, 35–42. More than half of the houses illustrated were by Cutter. See also David Allison, "Seven Years of Architectural Control in Palos Verdes," *Architect and Engineer,* January 1930, 53–74.

Chapter 15 Long Beach: The Last Years (1925–1939)

1. Author's interview with Richard Jones, son of Jess Jones, January 18, 1985.

2. The Anderson drawings are signed with Ford's distinctive logo. Albert Ford was not a qualified architect, but an excellent designer who won several awards. He designed a number of motels in Long Beach and a church in San Diego. He did all the designing for the Long Beach Exposition of 1928, for which Hugh Davis was architect. Vance Clarke executed the drawings. Author's interview with Vance Clarke (1902–89), March 13, 1985.

3. Vance Clarke interview.

4. The Andersons' intention to employ Cutter as their architect is mentioned in a letter from Mrs. Helen Falk of Boise to Cutter, July 15, 1923.

5. See *Historic Resource Inventory*, City of Portland, Oregon.

6. Although the neighborhood is physically continuous, these houses are now in Pasadena.

7. Author's interview with Karl Von Platen, January 25, 1985.

8. Von Platen interview.

9. Edwards house building permit, City of Long Beach, December 7, 1929; completion May 5, 1930, and cost $30,000. Condit house building permit, City of Long Beach, May 6, 1929; completion September 16, 1929, and cost $15,000.

10. Date given by Mrs. Clock in an interview with the author, March 11, 1985.

11. *Spokesman-Review*, May 18, 1930, announced construction of the Jergins house; also an undated cutting from a Long Beach newspaper: "Oil Magnate's Residence of Italian Type." Vance Clarke described the Peyton house as Italian. Working drawings of the Peyton house, executed by Vance Clarke, were dated 1932.

12. *Architectural Digest* 9, no. 1 [1933]: 85, and 9, no. 2 [1933]: 69, 70, 71.

13. Author's interview with Mrs. Peggy Bayless, January 19, 1985.

14. Helen Louise Walker, "The Home of a Wise Young Man," *Movie Mirror*, April 1933, 40–41 and 73.

15. The dating of the Fleming and Honeyman beach cottages is uncertain. The Fleming cottage was illustrated in *Architectural Digest* 9, no. 2 [1933]: 20–21. The Honeyman house is shown on page 32 of the same issue.

16. Joseph K. Horton, *A Brief History of Bel Air Historical Society* (Los Angeles, 1982).

17. Phyllis Poper's audio-taped interview with Dana Agergaard, November 1979.

18. Author's interview with Victoria Fleming, March 15, 1985.

19. These houses have been dated by means of building permits in Long Beach City Hall.

20. Jimmerson was a founder of the Long Beach Children's Clinic. See *Long Beach Review*, October 1978.

21. Jimmerson to Cutter, June 25, 1937 (Poper Collection).

22. A photograph of Lowell Elementary School in the Poper Collection shows the earthquake damage. Drawings of the Abraham Lincoln School are dated 1934.

23. Several drawings survive of a large house for Maurice Von Platen. His nephew Karl stated that his uncle could never have afforded to build such a house. Interview with the author, January 25, 1985.

24. Names of some clients appear on drawings.

25. *Spokesman-Review*, May 18, 1930.

26. This description of Cutter was corroborated by Richard Jones, Vance Clarke, and Hugh Gibbs.

27. Author's interview with Hugh Gibbs, January 24, 1985.

28. Corbin Corbin Jr. knew nothing of his granfather's achievements until late in life when Mary Olsen and Jean Oton of the Eastern Washington Historical Society Museum found and befriended him. They were able to tell him

about Kirtland's successful career. When they showed him a photograph of his grandfather and stepgrandmother, he identified them as the elderly couple he often met as a child. Corbin Corbin Jr. never married. He lives quietly in California and says that he is happy to have discovered his heritage.

29. Dana Agergaard interview by Phyllis Poper (see note 17 above).

30. Richard Jones interview (see note 1 above).

31. Margaret Bean in the *Spokesman-Review*, June 13, 1937, quoting an unidentified Los Angeles columnist, probably with some exaggeration.

32. Richard Jones interview.

33. Undated typed note signed K. C. The signature appears weak.

34. Author's interview with Dr. William Stanton, Sr., January 25, 1885. The chauffeur was probably Jess Jones.

35. Jess Jones to Richard Poper, July 28, 1971:

"Cutter had never openly allowed me much credit for what I was doing. So after his death, I was only considered Cutter's office boy. It took several years for me to overcome this handicap." Poper Collection.

36. Richard Jones interview.

37. Kirtland Cutter obituary, *Spokesman-Review*, September 29, 1939.

38. Dana Agergaard interview with Phyllis Poper.

39. Hugh Gibbs. Gibbs practiced architecture in Long Beach and was still professionally active when interviewed by the author in 1985.

40. Jess Jones continued the practice until his retirement. His assistant and later partner, Richard Poper, carried on the practice, which is still in business.

41. Richard Jones interview. He recalls carrying the box that contained Cutter's ashes.

BIBLIOGRAPHY

Until 1983, when Larry Schoonover of the Eastern Washington State Historical Society (EWSHS) discovered a large collection of Kirtland Cutter's drawings, books, and office records, there was almost no documentary material to support the study of Cutter's life and architeture. Nor did his name appear in architectural bibliographies. In the course of research for this book I have discovered many brief references that have provided information on specific projects, and there are a few significant articles discussing his architecture more fully. I have cited all useful references in notes, but for the sake of brevity I have included in this bibliography only materials that shed a broader light on Cutter's career.

Since the primary focus of this book is Kirtland Cutter as architect, I have not included writings that provide information on his family background and the context of his student years; these can be found in the notes. From the many books on the Northwest, the city of Spokane, and other places where Cutter worked, I have included only those that provide useful information on his architecture or the social context of his life and professional career. There is also now a large volume of literature on the architecture of Cutter's era, from which I have made a short selection.

Unpublished and archival material

Washington

Cutter Collection, Eastern Washington State Historical Society, Spokane
    This collection consists mainly of architectural drawings of over 290 projects dating from 1889 to 1922 and office accounts from 1906 to 1923. It includes a limited quantity of other documentary materials and some books from Cutter's library.

Letterbook: Cutter and Poetz kept a record in a letterbook of the letters and telegrams they sent to clients, contractors, and suppliers. Each handwritten letter was pressed in the book beneath a dampened page, which absorbed enough of the ink to be legible on the other side. The book, containing impressions of letters from August 29, 1889, to August 31, 1891, provided valuable information about the first two years of the practice and led to the identification of several buildings not previously attributed to Cutter. The letterbook is now in the hands of a private collector; however, copies, transcribed onto index cards by the author, are in the EWSHS archives.

Photograph Collection, Eastern Washington State Historical Society

Peggy Hoyt Bayless Family Papers
Copies of most of the papers and photographs relevant to Kirtland Cutter have been donated to the Eastern Washington State Historical Society.

University of Washington Libraries, Special Collections and Preservation Division, Seattle

Whitman College Archives, Walla Walla

California

Architectural Drawings collection, University of California at Santa Barbara. This collection includes drawings from Cutter's Long Beach office, donated by Richard and Phyllis Poper.

Malaga Cove Library, Palos Verdes Estates, California. Photographs and a few documents. Bound copies of *Palos Verdes Bulletin and Social Review.* The Palos Verdes Home Owners Association holds plans and building permits.

Kirtland Cutter and his architecture

Bean, Margaret. *Campbell House.* Spokane: Eastern Washington State Historical Society, 1965.

Clausen, Meredith. "The Clark Mansion: Adaptive Reuse," *Landmarks: Magazine of Northwest History and Preservation* 3, no. 1 (1984): 15–17.

Cornell, Judy C. "Kootenai Lodge: Historic Treasure on Swan Lake." *Big Sky Journal* 1, no. 2 (Summer 1994): 56–62.

Cutter, Kirtland. "Architecture in the Northwest: Modern Architecture and Its Relation to the American Home." *Pacific Builder and Engineer*, December 11, 1909, 484–85.

Hibbard, Don. "Chicago 1893: Idaho at the World's Columbian Exposition." *Idaho's Yesterdays*, Summer 1980, 24–29.

Hopkins, Mary Alden. "Building on a Spokane Hillside." *House Beautiful* 50, no. 1 (September 1921): 190-91.

Jennings, Frederick. "The Most Notable Architecture and Landscape Architecture of Spokane, Washington." *Architect and Engineer* 65, no. 3 (June 1921): 47-91.

Kreisman, Lawrence. *The Stimson Legacy: Architecture in the Urban West.* Seattle: Willows Press and University of Washington Press, 1992.

Matthews, Henry C. "Kirtland Cutter and the Shingle Style." *Arcade: Northwest Journal for Architecture and Design* 9, no. 9 (December 1989): 12-15.

———. "A Decade of Hopes and Fears: The Preservation of Spokane's Davenport Hotel." *Arcade: Northwest Journal for Architecture and Design* 10, no. 6 (February 1991).

———. "Kirtland Cutter: Spokane's Architect." In David H. Stratton, ed., *Spokane and the Inland Empire*, 142-77. Pullman: Washington State University Press, 1991.

———. "A Marriage of Function and Fantasy: Spokane's Davenport Hotel." *Columbia* 5, no. 3 (September 1991): 3-11.

———. "Kirtland Cutter and the Search for a Northwest Vernacular." In Nicola Gordon Bowe, ed., *The Search for Vernacular Expression in Turn-of-the-Century Design*, 69–80. Dublin: Irish Academic Press, 1993.

———. "Kirtland K. Cutter." In Jeffrey Karl Ochsner, ed., *Shaping Seattle Architecture*, 78-83. Seattle: University of Washington Press, 1994.

Nolan, Edward W. *A Guide to the Cutter Collection.* Spokane: Eastern Washington State Historical Society, 1984. 36p.

Shissler, William K. *Davenport Hotel, Spokane, U.S.A.* Spokane: McKee, 1915.

Architectural Digest 9, no. 1 [1933?]: 85; 9, no. 2 [1933?]: 20-21, 32, 69-71.

Garden Home Builder, November 1927, 220–24.

House and Garden 37, no. 1 (January 1920): 22–24 (C. D. Stimson house in the Highlands).

House Beautiful 59 (March 1926): 273-77.

Inland Architect 43 (February 1904): 8, 24; 45 (July 1905): 68; 46 (August 1905): 12.

Pacific Builder and Engineer (originally *Pacific Building, Real Estate, and Financial Record*; then *Pacific Building and Engineering Record*). Many short, factual entries are footnoted in this book. See especially, for Seattle buildings, June 30, 1906, 3; December 8, 1906, 3; June 29, 1907, 11; March 7, 1908, 10; and June 13, 1908, 228.

Pacific Coast Architect (Portland, Oregon), 2, no. 6 (March 1912): 266, followed by six pages of pictures (Thornewood).

Palos Verdes Bulletin and Social Review (many entries beginning with volume 1, no. 1, November 1924).

Wasmuths Monatshefte 12, no. 8 (1928): 372-75.

Western Architect 12, no. 3 (September 1908): 21-38; 14 (July 1909): 10 (Seattle Golf and Country Club and C. J. Smith house); 19 (July 1913): 65.

The Northwest

Bean, Margaret. *Age of Elegance.* Spokane: Eastern Washington State Historical Society, 1968.

Durham, Nelson W. *History of the City of Spokane and Spokane County, Washington, from Its Earliest Settlement to the Present Time.* [Also entitled: *Spokane and the Inland Empire.*] 3 vols. Chicago: S. J. Clarke, 1912.

Fahey, John. *Inland Empire: D. C. Corbin and Spokane.* Seattle: University of Washington Press, 1965.

———. *The Inland Empire: Unfolding Years, 1879-1929.* Seattle: University of Washington Press, 1986.

———. "When the Dutch Owned Spokane." *Pacific Northwest Quarterly* 72 (January 1981): 2-10.

Hook, H. H., and Francis J. McGuire. *Spokane Falls Illustrated.* Minneapolis: Frank L. Thresher, 1889.

Murphy, James E. *Half Interest in a Silver Dollar: The Saga of Charles E. Conrad.* Missoula: Mountain Press Publishing Co., 1983.

The Oregonian, July 30, 1888, Spokane Falls Supplement.

Spokane Falls and Its Exposition. Buffalo: Matthews, Northrup and Co., 1890.

Stratton, David H., ed. *Spokane and the Inland Empire.* Pullman: Washington State University Press, 1991.

Northwest architecture

Calvert, Frank, ed. *Homes and Gardens of the Pacific Coast, Volume 1: Seattle.* Beaux Arts Village, Lake Washington: Beaux Arts Society, 1913.

Croly, Herbert. "The Building of Seattle" and "The Domestic Architecture of Seattle." *Architectural Record* 32 (July 1912): 4-18.

Dunn, Jerry C., Jr. *The Smithsonian Guide to Historic America: Rocky Mountain States.* New York: Stewart, Tabori and Chang, 1989.

Hart, Arthur. *Historic Boise: An Introduction to the Architecture of Boise, Idaho, 1863-1938.* Boise: Historic Boise Inc., 1985.

———. *The Boiseans at Home.* Boise: Historic Boise Inc., 1985.

Hyslop, Robert B. *Spokane's Building Blocks.* Spokane: R. B. Hyslop, 1983.

Kundig, Moritz, ed. *Historic Landmarks Survey: A Report and Site Inventory of Spokane's Historic Resources.* Spokane: City Planning Commission, 1979.

Logan, William B., and Susan Ochshorn. *The Smithsonian Guide to Historic America: The Pacific States.* New York: Stewart, Tabori and Chang, 1989.

McDonald, Lucile, and Werner Lenggenhager. *Where the Washingtonians Lived.* Seattle: Superior Publishing Company, 1969.

Ochsner, Jeffrey Karl, ed. *Shaping Seattle Architecture: A Historical Guide to the Architects.* Seattle: University of Washington Press, 1994.

Vaughan, Thomas, and Virginia Guest Ferriday. *Space, Style and Structure: Building in Northwest America.* 2 vols. Portland: Oregon Historical Society, 1974.

Woodbridge, Sally B., and Roger Montgomery. *A Guide to Architecture in Washington State: An Environmental Perspective.* Seattle: University of Washington Press, 1980.

Architecture of California

Cheney, Charles H. "Palos Verdes: Eight Years of Development." *Architect and Engineer* vol. C, no. 1 (January 1930).

———. "Palos Verdes Estates: A Model Residential Suburb," *Pacific Coast Architect* 31, no. 4 (April 1927): 14–15.

Fink, Augusta. *Time and the Terraced Land.* Berkeley: Howell-North Books, 1966.

Gates, Thomas P. "Palos Verdes, the City Beautiful." *Society of Architectural Historians, Southern California Chapter Review*, 1984, no. 2, 1–7.

Gebhard, David. "Architectural Imagery, the Mission and California." *Harvard Architecture Review* 1 (Spring 1980): 336-45.

———. "The Spanish Colonial Revival in Southern California (1895-1930)." *Journal of the Society of Architectural Historians* 26, no. 2 (1967): 131-47.

Hunt, Myron. "Palos Verdes, Where Bad Architecture Is Eliminated." *Pacific Coast Architect* 31, no. 4 (April 1927): 3–13.

Olmsted, Frederick Law, Jr. "Palos Verdes Estates." *Landscape Architecture*, July 1927, 10-12.

Weitze, Karen J. *California's Mission Revival.* Los Angeles: Hennessey and Ingalls, 1984.

Architecture of Cutter's era

Brooks, H. Allen. *The Prairie School: Frank Lloyd Wright and His Midwest Contemporaries.* New York: W. W. Norton, 1976.

Hewitt, Mark A. *The Architect and the American Country House, 1890-1940.* New Haven: Yale University Press, 1990.

Jordy, William H. *American Buildings and Their Architects: Progressive and Academic Ideals at the Turn of the Century.* Garden City: Doubleday, 1970.

Kaiser, Harvey H. *Great Camps of the Adirondacks.* Boston: David Godine Inc., 1982.

Lancaster, Clay. *The American Bungalow, 1880-1930.* New York: Abbeville Press, 1985.

Landau, Sarah Bradford. "Richard Morris Hunt, the Continental Picturesque, and the 'Stick Style.'" *Journal of the Society of Architectural Historians* 42, no. 13 (October 1983): 272–89.

Longstreth, Richard W. *On the Edge of the World: Four Architects in San Francisco, at the Turn of the Century.* Cambridge: MIT Press, 1983.

———. "Academic Eclecticism in American Architecture." *Winterthur Portfolio* 17 (Spring 1982): 55-82.

McCoy, Esther. *Five California Architects.* New York: Praeger Publishers, 1975.

Roth, Leland M. *McKim, Mead and White, Architects.* New York: Harper and Row, 1983.

Scully, Vincent J., Jr. *The Shingle Style and the Stick Style: Architectural Theory and Design from Richardson to the Origins of Wright.* New Haven: Yale University Press, 1971.

Segger, Martin. *The Buildings of Samuel Maclure: In Search of an Appropriate Form.* Victoria, B.C.: Sono Nis Press, 1986.

INDEX

Page numbers in italic refer to illustrations.

clients' wives, 113; and classicism and romanticism, 113; expressing clients' individuality, 122,
381, 383; progresses to mature professional, 140;
156; marriage to Katharine Williams, 187; portrait with Katharine, *186*; and Prairie and Craftsman styles, 195; opens Cutter and Plummer, 212;
with Davenport in New York, 236; juror for
Washington State Capitol Competition, 260; and
Old English styles, 267–69; financial problems,
315, 317; home seized by court order, 317; corre-
sponds with benefactors in California, 319–24;
move to California, 324–25, 326; elected fellow of
AIA, 325; appointed consulting architect for
Palos Verdes, 327; character in old age, 376–78;
death, 379
Cutter, Laura: birth, 9; in Europe, 29, in Spokane,
48; marriage, 85; Cutter's studio in her home,
110; shares her home, 185; in Long Beach, 379
Cutter, Malmgren and Wager, 174
Cutter, Mary Corbin: marriage to Kirtland, 87;
birth of son, 99; divorce, 109–10, 185; remarries,
377
Cutter, Norman, 16
Cutter, Orlando, 15–16, 37
Cutter, William Lemen, 9, *10*, 16, 29
Cutter and Malmgren: partnership formed, 100;
open office in Cleveland, 109; practice in late
1890s, 111; peak of success, 113; professional fees,
149, 313; houses analyzed, 156; open office in
Portland, 174; open office in Seattle, 174, 192–93;
residential commissions diminish, 189; close
Seattle office, 211; reputation for hotel design,
235; move office, 253–54; partnership dissolves,
312–13
Cutter and Plummer, 212
Cutter and Poetz: partnership formed, 64; establish
office in First National Bank Building, 72;
review of work 1889–91, 83–84; in 1892 Depression, 87–88; win prize at World's Columbian
Exposition,94; end of partnership, 99

Daly, Marcus, 124
Davenport, Louis: biography, 160–61; praised by
Elbert Hubbard, 168–69; partner in Cutter and
Plummer, 212; and Davenport Hotel, 235–37, 249;
and Western Union Life Insurance Co., 254
Davenport, Louis, house, Spokane, 275–81, *277, 278,
279, 280,* 285, 316
Davenport Hotel: as symbol of Spokane, 8; first
Davenport Hotel (*continued*)
design, 235–37, *237*; environmental systems, 236,
249; revised designs, 238–40, *239, 240*; final
design, 240–50, *241, 242, 243, 344, 245, 246, 247*;
opening, 249–50; mentioned, 160, 311, 316, 316
Davenport's Restaurant, Spokane, 160–68, *161, 162,
164, 165, 166,* 235, 384

Davies, Hugh, 355
Dawson, James: at Western Union Life Insurance
Co., 254; at Thornewood, 267, 270; at "Waikiki,"
285; at Palos Verdes, 317; offers Cutter support,
318–20; at Palos Verdes, 332, 333, 354
Delhi, Red Fort, 129
Depression of 1893, 87–88, 99
Dewart, Frederick, house, 195
De Wolfe, Mrs. Edgar, 267
Dickens, Charles, 30
Dolge, Ernest, house, Steilacoom Lake, Wash.,
293–94, *293*
Domestic technology: at Conrad house, 106–7; at
Campbell house, 118; at Stimson house, 299; at
Carman house, 307
Donald, William, 276, 278
Donaldson, Alfred, 214
Dow, J. K., 237
Downing, Andrew Jackson, 21, 44
Doyle, Albert E., 230, 316
Dresden: Cutter in, 26, 30; architecture of, 58, 112
Drumheller, David, house, Spokane, 189
Dunn, Thomas, house, Newport, R.I., 52–53, *53*
Durant, William West, 214–16
Duveneck, Frank, 25, 26, 29

East Indian Building, World's Columbian Exposi-
tion, 129, *129*
East Rockport, Ohio, 9, 11
École des Beaux Arts, Paris, 26
Edison, Thomas, 279
Edwards, L. T., house, Long Beach, 358–59, *359*
Ehrhardt, M., 310
Eiffel Tower, Paris, 89
Elks Temple, Spokane, 316
Emerson, Ralph Waldo, 214
Estabrook, Colonel, log house, Idaho City, 223–24,
224
Evans, L. O., 231
Exchange National Bank, Spokane, 160
Eyre, Wilson, 269

Fairhaven, Wash., 77–78
Fairmont Cemetery Chapel, Spokane, 74–77, *75,*
262, 382
Falk, Helen, 325
Falk, Leo J., house, Boise, Idaho, 308–9, *309,* 329
Farquhar, Robert, 332
Farrell, J. D., 192, 194
Fatehpur Sikri, India, 128
Faville, William, 260
Finch, Charlotte, 122, 134
Finch, John A., 121, 124
Finch, John A., chalet, Hayden Lake, Idaho, 219–20,
220, 226
Finch, John A., house, 113, 119–21, *119, 120,* 156, 174